THE JEWISH YEAR BOOK:
AN ANNUAL RECORD OF MATTERS
JEWISH, 5657 (1896–1897)

A Centenary Facsimile

Alderman George Faudel Phillips, Lord Mayor of London, 1896–97, from *Illustrated London News,* 7 November 1896.

The Jewish Year Book:

An Annual Record of Matters Jewish, 5657 (1896–1897)

A Centenary Facsimile of the
First Jewish Year Book

Preface by
STEPHEN W. MASSIL

Historical Introduction by
Anne J. Kershen

VALLENTINE MITCHELL
LONDON • PORTLAND, OR

This edition published in 1996 in Great Britain by
VALLENTINE MITCHELL & CO. LTD
Newbury House, 900 Eastern Avenue,
London IG2 7HH

and in the United States of America by
VALLENTINE MITCHELL
c/o ISBS, 5804 N.E. Hassalo Street, Portland, Oregon 97213–3644

First edition published in 1896 by Greenberg & Co. and Simpkin,
Marshall, Hamilton, Kent & Co. Ltd., London

'The Jewish Year Book, 5657 (1896):
A Defence of British Jewry?' © 1996 Anne J. Kershen

This edition copyright © 1996 Vallentine Mitchell & Co. Ltd.

British Library Cataloguing in Publication Data

The Jewish year book : an annual record of matters Jewish, 5657
(1896–1897) : a centenary edition of the first Jewish year book
1. Jews – Great Britain – Periodicals 2. Jews – Great Britain
– History – 1789–1945 3. Judaism – Great Britain – History –
Modern period, 1750–
I. Massil, S.W. (Stephen Whitney)
296'.0941

ISBN 0-85303-321-8 (hardback)
ISBN 0-85303-322-6 (limited edition binding)

Library of Congress Cataloging in Publication Data

A catalog record for this book is available from the Library of Congress.

All rights reserved. No part of this publication may be reproduced
in any form or by any means, electronic, mechanical, photocopying, recording or
otherwise, without the prior permission of Vallentine Mitchell & Co. Ltd.

Printed in Great Britain by
Bookcraft (Bath) Ltd, Midsomer Norton, Avon

Contents

Acknowledgement [vi]

Preface to Facsimile Edition   *Stephen W. Massil* [vii]

The Jewish Year Book,
   5657 (1896): A Defence of
   British Jewry? *Anne J. Kershen* [xv]

FACSIMILE

The Jewish Year Book 5657
   edited by Joseph Jacobs v

Contents xi

Acknowledgement

The facsimile is reproduced from the copy in the possession of the family of David Jacobs, which was formerly in the library of the London Society for the Promotion of Christianity amongst the Jews.

Preface to Facsimile Edition

Of the marking of centenaries there is no end, but the celebrations of centenarians are few. Anglo-Jewry is blessed in possessing several institutions that have attained their centuries and more and remain active. In 1991, I signalled the wish to mark the centenary of the *Jewish Year Book* and I am happy that Vallentine Mitchell have seen fit to commemorate the occasion by way both of a special Centenary Edition of the current 1996 edition, enlarged by celebratory and critical essays, and of this facsimile of the first volume that appeared in August 1896, which so quickly went into a reprint in the fortnight before the High Holy Days of 5657.[1] The Jewish press of the time was full of enthusiastic advertisements for it: 'demand so exceeded [the] most sanguine expectations.'

If the longevity of human institutions that survive and outlast their founders is remarkable, the study of their origins is also worth while. The *Jewish Year Book* for 1896/5657 appeared, fully fledged and ample, on 28 August 1896 and was immediately recognised as the 'Hebrew Whitaker' (Whitaker's *Almanack* itself having begun publication in 1868, the Statesman's *Yearbook* in 1862, Dod's *Parliamentary Companion* in 1832, the *Catholic Calendar* in 1887). It is this achievement that is best recognised in the form of a facsimile reproduction carrying the full text of the work and its accompanying advertisements, which have a breadth and flavour that our current advertisers cannot hope to emulate. (No doubt, in time to come, they will be viewed with equal fascination for their tone and the light they reflect on communal needs and assumed appeal.) I have commissioned a historical introduction to the text so as to set the *JYB* in its context. It is the fact that the *JYB* is more than a directory that makes its reproduction the more worth while at a time when 'immigration control' remains an issue of the British polity, and if it be a coincidence that the current Home Secretary is a Jew, Leopold Greenberg's preoccupation with the subject has resonances that give Anne Kershen her focus.

The book is a very confident production but it had its precursors, as Joseph Jacobs recognised, in Asher Myers' *Jewish Directory for 1874* (which would have made an excellent companion volume to this, the pair documenting together the full-flowering of Victorian Jewry in Britain), a tentative volume which had no immediate follow-up, although I have seen an annotated copy marked for future publication. Asher Myers (1846–1902) expressed himself modestly in the preface (hoping that it would be 'found as correct and ample as may be expected in respect of a first production of this character'), while the *Jewish Chronicle* puff (April 1874) proclaimed it an 'indispensable volume – how have we done without?'. But they did so again for a further 20 years and I surmise that this may have been because the leaders of the community were still a close-knit group and communal business, certainly in London, was very cohesive in a 'self-contained and self-administering community', as the *London Mirror* put it. It may also have been the sheer effort for Myers, P. Vallentine, his co-publisher, and their colleagues on the *Jewish Chronicle* that defeated the intention to maintain the momentum; and the hiatus smacks of the delay that prevailed between the inspiration of the 'Anti-Demolition League' of 1886 and the establishment of the Jewish Historical Society in 1893. Rachel Myers began publishing a series of directories attempting to cover the institutional fabric of the London community in the 1880s (I have seen volumes for 1887 and 1889[2]) and announced in 1893, although not published until late in 1894, came G. Eugene Harfield's *A Commercial Directory of the Jews of the United Kingdom* (London and Richmond: Hewlett and Pierce, 5654, 1894). This appeared in a second edition in 1896 and is not superseded by the *JYB* except in respect of its rudimentary communal listings.

That the *Jewish Year Book* when it appeared filled a need, subsequently flourished and has survived owes much

PREFACE TO FACSIMILE EDITION [ix]

to the circumstances of its origins and the state of the community which it charts. It was a product of that remarkable era of the 1890s which saw the spiritual, cultural and intellectual efforts of the Jewish renaissance of the 1880s come to fruition, largely through the efforts of the group that Norman Bentwich called the 'Wanderers and other Jewish scholars of my youth';[3] other achievements included the *Jewish Quarterly Review* (1888–), the *Singer's Prayerbook* (1890), the Maccabeans (1891) and the Jewish Historical Society of England (1893), itself a culminating outcome of the Anglo-Jewish Exhibition of 1887 and given in its time a wholehearted welcome by the London press. These had been preceded by the establishment of the JPSA in Philadelphia in 1887, many of whose first publications were works by British Jewish authors. And Jacobs himself, when he moved on, went to America to become literary editor of the *Jewish Encyclopaedia*.

Judging by its metropolitan reception, the *JYB* was received by the Victorians as a key document at the coming-of-age of the Jewish Community of the Emancipation (1858). Despite the growing impact of immigration and the emphatic cultural anti-semitism which had centred on Disraeli as Prime Minister throughout his ministry in the 1870s (by way of his being a focus of press and political stereotypes), the settled Jewish community undoubtedly held a proper place in British society. New peerages for Jews had doubled in 1895, and in 1896, moreover, Alderman Phillips was about to become the fourth Jewish Lord Mayor of London in 40 years (eminent son of an eminent father whose double achievement in civic merit stood unique in the history of the City at that era), itself a recognition that an appropriate honorand would hold office at the Queen's forthcoming Diamond Jubilee and at the marking of the bicentenary of the first tolerant recognition of the Jewish presence in the City (1697). The commercial success of the *JYB* perhaps owed a good deal to the plethora of advertising which makes it indistinguishable from other publications of the age, but it is surely of note that such a directory could be relied on by advertisers anticipating demand from the Jewish community as from any other group in the general society.

Unlike Asher Myers' book, the *JYB* did remain indispensable. It was put together between 15 April and 15 July 1896, and this achievement owes much to its first editor, Joseph Jacobs, his advisers and proprietor Leopold Greenberg. They could draw upon literary, biographical and statistical work already under way (the list of Jewish celebrities was originally compiled in 1885). But the alacrity with which the officers of communal organisations came forward with their records and the fullness of the entries also indicates an immediate appreciation of the need to sustain such a volume of record. There are omissions, of course, and the references to its shortcomings began to appear in the *Jewish Chronicle* from early October 1896, but many of these were certainly made good in 1897 when the entry for Bradford, for instance, was rectified by the inclusion of its (senior) Reform Synagogue, and the second volume ran to 370 pages (in addition to its advertisements) and was a more polished publication. Other errors, such as the over-zealous inclusion of the possible Jewish connections of prominent figures of the time, have not been cleared up until very recently,[4] and have been harder to detect and eradicate – a salutary warning for any editor.

The book shows the extent of a self-confident community, its organisation stable and extensive, and its institutions numerous and far-flung. Perhaps the most notable (and general) reflection made on Asher Myers' 1874 directory was the range of Jewish philanthropy and communal charitable organisations that it conveyed.[5] By 1896 there were many more, meeting especially the needs of the expanding labouring and (transitory) immigrant commu-nity. It is worth noting that the Board of Guardians moved to imposing new premises in 1896. The inauguration of the new synagogue in Lauderdale Road, Maida Vale in 1896 finally absolved the Mahamad of its intentions towards Bevis Marks Synagogue in the mid-

PREFACE TO FACSIMILE EDITION [xi]

1880s. And 1896 also saw the election of Sir Joseph Sebag-Montefiore as President of the Board of Deputies.

The century of the *JYB* is of course a remarkable one and this is not the place to give a full account of it (Chaim Bermant's contribution to the centenary essays in the 1996 *Jewish Year Book* goes some way towards it). I do, however, need to commemorate the succession of its editors, starting with Joseph Jacobs (1854–1916) who founded the *Year Book* in 1896 but remained its editor only until 1899. Jacobs established the format of the book and its excellence; he gave it initially a distinctly literary cast which was not sustained. The reference library and list of notables remained features and were steadily increased; the 'Glossary of Jewish Terms', which here fills 90 pages, was removed after 1899 in favour of an expanded 'Who's Who', an extensive obituary list of nineteenth-century Jewish celebrities, and 'Anglo-Jewry's Roll of Honour listing the British Jews serving at the front in the South African War'. These changes were introduced by Jacobs' successor, the Reverend Isidore Harris (1853–1925), from 1900 until 1924, who greatly increased the detail of entries; he sought as well to enlarge the scope of the book among the Provincial congregations and the Colonial communities. The Reverend Solomon Levy (1876–1957) served as editor from 1925 until 1938; the responsibility was shared between him and Cecil Roth from 1935 until 1938; and Cecil Roth (1899–1970) acted alone in 1939. Albert M. Hyamson (1875–1954), on his return from the Palestine Civil Service, was editor from 1940 until 1952, and Hugh Harris (1898–1981) from 1953 until 1968. Michael Wallach (1918–82) was editor from 1969 until 1983, when he died on the eve of publication, as did his successor, Roger Japhet (1915–88), editor from 1984 until the 1989 edition, after which the present incumbent succeeded. Hugh Harris, Wallach and Japhet were newspapermen at the offices of the *Jewish Chronicle*; Jacobs, Isidore Harris, the Reverend Levy, Roth and Hyamson were all pillars of the Jewish Historical Society of England, and the current editor looks forward to claiming a place among their number. I have already drawn attention to the conjunction of centenaries in quick succession in this last decade at the *fin de siècle*.

The editors record a multitude of assistants and advisers over the years, the most significant of these (aside from the compilers of the calendar) was Leopold Greenberg (1861–1931) who aided Jacobs from the start, published the series from 1897 until 1910 and was editor of the *Jewish Chronicle* when the newspaper took over proprietorship of the *Year Book* in 1911. The 'Hebrew Whitaker' was always at the heart of the Jewish media. The transfer from the *Jewish Chronicle* to Vallentine Mitchell from the 1994 edition was thus a major shift (and from EC4 to Leytonstone and Newbury Park).

Jacobs notes that the pundits of the infant JHSE had in 1896 been debating the function of Moyses Hall as a medieval synagogue; now we have news at the point of going to press of a discovery of what might prove to have been a synagogue in medieval Guildford, *c.*1180. In the editions of the 1990s I have been reporting the latest demographic figures showing the British Jewish community declining now to the numbers it attained just after the Great War. Matters of concern these days are continuity, education, out-marriage, women's place in synagogue management and prayer, and the prospects for the next generation; a place for diaspora communities in Israel's perception of its own future development; establishment of new communities at places like Hereford, Winchester and Lincoln, none, of course, connected with their historical predecessors but reflecting social trends of society at large; transfer of such bodies as the Anglo-Jewish Archive out of communal hands (to Southampton University), and the establishment at a remove from the community of such institutions as Holocaust, German–Jewish and Gentile–Jewish centres of study. It is fitting, of course, that the centenary of James Parkes's birth should be marked in this way this year. But the naming of lectureships at universities and the diffusion of Jewish philanthropic support for education and the promotion of

PREFACE TO FACSIMILE EDITION [xiii]

study of matters Jewish in the wider society through these new bodies is significant.

I am grateful to David Jacobs for use of his copy of the book (and it makes an interesting sidelight to know that it was once in the possession of the Society for the Promotion of Christianity amongst the Jews!) and for his advice on the illustrative material used on the jacket; thanks are also due to Esra Kahn, librarian at Jews' College, the Library of the *Jewish Chronicle* and staff of the Jewish Museum (Finchley) for their assistance in the preparation of this facsimile.

STEPHEN W. MASSIL

London,
28 January 1996, 8 Shebat 5756

NOTES

1. I have compared the first edition presented here with one in which the title-page proclaims it a '2nd ed.', but there is no difference at all in the texts and we would now call the latter a second impression. Extant copies do not necessarily carry all the advertisements, especially those numbered as pages i and 299.
2. *The Jewish Calendar, Manual and Diary, 1888–9/5649*, edited for Mrs Rachel Myers (L. Schaap, 1888).
3. *Transactions of the Jewish Historical Society of England*, Vol. 20 (1964), p.51.
4. For example, Arthur Jacobs disposed of Sir Arthur Sullivan's 'supposed Jewish connection' only in his *Arthur Sullivan ...* (OUP, 1984), pp.434–5; and Asher Tropp in his *Jews in the Professions in Great Britain, 1891–1991*, published to mark the centenary of the Maccabeans, drew attention to other long-standing errors, as have other writers.
5. The *London Mirror* commented: 'It cannot but enhance the respect which Christians entertain towards Jews when they learn through its pages the number of works of charity in which those who are settled in this country and happily enjoy all the benefits of its citizenship, are engaged.'

The Jewish Year Book, 5657 (1896): A Defence of British Jewry?

Anne J. Kershen

In the preface to the first *Jewish Year Book* its compiler, Joseph Jacobs, tells us that though 'nothing ... was written on April 15'[1] it had gone to press four months later. A few sentences on, Jacobs informs his readers that the need for such a volume, referred to by the *Jewish Chronicle* as 'A Jewish version of Whittaker',[2] was 'undeniable'. Why was there a 'need', an urgency to publish at that moment in time? For behind the advertisements for luxury Atlantic crossings and expensive seminaries for young ladies there is a discernible subtext, an intensity in the glorification of Jews who had become peers of the realm, members of the armed forces and government ministers. What was the climate in which the *Year Book*'s editor and publisher found it imperative to produce such a fact-filled volume? In order to answer these questions, I have chosen to take the temperature of the times without the benefit of hindsight. So as to avoid the impression of having 'finished the chapter', I have used only material that would have been available to concerned individuals such as editor Joseph Jacobs and publisher Leopold Greenberg. It would be wrong however, and indeed unhelpful to the late twentieth-century reader, to avoid all mention of that which confirms or contradicts statements and images appearing in that very first volume

---

Anne J. Kershen is Barnet Shine Senior Research Fellow and Director of the Centre for the Study of Migration at Queen Mary and Westfield College, University of London and a member of the Faculty of Leo Baeck College. She has appeared on radio and television and is the author of *Tradition and Change: A History of Reform Judaism in Britain, 1840–1995* (with Jonathan A. Romain) (1995), *Uniting the Tailors* (1995), *150 Years of Progressive Judaism* (1990), *Off the Peg* (1988), as well as chapters in G. Alderman and C. Holmes (eds), *Outsiders and Outcasts* (1990), and D. Cesarani (ed.), *Making of Modern Anglo-Jewry* (1990).

of the *Jewish Year Book*, so, where pertinent, I have provided some follow-up information.

Let us look at the *Year Book* as it appeared in the bookshops on 28 August 1896. It was indeed a valuable addition to the library of Jewish publications, providing its, assumedly middle and upper class, Jewish readership with the 'knowledge' which Jacobs believed would offer the community the 'power for improvement'. Who were those who sought to influence and improve late nineteenth-century British Jewry through the provision of an almanack for the Jewish community? The publisher, Leopold Greenberg, was a journalist, Zionist and later editor-in-chief of the *Jewish Chronicle*. A member of the north-west London group of Jewish intellectuals, 'The Wanderers', a founder member of the Maccabeans, and a confirmed liberal, he was absolutely opposed to controls on immigrant entry[3] and thus would have been eager to support and publish a volume that presented a favourable image of Anglo-Jewry, that identified a successful and continuing assimilation process and that chronicled the existence of a host of Jewish charitable organisations which accommodated the material and spiritual needs of the immigrants, thus avoiding recourse to English Poor Law Guardians. As his article on alien immigration in the *Year Book* illustrates,[4] Greenberg was keen to refute allegations of an 'alien invasion' by focusing upon the more sympathetic findings of government commissions and select committees. He was eager for his readership, and through it the wider public, to know that more people were leaving England than entering it and that it was America that was admitting large numbers of eastern European immigrants, many of them having come via the United Kingdom.

In the *Jewish Year Book*'s first editor, Joseph Jacobs, we find a man who dedicated himself to understanding the Jewish race in a scientific manner. Australian born, Jacobs arrived in Cambridge in 1872, at the age of 18; just over two years later he graduated with a First in Moral Science.[5] Influenced by his reading of George Eliot's *Daniel*

Deronda and its Darwinistic theme, Jacobs decided to attack contemporary antisemitism by combining physical anthropology with sociology in order to highlight the Jewish contribution to history.[6] In other words, he set out to use science and statistics as a force against antisemitism. From this we can locate Jacobs within the school of other early empirical social scientists, such as Charles Booth,[7] who used the tool of statistics in their attempts to resolve contemporary issues and problems. Jacobs believed that environment more than biology was the determining factor in the development of racial charateristics. Therefore, though on arrival eastern European Jewish immigrants might find the customs and climate of England strange and harsh, acclimatisation ran parallel to assimilation and, as history and his statistics proved, once assimilated, Jews were able to make valuable contributions at all levels of the economy and society.

Between 1882 and 1885 – a high point in alien immigration – Jacobs wrote a series of articles in the *Jewish Chronicle* which he published in 1891 in a volume entitled *Jewish Statistics*. Covering topics which included marriage patterns, morality, occupations and professions, he set out to defend, and indeed dispel, the Jewish myth by proving that consanguineous marriages were not harmful to the Jewish race, that the Darwinistic conditions of the ghetto created resourceful survivors not dependent paupers, and that not all Jews were wealthy. The latter thesis, argued through the provision of statistics which detailed levels of poverty amongst London Jewry, could well have proved counter-productive in the mid-1890s when it was the pauper aliens who were accused of taking the jobs of Englishmen.[8] In 1894 Jacobs's *Statistics of the Jewish Population in London 1873–1893* appeared. Having amassed this store of material Joseph Jacobs was ready to accommodate the 'need' and thus, he believed, facilitate communal improvement which, following his philosophy, would help fight the rising tide of anti-alienism.

As his 'Glance at 5656' shows, Jacobs was not concerned solely with British Jewry and we must, as he did, review events taking place in Britain within the context of the international scene. As is evident from the structure of his article,[9] events overseas took priority in the consensus of antisemitism. No one was more aware of the varying levels than the *Year Book*'s editor who, as a visitor to Germany, had witnessed 'jew hatred' at first hand. Yet, it does not appear in Jacobs's review, even though antisemitism was alive and thriving in the country where racism was beginning its journey towards hell. Throughout the second half of the nineteenth century, German radical intellectuals had been developing their anti-Jewish theses – some using Gobineau's theories of racial purity as vehicles to promote antisemitism. German Jews were considered separate in religious and sociological terms. As depicted in the music of Wagner and in the writings of Dühring and Marr, they were seen as alien and decadent. It was Wilhelm Marr who, in 1879 in his pamphlet *Jews' Victory over Teutonism*, coined the word 'antisemitism' as meaning Jew hatred. Perhaps the omission of Germany in Jacobs's overview can be explained by the attitude of the German Jewish people themselves. According to a letter that appeared in the *Jewish Chronicle* in September 1894 they displayed an 'apathetic attitude to antisemitism'.[10] The signs were there but, for the time, attention lay elsewhere.

There is no doubt that the harshest examples of Jewish separation and alienation were to be found in nineteenth-century Russia. Under what Jacobs considered the most repressive regime in Europe, over five million Jews were subjected to more than 1,400 statutes and regulations, including the notorious May Laws passed in 1882 following the assassination of Tsar Alexander II. Under Alexander III, the movement of nationalism spreading across Europe had reached the Russian Empire and a process of Jewish separation was pursued. Jews were geographically, educationally, domestically and economically confined. Hope for the future lay westward, in the promised lands of America and Britain. Jacobs's belief that

INTRODUCTION TO FACSIMILE EDITION [xix]

pressure on the Jews of Russia had eased during 1895[11] was optimistic and one that was to be disproved by the violence of the Kishinev pogrom of 1903.[12]

The next European country to come under the spotlight was Austria. Here, too, Jacobs's optimism shows through. A corollary to the emancipation of the Jews in Austria in the 1860s was an increase in antisemitism. During the 1870s and 1880s Jews began to take an over-representative part in Vienna's professional, financial and cultural activities. Not surprisingly, the 'Jewish conspiracy' theory began to feature in the arguments of the antisemites. The 'Dr. Lueger' referred to in Jacobs's article[13] was Karl Lueger, a Christian Socialist and overt antisemite, the man credited with 'creating a regime based on antisemitism anchored in the militant Catholic faith'.[14] It has been suggested that his more radical antisemitic articles and activities were held in check by the Emperor Franz Joseph who was concerned to uphold 'the equality of all religious faiths and of all Austrian citizens before the law'.[15] Lueger's position was strengthened the year after the publication of that first *Year Book* when he was elected Lord Mayor of Vienna, a position he retained for 13 years.

Jacobs concludes his report on 'the rest of the world' in one brief paragraph. He tells us that, according to received information, the Jews of Rumania were 'not perceptibly worse off' than they had been a year before. Rumania gained its sovereignty in 1881 and, with it, a free hand to subjugate the Jews. The country's strategic value was such that the western powers placed their desire for railway concessions above the emancipation of the Jews of Rumania. The Jewish position may not have deteriorated in 1895 but neither did it improve in the years ahead.

At the time of publication, 'Mons. Drumont' did indeed appear to be the chief orchestrator of French antisemitism in the closing decades of the nineteenth century. A Catholic journalist, Eduard Drumont published his diatribe against French Jewry, *La France Juive*, in 1886; three similar works followed. In 1889 he founded an Antisemitic League and subsequently, through his newspaper, continued his campaign, suggesting that Jews were set upon controlling French finance and de-Christianising France. Small wonder that, in the summer of 1896, it was the activities of Drumont and the growing number of antisemitic agitators in France that concerned Jacobs rather than the arrest and conviction of one Captain Alfred Dreyfus at the end of 1894. That is not to suggest that what was to become the 'Dreyfus Affair' went unnoticed in Britain. In January 1895 the *Jewish Chronicle* reported that 'Jews were being villified by the French press for a crime alleged to have been committed by a Jewish officer'.[16] In contrast, two weeks later the *Chronicle* reported that, for the first time, lay and clerical Jewish leaders had been invited by the Prime Minister to attend New Year's celebrations in the capital. From this Jacobs concluded that French antisemitism 'was not making much headway'.[17] Almost eight months later, two years before his famous *J'Accuse*, Emile Zola published an article in the French paper *Figaro*, which was reproduced in full in the *Jewish Chronicle* in September 1895. In this Zola argued that antisemitism in France was a form of insanity which had to be overcome. It was while the first *Jewish Year Book* was going to press that the campaign for a retrial of Dreyfus began, one which ignited a fresh, but ultimately unsuccessful, outbreak of antisemitism. As we know, events climaxed in 1898; the following year Dreyfus was released.

Mass immigration from eastern Europe was not without its repercussions on the other side of the Atlantic. As in Britain, so in America, Jewish aliens, with their strange language, different religion and somewhat exotic habits, who were prepared to work as sweated labour in order to enjoy the fruits of success, were bound to meet with antipathy from the white Anglo-Saxon Protestants of American society. We might ask what concerned Jacobs here, the fear of rising social antisemitism or the recent legislation restricting immigrant entry which, though not aimed directly at the Jewish incomers, could not help but affect them and perhaps influence activists in Britain? As Jacobs did, so shall we now turn 'to the quarter of the globe in which readers of this Year Book would be particularly interested'.

If that first *Year Book* is used as a guide to the structure of British Jewry *circa* 1896, the image is one of a stratified yet well-disciplined and well-organised community, its members fulfilling the requirements of the emancipation contract. Jews played their part in the running of the country and in its defence – the *Jewish Chronicle* was clearly delighted with this last fact and, in its review of the *Year Book*, stressed how astonished its reader had been to discover 'how many Jews held commissions in her Majesty's army and navy'.[18] Jews had entered the aristocracy while, at the other end of the scale, the extensive list of Jewish charitable organisations active in the capital and in the provinces was proof of the way in which the community was providing 'relief in kind' – training or providing for those who were unskilled or unemployed, sometimes even making funds available for them to return to eastern Europe. The advertisements which appeared were a clear pronouncement of the fact that the longer resident Jewish community of Britain was well assimilated and acculturated, enjoying the fruits of socio-economic success.

Hindsight would enable a lengthy analysis of the final paragraph in Joseph Jacobs's 'Glance at 5656'. His reference to the 'remarkable pamphlet on a Jewish State, written by Dr. Theodor Herzl', reveals the editor's cursory consideration of an issue which was to go right to the heart of the Jewish people and cause deep divisions within established British Jewry. However, this essay allows neither the time nor the space to consider the impact of the arrival of both Herzl and political Zionism in Britain at the end of the nineteenth century.[19]

The *Year Book* was clearly intended as a vehicle through which to dispel myths and legends. One avenue was by the provison of a Glossary which offered rational explanations for the expected, and sometimes the unexpected. At first glance we might question why there was a need to attach significance to the Jewish tradition of eating fried fish.[20] The answer lies in an anti-alien statement made at the 1895 Trade Union Congress Conference held in Cardiff, rather than in a culinary discourse. In a debate which considered the passing of a resolution to prevent the entry of pauper aliens, one delegate, Mr Newcombe, representing the watch industry, referred to the 'importation of the Jews and their well-known penchant for fried fish'.[21] Though this aside may not have swayed the delegates, it should be noted that the anti-alien resolution was finally passsed at that Conference.

The first *Jewish Year Book* appeared at a time of heightening socio-political unease. One manifestation was anti-alienism. A stance, it was argued by some, not to be confused with antisemitism. For there were those who declared that, whilst they were not against Jews because of their religious beliefs and practices, they were opposed to the 'invasion of the destitute and worthless of other lands'. We will now consider what form the forces of antisemitism and anti-alienism took and how long they had been building up.

Recent historians agree[22] that antisemitic sentiment became more apparent and English Jews more uneasy during the period of Benjamin Disraeli's second goverment, that is from the mid-1870s. The Tory Prime Minister's support for the Turks after they reportedly massacred 25,000 Bulgarian Christians in 1876 brought forth a storm of anti-Disraeli and antisemitic comments. In spite of his baptism, Disraeli was perceived, and portrayed by his opponents, as a Jew, an oriental Jew, 'the friend of the Turk and the enemy of the Christian'.[23] Disraeli's policy, 'my enemy's enemy is my friend' – the enemy of both the Turks and the British in the Balkans at the time being Russia – was interpreted by enemies of the Prime Minister as that of a Jew whose oriental blood 'was thicker than water'. To anglicised and assimilated Jews who believed themselves fully paid up members of British society following the entry of Baron de Rothschild into the House of Commons

INTRODUCTION TO FACSIMILE EDITION [xxiii]

in 1858, the vitriol which Disraeli's Balkan policy elicited marked a movement away from complacency to concern and unease, necessitating for some a re-examination of the Jew's place within British society.

By the close of the 1870s Goldwin Smith, a forceful opponent of Disraeli whom he had derided for his Hebrew flashiness during the Balkan Crisis, was publicly restating the dilemma that had haunted the emancipation debate in mid-century, could a Jew be a patriot?[24] The same topic was pursued by Smith three years later in his article 'The Jewish Question',[25] which appeared in the journal *Nineteenth Century*. In this he followed the themes of both Jewish separateness and Jewish power, the latter, manifested as it was in the worlds of finance and the press, posing a threat to the independence of the nation state. In his writings Smith was some 22 years in advance of the appearance of the *Protocols of the Elders of Zion* in Russia, and almost 40 years before its English equivalent, *The Jewish Peril*,[26] was published in Britain. The dangers of Jewish power and control were further pressed home by the author Richard Burton in his pamphlet *Lord Beaconsfield, A Sketch*,[27] which was published around 1882. The theme of a Jewish conspiracy was taken up by the *East London Leader* a year later in an editorial which warned that 'The Jewish mind is guiding the religious and moral movements ... the Jew is forging the chains with which he is prepared to flood those miserable gentiles'.[28]

It has been suggested that the influence of the Balkan Crisis and Disraeli's perceived anti-Christian stance is also apparent in the literature of the period.[29] The Jewish stereotype is a familiar literary device which can be traced back to Chaucer, through Shakespeare and on to Dickens. Did Joseph Jacobs notice subtle changes taking place in Anthony Trollope's characterisations during the years in question? Was the refusal of the Duke of Omnium's hand in marriage by the dark-skinned, dark-haired Jewess, Madame Max Goesler, Trollope's way of signalling the lower racial qualifications of the Jew? Similarly, when the

Jew, Lopez, in Trollope's *The Prime Minister*, published in 1876, is described as 'The greasy Jew adventurer out of the ghetto', was this interpreted as part of the old tradition or as a more sinister departure? Were contemporary writers, such as Kipling and du Maurier, sending out antisemitic messages? As, for example, when du Maurier's Trilby makes reference to that 'indelible [Jewish] blood which is of such priceless value in diluted homeopathic doses ... which is not meant to be taken pure ... which is not beautiful in itself'.[30] Du Maurier provides us with the Jew, Svengali, 'a tawdry and dirty' person with filthy habits who hypnotised the innocent Trilby to do his will. In the climate of the 1880s and 1890s did these literary figures really unnerve men such as Jacobs and Greenberg or were the characterisations taken as a natural progression from earlier writers? A far greater furore was created by the distasteful portrayal of the middle-class Jew by his co-religionist, the novelist Julia Frankau. In her work, *Dr. Philips: A Maida Vale Idyll*, which appeared in 1887, the author, who published under the pseudonym Frank Danby, was extremely critical of the race of her origins and painted an image of a 'corrupt' milieu. Dr Philips epitomised the vulgar, greedy, avaricious philistine Jew[31] who was 'ignorant of politics, literature and art' and took 'no interest in the world beyond their families and friends, businesses and homes'.[32] Not surprisingly, the book was ill received by the Jewish community who accused Frankau of 'feeding the fires of antisemitism'. It was no better received by the English press, whose reaction can best be summarised by the reviewer for *Punch* who declared that it should 'never have been written'. Frankau was not alone in condemning her race in print, Amy Levy's *Reuben Sachs*, which appeared the following year, was almost as vitriolic. Such publications, while doing nothing to help the cause of philosemitism, provided valuable amunition for antisemites like Arnold White to use in diatribes such as *The Modern Jew* which appeared in 1899.

During the 1880s, storm clouds of anti-alienism were

INTRODUCTION TO FACSIMILE EDITION [xxv]

gathering in Britain. There is no doubt that it was the growing number of eastern European Jewish immigrants that increased tension and raised the temperature. In order to appreciate the impact of that alien presence on British society and labour we have to locate it within the socio-economic framework of the last decades of the nineteenth century.

The development of the docks, the railways, the roads and the canals during the first half of the century had necessitated the demolition of slum houses and tenements, with the resultant dishousing of many thousands. This programme was followed by the Cross Act of 1875 which authorised the compulsory demolition of insanitary dwellings. The beneficiaries of this Act were the slum owners who received compensation and the developers who bought the land cheap for redevelopment. The losers in every case were those who had been dishoused and who, with no government policy for rehousing or provision of suitable alternative accommodation, were forced in upon themselves, drawn by the nexus of community and the need to live close to their place of employment. The problem of overcrowding reached its peak in the 1880s in East London with the full impact of the clearances taking their toll. What rebuilding there had been was let at far too high a price for those who needed it most.

With the exception of the short-lived boom years between 1888 and 1892, the 1880s and 1890s were years of stagnation and recession. From 1880 onwards unemployment increased, those worst affected being workers in the seasonal, casual, sweated trades in which the newly arrived semi-skilled and unskilled alien immigrants often sought work. It was only in the decade of the 1880s that the word 'unemployed', meaning jobless, appeared in the vocabulary of political economists and labour commentators. Between 1882 and 1886 unemployment rose dramatically. Newspaper exposures of the plight of the poorest members of society, such as those which appeared in the *Pall Mall Gazette*, acted as a catalyst. Many who had previously held the poor personally responsible for their poverty and for the resolution of their plight, who had clung to the ideology of *laissez-faire*, in which self-help reigned supreme, found themselves begining to question a society in which poverty was perceived as the fault of the individual. By the second half of the 1880s poverty, for many, had become a problem that had to be addressed. Changes in attitude were not solely due to altruism; there were other factors at work. New political ideologies, which sought to redress the balance for the deprived and the exploited, loomed on the horizon, while those very individuals who had been thought unorganisable, the semi-skilled and the unskilled, had formed 'new unions'; whispers of revolution and *frissons* of fear rippled through certain government quarters. At the same time there were those in Britain whose thoughts lay with national supremacy; a malnourished, diseased workforce could not secure the future. High on the agenda for debate was overcrowding and the misery, destitution and immorality that travelled with it. Allied to that was immigration and the alien's impact on jobs, housing and the health of the nation.

London, the magnet for immigrants, was the focus of attention.[33] It was to East London, the first point of settlement for incomers for hundreds of years, that the newcomers flocked. It was at the eastern edge of the City of London that the Jews of the Readmission made their home and it was at the eastern edge of the City of London, by the London Docks, that the ships from Hamburg and Bremerhaven disgorged their steerage cargoes of bedraggled, dirty, malodorous eastern European arrivals, half dead from the misery and deprivations of their voyage yet filled with the hope that only those who had left the Pale of Settlement and survived the journey could appreciate. Those immigrant ships off-loaded their human cargoes in an area which, by the 1880s, was becoming increasingly and disturbingly deprived.

It would not take long into the 1880s for the alien Jewish immigrants in the East End to be accused of 'taking the jobs and homes of Englishmen'. In an area where work was casual and wages barely enough to cover basic needs, new arrivals prepared to work for the lowest rates of pay were accused of, and in many instances were, undercutting wages and taking away jobs, if not from male workers, then certainly from English women. Frederick Engels noted the situation as one in which immigrants were reversing any improvements the workers might have come to enjoy. An ever-widening pool of immigrant labour would only result in further underemployment and hardship all round – or so the anti-alienists would have had you believe.

One of the worst forms of economic exploitation was the sweating system, that iniquitous form of slavery by which those employed worked the longest hours, in the worst conditions, for the lowest pay. The sweating of unskilled and necessitous labour far pre-dated the so-called 'alien invasion' but, as the Jewish ghettoes of Spitalfields in London and the Leylands in Leeds filled to overflowing, the system – its origin and perpetuation – was blamed on the economic greed of the Jewish master. Almost 40 years earlier the investigative journalist, Henry Mayhew, had attacked the Jewish sweater for his 'barbarous habits and mode of life',[34] but the time had not been ripe for such accusations to be taken up by the anti-alienist school. By the 1880s, however, *The Lancet*, journal of the British Medical Association, was able to add fuel to the fire when, in 1884, it carried out a special investigation into the 'Polish Colony of Jew Tailors' in East London, from which it was rumoured, diseases were transmitted in garments manufactured by workers employed in the most insanitary of East End workshops. The reporter from *The Lancet* found conditions in the Jewish sweatshops to be 'appalling' breeding places for disease. Levels of sanitation were foul, no doubt aggravated by the common practice of glazing poor quality fabrics with urine.[35] The eastern European immigrant was thus revealed as both exploitive and insanitary, presented by anti-alienists as a threat to the well-being of the nation. One who supported that view was Arnold

White. Over the next 20 years he carried out an increasingly virulent antisemitic campaign directed mainly against alien Jews, whom he described as the 'dregs of the Russian cities'. In the early 1890s he published a survey of poverty in London which centred on the East End.[36] From his findings he concluded that it was the immigrant who was responsible for the impoverishment of the English working man in East London.

It was only to be expected that, as unemployment levels grew, the spotlight would fall increasingly on the immigrants who, according to an article in the *Pall Mall Gazette* which appeared in February 1886, were 'becoming a pest and a menace to the poor native born East Ender'.[37] As the economic and domestic[38] impact of the immigrant presence featured increasingly in public debate, demands were made for regulation of the entry into Great Britain of destitute alien immigrants. Members of Parliament representing East End constituencies, such as Bow and Bromley and St George's in the East, warned of the dangers if no controls were imposed. Arnold White, in a letter to *The Times* written in July 1887, demanded 'England for the English'[39] (a phrase familiar to those who have studied the language of racism over the past 100 years).

The government's first response was to commission the Board of Trade's Labour Correspondent, John Burnett, to carry out an investigation into the sweating system in the East End. In his *Report to the Board of Trade*, which appeared in 1887, he described the 'filthy and unsanitary' conditions that were to be found in the small workshops:

> In small rooms not more than 9 or 10 feet square, heated by a coke fire for the pressers irons, and at night lighted by flaring gas jets, six, eight, ten and even a dozen workers may be crowded. The conditions of the Public Health Acts, and of the Factory and Workshop Regulation Acts, are utterly disregarded ... At a moderate computation there must be at least 2,000 sweaters in the East End of London ... A

tour of inspection of a few of these places and of the people therein employed gives some idea of the misery and extent of the system...

Burnett also reinforced the fear of disease that was a product of the sweatshop, a feature of *The Lancet* survey three years earlier. 'In this way has grown up in our midst a system so bad in itself and so surrounded by adherent evils as to have caused, not only among the workers themselves, great suffering and misery, but in the minds of others grave apprehensions of public danger.'[40] To a nation at the dawning of the eugenics debate, the immigrant was not only an immediate threat to jobs and houses, his presence as workshop master and exploiter was a major factor in the birth of enfeebled infants. Sweatshops reinforced the deskilling process, took jobs away from English males and gave them to females who later bore sickly children. Until sweating was eradicated English men would be denied their rightful employment. The eastern European alien was culpable on two levels, as the heartless, mercenary employer and the undercutting employee. Thus not only was the presence of the immigrant perceived as an immediate local danger, his method and form of employment presented a greater and more ominous threat to the nation at large.

Government reaction to Burnett's findings were not as positive as the advocates of immigration control wished. A House of Lords Committee to Investigate the Sweating System was established and began sitting in 1888. The original remit of the Committee was to concentrate solely on the East End sweated trades, but an outbreak of smallpox in the Leylands area of Leeds resulted in a decision to extend the investigation into one that was nationwide and inclusive of trades which were not traditional alien immigrant occupations, such as dock labour, chain making and lace making.

The recommendations of the Sweating Committee that appeared in 1889 did little to stem the flow of immigrants or to ameliorate conditions in the sweated trades. Beatrice

Potter, not always a friend to the Jewish immigrant, concluded from the findings of the Committee that 'the sweater is in fact the whole nation'.[41] How influential her words were is difficult to gauge but there was no immediate attempt to implement Burnett's recommendation, made in his earlier Report, for 'the restriction, by poll tax or otherwise, of the immigration of foreigners',[42] in spite of the *East London Advertiser*'s report that 'swarms of foreign jews' were continuing to invade and dominate the East End labour market.[43]

As the numbers of eastern European immigrants in the East End and the ghettoes of Leeds and Manchester continued to grow, criticism mounted. The national press and journals such as *Nineteenth Century* and *Fortnightly Review* carried articles which lambasted the alien for his 'lack of morality and love of gain'. In a scaremongering series of articles, the *Evening News* revealed in 1891 that the aliens were coming over 'in battalions and taking the bread out of the mouths ... of English women and children'.[44] The Jew might be 'self-supporting, self-creating and self-governing',[45] but, as Beatrice Potter wrote in Booth's *Life and Labour of the People in London* in 1889, he 'bought cheap and sold dear' and 'totally ignores all social obligation other than keeping the law of the land, the maintenance of his own family and the charitable relief of co-religionists'.[46] The Jew was, in his enlightened selfishness, as J.A. Hobson described him at the beginning of the 1890s, 'The ideal economic man' who acquired 'a thorough mastery of all the dishonorable tricks of the trade'.[47] The cultured, affluent Jew had long been stereotyped as an economic opportunist and financial climber; now, at the end of the nineteenth century, his poorer co-religionist was being portrayed as economically immoral.

It was not only for his unsocial economic behaviour that the eastern European alien immigrant was criticised. His domestic environment and sexual practices were also on the anti-alienists' agenda. The corollary of taking the Englishman's job was the taking of his home. As we have

INTRODUCTION TO FACSIMILE EDITION [xxxi]

seen above, the problems of the housing of the poor had existed long before the alien invasion began but it was not until the 1880s that overcrowding became a major issue. It was thought to be at its worst in the East End of London, in the alien-dominated areas of Whitechapel and St George's in the East, where more than 55 per cent of the population lived in overcrowded conditions.[48] A survey carried out in 1881 revealed that in Whitechapel the number of persons per house had risen from 8.98 in 1861 to 11.28 in 1881.[49] In a city in which overcrowding was considered to be 56 persons per acre, no fewer than 286 persons per acre[50] were estimated to be living in Spitalfields. The abyss was filled to overflowing. And the alien invasion had barely begun.

It was Andrew Mearn's pamphlet, *Bitter Cry of Outcast London*, which appeared in 1883, that first pricked the public conscience with its horrifyingly graphic descriptions of abject domestic misery. Where accommodation was scarce, rents were high. Subletting, frequently with several families to a room, was common practice. High rents charged to poor people – in the poorest parts of London between one-quarter and one-half of weekly earnings went on rent – allowed little for food. Shortage of food caused malnutrition and disease, inablity to work and ever increasing poverty. The alien presence exacerbated an already desperate situation. In March 1887 the Committee of Guardians of the Whitechapel Union demanded that something 'be done to prevent the landing of foreign paupers'.[51] In that same year Charles Booth gave a paper on poverty to the Royal Statistical Society. In it he criticised the Jews for taking over whole buildings, even streets, and for being 'unpleasant neighbours'.[52] Anglo-Jewry, too, was conscious of the unfortunate image projected by the aliens' propensity for voluntary ghettoisation. An editorial which appeared in the *Jewish Chronicle* reflected the sentiments of the Jewish establishment.

> If poor Jews will persist in appropriating whole streets to themselves in the same district, if they will

> persevere in the practice of congregating as a body at prominent points in the great public thoroughfare of Whitechapel, drawing to their peculiarities of dress, of language and of manner, the attention which they might otherwise escape, can there be wonder that the vulgar prejudices of which they are the object should be kept alive and strengthened? What can the tutored unthinking denizens of the East End believe in the face of such facts, but that the Jew is an alien in every sense of the word, alien in ideas, in sympathy and in interests from the rest of the population.[53]

The image of the alien was not helped by his being landlord as well as impoverished tenant. Jewish landlords in the Leylands in Leeds were considered rack-renting capitalists who had taken the homes of honest Englishmen.[54] Reinforcing Booth's findings, the anti-alienist W.H. Wilkins described how in Leeds, as in the East End of London, Jews had taken over whole streets. In the Leylands, 900 of the 1,300 houses were occupied by Jews. The blame for the social and economic evils of the times was placed fairly and squarely on the shoulders of the immigrants.

In its article on the tailors' colony in the East End, *The Lancet* had highlighted the shortage of property and the increasing number of alien immigrants. It had also focused on their insanitary and unhealthy habits. The aliens 'didn't know how to pull the chain and flush and clean the pan ... some tenants just threw soil out of the window'.[55] Theories of the threat to the nation's health posed by the immigrants did not gain full exposure until the beginning of the twentieth century, when they became part of the anti-alienists' weaponry. The aliens were attacked for their lack of cleanliness, for their evil odour and for their propensity to carry and spread disease.[56] But the shadows of concern over the importation of trachoma, lupus and other so-called 'Jewish' degenerative diseases began to fall from the late 1880s onwards.

In his monograph, *The Alien Invasion*, which was published in 1892, W.H. Wilkins referred to the alien immigrants as the 'invading hordes'. He deemed Jewish charities such as the Poor Jews' Temporary Shelter responsible as they 'drew immigrants'[57] from overseas with their provision of food and lodging, albeit for only two weeks. The Shelter, established in the East End of London in 1885, acted both as a starting point for immigrants and as a staging post for those travelling further, to America and South Africa. In his monograph Wilkins was adamant that something had to be done to stop the influx of pauper aliens, be they long- or short-term arrivals. He did not look to his fellow countrymen for the resolution. As far as he was concerned it was 'A question for English Jews themselves ... they will be caught up in the antisemitism, they are doing nothing. The wealthy Jews must do something, in gratitude to the country under whose enlightened rule they have amassed their wealth and attained their present influence.'[58]

The alien threat to homes and jobs was augmented by another characteristic of xenophobia, fear of the alien's sexuality. The Jew was perceived as the sexual exploiter of desperate females who, in order to survive on sweated wages, had no alternative but to take to the streets. The alien was not just the cruel sweater who by his harsh method of employment drove women onto the street, he was also the pimp, brothel owner and supplier of girls to the brothels of Buenos Aires, Bombay, Constantinople and Rio de Janeiro. As one anti-alienist wrote in 1892, the alien Jew 'imported vices common to the deeper depths of continental cities'.[59] The dangers of young innocent Jewish girls being drawn into the white slave trade spread from the Pale of Settlement – where promises of marriage and affluence in distant lands led to, at best, false marriages and, at worst, rape – to London where newly arrived, unescorted virgins could end up in the brothels of London or South America.

In order to protect young girls and women on their arrival at the London Docks, the Jewish Ladies Association for Preventive and Rescue Work – to become better known as the Jewish Association for the Protection of Girls and Women – was established by Lord Rothschild's daughter, Constance Flower, later Lady Battersea, in 1885. Some of the Association's most important work was carried out at Liverpool Docks where innocents in transit were ripe pickings for the white slave traders. Inevitably, some girls fell through the net, whilst others may have chosen the course of prostitution as an alternative to starvation. The *Jewish Chronicle* considered Jewish prostitution in the East End of London to be 'a blot upon our community at large'.[60] Chief Rabbi Adler had no doubt that the hundreds of young Jewesses engaged in prostitution (by 1909 the number of Jewish prostitutes operating in the East End was approximately 500[61]) was a consequence of the high levels of immigration and an ever-expanding labour pool. Arnold White adopted this theme in his fight to end pauper alien immigration. Even though the number of English prostitutes active at this time could be counted in the many thousands, the spotlighting of Jewish immorality, male and female, did little to project the alien Jew in an attractive light.

The increasing anti-alien tensions of the first half of the 1890s can be attributed to a combination of the antipathies that arose from concerns over jobs and homes and the impact of numbers. The *Decennial Census* of 1891 identified an increase of 31,249 in the number of Russians, Russian Poles and Rumanians in England and Wales over the previous decade, a rise of over 200 per cent. This was a substantial increase by any reckoning; however, certain further points need to be noted. Firstly, the census returns were not accurate, some aliens falsified their returns or evaded the enumerators whilst many simply did not understand the questions, thus numbers were undoubtedly higher than recorded. Secondly, the visual impact of the increase in numbers was even greater because the alien arrivals were not evenly dispersed but heavily concentrated within the accepted ghetto areas.

Those using statistics in their battle against the alien invasion also took advantage of the none too accurate, but unusually high, Alien Lists which were published every month with details of incoming vessels and the number of aliens aboard. The lists were unchecked and frequently failed to differentiate between those *en route* and those intending to stay in England, thus the numbers of aliens could appear to have reached frightening proportions. This inconsistency was identified by the 1894 *Report on the Volume and Effects of Recent Immigration from Eastern Europe into the United Kingdom* which found that 'the numbers of aliens coming to this country for residence had been grossly exaggerated'[62] and that 'the great majority of aliens who arrive from Continental ports are reported to be on the way to America'.[63] Findings such as these were studiously ignored by the anti-alienists.

The renewed recession of the 1890s did little to lessen demands for immigration controls. The throngs of eastern European Jews on the streets of Whitechapel were a visible reminder of the pressure on jobs and housing. The anti-alienists found an ally in the politician Joseph Chamberlain, who expressed his concern at the 'tens of thousands of foreigners who come to our shores every year who are destitute of all apparent means of subsistence and who are accustomed to so low a standard of living that they can very easily undersell the British workman'. England, he feared, was fast becoming 'the dumping ground of Europe'.[64] Further attacks on the destitute alien came from trade unionists at their annual conference in September 1895. For the fourth year running a resolution was laid down demanding an end to pauper alien immigration. One delegate classified the aliens as the 'refuse of the world' and the Polish Jew as 'a blighted blister on the shoe of industry'.[65] With the economy in recession and unemployment rising it is not surprising that the resolution was finally passed, the trade unionists' delegation to the government welcomed, and their demands sympathetically received. The Jewish trade union movement immediately responded.

Led by the socialist trade unionist Joseph Finn,[66] nine Jewish trade unions published a defence entitled *A Voice From The Alien*. In the pamphlet, Finn used the evidence of the 1894 *Report on the Volume and Effects of Immigration and Migration* to emphasise the fact that England had experienced more emigration than immigration in the years 1891–93. He then identified a number of trades which did not employ immigrant labour but which were still renowned for their low wages and appalling conditions. Finn borrowed a leaf out of Joseph Jacobs's book when describing the way in which Jewish immigrants in the tailoring trade had made a major contribution to the British economy. The example he gave was that of the wholesale mantle trade which had been started in the East End by a Russian immigrant, Morris Cohen, in 1880. Within 15 years Cohen had reversed the trend of importing to one of exporting, and substantially improved Britain's balance of trade.[67] Even though *A Voice From The Alien* put forward a solid argument, backed by valid facts, it did little to alter the views of those determined to ensure that Britain's traditional open-door policy towards immigration was brought to a close.

From the second half of the 1880s moves had been afoot to introduce legislation to control alien immigration. In 1887 there were rumours that a bill was about to be introduced but, instead, the goverment set up its Sweating Commission which found that the 'evils of sweating' were grossly exaggerated and recommended no immediate restrictions on alien entry. The same conclusions were drawn by the goverment's Immigration Committee. The restrictionists were not satisfied. In 1891 they established the (short-lived) Association for Preventing the Immigration of Destitute Aliens. In 1894 a further attempt was made to pass an aliens bill. It failed. Two years later, in March 1896, following hard on the deputation from the TUC Cardiff Conference, a draft bill was drawn up to restrict 'the importation of destitute aliens'[68]. This too went no further.

It was within this climate that the first *Jewish Year Book* was conceived. A volume intended, as its author suggested, to provide knowledge in order to facilitate improvement; to enable its readership to recognise the dangers, as social scientist Jacobs saw them, of presenting an inaccurate image of British Jewry. Jacobs was determined to press home his thesis, that with the right guidance and information the eastern European aliens could, within a short period of time, become anglicised, assimilated and acculturated, and ready to make their worthwhile contribution to the British way of life. By contrast, vulgarity, over-representation and ignorance of the mores of the society of which they should become a part would only antagonise the antisemites and anti-alienists. This message was intended for the alien and the more anglicised members of British Jewry. Not everyone heeded Jacobs's warnings. In 1902, the Senior Minister of the West London Synagogue of British Jews, the Reverend Morris Joseph, in the light of growing antisemitism, called for Jews to 'eschew vulgarity and extravagance and adopt a more sober way of life', a call he repeated 11 years later in the wake of the Marconi and Indian Silver scandals.[69]

In view of the tensions which manifested in the 1880s and first half of the 1890s it would be surprising if there had not been subtexts to that first *Jewish Year Book*. One was clearly addressed to British Jewry, telling them that though, compared with countries overseas, antisemitism was not yet a major problem in Britain, there was a need for vigilance and good practice if this was to remain so. Provision had been made for needy immigrants to be taken under the wing of the community, not the state, in order that, wherever possible, the 'ghetto bends' be ironed out.[70] It was vital that those provisions did not appear too attractive. This had clearly been a factor in the minds of those who had closed down the forerunner to the Poor Jews' Temporary Shelter in 1884 and those who had placed advertisements in newspapers in eastern Europe recommending that would-be emigrants stay where they were.

The message going out to Jew and non-Jew alike who

might read the *Year Book* of 5657 was very similar to that which appeared in Board of Trade's *Reports on the Volume and Effects of Recent Immigration from Eastern Europe into the United Kingdom* – one which might have been taken directly from Joseph Jacobs's lips. It was that, providing the aliens took note of the advice Jacobs had to offer, they too could assimilate 'with marvellous rapidity to English habits and ideas, producing in the second generation at least, a people of whom any State might well be proud'. With the benefit of hindsight we know that this did not satisfy the impatience of the anti-alienists. As the alien presence increased, tensions rose. In 1901 the British Brothers League, arguably a precursor of later fascist organisations, was founded in the East End of London. Its main objective was to put an end to alien immigration. Two years later the goverment established the Aliens' Commission. In 1905 the Aliens Act was passed by a Conservative government and, ironically, as a result of that year's general election, was put into operation by the party that had always been the friend of the immigrant, the new Liberal government of 1906. By the passage of that act, Greenberg believed, 'Great Britain bowed its neck to clamour nurtured and fostered by racial prejudice, and for the first time for centuries, yielded up its proud privilege of rendering free asylum to the oppressed of the world'.[71] It was this act that heralded the beginning of immigration control in Britain. Subsequent acts, in 1914 and 1919, tightened controls still further, so that by the 1930s what had appeared harsh in the 1900s might have saved thousands of lives between 1933 and 1945.

NOTES

1. *Jewish Year Book 1896*, p.ix (future references, unless otherwise stated, to the *Jewish Year Book* will refer to the 1896 edition).
2. *Jewish Chronicle*, 28 Aug. 1896.
3. D. Cesarani, *The Jewish Chronicle and Anglo-Jewry 1841–1991* (London, 1994), p.106.

INTRODUCTION TO FACSIMILE EDITION [xxxix]

4. *Jewish Year Book*, pp.213–24.
5. His contacts in Cambridge were Lucien Wolf and his family.
6. See J. Efron, *Defenders of the Race* (Yale, 1994), Ch.4.
7. See A.J. Kershen, 'Henry Mayhew and Charles Booth: Men of Their Times' in G. Alderman and C. Holmes (eds), *Outsiders and Outcasts* (1993), Ch.6.
8. See below.
9. *Jewish Year Book,* pp.203–10.
10. *Jewish Chronicle,* 7 Sept. 1894.
11. *Jewish Year Book* p.203.
12. During the pogrom 1,300 Jewish homes and shops were destroyed, 400 Jews injured and 45 Jews killed. These incidents resulted in a world-wide protest to the Tsar from the President of the USA, the heads of the governments of Britain, France and Germany and the Austrian Emperor. See H.M. Sacher, *The Course of Modern Jewish History* (New York, 1977), pp.248–9.
13. *Jewish Year Book*, p.204.
14. G.L. Mosse, *Toward the Final Solution* (New York, 1985), p.141.
15. R. Wistrich, *Antisemitism: The Longest Hatred* (1992), pp.63–4.
16. *Jewish Chronicle*, 11 Jan. 1895.
17. Ibid., 25 Jan. 1895.
18. Ibid., 5 Sept. 1896.
19. For an account of British Jewry's attitudes towards Zionism between 1895 and 1920 see S. Cohen, *English Zionists and British Jews* (Princeton, 1982).
20. *Jewish Year Book,* p.154.
21. *Jewish Chronicle*, 13 Sept. 1895.
22. See, among others, D. Feldman, *Englishmen and Jews* (1994) and C. Holmes, *Antisemitism in British Society* (1979).
23. For a detailed account of Disraeli and attitudes during the Balkan Crisis see D. Feldman, op.cit., Ch.4.
24. Goldwin Smith, 'Can Jews be Patriots?', *Nineteenth Century* (May 1878), pp.878–97.
25. Goldwin Smith, 'The Jewish Question', *Nineteenth Century* (Oct. 1881), pp.494–515.
26. Both were works which purported to reveal the Jewish plot to dominate the world.
27. See C. Holmes, op.cit., pp.55–7.
28. *East London Leader and Tower Hamlets Record and Parliamentary and Parochial News*, 2 June 1883.
29. See B. Cheyette, *Constructions of the Jew in English Literature and Society* (Cambridge, 1993).
30. G. Du Maurier, *Novels* (London, 1947), p.224.
31. See T. Endelman, 'The Frankaus of London', *Jewish History*, Vol. 8, Nos 1–2 (1994), pp.128–32.
32. Ibid.

33. In the Jewish ghettoes of both Leeds and Manchester conditions very similar to those which existed in London could be found.
34. *Outsiders and Outcasts*, op.cit., p.99.
35. *The Lancet*, 5 March 1884, and A.J. Kershen, *Uniting the Tailors* (London, 1995), p.110.
36. As did other social commentators, most notably Charles Booth who chose to carry out his 1887 survey of poverty in Tower Hamlets as he believed that to be the most impoverished area in Britain. See A.J. Kershen in *Outsiders and Outcasts*, op.cit.
37. Quoted in *Jewish Chronicle*, 26 Feb. 1888.
38. See below.
39. *The Times*, 13 July 1887.
40. *Report to the Board of Trade on the Sweating System at the East End of London* by the Labour Correspondent of the Board, 12 Sept. 1887 (London, 17 Feb. 1888), pp.4–7.
41. B. Potter, The House of Lords Committee on the Sweating System, *Nineteenth Century*, Vol.clx (June 1890), p.889.
42. Burnett, op.cit., p.19.
43. *East London Advertiser*, 3 March 1888.
44. *Evening News*, 9 Oct. 1891.
45. C. Booth (ed.), *Life and Labour of the People in London*, First Series, Poverty, Vol. 3 (1902 edn), p.171.
46. Ibid.
47. J.A. Hobson, *Problems of Poverty* (1892), p.60.
48. See G. Stedman Jones, *Outcast London* (London, 1971), Chs.8–11, for a full account of overcrowding in London during the last half of the nineteenth century.
49. G. Stedman Jones, op.cit., p.176.
50. H. Boult, 'The Housing of the Poor', *Fortnightly Review*, Vol.xliii (1 Feb. 1888), p.147.
51. Ibid., p.149.
52. *Outsiders and Outcasts*, op.cit., p.99.
53. *Jewish Chronicle*, 29 Sept. 1888.
54. See B. Gainer, *The Alien Invasion* (1972), p.42.
55. *The Lancet*, op.cit.
56. For an account of the way in which the health hazard was used as a tool in the anti-alienist attack see Holmes, op.cit., Ch.3.
57. W. H. Wilkins, *The Alien Invasion* (1892), p.51.
58. Wilkins, op.cit., p.53.
59. Quoted in C. Holmes, *Antisemitism in British Society 1879–1939* (1979), p.24 n57.
60. *Jewish Chronicle*, 12 Oct. 1888.
61. L. Gartner, *The Jewish Immigrant in England* (1960), pp.185–6.
62. A.J. Kershen, *Uniting the Tailors*, op. cit., p.50.
63. *Jewish Year Book*, p.219.
64. Quoted in G. Drage, 'Alien Immigration', *Fortnightly Review*,

Vol.lvii (1895), pp.37–46.
65. Reported in *Jewish Chronicle*, 13 Sept. 1895.
66. For details of Finn see A.J. Kershen, *Uniting the Tailors*, op. cit., Ch.2.
67. Ibid., Ch.4.
68. Gainer, op.cit., p.178.
69. See A.J. Kershen and J.A. Romain, *Tradition and Change: A History of Reform Judaism in Britain 1840–1995* (1995), pp.117–18.
70. One way was by the formation of clubs for the children of the immigrants, such as the Jewish Lads' Brigade. For the history of the Brigade, which was established in 1895, see S. Kadish, *'A Good Jew and a Good Englishman': The Jewish Lads' & Girls' Brigade, 1895–1995* (1995).
71. J. Greenberg, *Jewish Year Book, 1905 [5666]*, p.464.

ALLIANCE ASSURANCE COMPANY.

Head Office—BARTHOLOMEW LANE, LONDON, E.C.

Established 1824.

CAPITAL—£5,000,000.

DIRECTORS:

...rd ROTHSCHILD, *Chairman*.

JAMES ...	Sir GEORGE C. LAMPSON, Bart.
CHARLES EDWARD BAR...	FRANCIS ALFRED LUCAS, Esq.
Right Hon. Lord BATTERSEA,	...ARD HARBORD LUSHINGTON, Esq.
Hon. KENELM P. BOUVERIE.	HUGH COLIN SMITH, Esq.
T. H. BURROUGHES. Esq.	Right Hon. Lord STALBRIDGE.
FRANCIS WILLIAM BUXTON, Esq.	Lieut.-Col. F. ANDERSON STEBBING.
JAMES FLETCHER, Esq.	Sir CHARLES RIVERS WILSON,
RICHARD HOARE, Esq.	G.C.M.G., C.B.

Auditors—

VICTOR C. W. CAVEN... ...sq., M.P.   Major-Gen. ARTHUR E. A. ELLIS, C.S.I.
Hon. H. BERF... ...ORTMAN.   Hon. LIONEL WALTER ROTHSCHILD.

ROBERT LEWIS, *Chief S...* ...*ry*.   D. MIRYLEES and P. MYERS, *Assistant Secretaries*.
M. N. ADLER, *A...* ...*y*.   G. J. LIDSTONE, *Assistant Actuary*.

ST. JAMES... BRANCH—ST. JAMES'S STREET, LONDON, S.W.
CHANCERY LANE BRANCH—64, CHANCERY LANE, W.C.
NORFOLK STREET BRANCH—3, NORFOLK STREET, STRAND, W.C.
WESTMINSTER BRANCH—1, GREAT GEORGE STREET, WESTMINSTER.
MINCING LANE BRANCH—3, MINCING LANE, E.C.

The Company have Branch Offices at Edinburgh, Glasgow, Dublin, Liverpool, Manchester, Sheffield, Birmingham, Ipswich, Bury St. Edmunds, Newcastle-on-Tyne, Bristol, Shrewsbury, Leicester, Wrexham, and Nottingham.

FIRE INSURANCES GRANTED AT CURRENT RATES.

LIFE DEPARTMENT.

Moderate Rates of Premium. Large Bonuses, including interim Bonuses. Policies Whole World and Indisputable.

DEATH DUTIES.—Special forms of Policies have been prepared in order to enable the owners of property to make provision for the new ESTATE DUTY. Full particulars will be forwarded on application.

LEASEHOLD AND SINKING FUND POLICIES

are granted (on terms which may be ascertained on application) enabling Leaseholders to recoup their expenditure by a small Annual Premium, or by a Single Payment in advance.

Full Prospectuses and Statements of Accounts may be had on application to the Head Office of the Company, or to any of the Branch Offices.

ROBERT LEWIS, *Chief Secretary*.

"*No flaw in its claim to be Absolutely Pure.*"
Medical Annual.

Fry's

PURE CONCENTRATED

Cocoa

"**STRONGEST and BEST.**"—*Health.*

OVER 180 GOLD MEDALS AND DIPLOMAS.

"FRY'S PURE CONCENTRATED COCOA."

ADVERTISEMENTS.

217, PICCADILLY, W. ALLEN & WRIGHT, 26, POULTRY, E.C.

MAKERS OF HIGH-CLASS BRIAR & MEERSCHAUM PIPES. Every Pipe Guaranteed.

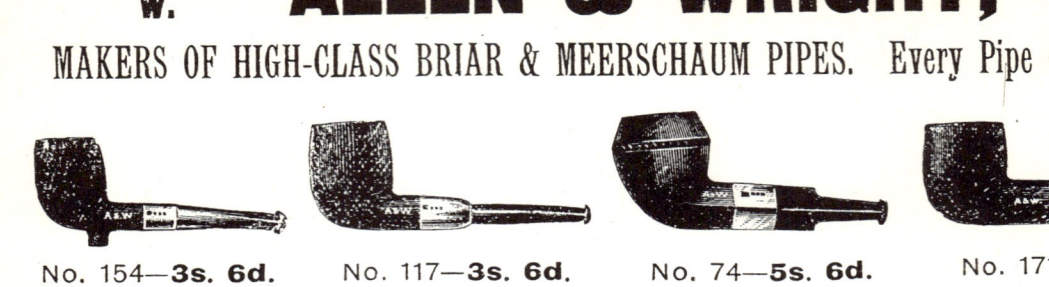

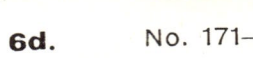

No. 154—**3s. 6d.** No. 117—**3s. 6d.** No. 74—**5s. 6d.**  No. 171—**4s. 6d.**

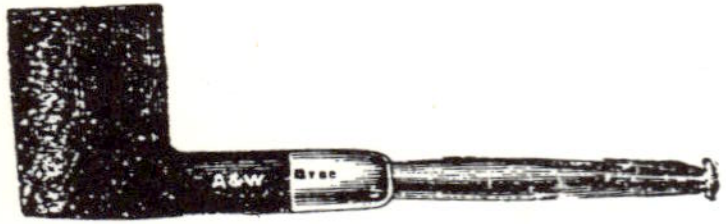

No. 38—**3s. 6d.**  No. 184—**3s. 6d.** 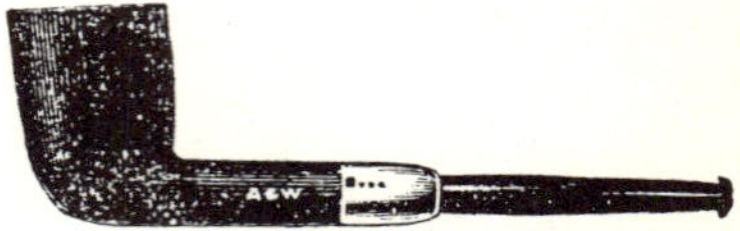 No. 179—**3s. 6d.**

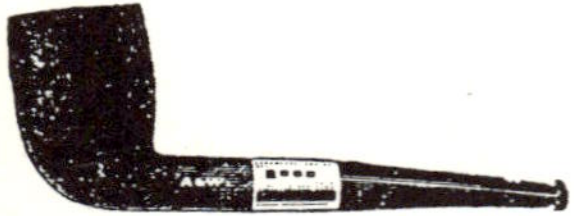

No. 53—**3s. 6d.**  No. 117—**3s. 6d.**  No. 118—**3s. 6d.**  No. 156—**4s. 6d.**

ILLUSTRATED CATALOGUE POST FREE TO ANY PART OF THE WORLD.

THE JEWISH YEAR BOOK

5657.

FAMILY EVENTS.
5657 (1896-7).

THE JEWISH YEAR BOOK.

An Annual Record of Matters Jewish.

5657.

8th SEPTEMBER, 1896—26th SEPTEMBER, 1897.

EDITED BY

JOSEPH JACOBS,

Author of "Studies in Jewish Statistics," "The Jews of Angevin England," "Jewish Ideals," etc.

למנות ימינו כן הודע

"So teach us to number our days."—Ps. xc. 12.

LONDON:
GREENBERG & CO., 80, CHANCERY LANE, W.C.
SIMPKIN, MARSHALL, HAMILTON, KENT & CO., Ltd.

1896.

Price Two Shillings net.

LONDON:
PRINTED BY WERTHEIMER, LEA AND CO.,
CIRCUS PLACE, LONDON WALL.

PREFACE.

THERE is no need for any apology for the appearance of such a work as this. I feel none the less that some words of excuse should be given for any imperfections which must appear in this first attempt at a somewhat complicated task. Nothing of the book, however, was written on April 15th of this year, and it went to press on July 15th. This fact will, perhaps, serve as my best excuse for its failings, and any errors of omission or commission will be gladly amended in subsequent issues, and I shall be grateful to any one who will kindly draw my attention to them, at the address given below. That they are not more numerous is due, in the first place, to the promptitude with which the secretaries of the Metropolitan Institutions have responded to my appeals for information in regard to their activities. Truly, we are a business people.

For the first time since the appearance of Mr. Asher I. Myers' *Jewish Directory* (in 1874), English Jews are now put into possession of a summary account of their present position and organisation in the British Empire. The need of such a work is undeniable. Knowledge is power for a community as well as for an individual, and in many directions communal improvement has been impaired and often rendered nugatory for the want of such information as is contained in the present volume.

I have attempted to mitigate the aridity which must characterise such a collection of facts and figures by adding a certain amount of material which can claim to be, in a certain sense, literature. It will doubtless be of interest both to Jews and others to find in the Glossary a succinct account of technical terms covering almost all aspects of Jewish life. I can offer this list with some confidence, since most traces of my Am haaretsuth (*q.v.*), have been removed by the kind revision of such eminent scholars as Dr. Friedlander, Mr. S. Schechter, and Mr. Israel Abrahams, from whose work on "Jewish Social Life in the Middle Ages" I have picked some of its plums. These gentlemen, however, are not to be held responsible for the errors that doubtless still remain. Besides these, my friend, Mr. Israel Zangwill, has given permanent value to the book by allowing me to include in it a series of poems which will reveal him, I fancy, in an unexpected light to the Jewish public.

The Very Rev. the Chief Rabbi has throughout shown the greatest possible interest in the work, and has freely placed at my disposal the information stored in the archives of his office. At his suggestion there is included in the calendar a list of the Minhagim, which has been compiled by Dr. Hirsch. Dr. Adler has also allowed excerpts to be made from his lists of Jewish celebrities, which have rendered the one contained in this work much more complete than it would otherwise have been. I have also to thank Prof. Bacher, of Buda-Pesth, Mons. Theodore Reinach, of Paris, and Dr. C. Liebermann, of Berlin, for kind help in this direction. The Rev. F. L. Cohen, has contributed to the book from his intimate acquaintance with the Jewish elements in the British Army, and Mr. M. Duparc has placed at my disposal his extensive and peculiar knowledge of Metropolitan Judaism.

Finally, it would be unfair not to acknowledge in most grateful terms the ready assistance I have received throughout from my friend, Mr. L. J. Greenberg, who first suggested the work to me, and to whom many of the most valuable items of the book owe their existence. The succinct yet comprehensive account of Alien Immigration is from his pen.

JOSEPH JACOBS.

80, CHANCERY LANE, LONDON, W.C.,
15th July, 1896—*Ab 5th,* 5656.

CONTENTS.

	PAGE.
JEWISH CALENDAR AND NOTABLE DAYS	1
EXPLANATION OF CALENDAR	15
JEWISH HOLIDAYS AND FESTIVALS	20
JAHRZEIT AND BARMITZVAH TABLES	21
GENERAL JEWISH STATISTICS	27
JEWS OF THE BRITISH EMPIRE	28
COMMUNAL STATISTICS	30
COMMUNAL INSTITUTIONS, METROPOLIS—	
Synagogues	34
Charities (with Charity Guide)	40
Schools	53
Miscellaneous Jewish Institutions	57
Ecclesiastical Authorities, and Persons authorized by them	61
COMMUNAL INSTITUTIONS, PROVINCIAL	64
COLONIAL CONGREGATIONS	91
JEWISH CLERGY LIST	95
JEWISH PEERAGE, KNIGHTHOOD AND BARONETCY	100
JEWISH MEMBERS OF PARLIAMENT	113
JEWS IN THE ARMY, NAVY, AND RESERVE FORCES	115
JEWISH CELEBRITIES	118

	PAGE
BOOKS OF REFERENCE	126
ACTS OF PARLIAMENT	129
GLOSSARY OF JEWISH TERMS	135
A GLANCE AT 5656	203
NOTABLE EVENTS OF 5656	211
OBITUARY OF 5656	212
ALIEN IMMIGRATION	213
LITERARY SUPPLEMENT—	
"Moods of the Jewish Year," I. ZANGWILL	225
"Jewish Table Customs," I. ABRAHAMS	235
"Jewish Messiahs," J. JACOBS	253
ALPHABETICAL TABLE OF CONTENTS	259
INDEX OF NAMES	267
INDEX OF ADVERTISERS	276

The Jewish Year,
5657,

is known as 657 (תרנ"ז) on the short system (לפ"ק), and is a **regular** *Leap Year* of 13 months, 55 Sabbaths, and 384 days. Its first of Tishri begins on Tuesday, the third day of the week, and the first day of Passover on Saturday the seventh. Therefore its sign is גכ"ז, *i.e.* 'ג for third, 'כ for regular (כסדרה), and 'ז for seventh.

It is the fourteenth year (י"ד) of the 298th (רצ"ח) minor (למ"ק) or lunar (ללבנה) cycle (of 19 years each) since the Era of Creation, and the first ('א) of the 203rd (ר"ג) major (למ"ג) or solar (לחמה) cycle (of 28 years each) since the same epoch.

It begins on September 8th, 1896, and concludes on September 26th, 1897.

The hours of the beginning of Sabbaths and Festivals are for the latitude of London, and as established by Haham David Nieto, and the hour of the close of the same as settled by the late Chief Rabbi, the Very Rev. Dr. N. M. ADLER.

Marriages may not be solemnised September 16th (day preceding Day of Atonement), September 21st (day preceding Tabernacles), September 24th to 27th (Middle days of Tabernacles), March 18th and 19th (Purim), April 16th (day preceding Passover), April 19th to 22nd (Middle days of Passover), May 3rd to 19th and 20th to 31st (Sephira), June 5th (day preceding Pentecost), July 19th to August 7th (from Fast of Tamuz to that of Ab), nor on any Sabbath or Festival.

1896, Sept. 8–Oct. 7] **TISHRI XXX. DAYS.** [תשרי 5657

תקופה: Oct. 6. 3 a.m.   Monday: 4h. 17m. 13s. p.m. מולד

Night. h. m.	Day.	D. of Month Heb. / Eng. SEPT	Sabbaths, Fasts, Festivals, Events, Remarkable Days, Portions of Pentateuch, Haphtorahs.
7.12	T	א / 8	**New Year** א' דר' השנה { *Por.*, Gen. xxi., Num. xxix. 1-6. / *Haph.*, 1 Samuel i., ii. 1-10.
7.10	W	ב / 9	**2nd Day** ב' דר' השנה { *Por.*, Gen. xxii., Num. xxix. 1-6. / *Haph.*, Jeremiah xxxi. 2-20.
7.8	Th	ג / 10	*Fast of Gedaliah* צום גדליה { *Por.*, Ex. xxxii. 11-14, xxxiv. 1-10. / *Haph.*, Is. lv. 6—lvi. 8.
	F	ד / 11	Jews burnt alive in Prague, 1400. 6.0 שבת
7.3	S̃	ה / 12	וילך , שבת שובה { *Por.*, Deut. xxxi. / *Haph.*, Hos xiv. 2-10, Joel ii. 15-27.
	S	ו / 13	
	M	ז / 14	R. Jacob Möln Halevi (Maharil) d. in Worms, 1427.
	T	ח / 15	Rodrigues Pereyra, inventor of deaf and dumb oral method, d. 1780.
	W	ט / 16	Grace Aguilar, d. 1847. ערב יום כפור
6.51	Th	י / 17	**Day of Atonement** יום כפור { *Por.*, Lev. xvi., Num. xxix. 7-11, *Aft.* Lev. xviii. / *Haph.*, Is. lvii. 14—lviii. 14, *Aft.* Book of Jonah
	F	יא / 18	Jon. Eibeschütz, d. 1764. 5.30 שבת
6.47	S̃	יב / 19	האזינו { *Por.*, Deut. xxxii. / *Haph.*, 2 Sam. xxii.
	S	יג / 20	Gedalyah Jachya d. 1487
	M	יד / 21	ערב סכות
6.40	T	טו / 22	**Tabernacles** א' דסכות { *Por.*, Lev. xxii. 26—xxiii. 44, Num. xxix. 12-16. / *Haph.*, Zech. xiv.
6.37	W	טז / 23	**2nd Day** ב' דסכות { *Por.*, Lev. xxii. 26—xxiii. 44, Num. xxix. 12-16. / *Haph.*, 1 Kings viii. 2-21.
	Th	יז / 24	Lady Montefiore d. 1862. *Por.*, Num. xxix. 17-25.
	F	יח / 25	5.30 שבת *Por.*, Num. xxix. 20-28.
6.30	S̃	יט / 26	שבת חו"ה { *Por.*, Ex. xxxiii. 12—xxxiv. 26, Num. xxix. 23-28. / *Haph.*, Ezech. xxxviii. 18—xxxix. 16.
	S	כ / 27	*Por.*, Num. xxix. 26-34.
	M	כא / 28	Hoshana Rabba הושענא רבה *Por.*, Num. xxix. 26-34.
6.23	T	כב / 29	**8th Day of Feast** ש' עצרת { *Por.*, Deut. xiv. 22—xvi. 17, Num xxix. 35—xxx. 1. *Haph.*, 1 Kings viii. 54-66.
6.21	W	כג / 30	**Feast of Law** שמחת תורה { *Por.*, Deut. xxxiii.—xxxiv., Gen. i.—ii. 3, Num. xxix. 35—xxx. 1. *Haph.*, Josh. i.
	Th	כד / OCT. 1	Moses Zacuto, d. 1697. אסרו חג
	F	כה / 2	5.0 שבת
6.14	S̃	כו / 3	בראשית , מברכין החדש { *Por.*, Gen. i.—vi. 8. / *Haph.*, Is. xlii. 5—xliii. 10.
	S	כז / 4	
	M	כח / 5	J. P. Baratier, Christian, translator of Benjamin of Tudela, d. 1740.
	T	כט / 6	ערב ר"ח
	W	ל / 7	א' דר"ח

Minhagim—Sept. 8-17, days of penitence, during which say זכרנו etc., in Amidah, לעילא ולעילא in Kadish,—אבינו מלכנו, morning and afternoon, except on 11th in afternoon, the 12th and the 16th, and Selichot on weekdays.—Sept. 8th, תשליך.—Sept. 16th, omit מזמור לתודה, תחנון said in מנחה. From the 18th of Sept. till 1st Oct. תחנון omitted.—השענות : on the 22nd Sept., למען אמתך; 23rd, אבן שתיה; 24th. אערוך ישועי; 25th, אום אני חומה; 26th, אום נצורה; 27th, אדון המושיע.—Sept. 26th, omit צדקתך in מנחה.—Sept. 29th, משיב.

1896, Oct. 8–Nov. 5] CHESHVAN XXIX. DAYS. [חשון 5657

Wednesday : 5h. 1m. 14s. a.m. מולד

Night. h. m.	Day.	D. of Month Heb.	D. of Month Eng.	Sabbaths, Fasts, Festivals, Events, Remarkable Days, Portions of Pentateuch, Haphtorahs.
	Th	א	Oct. 8	ב' דר"ח
	F	ב	9	שבת 5.0
5.58	S	ג	10	Elia Wilna, d. 1797. נח { *Por.*, Gen. vi. 9—xi. 32. / *Haph*., Is. liv. 1—lv. 5.
	S	ד	11	Ninety Jews massacred at Munich, 1285.
	M	ה	12	
	T	ו	13	
	W	ז	14	
	Th	ח	15	
	F	ט	16	Joseph del Medigo, d. 1655. 4.30 שבת
5.44	S	י	17	לך לך { *Por.*, Gen. xii.—xvii. / *Haph*., Is. xl. 27—xli. 16.
	S	יא	18	
	M	יב	19	Jews martyred at Heilbronn, 1298.
	T	יג	20	
	W	יד	21	S. M. Ehrenberg, Zunz's teacher, d. 1853.
	Th	טו	22	
	F	טז	23	Gesenius d. 1842. 4.30 שבת
5.30	S	יז	24	Moses Montefiore, b. 1784. ויראָ מב' ב'ה'ב' { *Por.*, Gen. xviii.—xxii. / *Haph*., 2 Kings iv. 1-37.
	S	יח	25	Asher b. Jechiel d. Toledo 1327.
5.26	M	יט	26	*First Fast* תענית שני קמא
	T	כ	27	
	W	כא	28	Moses Nachmanides d. 1270.
5.21	Th	כב	29	*Second Fast* תענית חמישי
	F	כג	30	שבת 4.0
5.17	S	כד	31	חיי שרה, מברכין החדש { *Por.*, Gen. xxiii.—xxv. 18. / *Haph*. 1 Kings i. 1-31.
	S	כה	Nov 1	Jews expelled from England, 1290.
5.14	M	כו	2	*Third Fast* תענית שני תניינא
	T	כז	3	
	W	כח	4	Auto da fé in Seville, 1481.
	Th	כט	5	David Sassoon. d. 1864. ערב ר"ח

הרוח commenced in מוסף.—Oct. 3rd, ברכי נפשי commenced in מנחה on Saturdays.—Oct. 6th, תחנון omitted in מנחה.—Oct. 7th, הלל (omitting the pieces לא לנו and אהבתי), omit תחנון and למנצח.

Minhagim—Oct. 8th, הלל (omitting the pieces לא לנו and אהבתי), omit תחנון and למנצח.—Oct. 26th and 29th, Nov. 2nd, סליחות in עמידה.—Nov. 5th יום כפור קטן, omit תחנון in מנחה.

B 2

1896, Nov. 6–Dec. 5] KISLEV XXX. DAYS. [כסליו 565 7

Thursday : 5h. 45m. 15s. p.m. מולד

Night.	Day.	D. of Month Heb.	D. of Month Eng.	Sabbaths, Fasts, Festivals, Events, Remarkable Days, Portions of Pentateuch, Haphtorahs.
h. m.	F	א	Nov. 6	ראש חדש שבת 4.0
5.6	S	ב	7	תולדות { *Por.*, Gen. xxv. 19—xxviii. 9. *Haph.*, Malachi, i. 1—ii. 7.
	S	ג	8	
	M	ד	9	
	T	ה	10	P. Beer d. 1838.
	W	ו	11	
	Th	ז	12	First number of *Jewish Chronicle* published, 1841.
	F	ח	13	שבת 4.0
4.57	S	ט	14	ויצא { *Por.*, Gen. xxviii. 10—xxxii. 3. *Haph.*, Hosh. xii. 13—xiv. 10.
	S	י	15	Baron James de Rothschild d. 1868.
	M	יא	16	Jews executed for imaginary crime at La Guardia, 1491.
	T	יב	17	
	W	יג	18	First Meeting of Board of Deputies, 1760.
	Th	יד	19	Interpellation in Prussian Landtag on Judenhetze, 1880.
	F	טו	20	Menasse b. Israel d. 1657 שבת 3.30
4.49	S	טז	21	וישלח { *Por.*, Gen. xxxii. 4—xxxvi. 43. *Haph.*, Hosh. xi. 7—xii. 12.
	S	יז	22	S. Maimon d. 1800. Geo. Eliot b. 1819.
	M	יח	23	
	T	יט	24	Spinoza b. 1632.
	W	כ	25	
	Th	כא	26	תענית ח' גמילת חסדים
	F	כב	27	שבת 3.30
4.43	S	כג	28	וישב, מברכין החדש { *Por.*, Gen. xxxvii.—xl. *Haph.*, Amos ii. 6—iii. 8.
	S	כד	29	
	M	כה	30	John Selden d. 1654. *Por.*, Num. vii. 1-17.
	T	כו	Dec. 1	*Por.*, Num. vii. 18-29.
	W	כז	2	חנוכה Hanucah Dedication of the Temple by the Maccabeans *Por.*, Num. vii. 24-35.
	Th	כח	3	*Por.*, Num. vii. 30-41.
	F	כט	4	ערב ר"ח שבת 3.30 *Por.*, Num. vii. 36-47.
4.40	S	ל	5	מקץ א' דר"ח, טל ומטר במעריב { *Por.*, Gen. xli. 1.—xliv. 17, Num. xxviii. 9-15, vii. 42-53. *Haph.*, Zech. ii. 14—iv. 7.

Minhagim—Nov. 6th, הלל (omitting אהבתי and לא לנו), omit תחנון and למנצח.—Nov. 29th, omit תחנון in מנחה; First Night of lighting the Hanucah light.—During Hanucah say אל ארך אפים, and למנצח.—Dec. 5th omit צדקתך in תחנון, omit הלל and על הנסים, commence saying טל ומטר in מעריב.

1896, Dec. 6–1897, Jan. 3] TEBETH XXIX. DAYS. [טבת 5657

Saturday : 6h. 29m. 16s. a.m. מולד

Night.	Day.	D. of Month Heb.	D. of Month Eng.	Sabbaths, Fasts, Festivals, Events, Remarkable Days, Portions of Pentateuch, Haphtorahs.
h. m.			Dec.	
	S	א	6	Lightfoot d. 1675. חנוכה, דר״ח ב׳ *Por.*, Num. xxviii. 1-15, vii. 48-59.
	M	ב	7	חנוכת מזבח *Por.*, Num. vii. 54—viii. 4.
	T	ג	8	Abraham ibn Ezra composed his Sabbath Epistle, London, 1158.
	W	ד	9	
	Th	ה	10	Averroes d. 1198
	F	ו	11	שבת 3.30
4.39	S	ז	12	ויגש {*Por.*, Gen. xliv. 18–xlvii. 27. *Haph.*, Ezech. xxxvii. 15-28.
	S	ח	13	Maimonides d. 1204.
	M	ט	14	
4.39	T	י	15	**Fast of Tebeth** צום עשרה בטבת {*Por.*, Ex. xxxii. 11-14, xxxiv. 1-10. *Haph.*, Is. lv. 6—lvi. 8.
	W	יא	16	Jews expelled from France, 1394.
	Th	יב	17	
	F	יג	18	שבת 3.30
4 40	S	יד	19	Tebele Schiff d. 1791. ויחי {*Por.*, Gen. xlvii. 28–l. 26. *Haph.*, I Kings ii. 1-12.
	S	טו	20	Joseph Cohen, historian, b. 1496.
	M	טז	21	*Shortest Day* ליל ארוך Benjamin Disraeli b. 1804.
	T	יז	22	Geo. Eliot d. 1880.
	W	יח	23	Salomon Heine d. 1844.
	Th	יט	24	
	F	כ	25	*Christmas*
4.44	S	כא	26	*Bank Holiday* שמות {*Por.*, Ex. ii.–vi. 1. *Haph.*, Is. xxvii. 6—xxviii. 13, xxix. 22-23.
	S	כב	27	Complete emancipation in Hungary, 1867.
	M	כג	28	Macaulay d. 1859.
	T	כד	29	
	W	כה	30	Joseph ibn Nagdila, d. 1066.
	Th	כו	31	
	F	כז	Jan. 1897 1	Chajim Bacharach d. 1702.
4.50	S	כח	2	וארא, מברכין החדש {*Por.*, Ex. vi. 2–ix. 35. *Haph.*, Ezech. xxviii. 25–xxix. 21.
	S	כט	3	Rachel d. 1858. ערב ר״ח

Minhagim—Dec. 6th, על הנסים, הלל, Num. xxviii. 3 not repeated. Omit תחנון and למנצח.—Dec. 7th, על הנסים, הלל, omit תחנון and למנצח.—Dec. 15th, סליחות, ענגו.—Jan. 3rd, omit תחנון in מנחה.

1897, Jan. 4–Feb. 2] SHEBAT XXX. DAYS. [שבט 5657

תקופה: Jan. 5. 10.30 a.m.   Monday: 7h. 13m. 17s. p.m. מולד

Night.	Day.	D. of Month Heb.	D. of Month Eng.	Sabbaths, Fasts, Festivals, Events, Remarkable Days, Portions of Pentateuch, Haphtorahs.
h. m.	M	א	Jan. 4	Mendelssohn d. 1786. ראש חדש
	T	ב	5	J. Salvador b. 1796.
	W	ג	6	First auto da fé at Seville, 1481.
	Th	ד	7	Sir Julian Goldsmid d. 1896.
	F	ה	8	שבת 3.30
4.58	S	ו	9	בא { *Por.*, Ex. x. 1-xiii. 16. / *Haph.*, Jeremiah xlvi. 13-28.
	S	ז	10	David Nieto d., London, 1728.
	M	ח	11	Marquis d'Argens, author of *Lettres juives*, d. 1771.
	T	ט	12	
	W	י	13	
	Th	יא	14	Emancipation of Swiss Jews, 1866.
	F	יב	15	שבת 4.0
5.7	S	יג	16	בשלח, שבת שירה { *Por.*, Ex. xiii. 17—xvii. 16. / *Haph.*, Judges iv. 4—v. 31.
	S	יד	17	
	M	טו	18	*New Year for Trees* חמשה עשר, ר"ה לאלנות
	T	טז	19	Dr. Marcus Herz d. 1803. Isaac D'Israeli d 1843.
	W	יז	20	
	Th	יח	21	Jews expelled from France, 1306.
	F	יט	22	שבת 4.0
5.18	S	כ	23	Abraham Ibn Ezra d. 1167 יתרו { *Por.*, Exod. xviii.—xx. / *Haph.*, Isaiah vi. 1—vii. 6, ix. 5, 6.
	S	כא	24	
	M	כב	25	
	T	כג	26	
	W	כד	27	
	Th	כה	28	Jews of Bayonne and Bordeaux received full civil rights, 1790.
	F	כו	29	שבת 4.30
5.29	S	כז	30	משפטים, מברכין החדש { *Por.*, Ex. xxi.—xxiv. / *Haph.*, Jeremiah xxxiv. 8-22, xxxiii. 25-26.
	S	כח	31	Dr. Michael Sachs d. 1864.
	M	כט	Feb. 1	ערב ר"ח, יום כפור קטן
	T	ל	2	א' דר"ח

Minhagim—Jan. 4th אל ארך, תחנון, omit (אהבתי and לא לנו omitting the piece) הלל תחנון.—Feb. 1st, ואפים, and למנצח.—Jan. 17th, omit תחנון in מנחה.—Jan. 18th, omit תחנון omit תחנון in מנחה.—Feb. 2nd, הלל (omitting the pieces אהבתי and לא לנו), omit תחנון and למנצח.

1897, Feb. 3–Mar. 4] 1st **ADAR XXX. DAYS.** [אדר ראשון 5657

Tuesday : 7h. 58m. 0s. am. מולד

Night.	Day.	D. of Month Heb. / Eng.		Sabbaths, Fasts, Festivals, Events, Remarkable Days, Portions of Pentateuch, Haphtorahs.
h. m.			Feb.	
	W	א	3	ב׳ דר״ח
	Th	ב	4	Resettlement Day—Jews admitted to England by Cromwell, 1656.
	F	ג	5	שבת 4.30
5.41	S	ד	6	תרומה {*Por.*, Ex. xxv. 1—xxvii. 19. / *Haph.*, 1 Kings v. 26—vi. 13.
	S	ה	7	S. Munk, 1867.
	M	ו	8	
	T	ז	9	Emancipation in Tuscany, 1848.
	W	ח	10	Jews permitted to return to Spain, 1855. Eötvös d. 1870.
	Th	ט	11	
	F	י	12	שבת 4.30
5.52	S	יא	13	L. Börne, d. 1837. תצוה {*Por.*, Ex. xvii. 20—xxx. 10. / *Haph.*, Ezech. xliii. 10-27.
	S	יב	14	
	M	יג	15	Lessing d. 1781.
	T	יד	16	*Minor Purim* פורים קטן
	W	טו	17	*Minor Purim* פורים קטן Heine, d. 1856.
	Th	טז	18	Luther d. 1546.
	F	יז	19	שבת 5.0
6.5	S	יח	20	Joseph II., d. 1790. כי תשא {*Por.*, Ex. xxx. 11—xxxiv. 35. / *Haph.* 1 Kings xviii. 1-39.
	S	יט	21	Spinoza d. 1677.
	M	כ	22	J. M. Jost b. 1793.
	T	כא	23	
	W	כב	24	
	Th	כג	25	Bensew d. 1811.
	F	כד	26	שבת 5.0
6.17	S	כה	27	ויקהל פ׳ שקלים, מברכין החדש {*Por.*, Ex. xxxv. 1—xxxviii. 20, xxx. 11-16. / *Haph.*, 2 Kings xii. 1-17.
	S	כו	28	
			Mar.	
	M	כז	1	Jews slain at Worms, 1349.
	T	כח	2	
	W	כט	3	ערב ר״ח
	Th	ל	4	א׳ דר״ח

Minhagim—Feb. 3rd, הלל (omitting the pieces לא לנו and אהבתי), omit תחנון and למנצח.—Feb. 15th, omit תחנון in מנחה.—Feb. 16th and 17th, omit תחנון and למנצח.—March 3rd, תחנון omitted in מנחה.—March 4th, הלל (omitting the pieces לא לנו and אהבתי), omit תחנון and למנצח.

1897, March 5–April 2] 2nd ADAR XXIX. DAYS. [אדר שני] 5657

Thursday : 8h. 42m. 1s. p.m. מולד

Night. h. m.	Day.	D. of Month Heb.	D. of Month Eng.	Sabbaths, Fasts, Festivals, Events, Remarkable Days, Portions of Pentateuch, Haphtorahs.
6.28	F ⛌	א ב	Mar. 5 6	ב׳ דר״ח שבת 5.30 פקודי, הפסקה ראשונה {*Por.* Ex. xxxviii. 21—xl. 38. *Haph.*, 1 Kings vii. 51—viii. 21.
	S	ג	7	Joseph Almanzi d. 1860.
	M	ד	8	
	T	ה	9	
	W	ו	10	Moscheles d. 1869.
	Th	ז	11	
6.41	F ⛌	ח ט	12 13	שבת 5.30 ויקרא, פרשת זכור {*Por.*, Lev. i-v., Deut. xxv. 17-19. *Haph.*, 1 Samuel, xv. 2-34.
	S	י	14	
	M	יא	15	
	T	יב	16	Jews of York slay themselves, 1190.
6.47	W	יג	17	**Fast of Esther** תענית אסתר {*Por.*, Ex. xxxii. 11-14—xxxiv. 1-10. *Haph.*, Is. lv. 6—lvi. 8.
	Th	יד	18	**Purim** פורים *Por.*, Ex. xvii. 8-16.
	F	טו	19	**Shushan Purim** 6.0 שושן פורים שבת
6.52	⛌	טז	20	צו, הפסקה שניה {*Por.*, Lev. vi.-viii. *Haph.*, Jeremiah vii. 21—viii. 3, ix. 22-23.
	S	יז	21	Leo di Modena d. Venice, 1648.
	M	יח	22	Michael Beer d. 1833.
	T	יט	23	N. H. Wessely d. 1805.
	W	כ	24	
	Th	כא	25	Anglo-Jewish Association founded 1871.
	F	כב	26	שבת 6.0
7.4	⛌	כג	27	שמיני, פ׳ פרה, מברכין החדש {*Por.*, Lev. ix.-xi.—Num. xix. *Haph.*, Ezech. xxxvi. 16-38.
	S	כד	28	Jews expelled from Moscow, 1891.
	M	כה	29	Meir Abulafia d. Toledo, 1244.
	T	כו	30	Chiera Esther d. Constantinople, 1600.
	W	כז	31	
	Th	כח	April. 1	יום כפור קטן
	F	כט	2	ערב ר״ח, שבת 6.0

Minhagim—March 5th, הלל (omitting the pieces אהבתי and לא לנו), omit התחנון and למנצח.—March 17th, סליחות, עננו, omit תחנון in מנחה, מחצית השקל given, על הנסים said in מעריב.—March 18th, על הנסים, omit תחנון, אל ארך אפים, and למנצח.—March 19th, omit תחנון and למנצח.

1897, April 3–May 2] NISSAN XXX. DAYS. [ניסן 5657

תקופה: April 6. 6 p.m.   Friday: 9h. 26m. 2s. a.m. מולד

Night.	Day.	D. of Month Heb. / Eng.	Sabbaths, Fasts, Festivals, Events, Remarkable Days, Portions of Pentateuch, Haphtorahs.
h. m. 7.16	S	א / April. 3	ר"ח, תזריע, פ' החדש { *Por.*, Lev. xii.-xiii., Num. xxviii. 9-15. Ex. xii. 1-20. *Haph.*, Ez. xlv. 16–xlvi. 18.
	S	ב / 4	Isaac Aboab d. Amsterdam, 1693.
	M	ג / 5	E. M. Kuh, German poet, d. 1790.
	T	ד / 6	
	W	ה / 7	*New Solar Cycle* קדוש החמה
	Th	ו / 8	
	F	ז / 9	שבת 6.30
7.29	S	ח / 10	מצורע, שבת הגדול { *Por.*, Lev. xiv.-xv. *Haph.*, Malachi iii. 4-24.
	S	ט / 11	Lassale b. 1825.
	M	י / 12	
	T	יא / 13	
	W	יב / 14	Seven Jews burnt at an Auto da fé, Seville, 1660.
	Th	יג / 15	בדיקת חמץ
	F	יד / 16	*Good Friday* 6.30 שבת *Fast of Firstborn* { ערב פסח, תענית בכורים
7.42	S	טו / 17	**Passover 1st Day** א' דפסח { *Por.*, Ex. xii. 21-51, Num. xxviii. 16-25. *Haph.*, Josh. v. 2–vi. 1.
			D. of Omer
7.44	S	טז / 18	1 — **Passover 2nd Day** ב' דפסח { *Por.*, Lev. xxii. 26–xxiii. 44, Num. xxviii. 16-25. *Haph.*, 2 Kings xxiii. 1-25.
	M	יז / 19	2 — *Easter Monday* Baron de Hirsch, d. 1896. { *Por.*, Ex. xiii. 1-16, Num. xxviii. 19-25.
	T	יח / 20	3 — Gersonides, d. 1344. { *Por.*, Ex. xxii. 24–xxiii. 19, Num. xxviii. 19-25.
	W	יט / 21	4 — Duke of Sussex, d. 1843 — *Por.*, Ex. xxxiv. 1-26, Num. xxviii. 19-25.
	Th	כ / 22	5 — ערוב תבשילין — *Por.*, Num. ix. 1-14, Num. xxviii. 19-25.
	F	כא / 23	6 — **Passover 7th Day** 6.30 ש/ז' דפסח { *Por.*, Ex. xiii. 17–xv. 26, Num. xxviii. 19-25. *Haph.* 2 Samuel xxii.
7.55	S	כב / 24	7 — ,, **8th Day** ח' דפסח { *Por.*, Deut. xiv. 22–xvi. 17, Num. xxviii. 19-25. *Haph.*, Is. x. 32–xii. 6.
	S	כג / 25	8 — אסרו חג
	M	כד / 26	9
	T	כה / 27	10 — Anti-Semitic riot at Elizabethgrad, 1881. Meir of Rothenburg d. 1293.
	W	כו / 28	11
	Th	כז / 29	12 — Isaac of Corbeil, author of *Semak*, d. 1280.
	F	כח / 30	13 — Cremieux b. 1796. 7.0 שבת
8.8	S	כט / May 1	14 — אחרי, מברכין החדש, מחר { *Por.*, Lev. xvi.–xviii. חדש, פרק א' *Haph.*, 1 Samuel xx. 18-42.
	S	ל / 2	15 — א' דר"ח

Minhagim—Omit תחנון and צדקתך during the whole of the month.—April 3rd, הלל (omitting the pieces לא לנו and אהבתי), omit ברכי נפשי after this Sabbath.—April 7th, ברכת החמה said before 9 o'clock a.m.—April 10th, say in מנחה from עברים היינו till לכפר על כל עונתינו (*see* Passover Night Service).—April 16th, abstain from חמץ by 9.15 a.m.

1897, May 3-31] IYAR XXIX. DAYS. [אייר 5657

Sunday : 10h. 10m. 3s. p.m. מולד

Night.	Day.	D. of Month Heb.	D. of Month Eng.	D. of Omer	Sabbaths, Fasts, Festivals, Events, Remarkable Days, Portions of Pentateuch, Haphtorahs.
h. m.	M	א	May. 3	16	ב׳ דר"ח Sir Francis Goldsmid d. 1878. "May laws" signed, 1882.
	T	ב	4	17	Meyerbeer d. 1864.
	W	ג	5	18	Napoleon d. 1821. E. Gans, jurist, d. 1839.
	Th	ד	6	19	M. C. Luzzatto d. 1747.
	F	ה	7	20	שבת 7.0
8.22	S	ו	8	21	קדושים, מברכין ב/ה'ב, פ"ב { *Por.*, Lev. xix.-xx. *Haph.*, Ezech. xxii. 1-19.
	S	ז	9	22	
8.25	M	ח	10	23	*First Fast* תענית שני קמא
	T	ט	11	24	A. Geiger b. 1810.
	W	י	12	25	Massacre of Jews by Crusaders, Worms, 1096.
8.31	Th	יא	13	26	*Second Fast* תענית חמישי
	F	יב	14	27	שבת 7.0
8.31	S	יג	15	28	אמר פרק ג׳ { *Por.*, Lev. xxi.-xxiv. *Haph.*, Ezech. xliv. 15-31.
	S	יד	16	29	פסח שני
8.38	M	טו	17	30	*Third Fast* תענית שני תניינא
	T	טז	18	31	
	W	יז	19	32	Isaac Alfasi (Rif.) d. Lucena, 1103.
	Th	יח	20	33	ל"ג בעומר
	F	יט	21	34	שבת 7.0
8.47	S	כ	22	35	בהר, פרק ד׳ { *Por.* Lev. xxv. 1—xxvi. 2. *Haph.*, Jeremiah xxxii. 6-27.
	S	כא	23	36	
	M	כב	24	37	Jews massacred Frankfort, 1241.
	T	כג	25	38	
	W	כד	26	39	Martyrs of Blois, 1171 (Fast day of pre-expulsion English Jews).
	Th	כה	27	40	Massacre of Jews by Crusaders, Mayence, 1096.
	F	כו	28	41	שבת 7.0
8.58	S	כז	29	42	בחקתי, מברכין החדש, פ׳ ה׳ { *Por.*, Lev. xxvi. 3—xxvii. 34. *Haph.*, Jeremiah xvi. 19—xvii. 14.
	S	כח	30	43	Massacre of Jews by Crusaders, Cologne, 1096.
	M	כט	31	44	ער"ח יום כפור קטן

Discontinue מזמור לתודה, omit —April 17th, Discontinue טל ומטר after מנחה—April 16-24th, omit מזמור לתודה. In the Evening commence counting the Omer.—April 17th & 18th, הלל, from 19-24th הלל, omitting the pieces אהבתי and לא לנו.—May 2nd הלל (omitting the pieces אהבתי and לא לנו), omit למנצח.

Minhagim—May 3rd, הלל (omitting the pieces אהבתי and לא לנו), omit אל ארך, תחנון.—May 10th, 13th and 17th, סליחות.—May 19th, תחנון omitted in מנחה.—למנצח, and אפים, May 20th תחנון omitted.—May 31st, omit תחנון in מנחה.

1897, June] **SIVAN XXX. DAYS.** [סיון 5657

Monday : 10h. 54m. 4s. a.m. מולד

Night.	Day.	D. of Month Heb. / Eng.	D. of Omer	Sabbaths, Fasts, Festivals, Events, Remarkable Days, Portions of Pentateuch, Haphtarahs.
h. m.	T	א / June. 1	45	Rappaport b. 1790. ראש חדש
	W	ב / 2	46	Tolerance Edict of Joseph II. of Austria, 1782.
	Th	ג / 3	47	שלשת ימי הגבלה
	F	ד / 4	48	שבת ס.7
9.7	S̄	ה / 5	49	במדבר, ערב שבועות, פ׳ ו׳ { Por., Num. i. 1.—iv. 20. / Haph., Hos. ii. 1-22.
9.8	S	ו / 6		**Feast of Weeks** א׳ דשבועות { Por., Ex. xix.-xx., Num. xxviii. 26-31. / Haph., Ezech. i., iii. 12.
9.9	M	ז / 7		**2nd Day** *Whit Monday* ב׳ דשבועות { Por., Deut. xv. 19—xvi. 17, Num. / Haph. Habak. iii. [xxviii. 26-31.
	T	ח / 8		אסרו חג
	W	ט / 9		R. Tam (Jacob b. Meir) d. Rameru, 1171.
	Th	י / 10		H. J. Michael, Hebrew book collector, d. 1846.
	F	יא / 11		שבת ס.7
9.14	S̄	יב / 12		נשא, פרק א׳ { Por. Num. iv. 21—vii. 89. / Haph. Judges xiii. 2-25.
	S	יג / 13		
	M	יד / 14		
	T	טו / 15		
	W	טז / 16		Jews massacred, Erfurt, 1221.
	Th	יז / 17		
	F	יח / 18		שבת ס.7
9.18	S̄	יט / 19		בהעלותך, פרק ב׳ { Por., Num. viii.-xii. / Haph., Zech. ii. 14—iv. 7.
	S	כ / 20		Four thousand Jews slain at Toledo, 1391.
	M	כא / 21		*Longest Day* יום הארוך
	T	כב / 22		
	W	כג / 23		Martyrdoms at Weissenburg, 1270.
	Th	כד / 24		Four hundred and ten Jews slain at Jacca, 1320.
	F	כה / 25		שבת ס.7
9.19	S̄	כו / 26		שלח לך, מברכין החדש, פ׳ ג׳ { Por., Num. xiii.-xv. / Haph., Josh. ii. 1-24.
	S	כז / 27		Jews of Xanten massacred, 1096.
	M	כח / 28		
	T	כט / 29		ער"ח, יום כפור קטן
	W	ל / 30		Reuchlin d. 1522. א׳ דר"ח Jews expelled from Prague, 1745.

Minhagim—June 1st, הלל (omitting the pieces לא לנו and אהבתי), omit תחנון and למנצח.—June 2nd 3rd 4th and 8th, omit תחנון.—June 5th, omit צדקתך, insert ותודיענו in מעריב.—June 6th and 7th, הלל.—June 30th, הלל (omitting the pieces לא לנו and אהבתי), omit תחנון and למנצח.

1897, July 1–29] **TAMUZ XXIX. DAYS.** [תמוז 5657

תקופה: July 7th, 1.30 a.m.   Tuesday: 11h. 38m. 5s. p.m. מולד

Night. h. m.	Day.	D. of Month Heb. | Eng.		Sabbaths, Fasts, Festivals, Events, Remarkable Days, Portions of Pentateuch, Haphtorahs.
	Th	א	July. 1	ב' דר"ח
	F	ב	2	שבת 7.0
9.17	S	ג	3	קרח, פרק ד' { *Por.*, Num. xvi.–xviii *Haph.*, I Samuel xi. 14–xii. 22.
	S	ד	4	
	M	ה	5	
	T	ו	6	Three hundred Jews murdered at Tarega in Catalonia, 1348.
	W	ז	7	
	Th	ח	8	
	F	ט	9	שבת 7.0
9.11	S	י	10	חקת, פרק ה' { *Por.*, Num. xix. 1–xxii. 1. *Haph.*, Judges xi. 1-33.
	S	יא	11	E. H. Lindo, Jewish historian, d. 1865.
	M	יב	12	
	T	יג	13	Rashi d. 1105. Berlin Treaty signed 1875.
	W	יד	14	
	Th	טו	15	Isaac Luria, Cabbalist, d. 1572.
	F	טז	16	שבת 7.0
9.3	S	יז	17	בלק פרק ו' { *Por.*, Num. xxii. 2–xxv. 9. *Haph.*, Micah v. 6–vi. 8.
9.2	S	יח	18	**Fast of Tamuz** { צום שבעה עשר בתמום נדחה } { *Por.*, Ex. xxxii. 11-14, xxxiv. 1-10. *Haph.*, Is. lv. 6–lvi. 8.
	M	יט	19	
	T	כ	20	Disputation at Barcelona, 1263. A. L. Davids, Turkish scholar, d. 1832.
	W	כא	21	Sehabtai Bass, Hebrew Bibliographer, d. 1718.
	Th	כב	22	Jews expelled from France, 1306. Emma Lazarus b. 1849.
	F	כג	23	שבת 7.0
8.52	S	כד	24	פנחס, מברכין החדש' פ' א' { *Por.*, Num. xxv. 10–xxx. 1. *Haph.*, Jeremiah i. 1–ii. 3.
	S	כה	25	Johann Christian Wolf, Hebrew Bibliographer, d. 1739.
	M	כו	26	First sitting of Paris Sanhedrin, 1806.
	T	כז	27	Baron Rothschild takes his seat in House of Commons, 1858.
	W	כח	28	Emancipation in Hungary, 1849. N. Rothschild d. 1836.
	Th	כט	29	ער"ח, יום כפור קטן

Minhagim—July 1st, הלל, (omitting the pieces לא לנו and אהבתי), omit תחנון, אל ארך אפים, and למנצח.—July 18th, סליחות, עננו.—July 29th, omit תחנון in מנחה.

1897, July 30–Aug. 28] AB XXX. DAYS. [אב 5657

מולד Thursday: 12h. 22m. 6s. p.m.

Night.	Day.	D. of Month Heb.	D. of Month Eng.	Sabbaths, Fasts, Festivals, Events, Remarkable Days, Portions of Pentateuch and Haphtorahs.
h. m.	F	א	July 30	ר״ח, שבת 7.0
8.40	S	ב	31	מטות ומסעי פרק ב׳ { *Por.*, Num. xxx. 2—xxxvi. 13. / *Haph.*, Jeremiah ii. 4-28—iii. 4.
	S	ג	Aug. 1	Mordecai ben Hillel d. in a riot, Nurenberg, 1298.
	M	ד	2	*Bank Holiday* Joseph Nasi d. 1579.
	T	ה	3	Jews expelled from Spain, 1492.
	W	ו	4	
	Th	ז	5	Jews massacred at Barcelona, 1391.
	F	ח	6	שבת 7.0
8.26	S	ט	7	דברים, שבת חזון { *Por.*, Deut. i. 1—iii. 22. / *Haph.*, Is. i. 1-27.
8.24	S	י	8	Fast of Ab צום תשעה באב נדחה { *Morning Por.*, Deut. iv. 25-40. / *Haph.*, Jeremiah viii. 13—ix. 23. / *Afternoon Por.*, Ex. xxxii. 11-14—xxxiv. 1-10. / *Haph.*, Is. lv. 6—lvi. 8.
	M	יא	9	M. Kormick, Jewish Calendar, d. 1821.
	T	יב	10	Zunz b. 1794.
	W	יג	11	
	Th	יד	12	E. Morpurgo, Hebrew translator of Pope's *Essay on Man*, d. Venice, 1835.
	F	טו	13	חמשה עשר, שבת 7.0
8.11	S	טז	14	ואתחנן, שבת נחמו, פ׳ ג׳ { *Por.*, Deut. iii. 23—vii. 11. / *Haph.*, Is. xl. 1-26.
	S	יז	15	Simeon b. Asher, astronomer, d. Toledo, 1342. Napoleon b. 1769.
	M	יח	16	Buxtorf, Christian Hebraist, d. 1664.
	T	יט	17	Frederick the Great, d. 1786.
	W	כ	18	
	Th	כא	19	
	F	כב	20	St. Bernard, d. 1153. שבת 6.30
7.55	S	כג	21	עקב מברכין החדש פ׳ ד׳ { *Por.*, Deut. vii. 12—xi. 25. / *Haph.*, Is. xlix. 14—li. 3.
	S	כד	22	Riot at Frankfort, under Fettmilch, 1614.
	M	כה	23	
	T	כו	24	Six thousand Jews slain at Mayence, 1349.
	W	כז	25	David Gans, historian, d. Prague, 1613. S. D. Luzzatto b. 1800.
	Th	כח	26	יום כפור קטן
	F	כט	27	ערב ר״ח, שבת 6.30
7.39	S	ל	28	ראה, א׳ דר״ח, פ׳ ה׳ { *Por.* Deut. xi. 26—xvi. 17, Num. xxviii. 9-15. / *Haph.*, Is. lxvi.

Minhagim—July 30th, הלל (omitting the pieces לא לנו and אהבתי), omit תחנון and למנצח.—Aug. 7th, No פרק said, omit צדקתך. In מעריב the Book of Lamentations is read, omit ואני זאת and ויתן לך and ויהי נועם.—Aug. 8th, קינות read, omit תחנון and למנצח and the verse ואני זאת

1897, Aug. 29–Sept. 26] ELLUL XXIX. DAYS. [אלול 5657

Friday : 1h. 6m. 7s. a.m. מולד

Night.	Day.	D. of Month Heb.	D. of Month Eng.	Sabbaths, Fasts, Festivals, Events, Remarkable Days, Portions of Pentateuch, Haphtorahs.
h. m.	S	א	Aug. 29	ב' דראש חדש Hugh of Lincoln's body discovered 1255.
	M	ב	30	
	T	ג	31	Lassalle d. 1864.
	W	ד	Sept. 1	A. Asher, editor of Benjamin of Tudela, d. 1833.
	Th	ה	2	
	F	ו	3	Coronation massacre, London, 1189. שבת 6.0
7.22	S	ז	4	שופטים פרק ו' { Por., Deut. xvi. 18—xxi. 9. / Haph., Is li. 12—lii. 12.
	S	ח	5	M. G. Saphir, Viennese humorist, d. 1858.
	M	ט	6	Moses Mendelssohn b. 1729.
	T	י	7	H. Graetz, Jewish historian, d. 1891.
	W	יא	8	Eight Jews burnt Murcia, 1560.
	Th	יב	9	"Caution" issued against Reformed Congregation, 1841.
	F	יג	10	Sabbatai Zewi, d. 1676. שבת 6.0
7.5	S	יד	11	כי תצא פרק א' ב' { Por., Deut. xxi. 10—xxv. 19. / Haph., Is. liv. 1-lv. 5.
	S	טו	12	Jacob Abendana d. London, 1695.
	M	טז	13	
	T	יז	14	Emancipation in Hanover, 1848.
	W	יח	15	Akiba Eger d. 1780.
	Th	יט	16	שבת 5.30
	F	כ	17	
6.49	S	כא	18	כי תבא פרק ג' ד' { Por., Deut. xxvi. 1—xxix. 8. / Haph., Is. lx.
	S	כב	19	Maier Rothschild, founder of the house, d. 1812.
	M	כג	20	Dr. Capadoce d. Amsterdam, 1826.
	T	כד	21	
	W	כה	22	Basnage, Christian historian of the Jews, d. 1723.
	Th	כו	23	
	F	כז	24	שבת 5.30
6.33	S	כח	25	נצבים פרק ה' ו' { Por. Deut. xxix. 9—xxx. 20. / Haph., Is. lxi. 10—lxiii. 9.
	S	כט	26	ערב ר"ה תרנ"ח זכור ברית

מנחה.—Aug. 13th, תחנון in מנחה, ענננו.—Aug. 12th, omit נחם in מנחה. Insert ובא לציון ברית in ברייתי, omit צדקתך.—Aug. 28th, הלל (omitting the pieces לא לנו and אהבתי), omit תחנון.

Minhagim—Aug. 29th, הלל (omitting the pieces לא לנו and אהבתי), omit תחנון and למנצח.—During the whole month the Shofar is blown on weekdays, except Sept. 26th.—Sept. 19-24th, 26th, סליחות.—Sept. 26th, omit תחנון.

EXPLANATION OF THE JEWISH CALENDAR.

THE Jewish Calendar is a lunar one, adapted to the solar year by various expedients. As at present constituted, it is founded upon the calculations of the Greek astronomers. The hour is divided into 1,080 portions, which we may call *minims*, and the month between one new moon and the next is reckoned as 29 days, 12 hours, 876 minims. This is exactly the month according to the Greek astronomer Hipparchus (146 B.C.). Again, the years are grouped in cycles of 19, according to the system of Meton, a Greek astronomer of the fifth century B.C. According to Jewish tradition, the present calendar was fixed by a Rabbi Hillel of Palestine. in A.D. 358, but there are certain indications that it went through further modifications after that date. In Biblical and early Talmudic times the new moons were fixed by actual observation, and were announced from Jerusalem to the surrounding countries.

If the time elapsing between one new moon (known by the Hebrew title of *molad*) to another were exactly 29½ days, the length of the months could be fixed at alternately 29 or 30 days, as they are in the common regular year. But there are three several corrections to make which disturb this regularity: (1) The excess of minims over the half day. (2) The combination with the solar year. (3) The arrangement that certain of the Jewish festivals shall not conflict with the Sabbath. To overcome these difficulties, the Jewish calendar recognises six different classes of years: three of them common, and three leap. The leap year is composed of thirteen months, an additional month of 29 days being added. This intercalary month is inserted immediately after the month of Adar, which in the ordinary year is of 29 days, but in leap year is 30 days. Both the common and the leap years may be either regular, defective, or redundant. The regular year has an alternation of 29 and 30 days, as already explained. The defective year makes Kislev, the third month, only 29 days. The redundant year makes Cheshwan 30 instead of 29 days. If, therefore, we know the number of days in Cheshwan and Kislev in any year, we can tell whether it is regular, defective, or redundant, while if we know the number of days in Adar, we know whether the year is common or leap.

The names of the Jewish months, as we now have them, are indeed mentioned in the Bible, but only in documents dated after the Exile. The conclusion is therefore forced upon us that they are derived from Babylon, and research in the cuneiform inscriptions has confirmed this view. Before the Exile we know the names of only four of the months: Abib, corresponding to Nisan (Exodus xl. 2-17); Siv, corresponding to Iyar (1 Kings vi. 1); Ethanim, corresponding to Tishri (*ib.* viii. 8), and Bul, corresponding to Cheshwan (*ib.* vi. 38).

The present names of the months are :—Tishri, Cheshwan, Kislev, Tebeth, Shivat, Adar, Ve-Adar, Nisan, Iyar, Sivan, Tamuz, Ab, Elul. The sacred Jewish year commences with Nisan, the civil with Tishri.

It is on the foregoing principles that the accompanying tables have been compiled, from which the reader can transfer the English into the Jewish year, or *vice versâ*, without difficulty. The English dates for the first of the Jewish months are given for the 40 years between 1865 and 1905. The whole number of days in each month is likewise given, and in addition the dates for the exceptional days in Cheshwan, Kislev and Adar are also given.

Thus, to find the Jewish date corresponding to January 4th, 1868, the reader will consult the column headed 1867-68, and find the nearest date to January 4th. This will be December 27th, corresponding to Tebeth 1st in the Jewish calendar. The simplest reckoning will enable the reader to see that January 4th will correspond with Tebeth 9th.

Suppose, now, we wish to find out a Jahrzeit occurring on the 9th of Tebeth for the year 1896-97. Looking under that column, we learn that the first falls upon December 6th, therefore that Tebeth 9th corresponds with the 14th of that month.

In order to ascertain the Sabbath on which a Jewish boy will attain his religious majority (Barmitzvah), a somewhat different method must be employed to that by which the occurrence of Jahrzeit can be ascertained. As a boy attains this proud position at the age of thirteen, it is obvious that for any given year we have only to consider the Hebrew dates, thirteen years previously, *e.g.*, for the current year's Barmitzvah we must go back to 5644 (1883-4). If the boy's Jewish birthday is known, it is, of course, simple to ascertain the next Sabbath occurring after that date in the year 5657. But if, as is usual, only the civil birthday is known for the years 1883-4, this must be translated into the corresponding Hebrew date of *that year*, and on the next Sabbath after that date in the year 5657, the boy will attain to the religious rights of manhood, and can be called to the Law. Thus, if a boy were born on February 5th, 1884, that would correspond to Shivat 9th, 5644, which exactly corresponds with January 9th, 1897, on which day the boy should celebrate his Barmitzvah and say his parasha.

Leap years occur seven times in each cycle of 19 years. It is easy to remember how they occur, if one begins at the eighth year, after which every third year is a leap year, till we reach the 17th year. As the third year after this would not fall within the cycle, the last year—the 19th year—is leap year, and counting from that, every third year is again leap. Thus the leap years in a cycle may be expressed thus :—3, 6, 8, 11, 14, 17, and 19.

Besides the lunar cycle of 19 years, there is a solar cycle of 28 years, in which the Tekufah of Nisan or Vernal Equinox recurs at the same period. It so happens that the solar cycle has just come round in 5657, and is celebrated in Jewish ritual by a special blessing, which will be found on page 26.

So far the arrangements have been to meet the first two of the difficulties of a lunar month, which has to be combined with a solar one. By the above expedients the cycle of Jewish years corresponds to 6,939 days and 16 hours, or 595 minims, 143 minutes, 33 seconds ; whilst the Julian cycle of the same number of years corresponds to exactly the same number of days, and exactly 18 hours over, and the Gregorian cycle, again, corresponds with the same number of days with an addition of 14 hours, 34 minutes, 28 seconds. The Jewish cycle is, therefore, about an hour and a-half less than the

EXPLANATION OF CALENDAR.

Julian one, and two hours more than the Gregorian one. In consequence of the latter fact, the first of Tishri tends to become later as each cycle passes, and if no remedy is found, the Jewish year is likely at some future time to commence in midwinter. But, for the present, this fault can be neglected, as it would only cause the difference of a week in 1,900 years.

If we divide the number of days in the Jewish cycle as given above by seven, it leaves a remainder of 2 days, 16 hours, 595 minims, which is the residuum of each cycle; in other words, the "molad" or New Moon of any one cycle is that amount in advance in the year of the preceding cycle. Working back to the traditional beginning of the Jewish reckoning of years—the Year of the Creation—it is found that the molad of this was October 7th, 11 hours, 204 minims p.m. This date is expressed by the Hebrew symbol בהרד, in which ב represents the second day of the week, ה and רד the hours and minims. This is the point of departure of the whole of the Jewish Calendar as at present constituted, and the molad of each succeeding cycle can be obtained from this by a simple arithmetical process.

The chief disturbing influence in the arrangement of the Jewish Calendar is to prevent the Day of Atonement from either immediately preceding or immediately succeeding the Sabbath. In other words, the Day of Atonement cannot fall upon either Friday or Sunday, for in either case the preparation for the Sabbath or for the fast would be put off two days. If, therefore, Tishri 10th cannot occur on a Friday or a Sunday, the first of that month—or the New Year—cannot occur either on a Wednesday or a Friday. Further, in order to prevent Hoshanna Rabba from falling upon the Sabbath, the first of Tishri cannot occur on a Sunday, thus leaving only four days of the week, second, third, fifth, and seventh, on which the Jewish New Year can fall. A further complication of a purely astronomical character is introduced by the consideration that the Jewish day formally commences six hours before midnight. If, therefore, the molad, or new moon, occurs after mid-day but before 2 o'clock, it cannot become visible until the next day, which has, therefore, to be reckoned as the day of the new moon. Owing to this difficulty, the first of Tishri can only occur on the Tuesday, when the year is regular. Indeed, we can tell, from the day upon which the Jewish New Year falls, what is the character of the year. If we express the days of the week by the numbers up to seven, beginning, of course, with Sunday as the first day of the week, and the character of the year by the letter r for the regular year, d for the defective year, and a for the redundant, giving the capital letters of the same class of year in leap year, we get fourteen types of the Jewish year which may be expressed by the following formulæ:—

Common Year—2d, 2a, 3r, 4r, 5a, 7d, 7a,
Leap Year— 2D, 2A, 3R, 5D, 5A, 7D, 7A.

It will thus be seen that the regular leap year can only fall upon a Tuesday, the regular common year only upon Tuesday or Thursday. The present Jewish year, 5657, being a regular leap year, follows this rule and begins on a Tuesday.

An ingenious aid to memory has been devised by which the days of the week on which the chief festivals of the year are determined by those on which the successive days of Passover fall. If we add the first letter of the Hebrew alphabet to the last, the second to the last but one, the third to the last but two, and so on up to the sixth letter, we obtain a guide to the whole Jewish ecclesiastical year as follows:—

א"ת ב"ש ג"ר ד"ק ה"ץ ו"ף

that is, the first day (א) of Passover occurs on the same day of the week as the fasts of Ab and Tammuz (ת), the second day (ב) coincides with Shabuoth (ש), Rosh Hoshana (ר) with the third (ג): the fourth day (ד) corresponds with Simchath (or Keriath) Torah, and the Fast (ץ) of Atonement coincides with the fifth day (ה) of Passover, while Purim begins on the same day as the sixth.

There are further some rather complicated astronomical reasons which determine the exact number of days in a cycle, which may vary between 6939 and 6942. Combining this with the other requirements of the fourteen types of Jewish year, we get no less than sixty-one different types of cycles, in each of which the order of the various types in the 19 years varies. Thus, the present year, 5657, is the 14th year in the 16th type of a cycle. Being the 14th year it is a leap year; being of the 16th cycle, the New Year falls upon a Tuesday, which we know can only happen in a common leap year. This being determined, the number of days in all the months is settled by the rule already given. If the reader is informed that the particular Tuesday in question corresponds with September 8th, he should now be in a position to draw out a Jewish Calendar for the whole year.

There are a few minor points connected with the calendar which must be here briefly referred to. The Jewish day begins with the night, if one may speak Hibernically. Its commencement, therefore, varies according to the time of year, and according to the latitude. For the beginnings of Sabbaths and festivals, rules were laid down for the latitude of London by David Nieto, Haham of the Sephardim, but with regard to the going out of these days, a difficulty occurs with regard to this process of determination. The Rabbinic rule is that the day is over when three stars can be seen together in the heavens. This is almost a subjective test, but within the last twenty years, three scholars have made it more precise by calling in the aid of astronomical science—Dr. Friedlander for England, Monsieur Hirsch for France, and Dr. Zuckermann for Germany. These three scholars differ somewhat as to the number of degrees the sun must sink below the horizon before three stars of the second magnitude can be seen in the heavens, but the variations are so slight as to make but little difference. This is one of the few points of Rabbinic Law which have been definitely decided only in this century. The hours of the close of night given in the accompanying calendar are those fixed by the late Chief Rabbi in accordance with Dr. Friedlander's formula.

Another point that has to be settled by astronomical calculations, is the hour at which the morning Shema can be read, which is of importance, especially for workmen beginning work. According to Rabbinic Law, this should not be said later than three hours of the

EXPLANATION OF CALENDAR.

day after sunrise, but, as the hours thus mentioned are not astronomic hours, but one-twelfth of the time elapsing between dawn and the appearance of the three stars, these in strictness ought to be calculated somewhat on the same principle as the close of night, according to the latitude and the time of the year. Dr. Zuckermann has drawn up tables in this direction.

Another point of importance for civil and religious life is the time of day at which the afternoon prayers can be combined with the evening prayers. This depends upon the length of the day since the combination of the two services must take place at latest an hour and a quarter before sunset, the hour being variable with date and place as before. Finally, the hour up to which leavened bread can be eaten upon the 14th of Nissan depends upon the length of the day, as the latest time is four hours after sunset, the hours again being variable.

TABLE SHOWING DATES ON WHICH JEWISH HOLIDAYS AND FESTIVALS OCCUR IN ALL YEARS, 1896-1905.

Festival.	Hebrew Date.	1896-97	1897-98	1898-99	1899-1900	1900-01	1901-02	1902-03	1903-04	1904-05
New Year ...	Tishri 1	Sept. 8	Sept. 27	Sept. 17	Sept. 5	Sept. 24	Sept. 14	Oct. 2	Sept. 22	Sept. 10
Day of Atonement	,, 10	,, 17	Oct. 6	,, 26	,, 14	Oct. 3	,, 23	,, 11	Oct. 1	,, 19
Tabernacle...	,, 15	,, 22	,, 11	Oct. 1	,, 19	,, 8	,, 28	,, 16	,, 6	,, 24
Feast of Branches...	,, 21	,, 28	,, 17	,, 7	,, 25	,, 14	Oct. 4	,, 22	,, 12	,, 30
,, 8th Day	,, 22	,, 29	,, 18	,, 8	,, 26	,, 15	,, 5	,, 23	,, 13	Oct. 1
,, the Law	,, 23	,, 30	,, 19	,, 9	,, 27	,, 16	,, 6	,, 24	,, 14	,, 2
Hanuca	Kislev 25	Nov. 30	Dec. 20	Dec. 9	Nov. 27	Dec. 17	Dec. 6	Dec. 25	Dec. 14	Dec. 3
Purim	Adar 14	—	Mar. 8	Feb. 24	Mar. 15	Mar. 5	—	Mar. 13	Mar. 1	Mar. 21
Purim (Leap Year)	Ve-Adar 14	Mar. 18	—	—	—	—	Mar. 23	—	—	—
Passover	Nisan 15	Apr. 17	April 7	Mar. 26	Apr. 14	Apr. 4	Apr. 22	Apr. 12	Mar. 31	Apr. 20
Feast of Weeks	Sivan 6	June 6	May 27	May 15	June 3	May 24	June 11	June 1	May 20	June 9
Fast of Ab	Ab 9	Aug. 7	July 28	July 16	Aug. 4	July 25	Aug. 12	Aug. 2	July 21	Aug. 10

JAHRZEIT AND BARMITZVAH TABLES. 21

TABLES FOR CALCULATING THE DATES FOR JAHRZEIT OR BARMITZVAH, 1864-1905.

		No. of Days in Jewish Month.	5625 1864–65	5626 1865–66	5627 1866–67	5628 1867–68	5629 1868–69	5630 1869–70	5631 1870–71	5632 1871–72*	5633 1872–73
Tishri	1	30	Oct. 1	Sept. 21	Sept. 10	Sept. 30	Sept. 17	Sept. 6	Sept. 26	Sept. 16	Oct. 3
Cheshvan	1	29	Oct. 31	Oct. 21	Oct. 10	Oct. 30	Oct. 17	Oct. 6	Oct. 26	Oct. 16	Nov. 2
,,	30 (red.)	—	—	—	Nov. 8	—	—	Nov. 4	Nov. 24	—	—
Kislev	1	30	Nov. 30	Nov. 19	Nov. 9	Nov. 28	Nov. 15	Nov. 5	Nov. 25	Nov. 14	Dec. 1
,,	29 (def.)	—	—	—	—	Dec. 26	—	—	—	Dec. 12	—
Tebeth	1	29	Dec. 30	Dec. 19	Dec. 9	Dec. 27	Dec. 15	Dec. 5	Dec. 25	Dec. 13	Dec. 31
Shevat	1	30	Jan. 28	Jan. 17	Jan. 7	Jan. 25	Jan. 13	Jan. 3	Jan. 23	Jan. 11	Jan. 29
Adar	1	29	Feb. 27	Feb. 16	Feb. 6	Feb. 24	Feb. 12	Feb. 2	Feb. 22	Feb. 10	Feb. 28
,,	30 (Leap)	—	—	—	Mar. 7	—	—	Mar. 3	—	Mar. 10	—
Ve-Adar	1	29	—	—	Mar. 8	—	—	Mar. 4	—	Mar. 11	—
Nisan	1	30	Mar. 28	Mar. 17	April 6	Mar. 24	Mar. 13	Apr. 2	Mar. 23	Apr. 9	Mar. 29
Iyar	1	29	Apr. 27	Apr. 16	May 6	Apr. 23	Apr. 12	May 2	Apr. 22	May 9	Apr. 28
Sivan	1	30	May 25	May 15	June 4	May 22	May 11	May 31	May 21	June 7	May 27
Tamuz	1	29	June 25	June 14	July 4	June 21	June 10	June 30	June 20	July 7	June 26
Ab	1	30	July 24	July 13	Aug. 2	July 20	July 9	July 29	July 19	Aug. 5	July 25
Elul	1	29	Aug. 23	Aug. 12	Sept. 1	Aug. 19	Aug. 8	Aug. 28	Aug. 19	Sept. 4	Aug. 24

* Civil leap year.

JAHRZEIT AND BARMITZVAH TABLES (continued).

		No. of days in Jewish Month.	5634 1873-74	5635 1874-75	5636 1875-76*	5637 1876-77	5638 1877-78	5639 1878-79	5640 1879-80*	5641 1880-81
Tishri	1	30	Sept. 22	Sept. 12	Sept. 30	Sept. 19	Sept. 8	Sept. 28	Sept. 18	Sept. 6
Cheshvan	1	29	Oct. 22	Oct. 12	Oct. 30	Oct. 19	Oct. 8	Oct. 28	Oct. 18	Oct. 6
,,	30	—	Nov. 20	—	Nov. 28	—	Nov. 6	Nov. 26	—	—
Kislev	1	30	Nov. 21	Nov. 10	Nov. 29	Nov. 17	Nov. 7	Nov. 27	Nov. 16	Nov. 4
,,	29	—	—	Dec. 8	—	—	—	—	—	Dec. 2
Tebeth	1	29	Dec. 21	Dec. 9	Dec. 29	Dec. 17	Dec. 7	Dec. 27	Dec. 16	Dec. 3
Shevat	1	30	Jan. 19	Jan. 7	Jan. 27	Jan. 15	Jan. 5	Jan. 25	Jan. 14	Jan. 1
Adar	1	29	Feb. 18	Feb. 6	Feb. 26	Feb. 14	Feb. 4	Feb. 24	Feb. 13	Jan. 31
,,	30	—	—	Mar. 7	—	—	Mar. 5	—	—	Mar. 1
Ve-Adar	1	29	—	Mar. 8	—	—	Mar. 6	—	—	Mar. 2
Nisan	1	30	Mar. 19	April 6	Mar. 26	Mar. 15	April 4	Mar. 25	Mar. 13	Mar. 31
Iyar	1	29	April 18	May 6	April 25	April 14	May 4	April 24	April 12	April 30
Sivan	1	30	May 17	June 4	May 24	May 13	June 2	May 23	May 11	May 29
Tamuz	1	29	June 16	July 4	June 23	June 12	July 2	June 22	June 10	June 28
Ab	1	30	July 15	Aug. 2	July 22	July 11	July 31	July 21	July 9	July 27
Elul	1	29	Aug. 14	Sept. 1	Aug. 21	Aug. 10	Aug. 31	Aug. 20	Aug. 8	Aug. 26

* Civil leap year.

JAHRZEIT AND BARMITZVAH TABLES. 23

JAHRZEIT AND BARMITZVAH TABLES (continued).

		No. of Days in Jewish Month.	5642 1881-82	5643 1882-83	5644 1883-84*	5645 1884-85	5646 1885-86	5647 1886-87	5648 1887-88*	5649 1888-89
Tishri	1 ...	30	Sept. 24	Sept. 14	Oct. 2	Sept. 20	Sept. 10	Sept. 30	Sept. 19	Sept. 6
Cheshvan	1 ...	29	Oct. 24	Oct. 14	Nov. 1	Oct. 20	Oct. 10	Oct. 30	Oct. 19	Oct. 6
,,	30	—	Nov. 22	—	—	Nov. 18	Nov. 8	—	—	Nov. 4
Kislev	1 ...	30	Nov. 23	Nov. 12	Nov. 30	Nov. 19	Nov. 9	Nov. 28	Nov. 17	Nov. 5
,,	29	—	—	Dec. 10	—	—	—	—	Dec. 15	—
Tebeth	1 ...	29	Dec. 23	Dec. 11	Dec. 30	Dec. 19	Dec. 9	Dec. 28	Dec. 16	Dec. 5
Shevat	1 ...	30	Jan. 21	Jan. 9	Jan. 28	Jan. 17	Jan. 7	Jan. 26	Jan. 14	Jan. 3
Adar	1 ...	29	Feb. 20	Feb. 8	Feb. 27	Feb. 16	Feb. 6	Feb. 25	Feb. 13	Feb. 2
,,	30	—	—	Mar. 9	—	—	Mar. 7	—	—	Mar. 3
Ve-Adar	1 ...	29	—	Mar. 10	—	—	Mar. 8	—	—	Mar. 4
Nisan	1 ...	30	Mar. 21	April 8	Mar. 27	Mar. 17	Apr. 6	Mar. 26	Mar. 13	April 2
Iyar	1 ...	29	April 20	May 8	April 26	Apr. 16	May 6	Apr. 25	Apr. 12	May 2
Sivan	1 ...	30	May 19	June 6	May 25	May 15	June 4	May 24	May 11	May 31
Tamuz	1 ...	29	June 18	July 6	June 24	June 14	July 4	June 23	June 10	June 30
Ab	1 ...	30	July 17	Aug. 4	July 23	July 13	Aug. 2	July 22	July 9	July 29
Elul	1 ...	29	Aug. 16	Sept. 3	Aug. 22	Aug. 12	Sept. 1	Aug. 21	Aug. 8	Aug. 28

* Civil leap year.

JAHRZEIT AND BARMITZVAH TABLES (continued).

		No. of Days in Jewish Month.	5650 1889-90	5651 1890-91	5652 1891-92*	5653 1892-93	5654 1893-94	5655 1894-95	5656 1895-96*	5657 1896-97
Tishri	1	30	Sept. 26	Sept. 15	Oct. 3	Sept. 22	Sept. 11	Oct. 1	Sept. 19	Sept. 8
Cheshvan	1	29	Oct. 26	Oct. 15	Nov. 2	Oct. 22	Oct. 11	Oct. 31	Oct. 19	Oct. 8
,,	30	—	—	—	Dec. 1	—	Nov. 9	—	Nov. 17	—
Kislev	1	30	Nov. 30	Nov. 13	Dec. 2	Nov. 20	Nov. 10	Nov. 29	Nov. 18	Nov. 6
,,	29	—	—	Dec. 11	—	—	—	Dec. 27	—	—
Tebeth	1	29	Dec. 24	Dec. 12	Jan. 1	Dec. 20	Dec. 10	Dec. 28	Dec. 18	Dec. 6
Shevat	1	30	Jan. 22	Jan. 10	Jan. 30	Jan. 18	Jan. 8	Jan. 26	Jan. 16	Jan. 4
Adar	1	29	Feb. 21	Feb. 9	Feb. 29	Feb. 17	Feb. 7	Feb. 25	Feb. 15	Feb. 3
,,	30	—	—	Mar. 10	—	—	Mar. 8	—	—	Mar. 4
Ve-Adar	1	29	—	Mar. 11	—	—	Mar. 9	—	—	Mar. 5
Nisan	1	30	Mar. 22	April 9	Mar. 29	Mar. 18	April 7	Mar. 26	Mar. 15	April 3
Iyar	1	29	April 21	May 9	April 28	April 17	May 7	April 25	April 14	May 3
Sivan	1	30	May 20	June 7	May 27	May 16	June 5	May 24	May 13	June 1
Tamuz	1	29	June 19	July 7	June 26	June 15	July 5	June 23	June 12	July 1
Ab	1	30	July 18	Aug. 5	July 25	July 14	Aug. 3	July 22	July 11	July 30
Elul	1	29	Aug. 17	Sept. 4	Aug. 24	Aug. 13	Sept. 2	Aug. 21	Aug. 10	Aug. 29

* Civil leap year.

JAHRZEIT AND BARMITZVAH TABLES (continued).

	No. of Days in Jewish Month.	5658 1897-98	5659 1898-99	5660 1899-1900	5661 1900-01	5662 1901-02	5663 1902-03	5664 1903-04*	5665 1904-05
Tishri 1	30	Sept. 27	Sept. 17	Sept. 5	Sept. 24	Sept. 14	Oct. 2	Sept. 22	Sept. 10
Cheshvan 1	29	Oct. 27	Oct. 17	Oct. 5	Oct. 24	Oct. 14	Nov. 1	Oct. 22	Oct. 10
,, 30	—	Nov. 25	—	—	Nov. 22	—	Nov. 30	—	Nov. 8
Kislev 1	30	Nov. 26	Nov. 15	Nov. 3	Nov. 23	Nov. 12	Dec. 1	Nov. 20	Nov. 9
,, 29	—	—	Dec. 13	—	—	Dec. 10	—	—	—
Tebeth 1	29	Dec. 26	Dec. 14	Dec. 3	Dec. 23	Dec. 11	Dec. 31	Dec. 20	Dec. 9
Shevat 1	30	Jan. 24	Jan. 12	Jan. 1	Jan. 21	Jan. 9	Jan. 29	Jan. 18	Jan. 7
Adar 1	29	Feb. 23	Feb. 11	Jan. 31	Feb. 20	Feb. 8	Feb. 28	Feb. 17	Feb. 6
,, 30	—	—	—	Mar. 1	—	Mar. 9	—	—	Mar. 7
Ve-Adar 1	29	—	—	Mar. 2	—	Mar. 10	—	—	Mar. 8
Nisan 1	30	Mar. 24	Mar. 12	Mar. 31	Mar. 21	April 8	Mar. 29	Mar. 17	April 6
Iyar 1	29	April 23	April 11	April 3	April 20	May 7	April 28	April 16	May 6
Sivan 1	30	May 22	May 10	May 29	May 19	June 6	May 27	May 15	June 4
Tamuz 1	29	June 21	June 9	June 28	June 18	July 6	June 26	June 14	July 4
Ab 1	30	July 20	July 8	July 27	July 17	Aug. 4	July 25	July 13	Aug. 2
Elul 1	29	Aug. 19	Aug. 7	Aug. 26	Aug. 15	Sept. 3	Aug. 24	Aug. 12	Sept. 1

* Civil leap year.

HAPHSAKOTH.

THE following information has been kindly forwarded by the Very Rev. the CHIEF RABBI :—

5657—1896-7.

הַפְּסָקָה on עֶרֶב יוֹם כִּפּוּר—The Fast of the Day of Atonement commences at 6 p.m. on Wednesday, September 16th. The Synagogue Service commences at 6.30 p.m.

הַפְּסָקָה on עֶרֶב פֶּסַח—Leavened Food may be eaten on the Eve of Passover, Friday, April 16th, until 9.15 p.m.

הַפְּסָקָה on עֶרֶב תִּשְׁעָה בְּאָב—The Fast of Ab commences at 8 p.m. on the Evening of Saturday, August 7th.

FORM OF PRAYER AT THE COMMENCEMENT OF THE NEW SOLAR CYCLE

ON WEDNESDAY, APRIL 7th, 1897—5657.

מִזְמוֹר ק"מ"ח — Psalm 148.

בָּרוּךְ אַתָּה ה' אֱלֹהֵינוּ מֶלֶךְ הָעוֹלָם עֹשֵׂה מַעֲשֵׂה בְרֵאשִׁית:

Blessed art Thou, O Lord our God, King of the Universe, who hast made the Creation.

מִזְמוֹר י"ט — Psalm 19.

קַדִּישׁ and עָלֵינוּ

The Blessing is to be said at the close of the Morning Service before 9 a.m.

GENERAL JEWISH STATISTICS.

The following Tables are the latest data given for the general Jewish population of the world, as far as can be ascertained :—

JEWS OF EUROPE.

Country.	1881.†	1891.
Austro-Hungary	1,643,708	1,860,106
Belgium	3,000*	3,000*
Denmark	3,946	4,080
England, &c.	60,000*	101,189*
France	63,000*	72,000*
Germany	561,612	567,884
Greece	2,652	5,792
Holland	81,693	97,324
Italy	40,430	50,000*
Luxembourg	777	1,000*
Norway	34	
Portugal	200*	300*
Roumania	265,000*	300,000*
Russia	2,552,145‡	4,500,000*
Servia	3,492	4,652
Spain	1,902	2,500*
Sweden	2,993	3,402
Switzerland	7,373	8,069
Turkey	115,000*	120,000*
Total	5,408,957	7,701,266

* Estimated numbers.
† After I. Loeb's article *Juifs* in "Dict. de Géographie," 1879.
‡ M. Loeb omitted 1,000,000 in Poland, 1881.

JEWS OF ASIA (after I. Loeb).

Turkey in Asia	150,000	
Persia	30,000	
Russia in Asia	47,000	
Turkistan, Afghanistan	14,000	
India and China	19,000	
		260,000

JEWS OF AFRICA (after I. Loeb).

Egypt	8,000	
* Abyssinia, Fellashas	50,000	
Carried forward	58,000	

* A. Loeb gives 200,000, but this is largely exaggerated.

Brought forward	58,000	
Tripolis	60,000	
Tunis	55,000	
Algeria and Sahara	43,500	
Morocco	100,000	
* Cape of Good Hope	1,500	
		318,000

* There are now probably some 20,000 in South Africa.

JEWS OF AMERICA.

*United States	750,000	
Canada, etc.	7,000	
Antilles	3,000	
South America	12,000	
		772,000

* In 1882 a statistical inquiry established that there were 250,000 Jews in the United States. Between that date and 1891, 380,000 were added by immigration, not to mention the natural increase.

JEWS OF AUSTRALIA.*

Australia 15,139

* For details *see* "Jews of British Empire."

JEWS OF THE WORLD.

Europe...	7,701,266
Asia	260,000
Africa	336,500
America	772,000
Australia	15,139
	9,084,005

There are probably eleven millions of Jews existing in the world at the present time (1896).

JEWS OF THE BRITISH EMPIRE.

It is possible to obtain exact statistics of the number of Jews in all parts of the British Empire, except Great Britain. All the British Colonies include a religious census in the decennial estimate of their numbers, and even Ireland follows in this the good example of the Colonies. But, for the centre of the Empire, for reasons into which we need not enter, this rubric is absent from the census returns. This laxity presses with peculiar harshness upon members of the Jewish faith in Great Britain, as it has given rise to all sorts of exaggerated notions as to their numbers in the past and the increase of their numbers in the present. But, while we have no figures endorsed with the authority of the Registrar-General, we are not entirely in the dark as to the number of Jews in England, Wales and Scotland. It will be allowed that few Jews are likely to be buried outside the Jewish "Houses of Life." Now, we have for the last quarter of a century full and accurate statistics of the number of Jews buried throughout the United Kingdom, and though, of course, we are unable to state the exact death rate ruling amongst them, one can be tolerably certain that it was not less than 15 per mil., or more than 25. So, too, we have for the purpose the number of marriages performed by Jewish clergymen, and here again we may be tolerably certain that these were not more than 12 per mil. of the Jewish population, or less than 7 per mil. If, then, we applied an average multiplier to the deaths and marriages of any one year, we could get, by averaging the two results, an approximate estimate of the Jewish population of England and Scotland which cannot differ from the true result by more than a few thousands. The last census of the British Empire was in 1891, and for that year we have the following figures :—

	Marriages.	Multiplier.	Population.	Deaths.	Multiplier.	Population.	Average Population.
London ..	724	100	72,400	1,431	40	57,240	64,280
Provinces.	327	120	39,240	538	50	26,900	33,070
Scotland ..	26	120	3,120	25	40	1,000	2,060

Taking these figures as approximately correct, we are enabled to draw up a complete census of the Jewish population of the British Empire as follows :—

JEWS IN THE BRITISH EMPIRE, 1891.

England and Wales		*c.* 97,350
Scotland		*c.* 2,060
Ireland—		
Connaught	8	
Leinster	1,135	
Munster	354	
Ulster	282	1,779
Australia—		
New South Wales	5,484	
Victoria	6,459	
South Australia	840	
Queensland	809	
New Zealand	1,463	
Tasmania	84	15,139
Canada—		
Ontario	2,501	
Quebec	2,703	
Nova Scotia	31	
New Brunswick	73	
Carried forward	5,308	116,328

Brought forward...	5,308	116,328
Manitoba ...	743	
British Columbia...	277	
Prince Edward's Isle	1	
North-West Territories	85	
		6,414
Trinidad ...		31
Barbadoes ...		21
Cape Colony		3,009
India—		
Ajmere	71	
Assam	5	
Bengal	1,447	
Berar	2	
Bombay	13,547	
Burma	351	
Central Provinces	167	
Madras	1,309	
North-West Provinces	60	
Punjab	33	
Quetta	23	
Haidarabad	26	
Baroda	36	
Mysore	21	
Rajaputana	15	
Central India	72	
		17,185
Aden		2,826
Gibraltar ...		c. 1,000
Straits Settlements		535
Malta		173
Cyprus		127
		147,649

COMMUNAL STATISTICS.

The following tables have been compiled from the returns made to the United Synagogue and to the Board of Deputies for the last quarter of a century. They convey important information as to the relative ages at which the Jews of London die, as to the increase in the number of burials, and the quarters of the town from which such burials take place.

The returns of the Visitation Committee of the United Synagogue, give information as to the number of Jewish inmates in public institutions of various kinds and may serve as a rough guide to the criminality of the Jewish population of London, while the returns of the Board of Deputies give the number of seatholders not only for the metropolis but for the Provinces, Scotland and Ireland.

UNITED SYNAGOGUE BURIALS, 1873—1895.

MALES AND FEMALES.

	undev.	stills.	under 1mo.	1 yr.	1-5	10	20	30	40	50	60	70	80	90	over 90	Total Burials	Char. & Free.	Non U.S.	E. and E.C.	Total less stills	
1873	21	97	45	189	117	21	18	45	27	34	59	62	60	21	8	824	496	701	662	706	1873
1874	6	110	52	151	191	43	18	42	36	39	51	62	57	30	5	881	486	720	745	771	1874
1875	0	123	73	169	156	21	24	35	34	27	46	51	55	34	3	851	462	663	685	728	1875
1876	28	97	55	161	128	13	15	33	32	32	56	46	66	30	10	802	423	620	688	677	1876
1877	16	106	74	194	136	25	20	31	40	43	42	65	62	35	11	900	474	703	694	778	1877
1878	6	124	74	211	133	26	26	46	30	36	61	65	65	35	7	960	522	792	743	832	1878
1879	15	61	121	198	224	27	16	46	49	40	59	85	68	52	6	1047	522	813	799	971	1879
1880	15	108	66	175	162	29	23	25	33	56	59	68	65	32	11	916	428	716	719	793	1880
1881	14	102	75	202	176	21	17	35	42	42	60	76	71	37	6	922	395	806	756	876	1881
1882	15	131	61	195	197	24	19	63	44	45	57	75	50	39	8	1012	512	915	781	866	1882
1883	21	108	91	199	175	37	33	32	46	41	78	49	57	28	8	1014	534	811	770	885	1883
1884	27	104	64	257	182	28	25	45	50	45	65	36	65	38	9	1038	574	853	812	907	1884
1885	49	122	89	252	205	24	29	41	39	59	52	82	74	33	16	1128	603	925	873	987	1885
1886	58	97	84	254	217	20	27	36	56	45	72	92	88	33	9	1202	673	993	919	1047	1886
1887	42	97	111	244	174	20	37	57	45	64	63	93	78	51	5	1172	645	972	894	1033	1887
1888	53	101	76	277	192	26	29	48	51	50	59	81	89	40	7	1177	647	957	874	1023	1888
1889	44	110	122	277	180	28	30	46	80	53	69	90	82	37	8	1261	725	1060	979	1107	1889
1890	48	99	143	337	262	29	25	63	55	49	73	93	90	45	5	1421	841	1210	1102	1274	1890
1891	42	119	105	327	188	33	33	66	60	71	73	107	102	39	16	1385	981	1164	1049	1224	1891
1892	54	143	151	310	188	63	40	76	67	77	73	101	108	44	15	1626	981	1383	1282	1429	1892
1893	45	142	181	414	321	47	30	70	86	81	99	108	99	47	6	1788	1102	1536	1436	1601	1893
1894	56	153	143	371	311	38	25	71	56	62	68	78	88	56	9	1570	976	1368	1227	1361	1894
1895	40	133	138	425	382	35	32	53	83	63	97	102	106	58	17	1764	1089	1545	1386	1591	1895

NOTE.—Char.=Charity; Non U.S.=not members of the United Synagogue; E. and E.C.=from the East and East Central districts of London; Undev.=undeveloped; Stills=stillborn.

JEWISH INMATES AT PUBLIC INSTITUTIONS, 1873—1895.

	Asylums.		Hospitals.		Workhouses*		Prisons.		Reformatories.		Distr. Schools	
	Max.	Av.	Max.	Av.	Max.	Av.	Max.	Av.	Max.	Av.	Max.	Recd.
1873	99	88	91	66	6	4	100	81	2	2		
1874	106	102	69	57	13	10	97	84	4	3		
1875	117	113	80	61	12	9	90	75	4	4		
1876	133	117	87	71	11	8	106	80	8	6		
1877	143	136	102	82	13	11	106	82	11	8		
	Max.	Recd.	Max.	Recd.	Max.	Recd.	Max.	Recd.	Max.	Recd.	Max.	Recd.
				deaths		deaths*						
1878	144	46	95	383	12	12	111	186	13	3	5	2
1879	149	35	89	364	11	8	117	202	10	2	6	5
1880	142	29	114	436	14	23	131	172	10	4	3	—
1881	144	27	105	444	12	17	162	223	20	10	3	5
1882	138	26	114	511 deaths	19	5	142	185	7	—	5	5
1883	141	20	90 71	506 79	22	23 16	165	227	7	3	3	4
1884	153	35	85 6	637 99	69	75 16	172	200	7	2	7	11
1885	148	26	134 18	726 111	38	71 29	181	237	8	3	14	14
1886	175	41	104 18	783 140	46	96 31	114	210	9	5	15	17
1887	183	33	103 29	771 111	47	106 45	112	244	10	6	8	4
1888	189	48	104 14	776 144	63	78 47	112	247	11	4	.2	1
1889	182	36	134 25	704 147	76	113 47	105	220	17	12	2	2
1890	190	42	139 18	830 186	57	87 38	134	270	36	23	7	3
1891	215	38	139 19	926 198	50	62 62	123	268	42	12	2	1
1892	218	77	143 24	1142 289	59	156 92	108	257	48	17	1	1
1893	200	51	184 22	1190 291	80	299 44	127	388	49	13	—	—
1894	261	98	180 27	1100 260	75	243 53	155	411	54	20	1	—
1895	270	92	192 27	1339 288	89	434 61	148	416	54	30	4	4

* "Workhouses" was the form used till recently but this is now changed to "Workhouse Infirmaries." The deaths noticed under this heading were not all from the infirmaries, some having been moved to the workhouse mortuaries after death.

COMMUNAL STATISTICS.

RETURNS MADE TO BOARD OF DEPUTIES OF THE NUMBERS OF

	LONDON.			PROVINCES.			IRELAND.			SCOTLAND.		
	Seat-holders.	Marriages.	Deaths.	Seat-holders.	Marriages.	Deaths.	Seat-holders.	Marriages.	Deaths.	Seat-holders.	Marriages.	Deaths.
1873	2,289	331	847	2,370	152	265	27	1	3	198	3	13
1874	2,287	309	875	2,642	144	302	31	1	2	226	10	13
1875	2,498	317	817	2,897	152	259	44	3	3	175	5	12
1876	2,435	275	755	2,833	175	271	48	1	5	190	5	15
1877	2,860	297	878	2,767	137	246	49	1	5	185	6	13
1878	2,972	377	985	2,640	127	271	63	5	11	151	7	22
1879	3,378	325	1,668	2,559	127	243	66	5	11	177	8	23
1880	3,199	349	883	2,820	120	261	68	4	5	170	3	25
1881	3,418	364	970	2,765	123	212	51	1	8	318	6	21
1882	3,274	372	930	2,715	152	261	45	3	8	192	10	15
1883	3,397	381	959	2,926	163	261	45	3	7	219	6	27
1884	3,428	439	991	3,025	176	333	53	4	4	240	11	22
1885	3,521	462	1,061	3,021	183	353	67	5	12	230	12	20
1886	3,689	472	1,148	2,937	201	354	64	9	8	240	6	25
1887	3,573	443	1,119	3,122	180	429	86	11	11	230	25	23
1888	4,108	589	1,129	3,359	223	389	84	7	18	230	17	24
1889	4,458	613	1,215	3,398	274	489	67	2	9	220	12	30
1890	4,578	654	1,450	5,785	275	513	87	4	9	220	25	24
1891	5,502	724	1,431	3,839	327	538	139	12	21	321	26	25
1892	5,669	743	1,625	4,114	314	567	165	8	17	306	22	28
1893	5,594	788	1,792	4,334	323	616	214	10	20	370	39	55
1894	6,561	839	1,620	4,751	321	619	231	12	31	400	46	51
1895	6,250	864	1,905	4,466	408	716	249	7	21	400	5	7

METROPOLITAN INSTITUTIONS.

SYNAGOGUES.

*UNITED SYNAGOGUE. (Founded 1870.)
President.—LORD ROTHSCHILD.
Vice-Presidents.—B. L. COHEN, Esq., M.P., and HENRY LUCAS, Esq.
Treasurers.—Messrs. DAVID DAVIS† and H. A. ABRAHAMS.
Council.—108 Members.
Income.—£28,703. *Expenditure.*—£28,058 (for details see p. 36).
Secretary.—P. ORNSTIEN.
Address.—2, Charlotte-street, Portland-place, W.

This important body was constituted by Act of Parliament (33 & 34 Vic. cap. 116), and now consists of the following 13‡ synagogues :—

Great Synagogue, Duke-street, Aldgate.
Wardens.—Rt. Hon. LORD ROTHSCHILD and A. ROSENFELD, Esq.
Financial Representative.—I. M. MARKS, Esq.
Reader.—Rev. M. HAST.
Assistant Reader and Secretary.—Rev. S. GORDON.

Hambro' Synagogue, Hall of Great Synagogue, Duke-street, Aldgate.
Wardens.—Messrs. JOSEPH JACOBS and EMANUEL SALOMON.
Financial Representative.—J. A. J. DE-VILLIERS, Esq.
Minister.—Rev. S. M. GOLLANCZ.
Secretary.—Mr. L. J. SALOMONS.

New Synagogue, Great St. Helen's, Bishopsgate, E.C.
Wardens.—Messrs. DANIEL JACOBS and HENRY ROSENBAUM.
Financial Representative.—A. M. WARTSKI, Esq.
Minister and Secretary.—Rev. S. LEVY.
Reader.—Rev. M. A. EPSTEIN.

Bayswater Synagogue, Chichester-place, Harrow-road, W.
Wardens.—Messrs. ISAAC A. JOSEPH and WOLF MYERS.
Financial Representative.—GEORGE BENDON, Esq.
Minister.—Rev. H. GOLLANCZ. *Reader.*—Rev. I. SAMUEL.
Reader and Secretary.—Rev. R. HARRIS.

Central Synagogue, Great Portland-street, W.C.
Wardens.—Messrs. SAMUEL E. MOSS and JOSEPH PYKE.
Financial Representative.—ASHER ISAACS, Esq.
Minister and Secretary.—Rev. D. FAY. *Reader.*—Rev. E. SPERO.

---

* Issues Annual Report.   † Resigned July, 1896.
‡ South Hackney Synagogue, p. 37, was admitted July 20th, 1896.

METROPOLITAN INSTITUTIONS.

Boro' Synagogue, Vowler-street, Walworth-road, S.E.
Wardens.—Messrs. JOHN A. COHEN and JACOB WOOLF.
Financial Representative.—A. LEON, Esq.
Minister and Secretary.—Rev. F. L. COHEN.

St. John's Wood Synagogue, 41, Abbey-road, St. John's Wood, N.W.
Wardens.—Messrs. A. SAUNDERS and R. SONNENTHAL.
Financial Representative.—ALBERT E. MOSS, Esq.
Minister.—Rev. B. BERLINER.
Reader and Secretary.—Rev. H. L. PRICE.

East London Synagogue, Rectory-square, Stepney-green, E.
Wardens.—Messrs. J. GREEN and LEWIS LEVY.
Financial Representative.—J. GREEN, Esq.
Minister and Secretary.—Rev. J. F. STERN.
Reader.—Rev. I. GREENBERG.

North London Synagogue, John-street-west, Thornhill-road, N.
Wardens.—Messrs. ADOLPH TUCK and J. GOLDHILL.
Financial Representative.—J. M. LISSACK, Esq., Jun.
Minister and Secretary.—Rev. J. A. GOULDSTEIN.
Reader.—Rev. S. MUNZ.

West End Synagogue, St. Petersburgh-place, Bayswater, W.
Wardens.—Messrs. STEPHEN S. HYAM and L. A. NATHAN.
Financial Representative.—LEONARD B. FRANKLIN, Esq.
Minister.—Rev. S. SINGER.
Reader.—Rev. J. L. GEFFEN.
Secretary.—Mr. H. J. PHILLIPS.

Dalston Synagogue, Poet's-road, Petherton-road, N.
Wardens.—Messrs. J. BIRN and W. ISAACS.
Financial Representative.—ALFRED POSENER, Esq.
Minister and Secretary.—Rev. M. HYAMSON.
Reader.—Rev. J. LESSER.

Hammersmith Synagogue, Brook-green, Hammersmith, W.
Wardens.—Messrs. J. M. LEVY and ADOLPH POSENER.
Financial Representative.—DELISSA JOSEPH, Esq.
Minister and Secretary.—Rev. M. ADLER, B.A.

Hampstead Synagogue, Dennington-park-road, N.
Wardens.—Messrs. FRANK I. LYONS and H. NATHAN.
Financial Representative.—SAMUEL MOSES, Esq., M.A.
Minister and Secretary.—Rev. A. A. GREEN.
Reader.—Rev. S. MANNE.

UNITED SYNAGOGUE REVENUE AND EXPENDITURE.

The following Tables give the Revenue and Expenditure for the United Synagogue for the year 1895:—

REVENUE.

	£ s. d.	£ s. d.
Constituent Synagogues:—		
Seat Rentals (including Temporary Seats let)	13,892 9 1	
Offerings	6,281 11 0	
Marriage Charges	522 6 6	
Communal Rates	4,888 12 0	
Other Items	231 19 10	
		25,816 18 5
Less 5 per cent. Building Tax	660 15 2	
		£25,156 3 3
United Synagogue:—		
Dividends and Income from Bequests	868 4 7	
Rents	1,024 10 4	
Board of Shechita	562 10 0	
Other items	21 17 0	
Marriage Fees	531 16 6	
Chief Rabbi's Fund	538 0 0	
		3,546 18 5
		£28,703 1 8

EXPENDITURE.

	£ s. d.	£ s. d.
Constituent Synagogues:—		
Salaries, excluding Doorkeepers, Assistants, & Choir, Rents, Rates, &c.	9,753 19 6	
All other items (except Recoupment of Stock sold out and interest thereon)	6,509 14 2	
		16,263 13 8
United Synagogue:—		
Charities (excluding Burial Rates)	2,816 8 9	
Salaries	3,006 6 10	
Pensions	1,254 3 4	
Votes of Council & all other Items	1,823 17	
		8,900 16 9
Jewish Religious Education Board	325 0 0	
		25,489 10 5
Funded Rent	192 7 2	
Funded Obligatory Charges	616 8 2	
Invested, Great Synagogue Rothschild Fund	100 0 0	
Final Surpluses	1,161 5 6	
„ „ Recoupments from	499 2 3	
		28,058 13 6
Less retained for payment of West End Synagogue Ground Rent		348 15 5
		27,709 18 1
Increase of Bank Balance (January 1st, 1894)		993 3 7
		£28,703 1 8

The following figures show at a glance the income, local expenditure, number of members, etc., of each synagogue:—

	Total Income.	Male Members.	Offerings.	Local Expend.	Surplus.	Deficit.
Great	£3,051	443	£745	£1,811	£325	—
Hambro	311	106	108	549	—	£315
New	1,473	316	322	1,065	—	—
Bayswater	4,321	359	1,064	2,391	801	—
Central	3,432	328	692	1,996	397	—
Borough	802	162	248	593	—	23
St. John's Wood	2,606	334	663	1,344	350	—
East London	1,054	306	236	847	—	83
North London	1,272	181	308	1,025	—	82
West End	3,940	279	854	1,876	480	—
Dalston	2,209	323	316	1,194	322	—
Hammersmith	486	117	129	312	—	—
Hampstead	2,220	213	427	1,027	317	—

METROPOLITAN SYNAGOGUES NOT INCORPORATED WITH THE UNITED SYNAGOGUE.

Spanish and Portuguese Jews' Congregation, London. (Founded 1656.)
Principal Synagogue, Bevis Marks, St. Mary-axe, E.C. (Erected 1701.)
Branch, Bryanston-street, W. (Erected 1861, after September, 1896, Lauderdale-road, Maida-vale.)
Wardens of both Synagogues, Messrs. JOSHUA M. LEVY, EUSTACE A. LINDO, EDWARD L. MOCATTA, and EDWARD SASSOON.
Treasurer.—M. A. N. LINDO, Esq.
Secretary.—Mr. SAMUEL I. COHEN.
Ministers (Bevis Marks).—Rev. S. J. ROCO and Rev. S. CONQUY.
Minister (Bryanston-street).—Rev. J. PIPERNO.
Offices of the Congregation.—Vestry Offices, Heneage-lane, E.C.
No. of Yehidim, 321.
Income, 1895.—£4,959. *Expenditure.*—£5,191.

Western Synagogue, St. Alban's-place, St. James's-street, S.W.
President.—MYER HARRIS, Esq. *Treasurer.*—E. J. LOEWE, Esq.
Minister.—Rev. H. DAVIDS. *Secretary.*—Mr. S. H. DAVIDS.
This Synagogue was removed from Denmark-street to St. Alban's-place in 1826. The present number of seatholders is 160.

Maiden Lane, Strand, W.C. (Founded 1821.)
Presidents.—Messrs. HENRY HARRIS and M. MOCH.
Treasurer.—J. S. LYON, Esq. *Secretary.*—Rev. P. PHILLIPS.
The seatholders number 75, and the income for 1895 was £679. 0s. 10d.

South Hackney Synagogue, Devonshire-road, Mare-street, N.E. (Founded 1879.)
Wardens—Messrs. A. B. SALMEN and L. ZACHARIAH.
Treasurer.—J. ROSENBERG, Esq.
Secretary.—Rev. M. J. HEILBRON.
Ministers.—Revs. M. J. HEILBRON and G. ISAACS.

There are also Religious Classes connected with this synagogue, founded in 1884. The Head Master is Rev. M. J. HEILBRON, and the scholars number 180; 90 boys and 70 girls, and 20 infants. The number of seatholders in the synagogue is 75.

Spital Square, Synagogue, Spital-square, Bishopsgate, E.
President.—H. BERLINER, Esq. *Treasurer.*—M. COHEN, Esq.
Minister—Rev. I. BLACHMAN. *Secretary.*—A. PRINS, Esq.
The seatholders number about 100.

New Dalston Synagogue, Birkbeck-road, Dalston, N.E.
President.—L. FREEDMAN, Esq.
Treasurer.—H. GOODMAN, Esq.
Reader.—Rev. C. DAVIES.
Secretary.—J. E. BLANK, Esq.
Income, 1895.—£585. *Expenditure.*—£498.

There are also religion classes connected with this Synagogue, Dr. Steinheim being the Head Master, and the scholars numbering about 100.

Sandy's Row Synagogue, Sandy's-row, Bishopsgate, E.
President.—JACOB FONTYN, Esq.
Treasurer.—JACOB VOGEL, Esq.
Secretary.—Rev. S. BRONKHORST.
Seatholders.—350.

North West London Synagogue, York-road, Camden-road, N.W.
(Founded 1889.)
President.—E. J. LOWE, Esq.
Treasurer.—ALFRED PYKE, Esq.
Minister.—Rev. WOOLF ESTERSON.
Secretary (pro tem.).—Mr. N. CHETHAM.
The seatholders number 52.

There is also a school attached to the synagogue which thirty children attend. Rev. W. ESTERSON is Head Master.

Finsbury Park Synagogue, 20, Portland-road, Finsbury-park, N.
(Founded 1884.)
President.—B. FULD, Esq.
Treasurer.—S. HAMBURGER, Esq.
Minister.—Rev. SALOMON FINEWICH.
Hon. Secretary.—S. ELDOV, Esq.

The income and expenditure is about £170 to £175, and the seatholders number 65.

South-East London Synagogue, Lausanne-road, Peckham, S.E.
Wardens.—Messrs. J. BERLINSKI and B. HERR.
Treasurer.—B. COHEN, Esq.
Reader and Secretary.—Rev. N. GOLDSTON.

There are also religion classes attached to the synagogue, 70 scholars attending.

West London Synagogue of British Jews. (Founded 1841.)
Chairman of Council.—F. D. MOCATTA, Esq.
Treasurers.—Messrs. B. ELKIN MOCATTA, and ALFRED WALEY.
Administration—by Council and Wardens elected annually.
Secretary.—Mr. ALFRED HENRY, F.C.A.
Address.—34, Upper Berkeley-street, W.

FEDERATION OF SYNAGOGUES.

Hon. President.—Right Hon. LORD ROTHSCHILD.

President.—Sir SAMUEL MONTAGU, Bart., M.P.

Vice-President.—H. LANDAU, Esq.

Treasurers.—M. MOSES, Esq.; I. WEBER, Esq.

Auditors.—M. HARRIS, Esq.; J. HOUTMAN, Esq.

Elders.—

S. ALEXANDER, Esq.
I. M. BOEKBINDER, Esq.
J. M. LISSACK, Esq.
J. LEVY, Esq.
E. OPPENHEIM, Esq.
S. S. OPPENHEIM, Esq.
S. STRELITSKI, Esq.

Secretary.—MR. J. E. BLANK.

Office: 34, Alvington Crescent, Dalston, N.E.

Synagogues represented.—

	President.	No. of Mem.
Sandys-row Synagogue, Bishopsgate	J. FONTYN	318
Old Montagu-st. Syn. (No. 36½), Whitechapel	K. SHEAR	150
West End Talmud Torah Synagogue, 9, Green's-court, Golden-square	J. DAVIS	148
New-road Synagogue, Whitechapel	J. SINGER	145
New Dalston Syn., Birkbeck-road, Dalston	M. FREEDMAN	135
Old Castle-steeet Synagogue, Spitalfields	M. MOSES	130
Spital-square Synagogue, Bishopsgate	H. BERLINER	120
Great Alie-st. Synagogue (No.40 & 41), Aldgate	K. SHEAR	120
White's-row Synagogue (No. 2), Spitalfields	W. GOODMAN	110
Lodz Syn., Davis Mans., Goulston-st., Aldgate	F. LITTMAN	104
Hope-street Synagogue, Spitalfields	J. SILVERMAN	104
Vine-court Synagogue, Whitechapel	B. RITTER	100
Greenfield-st. Synagogue, Commercial-road	A. JACOBS	89
Gun-street Synagogue (No. 37A), Spitalfields	Z. DIMANT	84
Princelet-street Synagogue, Spitalfields	J. DAVIDSOHN	80
Dunk-street Synagogue, Mile-end New Town	J. M. LIBGOTT	63
Mikvah Synagogue, New-court	H. GOLDBERG	62
Kehol Chasidim Synagogue, 5, Old Montagu-street, Whitechapel	S. GOLDSTEIN	60
St. Mary-st. Synagogue (No. 3), Whitechapel	H. ROSENTHAL (11 Booth-st.)	60
Spital-street Synagogue (No. 44), Spitalfields	H. ROSENTHAL (109, Brick-lane)	58
Fashion-st., Synagogue (No. 16), New-court	D. JACOBS	54
Scarborough-st. Synagogue, Goodman's-fields	H. PHILLIPS	52
Mansell-street Synagogue, Aldgate	H. HARRIS	50
Church-st. Syn.(No.29), Fournier-st., Spitlfds.	L. MOSES.	45
Konin Syn. 48, Hanbury-street, Spitalfields	N. GLÜCKSTEIN	45

METROPOLITAN INSTITUTIONS.

Guide to London Jewish Charities.

[*For fuller details see ensuing Alphabetical List.*]

THE following classified list gives under appropriate headings the names of the various charities contained in the succeeding alphabetical list, which gives full details in each case. When known, the mode of relief is shortly indicated in this list. Also, in some cases general charities, which are accessible to Jewish applicants, have been referred to. Where charities are marked with an asterisk no returns have been made, and all information that could be obtained is contained in this list. In order to obtain a sum total of Metropolitan Jewish Charity as also to serve as some guide to the relative importance of the various charities, the expenditure of each is given here as well as in the fuller list :—

1.—ORPHANS.

	£ s. d.
Jews' Hospital and Orphan Asylum, West Norwood (Election by Subscribers or admission by Committee)	7,592 14 6
*Royal Masonic Institution for Boys and Girls. For Orphans of Freemasons. Election by Subscribers. Candidates must be between 7 and 11. Jewish candidates, if elected, can at the request of their Guardians be educated outside the Institution. Secretary's Office, Great Queen-street, W.C.	
East London Orphan Aid Society (subsidiary to Jews' Hospital)	
Spanish and Portuguese Orphan Society (only for children of Sephardim)	618 0 0

2.—GIRLS.

Domestic Training Home	300 0 0
Jewish Ladies' Association for Preventive and Rescue Work	1,037 0 9

3.—DEAF AND DUMB, AND BLIND.

Jews' Deaf and Dumb Home (election by Committee)	1,300 0 0
Institution for the Indigent Blind	1,302 15 11

4.—EVENING CLASSES FOR STUDY OF ENGLISH.

English Evening Classes Committee	513 17 3

5.—WORKROOMS (for Women and Girls).

Jewish Board of Guardians, Widegate-street, Bishopsgate, E.C. ... ...

6.—LABOUR REGISTRY.

Free Employment Registry	
Location and Information Bureau	896 5 11
Carried forward	£13,560 14 4

METROPOLITAN INSTITUTIONS.

Brought forward	£13,560 14 4

7.—EMIGRATION.

Jewish Emigration Society	1,000 0 0

8.—LOANS.

Jewish Ladies' Benevolent Loan Society (for superior cases)
Board of Guardians for Relief of Jewish Poor (Loan Department)
Western Jewish Philanthropic Society

9.—RELIEF IN KIND—(a) Meals.

Soup Kitchen for the Jewish Poor (personal application)	1,766 6 0
Society for providing Penny Dinners (at Board and Jewish Schools)	482 8 4
*Nourishment Kitchen, Sandy's-row, Bishopsgate, E. (applicants must show a medical certificate)	

(b) Clothing.

Jewish Ladies' Clothing Association (upon Investigation by Visiting Committee)
Ladies' Clothing Committee (Board of Guardians)
*Jewish Boot Fund (at Board Schools)
Ladies' Guilds in connection with many synagogues

(c) Bread, Meat and Coals.

Meshivath Nephesh	2,036 12 11

10.—NURSING FOR INVALIDS.

Jewish Board of Guardians Conjoint Visiting Committee Nursing Home
Nurses for Invalid Children (apply to the secretary of the Jewish Board of Guardians)

11.—WATCHERS.

See List, page 63.
Chevra Kadisha (voluntary)

12.—HOSPITALS WHERE KOSHER FOOD IS PROVIDED FOR JEWISH PATIENTS.

Charing Cross Hospital, W.C.
Metropolitan Hospital, Kingsland-road, N.E.
London Hospital, Whitechapel-road, N.E.
Chelsea Hospital for Women, Fulham-road, S.W.
Ventnor Consumption Hospital

13.—LYING-IN WOMEN.

Ladies' Benevolent Institution	951 11 10
Honen Dalim, Menahem Abelim, Hebrat Yetomot and Hebrat Moalim (for Sephardim only)	65 0 0
East London Jewish Benevolent Society	28 16 0
Carried forward	£19,891 9 5

Brought forward	£19,981	9	5

14.—CONVALESCENT HOMES.

Jewish Convalescent Home (application with medical certificate, Great Synagogue-chambers, Mondays, 1.30 p.m.)...	838	14	0
*Convalescent Home for Jewish Children			

15.—INCURABLES.

Home and Hospital for Jewish Incurables (election by Committee)	104	0	0

16.—THE AGED—(a) Homes.

Home for Aged Jews (election by Committee) ...	2,045	0	0
Beth Holim Hospital (in connection with the Spanish and Portuguese Congregation)	1,040	0	0
*Salomon's Almshouses (in connection with the United Synagogue)			
*Marian Moses' Almshouses (Jewish Board of Guardians)			
*Abraham Lyon Moses' Almshouses, Devonshire-street, Mile-end, E.			

Pensions (b).

Society for Relieving the Aged Needy of the Jewish Faith (election by Subscribers)	1,396	0	0
Jews' Hospital and Orphan Asylum, West Norwood (election by Subscribers)			

17.—WORKHOUSES AND INFIRMARIES.

Parish of Whitechapel, Baker's-row, E. (Kosher food provided) ... ...
Parish of St. George's-in-the-East, Old Gravel-lane, Shadwell ... ...
Hamlet of Mile-end Old Town, Bancroft-rd., Mile-end
City of London Union : Offices, Bartholomew Close.

18.—WIDOWS.

City of London Benevolent Society for assisting widows of the Jewish Faith (election by Subscribers)	283	13	1½

19.—MARRIAGE PORTIONS.

Marriage Portion Society for assisting young men and virtuous girls of the Jewish Faith (election by Subscribers)	108	4	4
Israelite Marriage Portion Society (election by Subscribers)...	150	0	0
*Society for Granting Marriage Portions to Orphans (for Sephardim only)			

Carried forward	£25,947	0	10½

Brought forward	£25,947	0	10½

20.—BENEFIT SOCIETIES.

"Tree of Life" Confined Mourning Benefit Society	147	13	7½
Jewish Tradesmen's Benevolent Society			
East London Jewish Benevolent Society			
Sons of Plotzkar Benefit Society			
Lovers of Justice and Peace			

21.—GENERAL.

Ladies' Holy Vestment Society			
Jewish Branch of Children's Country Holiday Fund			
Society for Providing Strangers with Meals on Sabbaths and Holy Days	262	17	10
Metropolitan Promoters of Charity	742	18	5
Poor Jews' Temporary Shelter	1,334	0	0
East London Jewish Communal League			
Society for Relieving the Poor on the Initiation of their Children into the Holy Covenant of Abraham	386	19	11
Spanish and Portuguese Jews' Board of Guardians	1,500	0	0
Jewish Ladies' West-end Charity	200	0	0
Board of Guardians for the Relief of the Jewish Poor	35,738	0	0
TOTAL EXPENDITURE in 1895 of above-mentioned charities so far as known	64,259	10	8
To which must be added—			
Jewish contribution to Hospital Sunday, 1895	11,147	2	4*
Centennial Dinner Jews' Hospital	20,330	6	5
United Synagogue Charities	2,816	8	9
Building Fund of Board of Guardians	9,907	12	9
	£108,461	1	11

ALPHABETICAL LIST OF METROPOLITAN CHARITIES.

(Those presenting annual Reports are marked with an asterisk.)

*BETH HOLIM HOSPITAL, in connection with the SPANISH AND PORTUGUESE JEWS' CONGREGATION. (Founded 1747.)
Objects.—(*a*) For Sick Poor; (*b*) for Lying-in Women; (*c*) Asylum for the Aged.
President and Treasurer.—MANUEL CASTELLO, Esq.
Administration.—By Committee.
Income.—£1,105. *Expenditure.*—£1,040.
Secretary.—Mr. SAMUEL I. COHEN.
Address.—253, Mile End-road, E.

* Including special donation of £10,000.

*BOARD OF GUARDIANS FOR THE RELIEF OF THE JEWISH POOR. (Founded 1859.)

President.—BENJAMIN LOUIS COHEN, Esq., M.P.
Treasurers.—Messrs. LEOPOLD DE ROTHSCHILD and ARTHUR E. FRANKLIN.
Hon. Secretary.—MICHAEL A. GREEN, Esq.
Income, 1895.—£36,142. *Expenditure.*—£35,738.
Secretary.—Mr. M. STEPHANY.
Address.—Widegate-street, Bishopsgate, E.

Subsidiary Committees:—

Loan Committee.
Chairman.—S. SIMONS, Esq.
Hon. Secretaries.—Messrs. J. M. ANSELL and JOSEPH BERG.

Committee for Conducting the Workrooms.
Chairman.—CHARLES SAMUEL, Esq.
Hon. Secretary.—A. L. BIRNSTINGL, Esq.

Investigation Committee (for fixed allowances).
Chairman.—MAURICE BEDDINGTON, Esq.

Visiting Committee.
Chairman.—N. S. JOSEPH, Esq.
Hon. Secretaries.—Messrs. F. S. FRANKLIN, H. R. LEVINSOHN, and ERNEST MORLEY.

Emigration Committee.
Chairman.—A. ROSENFELD, Esq.
Hon. Secretary.—JULIUS SINGER, Esq.

Industrial Committee, to apprentice lads, supply tools, etc. (Rota meets every Monday at 4.30.)
Chairman.—STEPHEN S. HYAM, Esq.
Hon. Secretary.—H. T. MARCUS, ESQ.

Russo-Jewish and Jewish Board of Guardians Conjoint Committee. (Rota meets every Monday at 4.)
Chairman.—N. S. JOSEPH, Esq.

Sanitary Committee (to ensure Sanitary Acts being enforced).
Chairman.—N. S. JOSEPH, Esq.
Hon. Secretary.—DAVID SCHLOSS, Esq., M.A.

Ladies' Conjoint Visiting Committee.
President.—Mrs. LIONEL LUCAS.
Vice-President.—Mrs. LOUIS DAVIDSON.
Treasurer.—Mrs. ELLIS A. FRANKLIN.
Hon. Secretary.—Miss HYAM.

Ladies' Clothing Committee.
President.—Mrs. A. M. WOOLF.
Hon. Secretaries.—Mrs. S. HEILBRON, Miss F. ISAACS, Miss E. WOOLF, and Miss D. WCOLF.

Almshouses Committee.
Chairman.—MOSES H. MOSES, Esq.

CHEVRA KEDISHA. (Founded 1895.)
Object.—To perform the last rites to the dying and the dead.
President.—ARTHUR E. FRANKLIN, Esq.

Treasurer.—H. BENTWITCH, Esq.
Hon. Secretary.—S. ALEXANDER, Esq.
Address.—22, Duncan Terrace, Islington, N.

CHEVRATH TEHILLIM U - MISHMORIM. (Founded A.M., 5636.)
Object.—Allowances during Shiva, Death, and Visiting the Sick. Temporary relief to members in distress.
President.—MARK MOSES, Esq.
Treasurer.—JACOB DAVIDSON, Esq.
Secretary.—Mr. I. KALISKI.
Address.—18, Princelet Street, Spitalfields.

*CITY OF LONDON BENEVOLENT SOCIETY FOR ASSISTING WIDOWS OF THE JEWISH FAITH. (Founded 1867).
Object.—To assist Widows for the term of thirteen weeks with 5s. a week, and £1 at the expiration of that time.
Patronesses.—Lady ROTHSCHILD and Mrs. L. LUCAS.
Treasurer.—Mr. B. HARRIS.
Administration.—Voting by Proxy, and four elections a year. Subscribers vote according to the amount of their subscriptions. Annual Balance Sheet.
Income, 1895.—£421. 15s. 9½d.   *Expenditure.*—£283. 13s. 1¼d.
Secretary.—Mr. A. PRINS.
Address.—111, Brunswick Buildings, Aldgate, E.

*DOMESTIC TRAINING HOME, Branch of Jewish Ladies' Association. (Founded May 1st, 1894.)
Object.—To train Jewish girls for domestic service.
President.—Mrs. A. NATHAN.   *Treasurer.*—Mrs. HENRY NATHAN.
Matron.—Mrs. F. MEYER.
Income.—£250 to £300.   *Expenditure.*—Limited to Income.
Hon. Secretary.—Mrs. L. MODEL.
Address.—54, Hemstall Road, West Hampstead, N.W.

EAST LONDON JEWISH BENEVOLENT SOCIETY. (Founded 1869.)
Objects.—(*a*) To assist in procuring admission of indigent orphan children into an asylum ; (*b*) To disburse relief to poor lying-in women, sick persons, and persons in week of mourning ; (*c*) to lend sums of money to persons requiring assistance ; (*d*) to relieve all cases of want not above mentioned.
President.—A. MICHAELS, Esq.   *Treasurer.*—M. HEISER, Esq.
Administration.—By Committee elected by Subscribers.
Income, 1895.—£28. 16s.   *Expenditure.*—£28. 16s.
Balance Sheet issued annually.
Secretary.—Mr. LOUIS S. GREEN.   *Address.*—71, Stepney-green, E.

EAST LONDON JEWISH COMMUNAL LEAGUE.
Object.—To promote the religious, intellectual and social status of Jewish young men and women, and to enlist their sympathies and active co-operation in communal affairs.
President.—Rev. J. F. STERN.
Treasurer.—LAWRENCE LEVY, Jun., Esq.
Administration.—By Committee of twelve Members.
Hon. Secretary.—SAMUEL E. SAMUEL, Esq.
Address.—63, Stepney Green, E.

EAST LONDON ORPHAN AID SOCIETY. (Founded 1890.)
Objects.—Augmenting, by small weekly subscriptions, the funds of the Jews' Hospital and Orphan Asylum, West Norwood.
President.—LEWIS LEVY, Esq.
Treasurer.—J. M. LISSACK, Jun., Esq. *Collector.*—Mr. E. A. DIGHT.
Administration.—By Committee elected by Subscribers.
Income.—About £270, handed over, less working expenses, to the Jews' Hospital at Norwood. Balance Sheet issued annually.
Hon. Secretary.—Rev. J. F. STERN.
Address.—Synagogue Chambers, Rectory-square, Stepney, E.

FREE EMPLOYMENT REGISTRY. (Founded 1886).
Managers.—Rev. and Mrs. MORRIS JOSEPH.
Object.—To provide work for the Jewish unemployed.
Income derived from private sources, annual report being made privately to contributors to the funds.

*HOME AND HOSPITAL FOR JEWISH INCURABLES. (Founded 1889.)
Object.—The Care, Maintenance and Medical Treatment of persons of the Jewish Faith, resident in the United Kingdom, permanently disabled by chronic disease, accident or deformity.
President.—STUART M. SAMUEL, Esq., J.P.
Treasurers.—Messrs. M. DRUKKER and CHARLES D. SELIGMAN.
Administration.-By Board of Management and Subscribers' Votes.
Income.—About £800. *Expenditure.*—About £1,000.
Secretary.—Mr. L. J. SALOMONS.
Address.—49 and 51, Victoria Park-road, N.E.

*HOME FOR AGED JEWS (being the United Institutions formerly known as the Hand in Hand Asylum, Widows' Home, and Jewish Home respectively).
The amalgamation took place in December, 1894, but the constituent institutions were founded at various dates, the oldest more than fifty years ago.
President.—F. D. MOCATTA, Esq.
Treasurers.—Messrs. H. M. HARRIS and R. H. RAPHAEL.
Income, 1895.—£2,684. *Expenditure.*—£2,045.
Secretary.—I, BLOOMFIELD.
Address.—23 and 25, Well-street, Hackney, E., and 37 and 39, Stepney Green, E.

HONEN DALIM, MENAHEM ABELIM, HEBRAT YETOMOT AND HEBRAT MOALIM. (Founded 1724.)
Objects.—(a) To grant pecuniary aid to poor Lying-in Women, (b) to grant an allowance to persons in mourning, (c) to grant a marriage portion annually to one or more fatherless girls.
Treasurer.—MANUEL CASTELLO, Esq.
Administration.—By 24 Governors.
Income, 1895.—£144. *Expenditure.*—£65.
Secretary.—Mr. SAMUEL I. COHEN.
Address.—Vestry Offices, Heneage-lane, Bevis Marks, E.C.

INSTITUTION FOR THE RELIEF OF THE INDIGENT BLIND. (Founded 5579-1819.)
President.—Alderman GEORGE FAUDEL PHILLIPS.
Treasurer.—DAVID HYAM, Esq.

Income, 1895-6.—£1,366. 0s. 10d.   *Expenditure.*—£1,302. 15s. 11d.
Administration.—By Committee.   Balance-sheet issued yearly.
Secretary.—Mr. HENRY H. HYAMS.
Address.—8, Duke Street, Aldgate, E.C.

ISRAELITE MARRIAGE PORTION SOCIETY. (Founded A.M. 5636–1876.)

President.—L. MARCHANT, Esq.   *Treasurer.*—A. MOSES, Esq.
Income.—£150.   *Expenditure.*—£150.
Secretary.—Mr. I. KALISKI.
Address.—18, Princelet-street, Spitalfields (Prince's Street Synagogue).

JEWISH BRANCH OF CHILDREN'S COUNTRY HOLIDAY FUND. (Founded 1889.)

Object.—To send away poor Jewish children, selected from the various Board and Jewish schools, for a fortnight's stay in the country during the summer.
President.—E. L. FRANKLIN, Esq.
Treasurer.—L. SAMUEL MONTAGU, Esq.
Administration.—By Executive Committee, composed of ten Members. Supported by Subscriptions.
Hon. Secretaries.—Messrs. J. BERNBERG and J. KOSSICK.
Address.—11, East Mount Street, E.

JEWISH CONVALESCENT HOME. (Founded in memory of Judith, Lady Montefiore.)

Objects.—(*a*) To provide a Home for poor Jewish Patients recovering from illness; (*b*) to train Jewish Domestic Servants.
President.—Mrs. H. L. BISCHOFFSHEIM.
Treasurer.—Mrs. GEORGE C. RAPHAEL.   *Income*, 1895.—£838. 14s.
Hon. Secretaries.—Messrs. GEORGE S. JOSEPH and ELKAN N. ADLER.
Address.—Portland-road, South Norwood, and St. Patrick's-road, West Brighton.

*JEWISH LADIES' ASSOCIATION FOR PREVENTIVE AND RESCUE WORK. (Founded 1885.)

President.—LADY ROTHSCHILD.   *Treasurer.*—Mrs. F. B. HALFORD.
Income—for Rescue and Preventive Homes, £1,138. 13s. 11d.
Expenditure— - - - - - £1,037. 0s. 9d.
Hon. Secretary.—LADY BATTERSEA.
Address of Rescue Home.—Charcroft House, Beresford Terrace, Shepherd's Bush.
Address of Lodging House.—Sara Pyke House, 2a, Tenter Street North, Great Alie Street, E.

JEWISH LADIES' BENEVOLENT SOCIETY. (Founded, 5604—1844.)

Object.—To grant loans from £1 to £10, without interest or other charges, to the deserving Jewish poor.
President.—LOUISA, LADY DE ROTHSCHILD.
Treasurers.—Mrs. E. JACOB and Mrs. H. E. SYMONS.
Income, 1895-96.—£2,572. 4s. 2d.   *Expenditure.*—£2,581. 3s. 3d.
Administration.—by Committee. Balance-sheet issued annually
Secretary.—Mr. HENRY H. HYAMS.
Address.—8, Duke Street, Aldgate, E.C.

*JEWISH LADIES' CLOTHING ASSOCIATION. (Founded November, 1892.)
Object.—To supply articles of Clothing to various Schools, Charitable Institutions, and Visiting Committees for distribution among the needy.
President.—Mrs. LEOPOLD DE ROTHSCHILD.
Hon. Secretary.—Mrs. MEYER A. SPIELMANN.
Address.—23, Oxford-square, Hyde Park, W.

*JEWISH LADIES' WEST END CHARITY. (Founded 1842.)
Object.—The Relief of the Poor.
Treasurer.—Mrs. LIONEL LUCAS, 11, Westbourne-terrace, W., to whom subscriptions and donations are sent.
Hon. Secretary.—Mrs. ALFRED GOLDSMID.
Administration.—By Committee.
Income, 1895.—About £200. *Expenditure.*—About £200.
District Visitor.—Miss EMANUEL, 6, Ferntower-road, Canonbury, N., to whom gifts of clothing are sent.

JEWISH TRADESMEN'S BENEVOLENT SOCIETY. (Founded 1858.)
President.—ELLIS EMANUEL, Esq. *Treasurer.*—L. M. MYERS, Esq.
Income.—Depends upon theatrical speculation.
Expenditure.—Distribution to the poor, etc.
Administration.—By Members. *Secretary.*—Mr. HENRY HARRIS.
Address.—22, Great Prescot-street, E.

*JEWS' DEAF AND DUMB HOME. (Founded 1863.)
President.—Sir PHILIP MAGNUS.
Treasurer.—EDWARD D. STERN, Esq.
Administration.—By Committee.
Income, 1895.—About £800. *Expenditure.*—About £1,300.
No. of Pupils.—Boys, 17; Girls, 13.
Head Master.—Mr. S. KUTNER. *Hon. Sec.*—Rev. I. SAMUEL.
Address.—Walmer-road, Notting Hill, W.

*JEWS' EMIGRATION SOCIETY. (Founded 1852.)
Object.—To assist Emigrants going abroad in search of employment.
President.—LEOPOLD DE ROTHSCHILD.
Treasurer.—GASTON FOA, Esq.
Administration.—By Committee.
Income, 1895.—About £1,000. *Expenditure.*—About £1,000.
Hon. Sec.—G. L. LYON, Esq. *Address*—8, South-st., Finsbury, E.C.

*JEWS' HOSPITAL AND ORPHAN ASYLUM, WEST NORWOOD. (Founded 1795.)
Objects.—(a) Support of the Aged; (b) Maintenance, Education and Employment of Youth.
President.—Alderman G. FAUDEL PHILLIPS.
Treasurers.—Messrs. EDWARD LUCAS and DANIEL MARKS.
Hon. Secretary.—FELIX A. DAVIS, Esq., B.A., LL.B.
Income, 1896.—£6,929. 12s. 10d. *Expenditure.*—£7,592. 14s. 6d.
By a centennial dinner and legacies the Hospital obtained an additional extraordinary income of £20,330. 0s. 5d.
Secretary.—Mr. M. J. GREEN.
Address.—Hamilton-house, 149, Bishopsgate-street-without.

*LADIES' BENEVOLENT INSTITUTION.
Objects.—Clothing and otherwise Relieving Jewish Lying-in Married Women at their own houses.
Treasurer.—LADY ROTHSCHILD.
Administration.—By Committee.
Income, 1895.—£1,094. 11s. 2d. *Expenditure.*—£951. 11s. 10d.
Hon. Secretary.—Mrs. LIONEL LUCAS.
Address.—11, Westbourne-terrace, W.

LADIES' HOLY VESTMENT SOCIETY. (Founded April, 1893—5653.)
Object.—Providing holy vestments to the Prince's-street Synagogue.
President.—Mrs. J. ADLER.
Treasurer.—Mrs. J. JACOBS.
Income.—Varying from 10s. to 12s. weekly.
Hon. Secretary.—Miss KATE JOEL.
Address.—18, Princelet-street, Spitalfields.

*LOCATION AND INFORMATION BUREAU OF THE RUSSO-JEWISH COMMITTEE. (Founded 1892.)
Object.—To afford organised means whereby Russo-Jewish Refugees in London could obtain aid and information as to how and where to get work and where to reside.
President and Treasurer.—Sir SAMUEL MONTAGU, Bart., M.P.
Administration.—By Committee.
Income.—From the Russo-Jewish Committee. *Expenditure*, 1895.—£896. 5s. 11d.
Administrator.—Mr. J. E. BLANK.
Address.—84, Leman-street, Whitechapel, E.

LOVERS OF JUSTICE AND PEACE BENEFIT SOCIETY. (Founded 1823.)
President.—JACOB LOEZEN, Esq.
Treasurer.—A. N. NABARRO, Esq.
Income, 1895.—£1,457. 17s. 9d. *Expenditure.*—£1,408. 3s. 2d.
Secretary.—Mr. I. L. DEFRIES, 58, Artillery-lane, Spitalfields.
Address.—"Green Man," Mansell-street, Aldgate, E.C.

*MARRIAGE PORTION SOCIETY, FOR ASSISTING YOUNG MEN AND VIRTUOUS GIRLS OF THE JEWISH FAITH. (Founded 1850.)
Supported by Voluntary Subscriptions, Subscribers numbering about 300.
Dowry Allowed.—£25. 10s. 6d. marriage fee, and an allowance not exceeding 5s. to offer in Synagogue the Sabbath prior to the marriage.
Ages of Candidates.—From 18 to 35 years.
Patron.—Rev. Dr. ADLER, Chief Rabbi.
President.—A. SWAAB, Esq. *Treasurer.*—M. JOEL, Esq.
Administration.—By Board of Management. Voting by proxy.
Income, 1895-96.—£252. 16s. 2d. *Expenditure.*—£108. 4s. 4d.
Secretary.—Mr. A. PRINS.
Address.—111, Brunswick-buildings, Aldgate, E.

MESHIVATH NEPHESH. (Founded 5540-1780.)
Object.—To distribute bread, meat and coals amongst the Jewish poor, during the winter season.
President.—ISAAC A. JOSEPH, Esq.
Treasurers.—Messrs. HERMANN LANDAU and PHILIP S. WALEY.
Hon. Secretary.—ISAAC A. JOSEPH.
Income, 1895-96.—£2,012. 18s. 5d. *Expenditure.*—£2,036. 12s. 11d.
Administration.—By Committee. Balance-sheet issued annually.
Secretary.—Mr. HENRY H. HYAMS.
Address.—8, Duke-street, Aldgate, E.C.

***METROPOLITAN PROMOTERS OF CHARITY.** (Founded 1860.)
Object.—Relieving the Poor and necessitous by distribution of bread and fuel tickets during the winter.
President.—A. M. WARTSKI, Esq.
Vice-President.—S. F. FELDMAN, Esq.
Treasurer.—H. ROSENBAUM, Esq.
Administration.—By Committee.
Income, 1895-96.—£746. 7s. 8s. *Expenditure.*—£742. 18s. 5d.
Hon. Secretaries.—Messrs. SAMUEL WHARMAN, 119, Houndsditch, E.C., and HARRY RICHARDSON, 24, Finsbury-square, E.C.

PENNY DINNER SOCIETY. (Founded 1883.)
Object.—To provide dinners at schools during winter below cost for one penny.
President.—Mrs. ADLER.
Treasurer.—Mrs. B. BIRNBAUM. *Expenditure.*—£482. 8s. 4d.
Hon. Secretary.—E. D. LÖWY, Esq.
Address.—26, Sandy's-row, Whitechapel, E.

***POOR JEWS' TEMPORARY SHELTER.** (Founded 1885.)
Object.—Temporary accommodation of Immigrants.
President.—ELLIS A. FRANKLIN, Esq.
Treasurers.— Sir SAMUEL MONTAGU, Bart., M.P., and J. SCHWARZSCHILD, Esq.
Hon. Secretary.—F. H. HARVEY-SAMUEL, Esq.
Income, 1894-95.—£1,302. *Expenditure.*—£1,334.
Secretary.—Mr. J. E. BLANK.
Address.—84, Leman-street, Whitechapel, E.

***RUSSO-JEWISH COMMITTEE.** (Founded 1882.)
Object.—To promote the general welfare of Russian Jews who are the victims of religious persecution in their own country.
Chairman and Treasurer.—Sir SAMUEL MONTAGU, Bt., M.P.
Funds.—Collected in 1891, mainly distributed through the Conjoint Committee of the Jewish Board of Guardians and the Russo-Jewish Committee (*q.v.*), Information and Location Bureau (*q.v.*), and the English Evening Classes Committee (*q.v.*).
Secretary.—Mr. JOSEPH JACOBS, B.A.
Address.—61, Old Broad-street, E.C.

Subordinate Committees:
Location and Information Bureau.—84, Leman-street.
Chairman.—N. S. JOSEPH, Esq.
Administrator.—Mr. J. E. BLANK.

Intelligence Department.
Chairman.—Dr. A. WOLFF.
Hon. Secretaries.—B. A. ELKIN, Esq. and C. S. JOSEPH, Esq.

English Evening Classes Committee.
Chairman.—N. L. COHEN, Esq.
Hon. Secretaries.—H. R. LEVENSOHN, Esq., and B. B. HALFORD, Esq.
Address.—10, Throgmorton-avenue, E.C.
In conjunction with Board of Guardians, Conjoint Committee, and Fused Visiting Committee.

SOCIETY FOR PROVIDING STRANGERS WITH MEALS ON SABBATHS AND HOLYDAYS. (Founded 1869.)
President.—I. BIRNBAUM, Esq.
Treasurer.—I. WEBER, Esq.
Administration.—Tickets for meals issued weekly by Relief Committee, who meet at 84, Leman-street, E.
Income.—£358. 19s. 0½d. *Expenditure.*—£262. 17s. 10¼d.
Annual Balance Sheet.
Secretary.—Mr. H. SHMITH.
Address.—218, Whitechapel-road, E.

SOCIETY FOR RELIEVING THE AGED NEEDY OF THE JEWISH FAITH. (Founded 1829.)
President.—GILBERT E. SAMUEL, Esq.
Treasurers.—Messrs. M. H. SOLOMON and CECIL SEBAG MONTEFIORE.
Hon. Secretary.—EDWARD A. JOSEPH, Esq.
Administration.—By a Committee elected annually.
Income.—£988. *Expenditure.*—£1,396.
Secretary.—Mr. I. BLOOMFIELD.
Address.—68, Grove-road, Bow, E.
Meetings held at the Great Synagogue-chambers, St. James'-place, Aldgate.

SOCIETY FOR RELIEVING THE POOR ON THE INITIATION OF THEIR CHILDREN INTO THE HOLY COVENANT OF ABRAHAM. (Founded 1745—5605.)
President.—Sir SAMUEL MONTAGU, Bart., M.P.
Treasurer.—Dr. A. COHEN.
Income, 1895.—£416. 3s. 1d. *Expenditure.*—£386. 19s. 11d.
Secretary.—Mr. M. ABRAHAMS.
Address.—51, Pyrland-road, Canonbury, N.

SONS OF PLOTZKAR BENEFIT SOCIETY. (Founded June, 1873.)
Objects.—Payment during sickness, Shiva and Death, Members in distress relieved.
President.—A. W. SMITH, Esq.
Treasurer.—S. FRANKENSTEIN, Esq.
Secretary.—Mr. I. KALISKI.
Address.—Camperdown-house, Half Moon-passage, Whitechapel.

*SOUP KITCHEN FOR THE JEWISH POOR. (Founded 1858.)
Objects.— To provide (*a*) soup and bread during winter months (*b*) motzoth and grocery during Passover.
President.—ALFRED LOUIS COHEN, Esq.

Treasurer.—BERNARD BIRNBAUM, Esq.
Hon. Secretary.—BARRENT S. ELLIS, Esq.
Administration.—By Committee.
Income.—£1,982. 10s. 3d.   *Expenditure,* £1,766. 6s.
Clerk.—Mr. S. GILDER.
Address.—5, Fashion-street, Spitalfields, E.

*SPANISH AND PORTUGUESE JEWS' BOARD OF GUARDIANS.
(Founded 1837.)

Objects.—The Relief of the Poor.
President.—JOSEPH DE CASTRO, Esq.
Treasurer.—ABRAHAM LINDO HENRY, Esq.
Hon. Secretary.—EUSTACE A. LINDO, Esq.
Income 1894.—About £3,000.   *Expenditure.*—About £1,500.
Secretary.—Mr. NATHAN VAN KLEEF.
Address.—Heneage-lane, Bevis Marks, E.C.

*SPANISH AND PORTUGUESE JEWS' ORPHAN SOCIETY.
(Founded 1703.)

Object.—Educating, Clothing, Maintaining and Apprenticing Orphan Boys of the Congregation.
President.—ABRAHAM D. DE PASS, Esq.
Treasurer.—EDWARD L. MOCATTA, Esq.
Administration.—By Committee.
Income.—£655.   *Expenditure.*—£618.
Secretary.—Mr. SAMUEL I. COHEN.
Address.—9, Howley-place, Maida-hill, W. (after Sept., 1896, Lauderdale-road, Maida-vale).

* "TREE OF LIFE" MOURNING BENEFIT SOCIETY.

Supported by weekly contributions for the interment of free Members, allowance during Shiva, and in case of Member's or Member's wife's death, the Society also provides a tombstone.
Age Limit for Membership.—18 to 40 years.
Treasurer.—Mr. J. HESS.
Collector.—Mr. F. PENNAMACOOR.
Administration.—By Board of Management.
Income, 1895.—£490. 14s. 2d.   *Expenditure.*—£147. 13s. 7d.
Secretary.—Mr. A. PRINS.
Address.—111, Brunswick-buildings, Aldgate, E.

WESTERN JEWISH PHILANTHROPIC SOCIETY. (Founded 1827.)

Objects.—Relief of the Poor. To grant loans to tradesmen without interest.
President.—Rev. ISIDORE HARRIS, M.A.
Treasurer.—R. LYON, Esq.   *Secretary,*—Mr. S. H. DAVIDS.
Income, 1895.—£119.   *Expenditure.*—£41.
Address.—Synagogue-chambers, St. Alban's-place, St. James street, S.W.

JEWISH SCHOOLS.

The following list gives the chief Jewish Schools in the Metropolis, together with their addresses, Presidents, Head Masters and Mistresses and Secretaries:—

School.	Address.	President.	Head Master and Mistress.	Secretary.
Bayswater	St. James's-terrace, Harrow-rd.	J. Bergtheil	S. J. Heilbron	Rev. H. Harris (*Hon.*)
South London	Heygate-street, E.C.	A. H. Jessel	M. Kaizer	D. Singer and I. V. Albert (*Hon.*)
Jews' Free	Bell-lane, Spitalfields	Lord Rothschild	M. Angel	M. Duparc.
Gates of Hope	Heneage-lane	E. de Pass	...	S. I. Cohen.
Infants' Schools	Commercial-street	C. G. Montefiore	Miss Betteridge	Alfred Henry.
,, ,,	Buckle-street	,, ,,	Miss Sions	,, ,,
High Schl. for Girls	Chenies-st., Tottenham-crt.-rd.	Miss I. Goldsmid	Miss Levy	A. L Josephs (*Hon.*)
Stepney	71, Stepney-green	M. N. Adler	W. A. Payne	S. S. Hyam and E. Morley (*Hon.*)
Talmud Torah	Gt. Garden-st., Whitechapel, E.	H. Goodman	R. Rehfisch	
Villareal Girls	Heneage-lane	...	Miss Lyon	Miss Pinto (*Hon.*)
Westminster	Hanway-street	L. Davidson	J. Woolf	J. Woolf.

The tables on the next pages show the number of children attending these schools, and an additional table is added showing the number of children attending Board Schools in the East of London. By the kindness of the respective head masters and mistresses of these institutions, we are enabled to give information as to the origin of the children, showing whether they were born in England or abroad, and if in England whether of native or foreign parents.

JEWISH CHILDREN IN VOLUNTARY SCHOOLS.

	1894.							1896.						
	Boys.	Girls.	Infants.	Total.	Born Abro'd	Born in England of Fore'n Prnts.	Native Prnts.	Boys.	Girls.	Infants.	Total.	Born Abro'd	Born in England of Fore'n Prnts.	Native Prnts.
Jews' Free School	2,204	1,369	...	3,573	1,689	1,452	432	2,250	1,323	...	3,573	1,368	1,819	386
Infants, Commercial-street	...	...	1,095	1,095	103	943	49	...	...	1,063	1,063	42	927	94
Infants, Buckle-st.	...	...	917	917	355	499	63	...	...	898	...	299	525	74
Stepney Jewish	404	303	186	893	37	287	569	...	...	...	...	...	...	...
Borough "	109	63	43	215	13	79	123	118	84	47	249	15	79	155
Spanish and Portuguese, Heneage-lane	...	93	183	276	43	85	148	...	90	135	225	15	87	123
Bayswater Jewish	90	86	67	243	28	140	75	69	89	75	233	25	139	69
*Westminster "	243	244	134	611	209	331	71	280	232	44	556	203	289	44
Orphan Asylum, Norwood	145	120	...	265	13	151	101	142	109	...	251	28	128	95
Deaf & Dumb Home	23	15	...	38	8	17	13	16	14	...	30	8	16	6
Total	3,218	2,293	2,625	8,126	2,498	3,984	1,644	2,875	1,941	2,262	6,180	2,003	4,009	1,046

* At the time these figures were given for 1896, 23 Boys, 15 Girls, and 6 Infants were absent.

JEWISH CHILDREN IN BOARD SCHOOLS.

	1894.								1896.							
	Boys.	Girls.	Infants.	Total.	Born Abro'd	Born in England of Fore'n Prnts.	Born in England of Native Prnts.	Boys.	Girls.	Infants.	Total.	Born Abro'd	Born in England of Fore'n Prnts.	Born in England of Native Prnts.
Berner-street...	238	283	530	1,051	622	353	76	370	357	516	1,243	420	753	70
Buck's-row ...	66	78	283	427	125	199	103	100	102	200	302	77	145	180
Old Castle-street	495	403	534	1,432	162	865	405	400	417	500	1,317	482	746	89
Chicksand-street	457	466	543	1,466	342	771	353	400	418	760	1,588	400	1,060	118
Gravel-lane ...	236	397	375	1,008	268	305	435	346	405	503	1,254	316	504	434
Hanbury-street	231	317	288	836	542	209	85	312	413	280	1,005	292	433	290
Settles-street...	541	523	554	1,618	240	1,173	205	441	469	557	1,467	430	712	325
Baker-street ...	...	...	...	...	...	...	...	126	216	295	687	246	329	62
Deal-street ...	...	...	...	...	...	...	...	212	335	526	1,073	537	426	90
Dempsey-street	...	...	...	...	...	...	...	4	9	33	46	...	10	36
Total Board ...	2,264	2,467	3,107	7,838	2,301	3,875	1,662	2,711	3,141	4,170	9,982	3,200	5,118	1,694
Total Voluntary	3,218	2,293	2,625	8,126	2,498	3,984	1,644	2,875	1,941	2,262	6,180	2,003	4,009	1,046
Grand Total	5,482	4,760	5,732	15,964	4,799	7,859	3,306	5,586	5,082	6,432	16,162	5,203	9,127	2,740

THEOLOGICAL COLLEGES.

JEWS' COLLEGE, Tavistock House, Tavistock-square.
President.—The Very Rev. Dr. ADLER, Chief Rabbi.
Vice-President.—ARTHUR COHEN, Esq., Q.C.
Treasurers.—Messrs. CHARLES SAMUEL and JAMES H. SOLOMON.
Hon. Secretary.—Rev. J. CHAPMAN, Great Ealing School, Ealing, W.
Principal.—M. FRIEDLÄNDER, Ph.D.
Assistant Theological Tutor.—S. A. HIRSCH, Ph.D.
Masters.—Mr. G. WASHINGTON KILNER, M.A., Mr. ISRAEL ABRAHAMS, M.A., Rev. I. SAMUEL, Rev. F. L. COHEN, Mons. A. ANTOINE, and Mr. S. L. HASLUCK.

This institution, founded in 1846, is the chief seminary for the education of the Jewish Ministry. Scholars are admitted to the Preparatory class from the age of 13, after an examination in their knowledge of English and Hebrew, and to the Junior class from the age of 16. It grants nine scholarships, varying from £76 to £30 per annum on the result of examinations for the respective grades of Probationer Associate and Fellow. It also grants certificates to teachers of Hebrew and religion. During the year 1895 it expended £380 in scholarships and £1,478 15s. 1d. in general expenses.

There is also in connection with Jews' College a Jews' College Literary Society, at which Lectures are read on Sunday evenings, from October to May. The lectures are open to the public.

JUDITH MONTEFIORE COLLEGE, Ramsgate.
Temporarily closed.

ARIA COLLEGE, Portsea.
President.—The Very Rev. Dr. ADLER, Chief Rabbi.
Treasurer.—Alderman A. L. EMANUEL, J.P.
Principal and Secretary.—Rev. ISAAC S. MEISELS.
Income and Expenditure.—About £700.
Address.—St. George's Square, Portsea (Hants).

[Preferentially for candidates for the Jewish ministry born in Hampshire.]

CLUBS.

*JEWISH GIRLS' CLUB.
President.—Mrs. LOUIS DAVIDSON.
Treasurer and Secretary.—LADY MAGNUS.
Council.—26 Members.
Income 1895.—About £113. *Expenditure.*—About £94.
Address.—22, Great Prescot-street, E.

*JEWISH WORKING MEN'S CLUB AND LADS' INSTITUTE.
(Founded 1871.)
President.—Sir SAMUEL MONTAGU, Bart., M.P.
Treasurer.—Messrs. L. B. FRANKLIN and L. S. MONTAGU.
Administration.—Elected Committee.
Income, 1894.—£635. 17s. 11d.
Hon. Secretaries.—Messrs. J. M. LISSACK and J. CROCKER.
Address.—Great Alie Street, Aldgate, E.

THE MACCABEANS.
Object.—An Association of Jewish professional men and others to promote the higher interests of the Jewish race.
President.—SOLOMON J. SOLOMON, Esq., A.R.A.
Treasurer.—FELIX DAVIS, Esq.
Hon. Secretary.—H. J. COHEN, Esq.
Address.—St. James's Restaurant, Piccadilly, S.W.
In connection with this Association, there has been formed an

Educational Committee.
Chairman.—H. BENTWITCH, Esq.
Hon. Secretary.—J. HIRSCHKOVICH, Esq.;

and a **Jewish Lads' Brigade.**
Chairman.—Colonel GOLDSMID.
Hon. Secretary.—Dr. B. L. ABRAHAMS.

*WEST CENTRAL JEWISH GIRLS' CLUB. (Founded 1887.)
Objects.— (1) To provide evening continuation classes for working girls living in West Central district. (2) To provide amusement and recreation with a view to discourage girls from harmful amusements. (3) To encourage social intercourse between women of different education and varied occupation.
President.—Miss EMILY MARION HARRIS.
Treasurer.—Miss NATHAN.
Income, 1895.—£90. 18s. 8d. *Expenditure.*—£76. 2s. 8d.
Administration.—By Committee of workers, Sub-committee of Members, and Visiting Committee.
Hon. Secretary.—Miss LILY H. MONTAGU.
Address.—8, Dean-street, Soho, W.

EDUCATIONAL AND LITERARY INSTITUTIONS.

BETH HAMIDRASH. Library, St. James-place, Aldgate.

(1.) The Library is open daily from 11 to 1, and from 5 to 9 p.m.
(2.) Readings in Talmud, Bible with Commentaries, and other

branches of Hebrew Literature on Mondays and Thursdays from 7 to 9 o'clock p.m., and on Saturdays from 1 to 2 o'clock. These Classes are held in both German and English, and are presided over by the Rev. B. Spiers, who is the Librarian.

(3.) The Beth Din sits on Mondays and Thursdays from 11 a.m. to 3 p.m.

ENGLISH EVENING CLASSES COMMITTEE (In connection with the Russo-Jewish Committee).
Object.—To provide instruction in English at Board and Elementary Schools for Russo-Jewish refugees.
Chairman.—N. L. COHEN, Esq.   *Treasurer.*—C. DE PASS, Esq.
Expenditure.—£521. 0s. 5d. (Supplied by the Russo-Jewish Committee.)
Hon. Secretaries.—H. R. LEVINSOHN, Esq., and B. B. HALFORD, Esq.
Address.—c/o C. DE PASS, Esq., 10, Throgmorton-avenue, E.C.

The Committee has arranged for instruction to be given in English at the following Board Schools: Old Castle-street, Chicksand-street, Buck's-row (morning), and Settles-street.

***JEWISH HISTORICAL SOCIETY OF ENGLAND.** (Founded 1893.)
President.—LUCIEN WOLF, Esq.
Vice-Presidents.—Messrs. JOSEPH JACOBS, B.A., C. T. MARTIN, F.S.A., and ISIDORE SPIELMAN, F.S.A.
Treasurer.—E. L. FRANKLIN, Esq.
Hon. Secretaries.—Messrs. ISRAEL ABRAHAMS, M.A., and FRANK HAES.
Administration.—By Council of twenty-nine Members.
Address.—FRANK M. HAES, Esq., 28, Bassett-road, W.

***JEWISH RELIGIOUS EDUCATION BOARD.** (Founded 1895.)
Object.—The Diffusion of Religious Knowledge amongst Jewish Children.
President.—HENRY LUCAS, Esq.
Treasurers.—Messrs. M. A. SPIELMANN and LIONEL JACOB.
Income, 1895.—£1,674.   *Expenditure.*—£1,770.
Hon. Secretary.—Rev. DAVID FAY.
Address.—4, Charlotte-street, Portland-place, W.

***WEST END TALMUD TORAH.** (Founded Nov. 6th, 1892—5652.)
Object.—Hebrew and Religious Instruction.
President.—JOEL DAVIS, Esq.   *Treasurer.*—S. TRENNER, Esq.
Hon. Secretary.—B. A. FERSHT, Esq.
Income, 1895.—£280. 1s. 6d.   *Expenditure.*—£281. 4s. 7½d.
Secretary.—Mr. J. E. FURST.
Address.—10, Green's-court, Little Pulteney-street, W.

WESTERN HEBREW LIBRARY, in connection with the New West-end Synagogue. (Founded by Sir Samuel Montagu, Bart., M.P., in 1874.)
Librarian.—Rev. S. SINGER.
Address.—St. Petersburgh-place, Bayswater, W.

REPRESENTATIVE INSTITUTIONS.

*ANGLO-JEWISH ASSOCIATION. (Founded July, 1871.)
Objects.—(*a*) The Protection of Persecuted Jews; (*b*) the Education of Jewish Children in Eastern Countries.
President.—CLAUDE G. MONTEFIORE, Esq.
Treasurer.—ELLIS A. FRANKLIN, Esq.
Council.—60 Members.
Income, 1894-95.—£2,963. *Expenditure.*—£3,113.
Secretary.—M. DUPARC.
Address.—85, London-wall, E.C.

This Institution, founded in 1871, connected with the Alliance Israélite Universelle, has branches at the following places:—Ballarat, Birmingham, Bombay, Bradford, Brighton, Cambridge, Cardiff, Chatham, Dover and Canterbury, Edinburgh, Glasgow, Leeds, Leicester, Liverpool, Manchester, Middlesbrough, Newport, Nottingham, Otago, Plymouth, Sheffield, Sunderland, Sydney, Toronto, Tredegar, Wellington.

In addition to diplomatic correspondence with foreign Governments, conducted in combination with the London Committee of Deputies of the British Jews, the Association makes grants to Jewish schools at the following places:—Adrianople, Bagdad, Bombay, Bottuschani, Broussa, Chio, Constantinople, Crajova, Damascus, Fez, Haifa, Jassy, Jerusalem, Magnesia, Mogador, Philippopolis, Rustchuk, St. Jean d'Acre, Salonica, Smyrna, Tetuan.

The total number of the scholars attending these schools exceeds five thousand.

*LONDON COMMITTEE OF DEPUTIES OF THE BRITISH JEWS. (Founded 1760.)
Object.—To watch and take action with reference to all matters affecting the welfare of the British Jews as a religious community.
President.—JOSEPH SEBAG MONTEFIORE, Esq., J.P.
Treasurer.—MANUEL CASTELLO, Esq.
Administration.—By the entire Board.
Income.—Average £350. *Expenditure.*—Average £350.
Solicitor and Secretary.—LEWIS EMANUEL, Esq.
Address.—36, Finsbury-circus, E.C.

This body, the oldest representative institution of the British Jews, consists of 47 deputies, elected at the Triennial Meeting, May, 1895, of which 29 were elected by 16 Metropolitan synagogues, and 18 from the following provincial synagogues:—Birmingham, Chatham, Dover, Dublin, Hull (old), Liverpool (Fountain-road), Manchester (Great), Merthyr, Newcastle-on-Tyne, Newport (Mon.), Norwich, Pontypridd, Portsea, Sheffield, Southampton, Southport, Stockton-on-Tees, and Sunderland.

Its main activity consists in watching the domestic legislation which might affect Jews, and co-operating with the Anglo-Jewish Association in any action in which the intervention of the Foreign Office may be desirable.

MISCELLANEOUS INSTITUTIONS.

CHOYEVI ZION ASSOCIATION.
Object.—To encourage the Colonization of Palestine.
Chief of the Association.—Colonel ALBERT EDWARD W. GOLDSMID.
Treasurer.—I. BIRNBAUM, Esq.
Secretary.—Dr. S. A. HIRSCH.
The Association has "tents" at East and West London, Manchester, Dalston, Edinburgh, Glasgow, Sunderland, North and South Shields, Stockton-on-Tees, Leeds, Middlesbrough, Newcastle-on-Tyne, Liverpool, Cardiff, Birmingham, Newport, Hull, Merthyr Tydfil, Plymouth, Cork, and Cambridge. There are also cadet tents at Glasgow and Hull.
It has a publication issued quarterly, entitled *Palestina*, price sixpence.

*THE FOUR PER CENT. INDUSTRIAL DWELLINGS CO., LTD.
(Founded 1885.)
Object.—To provide the Industrial Classes with Commodious and Healthy Dwellings—maximum accommodation at minimum rent, compatible with yielding of a net four per cent. per annum dividend upon the Investment of the paid-up Capital, of the Company.
Chairman of Directors.—The Rt. Hon. Lord ROTHSCHILD.
Income, 1895.—£9,203. 5s. 11d.   *Expenditure.*—£5,692.
Secretary.—Mr. P. ORNSTIEN.
Address.—2, Finsbury-square, E.C.
Dwellings.—Thrawl-street, Spitalfields, Brady-street, Whitechapel, and Stepney Green, E.

THE SHECHITA BOARD. (Founded 1804.)
Object.—To take cognisance of and administer the affairs of the Shechita in the metropolis.
President.—Sir SAMUEL MONTAGU, Bart., M.P.
Vice-President.—MANUEL CASTELLO, Esq.
Secretary.—Mr. SAMUEL I. COHEN.
Address.—Vestry Offices of the Spanish and Portuguese Synagogue, Heneage-lane, Bevis Marks.
Income, 1895.—£9,590.   *Expenditure.*—£8,439.

The following figures give the number of animals slain, etc. :—

	Oxen.		Calves.		Sheep.	
	1894.	1895.	1894.	1895.	1894.	1895.
Slain ...	30,420	31,871	6,407	5,672	41,721	46,756
Kosher	24,920	27,261	5,361	5,013	30,965	33,122

besides some 300,000 fowls slain each year.

ECCLESIASTICAL AUTHORITIES, AND PERSONS AUTHORISED BY THEM.

The Chief Rabbi of the United Congregations of the British Empire, The Very Rev. Dr. HERMANN ADLER, Ph. D., 6, Cravenhill, W. Office of the Chief Rabbi, 22, Finsbury-circus, E.C.

Dayanim.—Revs. B. SPIERS and SUSMAN COHEN.

Beth Din meets at the Beth Hamedrash, St. James's-place, Aldgate, every Monday and Thursday between 11 and 2 o'clock.

The Chief Rabbi of the Spanish and Portuguese Congregations of England, Rev. Haham, Dr. MOSES GASTER, Ph.D., 37, Maidavale, W.

Persons Authorised by the Ecclesiastical Authorities.

BATHS (Mikvaoth).

Mrs. Levy Bensky, 2½, Heneage-lane, Bevis-marks, E.C.
Mrs. Bloomenthal, Burness-street, Commercial-road, E.
Mrs. Comer, Percy-street, Tottenham-court-road.
Mrs. Fonseca, 49, Westbourne-park-crescent.
Mrs. Golding, 28, Steward-street, Brushfield-street, E.C.
Mrs. Goodman, 9, Buckle-street, Commercial-road, E.
Mrs. Gouldinski, 3, Wilkes-street, Spitalfields, E.
Mrs. Rees, 17, Little Alie-street, Goodman's-fields, E.
Mrs. Rosenberg, 14a, Osborne-street, Whitechapel, E.

AUTHORISED MOHELIM IN LONDON.

M. Abrahams, Esq., 51, Pyrland-road, Highbury.
Lawrence Barnett, Esq., M.D., Lond., M.R.C.S., &c., 40, Broadhurst-gardens, N.W.
M. Clifford, Esq., L.R.C.P., M.R.C.S., 58, Clifton-gardens, Maida-vale, W.
A. Cohen, Esq., M.A., M.D., 67, Warrington-crescent, Maida-vale, W.
Rev. H. Danziger, Plumber's-row, Whitechapel.
Rev. M. A. Epstein, New Synagogue Chambers, Great St. Helen's, Bishopsgate, E.C.
S. Friedlander, Esq., 31, Duke-street, Aldgate.
Leonard M. Gabriel, Esq., M.D. (Lond.), M.R.C.S., Eng., 13, Porchester-terrace, W.
A. Gaster, Esq., M.D., M.R.C.P., Lond., 224, Belsize-road, N.W.
Rev. N. Goldston, 12, Ivydale-road, Nunhead, S.E.
Rev. I. Greenberg, Synagogue-chambers, Stepney-green.
Asher Gross, Esq., L.R.C.P., M.R.C.S., Eng., 7, South-side, Clapham-common.
H. L. Harris, Esq., 22, Great Prescot-street, Goodman's-fields, E.
Rev. S. Manné, 37, Kingdon-road, West Hampstead, N.W.
G. Michael, Esq., M.B., 188, Commercial-road, E.
Rev. P. Phillips, 100, New Oxford-street, W.C.
Rev. S. Rappaport, 67, Beresford-road, N.
Isaac Sandheim, Esq., 30, King-street, Hammersmith.
Rev. L. Simmons, 12, Cecil-street, Mile-end.

List of Names of **BUTCHERS AND POULTERERS** Licensed to sell Kosher Meat and Poultry for the Year 1896.

Those marked thus * are Licensed to sell Hind-Quarter Meat Porged.

M. VAN THAL, *Investigating Officer*, 9, Great Alie Street, E.

*Adelberg, M. Van, 49, Shirland-road.
Abrahams, A., 59, Middlesex-street.
Abrahams, B., 5, Lincoln-street, Bow-rd.
Abrahamson, K., 29, Church-lane, Whitechapel.
Angel, A., 215, Jubilee-street, Mile-end.
Ash, L., 2 ¹, Fairclough-st., Commercial-rd.
Amdur, N., 174, Commercial-road.
Abrahams, M., 75, Broadway, Londonfields.
*Barnett, E., & Co., 79 & 81, Middlesex-street, and 249, Euston-road.
Bannett, J., 236, Graham-road, Hackney.
Berner, 8, Union-street, Whitechapel.
Benjamin, I., 1, Freeman-st., Spitalfields.
Bloom, N., 4, Bell-lane, Spitalfields.
*Berlyn, J.,20, Commercial-street, Whitechapel.
Best, E., 68, Great Garden-street.
Blackstone, L. Mrs., 45, Broad-st., Soho.
Bermel, J., 16 Wentworth-street.
Bermel, L., 5, Davis Mansions, Goulston-st.
Cohen, Proops, Mrs., 14, Wentworth-st.
Cohen, I., 21, Old Montague-street.
Crook, M., 104, Hanbury-street, and 18, Wilks-street.
Cohen, M., 11, Bell-lane.
Cohen, I., 3, Montague-street, Bell-lane, and Goulston-street.
Cohen, S., Mrs., 16, Finch-st., Brick-lane.
Crisman, A., 26, East Mount-st., Whitechapel.
Cohen, S., 12, White's-row, Spitalfields.
Davis, J., 9, Green's Court, Soho.
Dvorsky, J., 196, Commercial-road.
Emmanuel, E., 123, White Horse-lane, Mile-end.
Erlinski, T., 10, Meard's-street, Berwickstreet, Soho.
Elsner, S, 83, Wellesley-st., Stepney-gr.
*Franks, L., 300, Harrow-road.
Faust, S., 10, Coke-street, Greenfield-st.
Fiescher, H., 29, Marshall-street, Soho.
Fraenkel, S., 104, Old Montague-street.
Fraenkel, W., 18, Chicksand-street, and 124, Green-Street, Bethnal-green.
Gabel, D., 57, Newark-street.
Galowitz, L., 71, Mare-street, Hackney.
Goldstein, H , 4, Wentworth-street.
Goldstein, J., 110, White-horse-lane.
Goodman, H., 15, Bell-lane.
Goldring, S., 2a, Wentworth-street.
Goodman, 19, New-street, Gravel-lane.
Gutman, J., 1, Ann's-place, Wentworthstreet.
Gedult, N., 142, Wentworth-street.
Grabovsky, 18, James-st, Cannon-st.-road.
Goodman, M., 2, Holloway-st., Commercial-road.
Goldberg, M., 5, Fleet-st.-hill, Brick-lane.
Green, J., 4, Chicksand-street.
Harris, L., 27, Grey Eagle-street.
Hart, L., 24, Hutchinson-st., Middlesex-st.
Hyams, S., 66, Middlesex-street.

Hamburger, S., 93, Green Lanes, Canonbury.
Israel, 16, Bedford-st., Commercial-road.
Isaacs, M., 74, Umberston-st., Commercial-road.
Joseph, S., 122, Sidney-street, Mile-end.
Joseph, H., 71, Hanbury-st., Spitalfields.
Jacobs, A., 43, Broad-street, Soho.
Jacobs, C. 132, Wentworth-street.
Jacobs, W., 161, Cambridge-road, Bethnalgreen.
Jacobs, P., Miss, 8, Bell-lane. [bury.
*Jacobs, J., 67, Newington-gr.-rd., Canon-
Jacobs, A., 13, Wentworth-street, and Bedford-street, Whitechapel.
Jacobs, A., 13, Palmer-street, Spitalfields.
Joel, M., 90, Mile-end-road.
Kulman, J., 41, Batty-st., Commercial-rd.
Kulman, J., 47, Great Garden-street.
Kunzler, A., 90, Oxford-st., Whitechapel.
Krotoski, P., 4, Montague-st., Bell-lane.
Krotoski, A., 67, Middlesex-street. [road.
Krotoski, J., 1, Stutfield-st., Commercial-
Krotoski, B., 14, Bell-lane.
Krotoski, M., 73, Nelson-street, New-rd.
Klichewski, 65, Brick-lane.
Koski, H. De, 5, Brook Green-road, Hammersmith.
Koninski, P.,15,Raven-row, Whitechapel-road.
Koninski, H., 28, Spital-street, Mile-end-new-town.
Konchinski, M., 17, Yalford-street.
Klapper, M., 16, Bell-lane.
Klein, M., 131, Back Church-lane.
Levy, D., Little or New Goulston-street.
Lipkind, J., Dalston-lane.
Lewis, Mrs., 9, Wentworth-street.
Liebowich, S, 50, Back Church-lane.
Levie, A., 9, Globe-road, Mile-end.
Lewis, Mrs., 75, Back Church-lane.
Levy, J., 27, Buxton-street, Mile-end-new-town.
Levy, M., Stepney-green.
Levy, J., 19, Charlotte-st., Whitechapel.
Levy, Z., 35a, Old Montague-street.
Levin, H., 16, Brick-lane, and 200, Walworth-road.
Lansberg, Mrs., 32, Charlotte-street.
Landsberg, L., 25, Leman-street.
Lazarus, S., 6, West-street, Soho.
Lissack, Mrs., 8, Bell-lane.
Lewis, H., 17, Wentworth-street.
Linda, D., 27, Wentworth-street.
Levy, Mrs., 14, Langdale-street, Commercial-road.
Lieberman, J., 9, Gun-st., Old Artillery-ground.
Lubinski, 11, Greenfield-street.
Levy, M., 149, Hanbury-street.
Messer, J., 2, Fieldgate-street.
Michael, L., 116, Wentworth-street.
Marcovitch, A., 74, Brady-street.
Morgenstern, L., 29, Hare-st., Brick-lane.

METROPOLITAN INSTITUTIONS.

Morris, A., 16, Fashion-street.
Mielzynski, 48, Cable-street.
*Nathan, J., 6, Artillery-passage, 105, High-rd., Kilburn, and 187, Mile-end-rd.
Neuman, M., 89, Berwick-street, Soho.
Oslofsky, S., 37, Wentworth-street.
Osmalofsky, E., Ruth House, Flower and Dean-street.
Pincus, M., 44, Baker's-row, Whitechapel.
Plaskofsky, F., 25, Tilley-st., Spitalfields.
Plaskofsky, L., 156, Brick-lane.
Phillips, G., 41, Whitechapel-road.
Petrikosky, K., 37, Pelham-street.
Rosenberg, 51, Shirland-rd., Paddington.
Raphael, D., 73, New-road, Whitechapel.
Raphael, Mrs., 34, Christian-street, Commercial-road.
Rosenthal, 110, Mare-street, Hackney.
Rosenberg, D., Mansell-street.
Rosenberg, J., 48, Umberston street, Commercial-Road
Reicher, J., 28, Baker's-row, Whitechapel
Reshowitz, L., 141, St. George's-street, E.
Schreiber, 15, Bell-lane
Solomons, Mrs., 48, Morgan-street
Seelig, Mrs., 5, Ridley-road, Dalston
*Swaebe, S., Mrs., 5, Stoney-lane, Houndsditch
Seelig, S., 8, Tenter-buildings, St. Mark-st.
Shear, W., 16, Hunt-street
Shershouski, S., 261, Commercial-road
Shershouski, I., 247, Commercial-road
Shershouski, J., 11, Fieldgate-street, Whitechapel, and 230a, Commercial-rd.
Silverstone, M., 136, Wentworth-street.
Schnitzer, A., 155, Cannon-street-road.
Strauss, H., 137, Commercial-road.
Silverberg, D., 8, Sandringham-rd., Dalston.
Smith & Son, 4, Crispin-st., Spitalfields.
Silverstone, S., 20, Bell-lane.
Stein, Mrs., 136, Wentworth-street.
Specterman, S., 72, Middlesex-street.
Specterman, M., 1, Wentworth-street.
Specterman, L., Davis-mans., Goulston-st.
Scoff, L., 37, Booth-street-buildings.
Shear, H., 5, Conduit-passage, Red Lion-st.
Shochet, S., Fashion-street.
Solomons, D., 26, Tenter-st., Spitalfields.
Solomons, J., 3, Wentworth-court, Wentworth-street.
Silberstein, 17, Andover-place, Paddington
Schneider, S., 15, Hutchinson-avenue.
Saunders, 29, Greenfield-street.
Tapor, R., 29, Booth-street, Spitalfields.
Tabaschnik, H., 13, King Edward-street, Mile-end-new-town.
Tobias, D., 9, Raven-street, Whitechapel.
Vigon, H., 128, Wentworth-street.
Vigon, M., 2, Edward-street, Soho.
Vigon, M., 6, Greenfield-street.
*White, L., 125, Harrow-road, and 196, Portobello-rd, Notting-hill, and shortly High-road, Kilburn.
White, J., 24, Wentworth-street.
Wolf De, Mrs., 55, Commercial-road, and 182, Cable-street.
Wolfsbergen, L., 124, Petherton-road.
Wolski, R., 357, Commercial-road.
Zargusky, 1, Bath-street, Brady-street, Whitechapel.
Zieskind, 24a, White's-row, Spitalfields.
Zissick, S., 142, Brick-lane.

MALE WATCHERS.

E. Best, 1, Fashion-street, Spitalfields.
J. Bierman, 98, Wentworth-buildings, E.
W. Franks, 107, Cleveland-street, W.
S. Harris, 8, Shirland-road, W.
S. Lewis, 9, Spital-square, E.
J. Michaels, 20, Hutchison-avenue, Houndsditch.
— Smith, 18, Grange-road, Bermondsey.
B. Vandersluis, 9, Westbourne-terrace North, W.

FEMALE WATCHERS.

Mrs. Denekamp, 160, Great Tichfield-street, W.
Mrs. Foluis, 7, Corea-place, Wentworth-street, E.
Mrs. Freedman, 16, Bell-lane, E.
Mrs. Hyams, 41, St. Peters-road, Mile-end.
Mrs. Jacobson, 93, Green-lanes, N.
Mrs. Lehman, 740, Harrow-road, W.
Mrs. Smith, 18, Grange-road, Bermondsey.
Mrs. Vandersluis, 9, Westbourne-terrace North, W.

JEWISH CEMETERIES.

Spanish and Portuguese, Beth Holim (disused).
 ,, ,, Mile-end-road, E.
United Synagogue, Willesden and West Ham. [monton.
Western Synagogue, Brompton (disused), and Green-lane, Ed-
Federation of Synagogues, Green-lane, Edmonton.
Maiden Lane Synagogue, Bancroft-road, Mile-end.

PROVINCIAL CONGREGATIONS.

ABERDARE.
President of Synagogue.—M. JACOBS, Esq., 14, Cardiff-street.
Shochet.—Mr. HIRSCH TAFFER.

ABERDEEN.
(Fifteen Jewish families.)
SYNAGOGUE, 34, Marischal-street. (Founded 1893.)
President.—A. ZAMCK, Esq. *Treasurer.*—J. BARNETT, Esq.
Minister.—Rev. JAMES LITTMAN. *Secretary.*—T. GEERSHON, Esq
There are twelve seatholders.

ALDERSHOT.
(Jewish population, 54; not including soldiers.)
SYNAGOGUE, 49, High-street. (Founded 1860.)
President.—MOSES PHILLIPS, Esq.
Treasurer.—J. LAZANECK, Esq.
Shochet.—Mr. LASSMANN. *Secretary.*—S. LAZANECK, Esq.
The seatholders number six, and the expenditure for 1895-6 was £78.

BANGOR.
(Jewish population, 30.)
SYNAGOGUE, Arvonia-buildings, High-street. (Founded 1894.)
President.—L. H. ARONSON, Esq. *Treasurer.*—M. WARTSKI, Esq.
Minister.—Rev. I. ROSENZWEIG.
Secretary.—I. WARTSKI, Esq.
There are 12 seatholders, and the weekly income is 20s.

BATH.
(1895. One Burial.)
SYNAGOGUE, Corn-street. (Founded 5502.)
Shochet.—Mr. ISIDORE BURMAN. *Secretary.*—Mr. M. FRANKS.
KOSHER RESTAURANT, 2, Sunnybank, Lyncombe-vale.

BELFAST.
(Jewish population, 400-500.)
SYNAGOGUE, Great Victoria-street. (Founded 1870.)
President.—OTTO JAFFE, Esq. *Treasurer.*—M. LEVENE, Esq.
Minister.—Rev. Dr. CHOTZNER. *Secretary.*—Mr. H. FOX.
There are 70 seatholders.
BOARD OF GUARDIANS. (Founded 1893.)
Object.—To assist resident Jewish poor and strangers.
President.—M. VEITEL, Esq. *Treasurer.*—H. BOAS, Esq.
Secretary.—Rev. Dr. CHOTZNER, 12, Eglinton-street.
Income and Expenditure.—About £50.
HEBREW AND RELIGION CLASSES. (Founded 1893.)
Head Master.—Rev. Dr. CHOTZNER, 27, Fleetwood-street.

BIRMINGHAM.

(Jewish Population 3,000 to 4,000.   1895, 22 marriages, 49 burials.)

SYNAGOGUE, Singer's-hill.   (Founded 1855. Congregation more than a century old.)
President.—B. H. JOSEPH, Esq.   Treasurer.—HENRY DAVIS, Esq
Minister.—Rev. G. J. EMANUEL.   Secretary.—M. BERLYN, Esq.
Income, 1895-96.—£3,565. 4s. 4d.   Expenditure.—£3,526. 5s. 10d.
The number of seatholders is 560.

LADIES' VISITING SOCIETY, Singer's-hill.
Objects.—Relief of Sick Women and Children. Care of Women during confinement. Visiting the Homes of the Poor generally.
President.—Mrs. A. BLANCKINSEE.   Treasurer.—Mrs. S. GORDON.
Hon. Secretary.—Miss J. M. LEVI.
Income, 1895-96.—£141. 2s. 2d.   Expenditure.—£119. 2s. 7d.
Managed by Committee of 24 ladies.

BIRMINGHAM JEWISH CHARITIES' AID SOCIETY, Singer's-hill.   (Founded 1892.)
Object.—To make annual grants to the Birmingham Jewish Charities.
President.—Mrs. C. KINO.   Vice-President.—Mrs. SILLDEIR.
Treasurer.—Mrs. MONTAGUE DAVIS.
Hon. Secretaries.—Miss MAY LOWENSTEIN and Miss HETTY COHEN.
Income, 1895-96.—£65. 14s. 4½d.   Expenditure.—£60.

BIRMINGHAM AID SOCIETY OF THE JEWS' HOSPITAL AND ORPHAN ASYLUM.   (Founded 1888.)
Object.—To assist Parent Institution by purchasing Life Governorships.
President.—M. L. DIGHT, Esq.   Treasurer.—Rev. G. J. EMANUEL.
Hon. Secretary.—ALEXANDER JOSEPH, Esq.
Income, 1895-96.—£54.   Expenditure.—£50.

JEWISH WORKING MEN'S INSTITUTE.
Object.—To provide an English Education for foreign co-religionists and Mutual Improvement.
President.—HENRY DAVIS, Esq.
Treasurer and Hon. Secretary.—LIONEL BARNETT, Esq.
Income, 1895-96.—£60. 1s. 2d.   Expenditure.—£55. 16s. 8d.

RECREATION CLASSES FOR GIRLS.   (Founded 1887.)
Object.—To instil into the minds of Jewish working girls a profitable method of spending their leisure time. To improve their tastes generally.
President.—Mrs. JOHN PHILLIPS.
Treasurer.—Miss LIZZIE SPIERS.
Hon. Secretary.—Mrs. M. BERLYN.

*HEBREW PHILANTHROPIC SOCIETY, Singer's-hill.   (Founded 1838.)
Objects.—(a) The relief of Indigent Tradesmen; (b) Granting Pensions to aged persons; (c) Undertaking all cases of deser-

ving people not eligible for consideration by the Board of Guardians.
President.—DAVID DAVIS, Esq. *Treasurer.*—HARRY P. PHILLIPS, Esq.
Secretary.—M. BERLYN, Esq.
Income, 1894-5.—£466. 6s. 4d. *Expenditure.*—£402. 9s. 7d.

*HEBREW EDUCATIONAL SOCIETY, Singer's-hill. (Founded 1851.)
Objects.—To pay all necessary expenses for support of the Hebrew Schools, and to apprentice Jewish children leaving school.
President and Treasurer.—A. M. BLANCKINSEE, and B. GOODMAN.
Secretary.—M. BERLYN, Esq.
Income, 1895-96.—£294. 16s. 11d.

*HEBREW BOARD OF GUARDIANS, Singer's-hill. (Founded 1870.)
Object.—Relief of the Jewish poor, resident and casual.
President.—S. J. DAVIS, Esq.
Treasurer.—JACOB JACOBS, Esq.
Hon. Secretary.—I. L. JACOBS, Esq.
Secretary.—Mr. J. D. REINOWITZ.
Income, 1894-95.—£909. 8s. *Expenditure.*—£898. 4s. 9d.

SABBATH MEALS SOCIETY, Singer's-hill.
Object.—To provide Meals on Sabbaths and Festivals to poor Jews passing through the town.
President.— *Treasurer.*—S. HILLNER, Esq.
Secretary.—Mr. J. D. REINOWITZ.
Income, 1894-95.—£29. *Expenditure.*—£23. 4s. 4d.

BIRMINGHAM HEBREW SCHOOL, Singer's-hill. (Founded 5601-1840.)
Head Master.—M. BERLYN, Esq.
There are 434 scholars, 168 boys, 124 girls, and 142 infants.

BLACKBURN.
(Jewish population, 120.)

SYNAGOGUE, Paradise-lane. (Founded 1893.)
Life President.—W. ARONSBERG, Esq., J.P.
Vice-President.—ISRAEL AARON, Esq.
Treasurer.—DAVID BLAIN, Esq. *Minister.*—HARRIS COHEN, Esq.
Secretary.—AARON PINKERS, Esq.
Assistant Secretary.—AARON MORRIS, Esq.
The number of seatholders is now 27, an advance of 11 on that of the first year.

BRIGHTON AND HOVE.
(Sixty Jewish Families, which does not include habitual visitors. 1895, 4 marriages, 12 deaths.)

SYNAGOGUE, Middle-street. (Founded 1874).
President.—LEWIS LEWIS, Esq. *Treasurer.*—WOOLF DAVIS, Esq.
Minister and Secretary.—Rev. A. C. JACOBS.
The seatholders number 64. Income about £1,400.

JEWISH BOARD OF GUARDIANS.
Object.—The relief of resident and casual poor.
President.—JACOB H. COHEN, Esq.
Treasurer.—SAMUEL COOK, Esq.
Relieving Officer.—W. DAVIS, Esq.
Hon. Secretary.—HYAM LEWIS, Esq.
Income, 1895.—£96. 11s. 9d.
270 persons were relieved, mostly men.

SYNAGOGUE CLASSES FOR RELIGIOUS INSTRUCTION.
The Classes are held three times a week, and the scholars number 20—12 boys and 8 girls.

BRADFORD.
(Population of 30 Jewish Families. 1895-96, 3 marriages, 1 burial.)
SYNAGOGUE, Houghton-place. (Founded 1886.)
President.—B. BERNSTEIN, Esq. *Treasurer.*—H. ROBINSON, Esq.
Shochet.—Mr. H. ANGEL. *Secretary.*—Mr. E. N. GERSHON.
Seatholders about 22.

BRISTOL.
(1895-6, 2 marriages, 7 burials.)
SYNAGOGUE, Park-row.
President.—J. M. JACOBS, Esq. *Treasurer.*—A. LAZARUS, Esq.
Secretary.—Mr. F. GOLDMAN.

BOARD OF GUARDIANS, Synagogue-chambers. (Founded 1894.)
Object.—The relief of the poor.
President.—Rev. J. POLACK, B.A. *Treasurer.*—J. M. JACOBS, Esq.
Secretary.—S. H. JACOBS, Esq.
Income and Expenditure between £40 and £50.

HEBREW SCHOOL, Synagogue-chambers. (Founded 1890.)
The *Head Master* is Rev. A. LEVINSON, and the number of scholars is 70.

BRYANMAWR.
(Twelve Jewish Families.)
There is a synagogue established here, the minister being Rev. — WALLMARS.

BURNLEY.
(Jewish Population, 30.)
SYNAGOGUE, 20, Sandy-gate. (Founded 1895.)
President.—S. SCHABATT, Esq. *Secretary.*—M. ZACHARIAS, Esq.
This Synagogue is the private property of the President, and is supported by voluntary contributions.
Ten children attend the Voluntary Sunday School for religious instruction, 6 boys and 4 girls.

CAMBRIDGE.
(Population of 47 Jews.)
SYNAGOGUE, Great St. Mary's-passage. (Founded 1888.)
President.—H. L. PASS, Esq. *Treasurer.*—O. E. D'AVIGDOR, Esq.
Secretary.—E. M. COHEN, Esq.
There are 27 seatholders, and the annual income averages £40.

CANTERBURY.

(1895-6, 12 Jewish Residents, 1 burial.)

SYNAGOGUE, King-street. (Said to be founded in 1680.)

President.—Alderman HENRY HART, J.P.
Secretary.—Mr. SAMUEL NATHAN.

There are 4 seatholders, and the annual income is about £30. Although there are no charitable institutions, from 50 to 100 poor casuals pass through the city during the year and are relieved.

CARDIFF.

(1895-96, 7 marriages, 15 burials.)

SYNAGOGUE, East-terrace. (Founded about 1853.)

President.—H. GOLDMAN, Esq.
Treasurer and Secretary.—A. COHEN, Esq.
Minister.—Rev. J. ABELSON.

JEWISH LADIES' BENEVOLENT SOCIETY. (Founded 1894.)

Object.—Relief of resident poor.
President.—Mrs. S. BARNETT.   *Treasurer.*—Mrs. I. SAMUEL.
Hon. Secretary.—Mrs. P. PHILLIPS.
Income 1895-96.—£130. 0s. 6½d.   *Expenditure.*—£101. 13s.

CHATHAM.

(Jewish Population, 70.   1895, 1 death.)

SYNAGOGUE, High-street, Rochester. (Founded 1870.)

President and Treasurer.—ISIDORE BERLINER, Esq.
Minister and Secretary.—Rev. BERNARD J. SALOMONS.

The number of seatholders is 15. The income and expenditure averaged £100 per annum.

PHILANTHROPIC SOCIETY.

Object.—Relief of local Poor, of whom ten were relieved during the last year.

The income and expenditure were £20, and the *Treasurer and Secretary* is ISIDORE BERLINER, Esq.

BRANCH OF ANGLO-JEWISH ASSOCIATION. (Founded 1887.)

President and Treasurer.—ISIDORE BERLINER, Esq.
Secretary.—Rev. BERNARD J. SALOMONS.

Six Jewish children are taught by the Rev. B. J. SALOMONS 4 boys and 2 girls.

CHELTENHAM.

(Seventeen Jewish Residents.   1895-6, 1 marriage.)

SYNAGOGUE, St. James-square. (Founded 1866.)

President and Treasurer.—E. L. FELDMAN, Esq.
Minister.—W. STOLOFF, Esq.

There are 3 seatholders, and the annual income is £48.

CORK.

(Jewish population, about 300 souls. 1895, 1 death.)
SYNAGOGUE, 24, South Terrace. (Founded 1883.)
President.—MARKS L. COHEN, Esq.
Minister.—Rev. J. E. MYERS.   *Treasurer.*—DAVID SCHAR, Esq.

COVENTRY.

(Jewish Population about 38.)
SYNAGOGUE, Barras-lane.
(Present one founded 1870, but one existed over a century ago.)
President.—F. SILVERSTON, Esq.   *Treasurer.*—M. KALKER, Esq.
Minister.—Rev. M. SHATZ.   *Secretary.*—A. E. FRIDLANDER, Esq.
There are ten seatholders, and the annual income is about £70.

DERBY AND BURTON-ON-TRENT.

(Jewish Population, 24).

There is no regular congregation at either of the above towns, but on New Year and Day of Atonement, a service is held in the Masonic Hall, Burton-on-Trent, the Jewish residents of both Derby and Ashby-de-la-Zouch joining in. Mr. S. BROWN, Shochet, officiates, and Mr. ISAAC BROWN is Secretary.

DOVER.

(Jewish Population, 104. 1895, 3 burials.)
SYNAGOGUE, Northampton-street. (Founded 1862.)
President.—ALDERMAN H. HART.
Treasurer.—SAMUEL HART, Esq.
Minister and Secretary.—Rev. ISIDORE BARNSTEIN.
The number of seatholders is 12, the income for 1895, £79, and the expenditure £102.

DOVER HEBREW AND RELIGION SCHOOL. (Founded 1873.)
There are 22 children attending this school, 12 boys and 10 girls.
Head Master.—Rev. I. BARNSTEIN.
Address.—Northampton Street.

DUBLIN.

(Jewish Population, 2,000.)
SYNAGOGUE, Adelaide-road. (Founded 1800.)
President.—M. DE GROOT, Esq., J.P.
Treasurer.—ADOLPH DAVIES, Esq.
Ministers.—Revs. L. MENDELSOHN, B.A., and I. LEVENTON.
Secretary.—JOHN ROSENTHAL, Esq., LL.D.
Income and Expenditure.—£510.   *Seatholders.*—120.

SYNAGOGUE, 8, Kevin's-parade. (Founded 1880.)
President.—R. BRADLAW, Esq.   *Treasurer.*—M. COHEN, Esq.
Secretary.—L. ROBINSON, Esq.   *Chazan.*—Mr. M. NEWMAN.
Income and Expenditure.—£125.   *Seatholders.*—80.

SYNAGOGUE, 52, Camden-street. (Founded 1892.)
President.—M. VANEE, Esq. *Treasurer*, E. ELIASAF, Esq.
Secretary.—Mr. M. SOLOMONS. *Chazan.*—Mr. L. JAFE.
Income and Expenditure.—£150. *Seatholders.*—90.

SYNAGOGUE, 32, Lennox-street. (Founded 1887.)
President.—E. WACHMAN, Esq. *Treasurer.*—T. LEVIN, Esq.
Secretary.—Mr. L. MARCUS. *Minister.*—Mr. JOSSELSON, Esq.
Income and Expenditure.—£175. *Seatholders.*—175.

SYNAGOGUE, 1, Oakfield-place.
President.—S. MILLER, Esq. *Treasurer.*—M. CORMICK, Esq.
Secretary.—Mr. S. ROBINSON.
Income and Expenditure.—£75. *Seatholders.*—45.

HEBREW SCHOOL, Adelaide-road. (Founded 1893).
The *Head Master* is Mr. M. HARTNET, and there are 130 scholars, 32 boys, 50 girls, and 48 infants.

JEWISH BOARD OF GUARDIANS. (Founded 1882.)
Object.—The relief of the poor, by loans or otherwise.
President.—M. NOYK, Esq. *Treasurer.*—E. ELIASAF, Esq.
Secretary.—Mr. S. BENSON.
Income and Expenditure.—£150. 200 persons relieved annually.

LADIES' BENEVOLENT SOCIETY. (Founded 1888.)
Object.—The relief of poor lying-in women.
President.—Mrs. LEVENTON. *Treasurer.*—Mrs. PUSHINSKY.
Secretary.—Mrs. LEVETT. *Income and Expenditure.*—£60,
Thirty cases relieved.

HAKHNOSAS ORKHIM. (Founded 1888.)
Object.—The relief of strangers, giving them shelter for three days.
President.—M. MITAFSKY, Esq.
Income and Expenditure.—£50 annually.

MEDICAL RELIEF SOCIETY. (Founded 1888.)
Object.—Relief of poor during Shiva, and medical attendance during sickness.
Treasurer.—Mr. GREENBERG. *Income and Expenditure.*—£110.

CHEVRA KADISHA.
Object.—Relief of poor in case of death, and cheap burials.
President.—R. BRADLAW, Esq. *Income*—about £80.

YOUNG MEN'S READING ROOMS. (Founded 1895.)
Object.—To foster taste for English and Hebrew literature amongst foreign residents.
President.—Rev. L. MENDELSOHN. *Treasurer.*—J. LEVENTON, Esq.
Income.—£50 a year. *No. of Members.*—80.

DUDLEY.

There is at present no synagogue established, but 9 families of Jews live here, and services are held.
Secretary.—Mr. LOUIS BERGENSKY, 12, Himley Road.

DUNDEE.
(Jewish Population, 50.)

SYNAGOGUE, 132, Murraygate. (Founded 1874.)
President.—DAVID CREE, Esq. *Treasurer.*—ISAAC ROSEN, Esq.
Minister.—Rev. SIMON WULF ROSENZWEIG.
Secretary.—NATHAN CREE, Esq.
The seatholders number 25, and the annual income averages £100.

HEBREW BURIAL GROUND, 10, Parker-street. (Founded 1889.)
Object.—Defraying funeral expenses of those unable to pay.
President.—HARRIS ESTERMAN, Esq.
Treasurer and Secretary.—EDWARD SAMUELS, Esq.
The average income is £12 yearly, and three persons were relieved during 1895.

HEBREW SCHOOL, 132, Murraygate. (Founded 1893.)
Head Master.—Rev. S. W. ROSENZWEIG.
There are 30 scholars—20 boys, 8 girls, and 2 infants.

HEBREW BENEVOLENT LOAN SOCIETY, 10, North Tay-street. (Founded 1895).
Object.—Lending sums of money without interest, which the borrower can pay back in weekly instalments; also relieving strangers in need.
Trustees.—Messrs. MAX ESTERMAN and EDWARD SAMUELS.
Treasurer.—DAVID CREE, Esq. *Secretary.*—NATHAN CREE, Esq.
Annual income about £10, and during 1895 14 persons were relieved.

EDINBURGH.
(Jewish Population, 250 families.)

SYNAGOGUE, Park-place. (Founded 1816—5576.)
President.—MAURICE ISAACS, Esq.
Treasurer.—PHILIP DRESNER, Esq.
Minister.—Rev. JACOB FURST.
Secretary.—ERNEST GOLDSTON, Esq.

BENEVOLENT LOAN SOCIETY, 5, Causeway-side. (Founded 1891.)
Object.—Loans to Industrious Poor.
Presidents.—Major J. P. SALAMANS and P. EPRILER, Esq.
Treasurer.—DAVID KISHINISKY, Esq. *Secretary.*—Rev. J. FURST.
Income for 1895.—£394. 2s. 4d. *Expenditure.*—£328. 10s.
Seventy-five persons obtained relief last year.

LADIES "LAID IN" SOCIETY. (Founded 1875.)
Objects.—To assist poor lying-in women.
President.—Mrs. M. ISAACS. *Treasurer.*—Mrs. J. MYERS.

BOARD OF GUARDIANS.
President.—H. MICHAEL, Esq. *Treasurer.*—C. ALEXANDER, Esq.
Secretary.—B. FREEMAN, Esq.

HEBREW AND RELIGION SCHOOL, Park-place.
Headmaster.—Rev. J. FURST.
The School meets every afternoon from five till seven o'clock.

BRANCH SYNAGOGUE, Dalry-road. (Founded 1880.)
President.—P. PHIN, Esq. *Treasurer.*—A. LEVENSON, Esq.
Shochet.—I. L. LEVINE. *Secretary.*—J. PHILLIPS, Esq.

SYNAGOGUE, Richmond-street. (Founded 1890).
President.—B. FURIANSKY, Esq. *Treasurer.*—S. MYERS, Esq.
Shochet.—J. LEVINE.

They have also an afternoon Religion Class.

EXETER.

SYNAGOGUE, St. Mary Arches, S.W. (Founded 130 years ago.)
President.—C. SAMUELS, Esq. *Treasurer.*—S. FREDMAN, Esq.
Minister.—Rev. I. LITOVITCH.

The seatholders number 8, and there is an average weekly income of 16s.

GATESHEAD-ON-TYNE.

SYNAGOGUE, 14, Redheugh Bridge-road.
President.—I. ZUCKER, Esq.

GLASGOW.

(Jewish Population, said to be 6,000. 1894, 42 marriages, 45 burials.)

SYNAGOGUE, Hill-street, Garnethill. (First Synagogue 5619–1858; present one, 5639—1878.)
President.—JULIAN FRANKENBURG, Esq.
Treasurer.—ADOLF SCHOMFELD, Esq.
Minister.—Rev. E. P. PHILLIPS.
Secretary,—Ex-Baillie MICHAEL SIMMONS, J.P.
No. of Seatholders.—160.
Income, 1895.—£1,300. *Expenditure.*—£1,250.

BRANCH SYNAGOGUE, Main-street, Garbals. (Founded 5645—1864.) 150 Seatholders.

JEWISH BOARD OF GUARDIANS, 173, St. Vincent-street.
Object.—To relieve and assist the poor.
President.—ISIDOR MORRIS, Esq.
Vice-President.—Ex-Baillie SIMMONS, J.P.
Treasurer.—CHARLES JACOBS, Esq.
Secretary.—PHILIP B. SIMONS, Esq.
Income.—£449. 10s. 6d. *Expenditure.*—£429. 5s. 2d.

293 Cases were relieved during the past year, involving about 1,172 persons.

The mode of election is by ballot at Annual Meeting of subscribers.

HEBREW BENEVOLENT LOAN SOCIETY, 95, George-street.
President.—Ex-Baillie M. SIMMONS, J.P.
Vice-President.—Rev. E. P. PHILLIPS.
Treasurer.—JACOB SAMUELS, Esq.
Hon. Secretary.—BENJAMIN STRUMP, Esq.
Income.—1895-6.—£515. 19s. 8d. *Expenditure.*—£510. 19s. 10d.

There are also a Ladies' Benevolent Society, Chovevi Zion Association, and an Anglo-Jewish Association,

HEBREW SCHOOL, 29, Thistle-street, Garnethill.
Head Master.—Rev. E. P. PHILLIPS.
220 children attend this School—90 boys and 130 girls.

GLASGOW HEBREW BENEVOLENT LOAN SOCIETY. (Founded 1888.)
Object.—To grant loans without interest to the deserving poor.
President.—MICHAEL SIMONS, Esq.
Treasurer.—JACOB SAMUELS, Esq.
Hon. Secretary.—BENJAMIN STRUMP, Esq.
Income, 1895.—£461. 15s. 11d. *Expenditure.*—£427. 2s. 1d.
106 loans granted. *Address.*—13, Portugal Street.

LITERARY AND SOCIAL SOCIETY. (Founded 1893.)
Hon. Secretary.—CHARLES B. MABON, Esq.
Address.—171, West Graham-street.

HEBREW LADIES' BENEVOLENT SOCIETY. (Founded 1879.)
Object.—To relieve the sick and unemployed with food and coals.
President.—Mrs. FRANKENBURG. *Treasurer.*—Mrs. BLOOM.
Secretary.—Mrs. E. P. PHILLIPS.
Address.—Synagogue Chambers, Garnethill.
Income, 1895.—About £120. *Expenditure.*—£110.
Over 250 families relieved yearly.

CLOTHING GUILD, Synagogue-chambers, Garnethill. (Founded 1893.)
Object.—To give blankets and clothing to the poor.
President and Treasurer.—Miss FRANKENBURG.
Secretary.—Miss SIMONS.

GREAT GRIMSBY.
(Jewish Population, 149. 1895, 5 marriages.)

SYNAGOGUE, Heneage Street, Grimsby. (Founded 1865.)
The present structure was consecrated in 1885, the Chief Rabbi officiating, Mr. F. D. MOCATTA having laid the Foundation stone.
President.—BENJAMIN COHEN, Esq.
Hon. Secretary.—ABRAHAM COHEN, Esq.
Minister.—Rev. B. H. ROSENGARD.
Reader and Shochet.—E. I. GOLDSMID, Esq.
Income and Expenditure average about £250 per annum, and the number of seatholders is 60.

RELIGION AND HEBREW SCHOOLS. (Founded 1865.)
Held at the St. Andrew's Denominational School, Albert-street, Grimsby.
Head Master.—Rev. B. H. ROSENGARD.
This School started with 10 boys, but now numbers 60 pupils, 23 boys, 19 girls, and 18 infants.

HALIFAX.
Secretary of Synagogue.—NATHANIEL LYONS, Esq., 7, Crossley-st.

HANLEY, STAFFORDSHIRE.
(Jewish Population of 40 Families.)
SYNAGOGUE, Hanover-street. (Founded 1873.)
President.—L. GOLDBERG, Esq. *Treasurer.*—M. EPSTEIN, Esq.
Minister.—Rev. S. SUMBERG.
Hon. Secretary.—M. ROTENBERG, Esq., Parliament-row, Hanley.
Income, 1895.—£150. *Expenditure.*—143.
The seatholders number 40.

SICK, BURIAL AND BENEFIT SOCIETY. (Founded 1892.)
Objects.—(1) Free Medical attendance. (2) 21/- Benefit during Shiva and Chevra Kadisha. (3) Advancing Loans up to £3 without interest.
President.—L. GOLDBERG, Esq. *Treasurer.*—M. EPSTEIN, Esq.
Income, 1895.—£11. *Expenditure.*—£6.
The conditions of relief are : (1) Medical attendance at once. (2) Shiva Benefit in six months. (3) Loan to all Jewish residents.
There were 19 men, 9 women, and 3 children relieved during 1895.
Election.—By Ballot for Committee ; President and Treasurer from Congregation.
Secretary.—M. ROTENBERG, Esq.
Address.—Synagogue-chambers, Hanover-street.

LADIES' BENEVOLENT SOCIETY, Pall Mall, Hanley.
Object.—To relieve poor Jewish Women during sickness.
President and Secretary.—Mrs. GOLDBERG.
Treasurer.—Mrs. EPSTEIN.
There were 30 women and 15 children relieved during 1895, and these must reside in Hanley District. The mode of Election is by ballot.

HANLEY RELIGIOUS CLASSES. (Founded 1887.)
Head Master.—Rev. S. SUMBERG.
Visiting Instructor.—Rev. N. COHEN, Nottingham.
Thirty children attend these classes, which are held at the Synagogue School Rooms, Hanover-street.

HUDDERSFIELD.
(Jewish Population, 50.)
No Synagogue as yet. First Minyan formed in 1895.
President.—HENRY KRUGER, Esq.
Treasurer.—JACOB HARRIS, Esq. *Minister.*—Mr. KAHN.
Secretary.—Mr. M. JACOBS. About 30 seatholders.
There is a small Fund to relieve tramps on their way to Leeds or Manchester, supplying them with meals and Railway fare.

HULL.
(1895-96, Jewish Population 1,350. 15 marriages, 38 deaths.)
SYNAGOGUE, Robinson-row. (Founded 1826.)
President.—M. SHAPEBS, Esq. *Treasurer.*—S. LIEBERMAN, Esq.
Minister.—Rev. I. LEVY. *Reader.*—Rev. E. PEARLSON.
Secretary—Mr. DAVID MOSS. *Seatholders.*—160.

HEBREW GIRLS' SCHOOL, Osborn-street. (Founded 1873.)
President and Treasurer.—Mrs. B. S. JACOBS.
Hon. Secretary.—Miss GLASSMAN.
Head Teacher in English.—Miss MORRIS.
Head Teacher in Hebrew.—Miss SIMON.

The pupils attending the school, which is under Government inspection, number 180.

LADIES' HEBREW BENEVOLENT SOCIETY. (Established 1861.)
Object.—To grant relief to necessitous persons of the Jewish Faith, and to Jewish married women during sickness and confinement.
President.—Mrs. V. DUMOULIN.   *Treasurer.*—Mrs. FARBSTEIN.
Hon. Sec.—Mrs. B. J. BARNARD.
Medical Officer.—Dr. H. FARBSTEIN.
Income, 1895.—£61. 1s. 1d.   *Expenditure.*—£59. 11s. 10d.

There is also a Dorcas meeting in connection with above.

"MALBISH AROOMIM" CLOTHING FUND. (Established 1880.)
This society purchases and distributes clothing to poor men and boys and school children. About £50 is raised annually.

HULL HEBREW BOARD OF GUARDIANS. (Founded 1880.)
Object.—Relief of resident and casual poor.
President.—B. S. JACOBS, Esq.   *Treasurer.*—J. H. BARNETT, Esq.
Hon. Sec.—E. E. COHEN, Esq.   *Income*, 1895.—£330. 11s. 5d.

HEBREW YOUNG MEN'S LITERARY AND DEBATING SOCIETY. (Founded 1895.)
President.—SOLOMON GOODMAN, Esq.
Treasurer.—ALFRED FELDMAN, Esq.
Hon. Secretary.—SIDNEY FRIEDMAN, Esq.

During the winter, on Sunday evenings, papers are read and discussions held on interesting and instructive popular subjects.

LEEDS.

(Jewish Population, 10,000.   1895, 102 marriages, 130 deaths.)

OLD HEBREW CONGREGATION SYNAGOGUE, Great Synagogue, Belgrave-street. (Founded 1846.)
President.—S. CAMRASS, Esq.   *Vice-President.*—H. STONE, Esq.
Treasurer.—J. LEVINSTEIN, Esq.
Minister and Secretary.—Rev. M. ABRAHAMS, B.A.

The number of seatholders is 300.

JEWISH BOARD OF GUARDIANS, Belgrave-street. (Founded 1878.)
Object.—Relief of resident and casual poor.
President and Treasurer.—PAUL HIRSCH, Esq.
Hon. Secretary and Hon. Relieving Officer.—Rev. M. ABRAHAMS, B.A.
Hon. Almoner.—M. HYMAN, Esq.
Income, 1895.—£664. 8s. 10½d.   *Expenditure.*—£496. 10s. 6d.

420 persons were relieved, 80 of whom were men, 125 women, and 215 children. Casuals are relieved at any time, but those seeking weekly relief must have been resident in Leeds for six months before application. Administration by subscribers.

JEWISH LADIES' BENEVOLENT SOCIETY, Belgrave-street. (Founded 1874.)
Object.—Relief of females during confinement.
President.—Mrs. LUCIEN MARCAN.
Treasurer.—LUCIEN MARCAN, Esq.
Hon. Secretary and Almoner.—Mrs. C. LANDA.

The income averages from £80 to £100 per annum. The number of persons relieved during 1895 were 250. In each case a grant of 10s. is made. A Committee investigates the case, and all deserving poor are relieved.

CHEVRA KADISHA BURIAL SOCIETY, Belgrave - street. (Founded 1895.)
Object.—To perform the last solemn rites to the dead, to assist the necessitous during the week of mourning, and to keep the cemetery in order.
President.—HERMAN FRIEND, Esq.
Vice-President.—J. LYONS, Esq.   *Treasurer.*—A. COHEN, Esq.
Hon. Secretary.—Rev. M. ABRAHAMS, B.A.
Income and Expenditure.—£30.

HEBREW SCHOOL, Gower - street Board School, Leylands. (Founded 1888.)
Head Master.—Rev. M. ABRAHAMS.   *Number of Children.*—200.

SYNAGOGUE, St. John's-place, New Briggate. (Founded 1876.)
President.—M. RAISMAN, Esq.
Vice-President.—M. ABRAHAMSON, Esq.
Treasurer.—J. GOTTLIFFE, Esq.
Reader and Secretary.—Rev. S. MANSON.
The seatholders number 200.

SYNAGOGUE (Marienpoler), Hope-street. (Founded 1888.)
President.—A. LEWIS, Esq.   *Treasurer.*—M. LIPMAN, Esq.
Reader and Secretary.—Rev. J. SAMUEL.
The seatholders number 100.

SYNAGOGUE (Polish), Byron-street. (Founded 1893.)
President.—ABRAHAM SOCKEL, Esq.   *Treasurer.*—S. JOSEPH, Esq.
Reader and Secretary.—Rev. MARK COHEN.
The seatholders number 80.

ACHNOSATH ORACHIM, 5 and 7, Templar-street. (Founded 1890.)
Object.—To provide poor strangers with shelter.
President.—C. LANDA, Esq.   *Treasurer.*—M. GLUK, Esq.
Income and Expenditure.—£30 per annum.

BIKKUR CHOLIM, 5 and 7, Templar-street. (Founded 1876.)
Object.—Relief of the sick poor.
President.—C. LANDA, Esq.   *Treasurer.*—S. HYMAN, Esq.
Income and Expenditure.—£80 per annum.

JEWISH LADIES' BENEVOLENT SOCIETY. (Founded 1888.)
Object.—Relief of ailing and confined females.
President.—Mrs. M. RAISMAN.   *Treasurer.*—P. GOLDMAN, Esq.
Secretary.—A. SAFFER, Esq.
Address.—Synagogue Chambers, New Briggate.

There were 400 persons relieved, and the Income and Expenditure for 1895 was £100.

PROVINCIAL INSTITUTIONS. 77

JEWS' FREE SCHOOL (Talmud Torah), Lady-lane. (Founded 1876.)
Head Master.—H. AGUSKY, Esq.
This is a boys' school, and numbers 140 scholars.

LEICESTER.

(1895-96, 2 marriages, 3 deaths.)

SYNAGOGUE, 15, Crofton-street. (Founded 1866.)
President.—Sir ISRAEL HART. *Treasurer.*—J. ALEXANDER, Esq.
Minister.—Rev. M. M. COHEN. *Secretary.*—B. SAMUEL, Esq.
The Income and Expenditure is £200, and there are 60 seatholders.

CHARITY ORGANISATION, Synagogue-chambers. (Founded 1886.)
Object.—To relieve poor immigrants and emigrants.
President.—Sir ISRAEL HART. *Treasurer.*—J. ALEXANDER, Esq.
Secretary.—B. SAMUEL, Esq. *Income.*—£50 annually.
250 persons were relieved during the past year, 3s. to 5s. being given to each person.

HEBREW AND RELIGION SCHOOL, Synagogue-chambers. (Founded 1881.)
Head Master.—Rev. M. M. COHEN.
There are 31 scholars, 11 boys, 16 girls, and 4 infants.

BIKKUR CHOLIM SOCIETY, Synagogue-chambers. (Founded 1896.)
Object.—To relieve its members during sickness, want of employment, and to give a helping hand when needed.
Patron.—Sir ISRAEL HART. *President.*—H. DAVIS, Esq.
Secretary.—HYMAN SIMMONS, Esq. *Treasurer.*—J. MAY, Esq.
The election of officers takes place annually. The invested funds are £30, and the Income is £18 annually.

The Leicester Hebrew Congregation is also in connection with the Anglo-Jewish Association and the Orphan Aid Asylum.

LIMERICK.

SYNAGOGUE, 18, Callooney-street.
President.—L. GOLDBERG, Esq. *Treasurer.*—B. GRAFT, Esq.
Minister.—Rev. E. B. LEVIN. *Secretary.*—A. NEWMAN, Esq.
The annual Income and Expenditure averages about £100, and there are 25 seatholders.

BIKKUR CHOLIM. (Founded 1888.)
Object.—To succour poor patients.
President.—J. BARRON, Esq. *Treasurer.*—J. HOVSBA, Esq.
Secretary.—D. CROPMAN, Esq. *Address.*—90, Edward-street.
Forty persons were relieved during the past year, 15 men and 25 women. The Income averages £30 per annum.

LIVERPOOL.

(Jewish population, 5,000. 1895, 43 marriages, 107 deaths.)

OLD HEBREW CONGREGATION, Princes-road. (Founded 1790.)
Wardens.—Messrs. D. GABRIELSEN and E. W. YATES.
Treasurers.—Messrs. S. J. HENSCHBERG and ELLIS K. YATES.

Minister.—Rev. S. FRIEDEBERG.   *Secretary.*—Rev. H. M. SILVER.
Income, 1895.—£1,880.   *Expenditure.*—£1,830.
The seatholders number 410.

The Princes-road Synagogue holds and administers several important bequests.
  (1) The Eliza Jackson Homes, North-hill-street. Giving a house and 10s. weekly for life to six spinsters, or widows without children, of the Jewish faith. Built and endowed by the late Eliza Jackson and Henrietta Braham.
  (2) About £13,300 from the late James Braham for the payment of stipend of Minister and Reader, provided they are English and born of English parents.
  (3) The Barned Annuity Fund, which provides four old people with a pension for life of £20 per annum.
  (4) The "Mozley and Elias Joseph" Coal and Blanket Fund for providing the poor with these necessaries during the winter. About 70 relieved.
  (5) £1,000 bequeathed by the late Mrs. Augustus Levy to provide annuities for two old deserving people.

PRINCES-ROAD SYNAGOGUE RELIGION CLASSES.
Superintendent.—Rev. S. FRIEDEBERG.
Average attendance 60.

SYNAGOGUE, Fountains-road, Kirkdale. (Founded 1887.)
President.—A. FAGIN, Esq.   *Treasurer.*—S. COHEN, Esq.
Minister.—Rev. S. M. HINDIN.
Hon. Secretary.—M. MORRIS, Esq.

There are 45 seatholders; the Income for 1895 was £315, and the Expenditure £200.

LIVERPOOL NEW HEBREW CONGREGATION.
Synagogue, Hope-place. (Consecrated 1857.)
President.—J. L. CURLENDER, Esq.   *Treasurer.*—J. LIPSON, Esq.
Minister.—Rev. A. RUTKOWSKI.
Hon. Secretary.—BARNARD LEVY, Esq.
There are 130 seatholders.

LIVERPOOL HEBREWS' EDUCATIONAL INSTITUTION AND ENDOWED SCHOOLS, Hope-place. (Founded 1840.)
President.—CHARLES S. SAMUELL, Esq.
Treasurer.—Baron L. BENAS.   *Secretary.*—Rev. H. M. SILVER.

Ladies' Committee :—
President.—Mrs. LOUIS S. COHEN.
Hon. Secretary.—Mrs. A. M. JACKSON.
Income, 1895.—£1,230.   *Expenditure.*—£1,384.
Head Master.—M. ROSENBERG, Esq., C.T.
Head Mistress.—Miss HART, C.T.
The children number 626, 271 boys, 243 girls and 112 infants.

LIVERPOOL BOARD OF GUARDIANS FOR THE RELIEF OF THE JEWISH POOR. (Founded 1875.)
President.—I. SILVERBERG, Esq.
Treasurer.—D. GABRIELSEN, Esq.

Hon. Secretary.—Rev. S. FRIEDEBERG.
Secretary.—Rev. H. M. SILVER.
Income, 1895.—£700. *Expenditure.*—£850.
Administrative Expenses.—£115. 548 persons relieved.

JEWISH LADIES' BENEVOLENT INSTITUTION. (Founded 1849.)
Object.—The relief of poor married women during sickness and confinement.
President and Treasurer.—Mrs. LOUIS S. COHEN.
Hon. Secretary.—Mrs. RUTKOWSKI.
Income, 1895.—£160. *Expenditure.*—£270. 83 persons relieved.

HEBREW PHILANTHROPIC SOCIETY. (Founded 1811.)
Object.—Giving weekly relief during the winter to the respectable Jewish poor.
President.—S. J. HENSCHBERG, Esq.
Treasurer.—ELLIS K. YATES, Esq.
Hon. Secretary.—ALEXANDER JONES, Esq., 127, Bedford-street.
Income and Expenditure, 1895.—About £200.
Administrative Expenses.—£18. 50 families relieved. Election by ballot.

HEBREW PROVIDENT SOCIETY, 46, Paradise-street. (Founded 1850.)
Object.—To provide old people with a pension of 5s. weekly for life.
President.—LOUIS SOLOMON, Esq.
Treasurer.—EDWARD W. YATES, Esq.
Hon. Secretary.—NATHAN MOSS, Esq.
Income and Expenditure.—About £100.
Administrative Expenses.—£7. The number of pensioners varies from six to nine.

SOCIETY FOR CLOTHING THE NECESSITOUS BOYS OF THE HEBREW SCHOOLS, Hope-place. (Founded 1867.)
President.—EDWARD W. YATES, Esq.
Treasurer.—PHILIP BARNETT, Esq.
Hon. Secretary.—RALPH ROBINSON, Esq. Number of Boys clothed—75 to 80.
Conditions of Relief.—Regular attendance at school. Cleanliness and tidiness in appearance. *Income and Expenditure.*—£85.

CHILDREN'S CLOTHING SOCIETY. (Founded 1884.)
Object.—Making and distributing clothes to poor Jewish children.
President.—Mrs. E. W. YATES. *Treasurer.*—Mrs. P. S. LEVY.
Hon. Secretary.—Mrs. H. SOLOMON. *Address.*—West Albert-road.
Income and Expenditure.—About £50. 71 persons relieved.

LIVERPOOL HEBREW SCHOOL CHILDREN'S SOUP FUND, Hope-place. (Founded 1870.)
Object.—Providing the children of the schools with hot dinners during the winter.
President.—Mrs. E. W. YATES. *Treasurer.*—Mrs. ELIOT LEVY.
Hon. Secretary.—Mrs. A. KATZ. *Address.*—22, Bentley-road.
Income and Expenditure.—About £85. 367 children fed daily.

ORPHAN AID SOCIETY.
Object.—To aid the Jews' Hospital and Orphan Asylum.
President.—HENRY D. BEHREND, Esq.
Treasurer.—ERNEST E. BARNETT, Esq.
Hon. Secretaries.—Rev. S. FRIEDEBERG and HERBERT J. DAVIES, Esq.
Income.—About £60.

SOCIETY FOR TEMPORARILY SHELTERING POOR STRANGERS OF THE JEWISH FAITH, 23, Moon-street.
President—J. LIPSON, Esq.   *Treasurer.*—D. BAKER, Esq.
Hon. Secretary.—A. MATTHEWS, Esq.
Income and Expenditure.—About £110.

CHILDREN'S JEWISH CHARITIES' AID SOCIETY. (Founded 1895.)
President.—Rev. S. FRIEDEBERG.   *Treasurer.*—Rev. J. HARRIS.
Hon. Secretary.—ERNEST ROSENHEIM, Esq.
Address—1, Croxteth-road.

LONDONDERRY.
(43 Jewish Residents.)

SYNAGOGUE, 18, Abercorn-road. (Founded 1894.)
President.—B. ROBINSON, Esq.   *Minister.*—Mr. F. HARRIS.
Secretary.—Mr. I. ROSEN.
There are 15 seatholders.

MANCHESTER.
(Jewish Population, 15,000. 1895-6, 139 marriages, 243 burials.)

GREAT SYNAGOGUE, Cheetham Hill-road.
President.—N. LASKI, Esq.   *Vice-President.*—L. COBE, Esq.
Treasurer.—M. A. MICHAELS, Esq.
Warden.—P. FRANKENSTEIN, Esq.
Minister.—Rev. Dr. B. SALOMON.
Secretary.—Mr. NATHANIEL H. HARRIS.
Seatholders.—477.

SHECHITA BOARD, Great Synagogue-chambers. (Founded 1890.)
President.—P. HART, Esq.   *Vice-President.*—B. I. BELISHA, Esq.
Treasurer.—G. SHAFFER, Esq.
Hon. Secretary.—H. M. FEINBERG, Esq.
Secretary.—Mr. NATHANIEL H. HARRIS.

MANCHESTER NATURALISATION SOCIETY, Jews' School, Derby-street, Cheetham.
Object.—To assist aliens to become naturalised by means of weekly subscriptions.
Chairman.—J. SALOMON, Esq.
Treasurers.—Messrs. H. L. ROTHBAND and N. LASKI.
Hon. Secretary.—Rev. H. LEVIN.

MANCHESTER JEWISH HISTORICAL SOCIETY, Jews' School Derby-street, Cheetham.
President and Treasurer.—G. C. MANDELBERG, Esq., J.P.
Hon. Secretaries.—Rev. H. LEVIN and J. S. BESSO, Esq.

PROVINCIAL INSTITUTIONS.

SYNAGOGUE, Park-place, Cheetham. (Founded 1856.)
President.—JAMES BAUER, Esq.
Treasurer.—ISIDOR DANZIGER, Esq.
Minister.—Rev. L. M. SIMMONS, LL.B., B.A.
Secretary.—ISAAC A. ISAACS, Esq.
The seatholders number 142, and the annual income is about £900.

JEWISH BOARD OF GUARDIANS, 18, Knowsley Street, Cheetham. (Founded 1867.)
Objects.—Relief, general and medical: also granting loans without interest, and apprenticing Jewish youths.
President.—DAVID S. BLES, Esq., J.P.
Treasurer.—A. J. S. BLES, Esq.
Hon. Secretaries.—E. M. HENRIQUES, Esq., J.P., and A. M. L. LANGDON, Esq.
Clerk.—ISAAC A. ISAACS, Esq.
Income, 1895-6.—£1,801.   *Loans.*—£3,251.
Administrative Expenses.—£447.
No. of Persons Relieved, 1,242.—382 men, 217 women and 623 children.
The conditions of relief are poverty, old age, and sickness. The mode of election is annually by ballot of the subscribers.

MANCHESTER JEWS' SCHOOL, Derby Street, Cheetham. (Founded 1838.)
Head Master and Mistress.—E. HARRIS, Esq., M.A., and Miss RAPHAEL.
Infants' Mistress.—Miss LEMON.
There are 2,300 scholars, 800 boys, 800 girls, and 700 infants.

JEWISH LADIES' VISITING COMMITTEE, Belmont, High Bringate. (Founded 1884.)
Objects.—Visiting the poor and attending to their sanitary condition.
President.—Mrs. BEHRENS.   *Treasurer.*—Mrs. DREYFUSS.
Secretary.—Rev. L. M. SIMMONS.
Income.—About £100.   *Expenditure.*—About £95.

BRODYER SYNAGOGUE, Waterloo-road. (Founded 1891.)
President.—B. BALABAN, Esq.   *Treasurer.*—K. MALLIS, Esq.
Minister.—Rev. J. KANTOR.
Hon. Sec. and Registrar.—MORITZ ABRAMOVITZ, Esq.
Income, 1895.—£227.   *Expenditure.*—£194.
The seatholders number 110.

MANCHESTER JEWISH WORKING MEN'S CLUB.
President.—B. STEEL, Esq.   *Treasurer.*—H. MYERSTON, Esq.
Hon. Sec.—L. DAVIS, Esq.   *Members.*—600.   *Lady Members.*—360.

LITERARY AND DEBATING SOCIETY.
Chairman.—Rev. L. M. SIMMONS, LL.B., M A.
Hon. Sec.—M. ABRAMOVITZ, Esq.

HEBREW SICK AND BURIAL BENEFIT SOCIETY.
President.—LOUIS COBE, Esq.   *Treasurer.*—J. ROSENBLUM, Esq.
Secretary.—B. A. STEINMARK, Esq.   *Members.*—About 100.

SOUTH MANCHESTER SYNAGOGUE, Sydney-street, All Saints. (Founded 1872.)
President.—EPHRAIM HARRIS, Esq., M.A.
Treasurer.—JOSEPH MYERS, Esq.
Minister and Secretary.—Rev. ISIDORE SIMON.
The annual income is £550, and the seatholders number 85.

NEW SYNAGOGUE, Cheetham Hill-road. (Founded 5649.)
President.—G. SCHAFFER, Esq.
Treasurer.—JACOB E. GOODMAN, Esq.
Minister.—Rev. JACOB MATZ. *Secretary.*—Rev. L. I. MUSCAT.
Income, 1895.—£550. *Expenditure.*—£600.
The seatholders number 225.

HOLY LAW SYNAGOGUE.
Secretary.—Mr. BERNARD LEWIS, 137, Red Bank.

CENTRAL SYNAGOGUE.
Secretary. — Mr. L. LEVINSON, Central Synagogue chambers, Cheetham Hill-road.

HIGHTOWN SYNAGOGUE.
Secretary.—Mr. JACOB SILVERBLATT, 170, Royal Mount, Hightown.

MERTHYR TYDVIL.
(1895-6, 1 marriage, 11 burials.)
SYNAGOGUE, Church-street.
President.—M. GOODMAN, Esq. *Secretary.*—Mr. JOSEPH PRAG.
A branch of the Chovevi Zion Association is formed here.

MIDDLESBROUGH.
1895, one marriage, two burials.
SYNAGOGUE, Brentnall-street. (Founded 1873.)
President.—J. WILKS, Esq. *Treasurer.*—J. HUSH, Esq.
Minister.—Rev. M. E. DAVIES. *Secretary.*—J. LEVY, Esq.
There are 40 seatholders, and the annual income is £500.

JEWISH BOARD OF GUARDIANS. (Founded 1893.)
Object.—To relieve town and casual poor.
President.—J. HUSH, Esq. *Treasurer.*—J. WILSON, Esq.
Secretary.—Rev. M. E. DAVIES.
Address.—Synagogue Chambers. *Income and Expenditure.*—£75.

JEWISH SCHOOL, Middlesbrough.
This school contains 50 children, 30 boys, and 20 girls.
Head Master.—Rev. M. E. DAVIES, Synagogue Chambers.
A Chovevi Zion Association was also established in 1888.

NEWCASTLE-ON-TYNE.
(1895-6, Population of about 400 Jewish Families; 15 marriages, 30 deaths.)
SYNAGOGUE, Leazes-park-road. (Founded 1880.)
There was a Jewish community here in 1830, and probably earlier.
President.—H. F. LEVINSON, Esq.
Treasurer.—J. ROSENBERG, Esq.

Minister.—Rev. M. ROSENBAUM.
Hon. Secretary.—HENRY BERNSTONE, Esq.
Income, 1895.—£1,017. *Expenditure.*—£918.
The number of seatholders is 180.

HEBREW PHILANTHROPIC FRIENDLY SOCIETY (Registered under the Friendly Societies' Act), Synagogue Chambers.
President.—D. MARKS, Esq. *Treasurer.*—J. ROSENBERG, Esq.
Secretary.—MOSES COHEN, Esq.
Income, 1895.—£53. *Expenditure.*—£23 (this does not include Administrative Expenses).
Object.—To provide Sick and Shiva benefits for its members.

AID SOCIETY TO THE JEWS' HOSPITAL AND ORPHAN ASYLUM.
President.—S. M. HARRIS, Esq. *Treasurer.*—M. LOTINGA, Esq.
Hon. Secretaries.—Miss ETHEL HENRY and Rev. M. ROSENBAUM.
Income.—About £70 per annum.

BRANCH OF THE CHOVEVI ZION ASSOCIATION.
Commander.—Rev. M. ROSENBAUM.
Treasurer.—J. ROSENBERG, Esq.
Hon. Secretary.—A. SOLOMON, Esq.

BETH HAMEDRASH, 12, Villa-place. (Founded 1891.)
President.—Mr. KRANZ. *Treasurer.*—N. MELTZER, Esq.
Hon. Secretary.—S. ROSENBERG, Esq.
In connection with the Beth Hamedrash there is a Chevrah Mishnayoth.

JEWISH LADIES' BENEVOLENT SOCIETY, Synagogue-chambers.
Object.—To provide medical attendance and a weekly allowance to poor Jewish women during confinement, and for the relief of the Jewish sick. There is also a Dorcas Society in connection with this, meeting every fortnight, which provides clothing for the deserving poor.
President.—Mrs. FRANKS. *Treasurer.*—Mrs. ROSE.
Hon. Secretary.—Mrs. H. ROSENBAUM.
Income, 1895.—£44. 5s. *Expenditure.*—£42. 6s. 6d.

JEWISH BOARD OF GUARDIANS. (Founded 1872.)
Object.—Relief of the deserving Jewish poor.
President.—DAVID FALK, Esq. *Treasurer.*—PHILIP COHEN, Esq.
Hon. Secretary.—Rev. M. ROSENBAUM.
Address.—Synagogue Chambers.
Income 1895.—£190. *Expenditure.*—£172.
Administrative Expenses.—£9. 17s.
710 applicants for relief.

ANCIENT HEBREW SACRED SOCIETY, Synagogue-chambers.
Object.—To perform the duties of a Chevra Kadisha for its members and the poor, and to bear part expenses of the burials of poor persons.
President.—JACOB WOOLF, Esq. *Treasurer.*—P. ROBINSON, Esq.
Hon. Secretary.—S. TURNER, Esq.

HEBREW BURIAL SOCIETY, Synagogue-chambers.
Objects.—To perform the duties of a Chevra Kadisha for its members and for the poor, and to bear part expenses of the burials of poor persons. The Hebrew Congregation and the Ancient Hebrew Sacred Society also bear part of such expenses.
President.—MICHAEL FALK, Esq. *Treasurer.*—A. FRANKS, Esq.
Hon. Secretary.—L COHEN, Esq.
Income 1895.—£30. *Expenditure.*—£26.

NEWPORT (Mon.).

SYNAGOGUE, Francis-street.
President.—L. S. ABRAHAMSON, Esq.
Minister.—Rev. Z. LAWRENCE.

NORTHAMPTON.

(Jewish Population, 100 to 200.)

SYNAGOGUE, Overstone-road. (Founded 1890.)
President.—D. SALOMON, Esq. *Treasurer.*—H. MICHAELSON, Esq.
Minister.—M. KREUGEL, Esq. *Secretary.*—E. SALOMON, Esq.
The seatholders number 15.

NORTH SHIELDS.

(1895-6, 1 burial.)

SYNAGOGUE, 29, Linskill-street.
President.—MEYER BARCZYNSKI, Esq.

NORWICH (Eastern Counties).

(Jewish Population, 50. 1895, 1 marriage, 8 deaths.)

SYNAGOGUE, Synagogue-street. (Founded 1842.)
President.—ALFRED J. HALDINSTEIN, Esq.
Minister.—Rev. J. JOSEPH.
Treasurer and Secretary.—J. CARO, Esq.
There are about 10 seatholders.

NORWICH JEWISH YOUNG MEN'S MUTUAL IMPROVEMENT SOCIETY.
President.—ALFRED J. HALDINSTEIN, Esq.
Treasurer.— SYMONS, Esq. *Secretary.*—Rev. J. JOSEPH.

HEBREW SCHOOL. (Founded in 1890.)
There are 16 children attending this school, 10 boys and 6 girls. The Head Master is the Rev. J. JOSEPH.

NOTTINGHAM.

(Jewish Population, 500. 1895-6, 6 marriages, 5 burials.

SYNAGOGUE, Chaucer-street. (Founded 1845. Synagogue built 1890.)
President.—RALPH GOLDMAN, Esq.
Treasurer.—JACOB RABINOVITCH, Esq.
Minister.—Rev. HARRIS COHEN.
Secretary.—GERSHON RABINOVITCH, Esq.
Income and Expenditure, 1895-96.—£380. 80 Seatholders.

HEBREW PHILANTHROPIC SOCIETY. (Founded 1885.)
Object.—Relief of resident poor and strangers ; medical assistance.
President.—RALPH GOLDMAN, Esq.
Treasurer.—DAVID BERNER, Esq.
Secretaries.—Rev. HARRIS COHEN and Rev. S. SCHLOSS.
Income and Expenditure, 1895-6.—£70.
Administrative Expenses.—£12. 10s.
About 150 persons per annum are relieved. The meetings of the society are held in the vestry of the synagogue, and the officers and committee are elected yearly by ballot.

HEBREW SCHOOL, Chaucer-street.
The *Head Master* is Rev. HARRIS COHEN, and the number of scholars is 53, 22 boys, 19 girls, 11 infants.

OXFORD.

(1895-6, 35 Resident Jews, and 10 Jewish University students. 1 burial.)

SYNAGOGUE, Worcester-place. (Founded 1841.)
President.—B. I. FRANKS, Esq.
Treasurer and Secretary.—J. ZACHARIAS, Esq.
Minister.—Rev. S. RADNITZKI.
The number of seatholders is 12, and the income for 1895-6 was £96. There is also a Jewish cemetery established here.

PLYMOUTH.

(Jewish Population 260. 1895-6, 5 burials.)

SYNAGOGUE, Catherine-street. (Founded 1767.)
President.—M. FREDMAN, Esq. *Treasurer.*—A. MORRIS, Esq.
Minister.—Rev. Dr. M. BERLIN.
Secretary.—MYER FREDMAN, Esq.
Income and Expenditure.—£400. Seatholders 70.

LADIES' SOCIETY. (Founded about 70 years ago.)
For charitable purposes.
President.—Mrs. ASHER LEVY.
Also branches of the Chovevi Zion Association, and Anglo-Jewish Association.

JACOB NATHAN DAY SCHOOL, 69, Well Street. (Founded 1869.)
The *Head Master* is Mr. JOSEPH GOLDSTON, and the average attendance of scholars is 15.

PONTYPRIDD.

(Jewish Population 150. 1895, 1 marriage, 4 burials.)

SYNAGOGUE, Wood-road.
President.—MARKS FREEDMAN, Esq.
Minister.—Rev. — ROSENBERG.
Secretary.—M. DIAMOND, Esq.
There are 23 seatholders, and the weekly income averages about £2. 5s.

SCHOOL, Wood-road.
Head Master.—Rev. — ROSENBERG.
Thirty-two children attend the school, 14 boys and 18 girls.

PORTSEA.

(500 Jewish Residents. 1895-6, 2 marriages, 5 deaths.)

SYNAGOGUE, Queen-street. (Founded 5507.)
President.—Councillor HENRY EDWARDS.
Treasurer.—EMANUEL HYAMS, Esq.
Minister and Secretary.—Rev. ISAAC PHILLIPS.
Income and Expenditure.—£400. *Seatholders.*—82.

HEBREW BENEVOLENT INSTITUTION, Queen-street. (Founded 1804.)
Object.—Relief of resident poor.
President.—M. HART, Esq.
Treasurer.—EDWARD ZACHARIAH, Esq.
Secretary.—SAMUEL MAY, Esq.
Income and Expenditure.—£90. *Administrative Expenses.*—£10.
There were six persons (four men and two women) relieved during the past year, the conditions of relief being twelve months' residence. Election takes place at meeting of subscribers.

HEBREW EDUCATIONAL CLASSES, Queen-street. (Founded 1856.)
Head Master—Rev. ISAAC PHILLIPS.
The scholars number 70, 36 boys and 34 girls.
There are three Kosher restaurants.

READING (Berkshire).

(Jewish Population between 60 and 70.)

SYNAGOGUE, 6, Anstey-road, Maidenhead. (Founded 1883.)
President.—S. A. PRASHUER, Esq.
Treasurer.—I. GOLDMAN, Esq.
Minister.—Rev. N. AARON. *Secretary.*—J. EHRENBERG, Esq.
There are 25 seatholders.

SHEFFIELD.

(Jewish Population, 400. 1895-6, 11 marriages.)

SYNAGOGUE (New Hebrew Congregation), West Bar-green. (Founded 1864.)
Warden.—M. H. AGAR, Esq. *President.*—S. COHEN, Esq.
Treasurer.—B. ALEXANDER, Esq. *Secretary.*—B. RESSER, Esq.
Minister.—Rabbi CHIAKIN. *Shochet.*—Rev. A. ALEXANDER.
The number of seatholders is 104, and the income and expenditure for 1895 were £5 weekly.

CHEVRA SHOLEM, Scotland-street. (Founded 1892.)
Object.—Aid to members, loans, etc.
President.—A. GREEN, Esq. *Secretary.*—A. HARTMAN, Esq.
Income and Expenditure.—£1 weekly.
The number of persons relieved is 83 per annum, consisting of 68 men, and 15 women. The mode of election is by ballot, and persons are relieved on application.

SYNAGOGUE, North Church-street. (Founded 1866.)
President.—Mr. H. LIPSON. *Treasurer.*—Mr. A. T. HARRIS.
Minister.—Rev. A. CHAIKIN. *Secretary.*—Mr. L. ABRAHAMS.
Income, 1895-96.—£397. 2s. 5d. *Expenditure.*—£429. 19s. 8d.
The seatholders number 80.

BOARD OF GUARDIANS. (Founded 1887.)
Object.—To relieve resident and casual poor.
President.—Mr. H. L. BROWN. *Treasurer.*—Mr. H. BUDRANZKI.
Hon. Secretary.—Mr. MAURICE FINESTONE.
Income, 1895-96.—£58. 8s. 2d. *Expenditure.*—£57. 12s. 4d.
404 persons relieved during the year.

SHEFFIELD JEWS' SCHOOL. (Founded 1892.)
Head Master.—Rev. A. CHAIKIN.
24 children attend this school, 17 boys and 7 infants.
Address.—North Church-street.

SOUTHAMPTON.

(Twenty-five Jewish Families. 1895, 2 burials.)
SYNAGOGUE, Albion Place, High-street. (Founded 1864.)
President.—M. EMANUEL, Esq., J.P. *Treasurer.*—M. COHEN, Esq.
Minister.—Rev. S. FYNE. *Secretary.*—N. LEVY, Esq.
The seatholders number 22.

JEWISH POOR RELIEF FUND, 18, Bridge-road. (Founded 1876.)
President.—J. HYAMS, Esq. *Treasurer.*—M. EMANUEL, Esq., J.P.

HEBREW AND RELIGION CLASSES, 2, Sussex-road.
Teacher.—Rev. S. FYNE.
Twenty-five children attend the school, 14 boys and 11 girls.

SOUTHPORT.

(Jewish Population, 200. 1895, 1 marriage.)
SYNAGOGUE, Sussex-road. (Founded 1893.)
President.—S. M. HARRIS, Esq. *Treasurer.*—A. PRICE, Esq.
Minister.—Rev. N. BLOSER. *Secretary.*—MAX. E. LAMBERT, Esq.
The annual income averages between £250 to £300, and the seatholders number 39.

RELIGION CLASSES.
These classes were founded in 1893, and are held at the Synagogue. The Head Master is the Rev. N. BLOSER, and the scholars number 33, 15 being boys, and 18 girls.

SOUTH SHIELDS.

(Jewish Population, 120.)
SYNAGOGUE, 33, Charlotte-street. (Founded 1890.)
President.—A. S. GOMPERTZ, Esq. *Treasurer.*—L. JOSEPHS, Esq.
Minister.—Rev. BENJAMIN LIPKIN.
Secretary.—J. GOMPERTZ, Esq.
The seatholders number 25, and the weekly income is 31s. 6d.

HEBREW SCHOOL.
The *Head Master* is the Rev. B. LIPKIN, and the scholars number 35, 30 boys and 5 girls.

STOCKTON-ON-TEES.
(About 100 Jewish Residents. 1895-96, 1 marriage, 1 burial.)

SYNAGOGUE, Skinner-street. (Founded 1884.)
President and Treasurer.—M. GETZ, Esq.
Minister and Secretary.—Rev. BENJAMIN COHEN.
There are 14 seatholders, and the annual income is £100.

BRANCH OF CHOVEVI ZION ASSOCIATION. (Founded 1891.)
President.—C. Z. A. MICHELSEN, Esq.
Treasurer.—A. BLOOM, Esq. *Secretary.*—Rev. B. COHEN.
Income, 1895-6.—£12.
There is also an Orphan Aid Society, the *President* of which is Mrs. MICHELSEN. The annual income is about £6, and the society has been established three years.

SABBATH SCHOOL. (Founded 1884.)
Head Master.—Rev. B. COHEN.
The scholars number 14, 11 boys and 3 girls.

STROUD.
(Jewish Population, 104. 1895-96, 6 burials.)

SYNAGOGUE, Lansdown, Stroud. (Founded 1879.)
President.—ELI GREENSWEIG, Esq.
Treasurer—SOLOMON SPERBER, Esq.
Minister.—Rev. D. JACOBS. *Secretary.*—ISAAC M. SHANE, Esq.
Seatholders, 12. Annual income, £75.

HEBREW SCHOOL, Lansdown, Stroud. (Founded 1879.)
The *Head Master* is Rev. D. JACOBS.
There are 22 scholars, 18 boys and 4 girls.

SUNDERLAND.
(Jewish Population, 1,000. 1895, 8 marriages.)

SYNAGOGUE, Moor-street, Sunderland. (Founded May, 1862.)
President.—B. JACOBY, Esq. *Treasurer.*—N. RICHARDSON, Esq., T.C.
Minister.—Rev. JACOB PHILLIPS. *Secretary.*—JOSEPH LEVY, Esq.
There are 108 seatholders, and the annual income is about £600

HEBREW BOARD OF GUARDIANS, Moor-street. (Founded June, 1869.)
Object.—Relief of the Jewish Poor.
President.—N. RICHARDSON, Esq., T.C.
Treasurer.—B. JACOBY, Esq. *Secretary.*—JOSEPH LEVY, Esq.
Five hundred persons were relieved in 1895; 480 men, and 20 women. The annual *Income* and *Expenditure* are about £120.

HEBREW SCHOOLS, Moor-street. (Founded May, 1862.)
Head Master.—Rev. JACOB PHILLIPS.
Mistress.—Miss SOPHY JACKSON.
Eighty children attend this school.

MATERNITY SOCIETY,
For assisting poor Jewish Women.
President.—Mrs. J. WOLFE. *Treasurer.*—Mrs. JACOB GALLEWSKI.
Hon. Secretary.—Mrs. ELIAS WOLFE.
Membership of 80.

HEBREW BENEFIT SOCIETY.
President.—SOLOMON GALLEWSKI, Esq.
Secretary.—HENRY JOSEPH, Esq.
Membership of 50.

CHEVRAH KEDISHA HACHNOSAS OURACHIM AND CHEVRA TEHILLIM SOCIETIES.
President.—A. JACKSON, Esq. *Hon. Secretary.*—B. JACOBY, Esq.

NATURALIZATION SOCIETY, Branches of the Orphan Aid and Anglo-Jewish Association.

SWANSEA.
(300 Jewish Residents. 1895-96, 7 marriages, 9 deaths.)

SYNAGOGUE, Goat-street. (Founded 1780.)
President.—S. LYONS, Esq.
Treasurer.—BARNETT GOLDBERG, Esq.
Minister.—Rev. PHILIP WOLFERS.

SWANSEA BENEVOLENT ASSOCIATION. (Founded 1893.)
Object.—To help the Resident Poor.
President.—A. LYONS, Esq. *Treasurer.*—Mrs. R. MARKS.
Secretary.—Rev. P. WOLFERS.
Income and Expenditure 1895-6.—£35.

CONGREGATIONAL HEBREW CLASSES. (Founded 1888.)
Head Master.—Rev. P. WOLFERS. *Scholars.*—30.

TREDEGAR.
(1895-96, Jewish Population, 102. 4 marriages, 8 deaths.)

SYNAGOGUE, Morgan-street. (Founded, 1870. Reorganised, 1884.)
President and Treasurer.—S. ROSENBAUM, Esq.
Minister.—Mr. J. B. ZACCHIEW.
Secretary and Registrar.—M. J. S. LYONS, Esq.
The number of seatholders is 20, and the annual income £100.

BRANCH OF THE ORPHAN AID AND POOR AID SOCIETIES.
(Founded 1890 and 1893 respectively.)
Object.—To relieve the Jewish itinerant poor.
President.—S. ROSENBAUM, Esq.
Treasurer and Secretary.—LIONEL L. HARRIS, Esq.
80 persons relieved per annum by voluntary subscriptions.

HEBREW CLASSES. (Founded 1888.)
Head Master.—Mr. J. B. ZACCHIEW.
25 children attend these classes, 10 boys, 10 girls, and 5 infants.

WATERFORD.
President of Synagogue.—J. W. GOLDRING, Esq., 8, John-street.

WEST HARTLEPOOL.
(Fifty Jewish Residents. 1895-96, 2 marriages.)
SYNAGOGUE, Whitby-street. (Founded 1872.)
President.—JACOB MOSESSON, Esq. *(pro tem.).*
Reader.—Mr. LEVY.   *Secretary.*—Mr. JACOB BROADY.
There are 13 seatholders, and the weekly income is 27s.

JEWISH CONGREGATIONAL SCHOOL.
The *Head Master* is Mr. LEVY, the Reader of the Synagogue; Rev. — DAVIS, the Visiting Minister, visits the school once a week. There are 10 scholars, an equal number of boys and girls.

WOLVERHAMPTON.
(Thirty-five Jewish Families. 1895-96, 3 marriages, 2 burials.)
SYNAGOGUE, Fryer-street. (Founded 1858.)
President.—M. GOLDENBERG, Esq.
Treasurer.—M. SCHWERIN, Esq.
Minister.—Rev. I. LEVY.   *Hon. Secretary.*—S. BENJAMIN, Esq.
The number of seatholders is 43. Annual income and expenditure £200.

BENEVOLENT SOCIETY AND SABBATH MEAL SOCIETY.
(Founded 1867.)
President.—M. GOLDENBERG, Esq.
Treasurer and Secretary.—E. RUDELSHEIM, Esq.
150 persons were relieved during the last year with money and food, the Income and Expenditure being £20.

HEBREW SCHOOL, Fryer-street. (Founded 1858.)
Head Master.—M. MORRIS, Esq.
There are 40 scholars, 30 boys and 10 girls.

WREXHAM.
(Jewish Population, 40.)
SYNAGOGUE, 10, Hill-street. (Founded 1890.)
President.—SOLOMON MYERS, Esq. *Treasurer.*—D. CARASON, Esq.
Minister.—Rev. E. BLOOM.   *Secretary.*—A. D. EPSTEIN, Esq.
The annual *Income* and *Expenditure* is £78, and the seatholders number 23.

YORK.
(Jewish Population, 60.)
SYNAGOGUE, Aldwark. (Founded 1892.)
President and Treasurer.—J. RUDOLPH, Esq.
Minister.—Rev. M. ISAACS.   *Hon. Secretary.*—J. COHEN, Esq.
There are 14 seatholders, and the annual *Income* and *Expenditure* is about £70. Children are taught by the Minister.

POOR RELIEF SOCIETY, Gillygate. (Founded 1896.)
Object.—To relieve poor Jewish families passing through the town.
President.—JACOB COHEN, Esq.   *Treasurer.*—J. RUDOLPH, Esq.
So far, 20 men have been relieved financially.

COLONIAL CONGREGATIONS.

AUSTRALIAN COLONIES.*

N.B.—*M.* stands for Minister; *P.* for President; *Sh.* for Shochet; *Sec.* for Secretary.

CONGREGATION.	MINISTERS, ETC.	ADDRESSES.
Adelaide (S. Aust.) ...	Rev. A. F. Boas, *M.* Mark Rosenthal, *Sh.*	West-terrace.
Auckland (N. Zealand)	Rev. S. A. Goldstein, *M.*	
Ballarat (Victoria) ...	Rev. J. M. Goldreich, *M.* Mem of Beth Din (Mel.). Aaron Bernstein, *Sh.*	
Brisbane (Queensland)	Rev. A. T. Chodowsky, *M.*	
Canterbury (N. Zeal.).	Ralph Levi, Esq. *P.* ... Louis Cohen, Esq., *Sec.*	
Christchurch (N.Zeal.)	Ralph Levoi, Esq., *P.*	
Dunedin (Otago, New Zealand).	L. H. Mendelsohn, Esq. *P.* Rev. Louis Harrison, *M.*	
Freemantle (W. Aust.)	A. Bennett, Esq., *P.*... B. J. Solomon, Esq., *Sec.*	
Melbourne (Bourke-street)	J. A. Cantor, Esq., *P.* Rev. Dr. Abrahams, *M.* Pres. of Beth Din. S. M. Solomons, Esq., *Sec.* Moses Saunders, Esq. *Sh*	
Melbourne (East) ...	Mendel Cohen, Esq., *P.* Rev. J. Lenger, *Reader.*	
Melbourne (St. Kilda)	M. Samuel, Esq., *P.*... Rev. E. Blaubaum, *M.* Member of Beth Din. Joel Freedman, Esq., *Sec. & Hebrew Master.*	Mozart-street.
Perth (W. Australia).	Nathaniel Nelson, Esq. *P.*	
Sydney (N. S. Wales).	Rev. A. B. Davis, *M.* ... Rev. J. H. Landau, *Assistant Master.* Simeon Frankel, Esq. *Sec.* Rev. P. Phillipstein, *Reader.* Rev. A. A. Levi, *Sh.*	Ardath, Victoria-street, N.

* Kindly supplied by the Chief Rabbi.

92   THE JEWISH YEAR BOOK.

Congregation.	Minister, etc.	Addresses.
Wellington (N. Zeal.).	Louis Pulver, Esq., *Head Master.* Rev. H. Vanstaveren, *M.*	
Rockhampton (Q'land).	Simon Lipstone, Esq.	William-street.

SOUTH AFRICAN COLONIES.

Congregation.	Ministers, etc.	Addresses.
Buluwayo (Mat'bele'd)	Joseph Saber, Esq., *P.* Emanuel Frank, Esq., *Sec.*	
Beaufort, W. (Calvinia)	Cohen, Esq., *P.*	
Uitenhagen		
Beaconsfield	Joseph Gross, *Jewish Resident.*	Market-square.
Blomfontein	Aaron Forman, *Sh.*	
Cape Town.	— Robel, Esq., *P.*	
	Rev. A. P. Bender, *M.*	Synagogue-house.
	A. L. Nathan, Esq., *Sec.*	
	L. Sytner, Esq., *Treas.*	Palmerston Hotel.
	Rev. E. D. Lyons, *Sh.*	
	Rev. S. Hoffenberg, 2nd *Sh.*	c/o Hoffmann, 59, Buitenkant-st.
Durban	J. H. Isaacs, Esq., *P.*	49, Gardiner-street.
	Sidney Sprinz, Esq., *Sec.*	Syn. Cham., Grey-street.
	Rev. — Pincus, *Sh. and Reader*	
Johannesburg	Rev. M. L. Harris, *M.*	Box 1311.
Johannesburg (New)	Simeon Sissack, Esq., *Sec.*	P.O. Box 511.
	Rev. H. Isaacs, *M.*	P.O. Box 1881.
Kimberley	H. Sezard, Esq., *Sec.* — Bronde, *Sh.*	
Ottoshoop (Malmani)	G. Belleville Stern, Esq., *Sec.*	
Oudtshoorn	A. Stusser, Esq., *P.* M. Morris, Esq., *Sec.* — Woolfson, Esq., *Sh.*	
Pretoria (Transvaal)	I. Rosenstein, Esq., *P.* M. Schwerman, Esq., *Sec.*	
Pietermaritzburg	J. H. Isaacs, Esq., *P.* Hyam Levy, Esq., *Sec.*	

COLONIAL CONGREGATIONS.

Congregation.	Ministers, etc.	Addresses.
Port Eliz. (C. Colony)	M. Joseph, Esq., *P.* .... Rev. D. Wasserzug, *M.* Rev. E. Eliasov, Esq., *Sh.*	51, Western-road.
Vryheid (New Republic, Zululand)...	Isaac Barnow, *Principal Resident* H. D. Lenusohn, *Sh.*	
Uitenhagen ...	J. Mizrache East, *Jew. Resident*	
Randfontein (?) ...		
Styllerville (?) ...		
Salisbury (Mashona.)	Rev. D. I. Freedman, B.A., *M.* ... Morris Freeman, Esq., *Sec.*	
The Paarl	A. Hertz, Esq., *P.* ... Moses Horwitz, *Sh.* ...	
Robertson	Benjamin Klein, *Sh.*	
Klerksdorff (?) ...		

MISCELLANEOUS COLONIAL CONGREGATIONS.

Congregation.	Ministers, etc.	Addresses.
Bombay Beni Israel	David Solomon, Esq., *Sec.* ...	5, Khuduk, Israel Moholla.
Hamilton (Canada)...	B. Rosenthal, Esq., *P.*	Syn. Ch. Hughson-street, South.
Halifax (Nova Scotia, Canada)	B. Benson, Esq., *P.* ... M. Dresdner, Esq., *Sec.* Rev. Simeon Schwartz, *Sh. & Reader*	116, Maitland-st.
Kingston (Jamaica)...	Rev. S. Jacobs, *M.* .	
United Hebrew Con.	S. S. Lawton, Esq., *Sec.*	
Montreal (Canada) Ger. and Eng. Con.	Rev. Friedlander, *M.*	
Shanghai	L. Moore, Esq., *P.* ...	
Toronto (Canada) ...	Rev. A. Lazarus, B.A., *M.*	272, George street.
Victoria (Brit. Col.)	Rev. Dr. Philo, *M.* ...	
Winnipeg (Canada)...	J. D. Freedman, Esq., *Sh.*	92, Ross-street.
Malta	Rev. Fragi Minni, *Rabbi*	

The following are the only Colonial returns which have reached the office up to the time of going to press :—

CAPE TOWN.

CAPE TOWN JEWISH BOYS' AND GIRLS' GUILD. Synagogue-chambers. (Founded 1895.)
President.—Miss MARTHA ROTHKUGEL.
Treasurer.—Miss DORA LORIE.
Hon. Secretary.—Master HENRY G. LEWIS.
Income and Expenditure.—About £70.
Managed by Committee of 11. Annual Report issued.

CAPE TOWN JEWISH PHILANTHROPIC SOCIETY. Synagogue-chambers. (Founded 1884.)
President.—DAVID ISAACS, Esq.   *Treasurer.*—R. HERMANN, Esq.
Hon. Secretary.—J. ARENSTEIN, Esq.
Income and Expenditure—over £200.
Managed by Committee of 9. Annual Report issued.

SYDNEY, N.S.W.

SIR MOSES MONTEFIORE JEWISH HOME. (Founded 1889.)
With which is incorporated Sydney Hebrew Philanthropic Society.
President.—Mr. SAMUEL COHEN.   *Matron.*—Mrs. J. BARNETT.
Income.—£824. 7s.   Inmates (all aged) seven men, four women.
Cost, maintenance of home £441. 3s. 4d. ; Relief (outside) £201. 13s. 4d. ; Pensions £78. 4s. ; Loans £127.

HEBREW LADIES' DORCAS. (Founded 1840.)
President.—Mrs. DAVID L. LEVY.
Treasurer.—Mrs. A. A. COHEN.   *Hon. Sec.*—Mrs. LOUIS JACOBS.
Income.—£299. 19s. 1d.   *Relief.*—£222. 19s. 8d.
The ladies of this society visit the homes of the poor, also the hospitals, and make up articles of clothing for distribution. It has funds amounting to £477. 4s. 9d.

JEWISH GIRLS' GUILD.
Object.—This society is established to visit the sick, and to distribute garments which they make up to the necessitous, and to help with other societies in giving relief.
President.—Mrs. J. H. LUMLAN.
Income for 1895.—£107. 13s. 4d.   *Expenditure.*—£136. 16s. 5d.
The number of contributing members is 198.

SYDNEY BRANCH ANGLO-JEWISH ASSOCIATION.
President.—Rev. A. B. DAVIS.
Receipts from 86 subscriptions £83. 10s. 3d.
There is also a Mutual Benefit Society having a fund of over £600.

HEBREW EDUCATION BOARD.
President.—Rev. A. B. DAVIS.
Children on roll 350.   Average attendance 265.
It has two Masters and 5 Lady Assistant Teachers.
Expenditure.—£450 per annum of which the Great Synagogue gives a yearly subvention of £150.

SABBATH SCHOOL.   *President.*—Rev. A. B. DAVIS.

JEWISH MINISTERS.

Abelson, J. *Cardiff Hebrew Congregation.* Born March, 1873, at Merthyr Tydvil. Educated Jews' College, and also University College, where he matriculated. B.A. London.

Abrahams, M. *Old Hebrew Congregation, Leeds* (Belgrave-street). Formerly Head Hebrew Master of Stepney Jewish Schools. Born October 10th, 1860, in London. Educated at Jews' and University Colleges. B.A. London.

Adler, Dr. Hermann. *Chief Rabbi of the United Hebrew Congregations of the British Empire* (appointed 1891). Previously Delegate Chief Rabbi since 1879. President of Jews' College, Examiner at College of Preceptors, Vice-President of the Jewish Religious Educational Board, of the Anglo-Jewish Association, etc., etc. Born at Hanover in May, 1839. Elucated at University College and University of London. Obtained Degree of Doctor of Philosophy at Leipzig University in 1861. In 1862, ordained Rabbi by Chief Rabbi Rappaport. Preached first sermon at consecration of Swansea Synagogue in 1859. Represented the Russo-Jewish Committee at Berlin in 1882, and at Paris in 1890. In 1863 Principal of Jews' College, and from 1864 to 1879 Theological Tutor of the same establishment. Minister of Bayswater Synagogue in 1864. Some of his published works are:—"Volume of Sermons on the passages adduced by Christian Theologians in support of the Dogmas of their Faith," "Ibn Gebirol and his relation to Scholastic Philosophy," Joint Authorship of "Jewish Reply to Bishop Colenso," etc., etc. Has contributed articles to *The Nineteenth Century*, *The Fortnightly Review*, *The North American Review*, etc.

Adler, Michael. *Hammersmith Synagogue.* Born July 27th, 1868, in London. Educated at Jews' Free School, Jews' College, and University College. B.A. Lond., with honours. Has contributed articles to *Jewish Quarterly Review*.

Barnstein, Isidore. *Dover Synagogue.* Born 1840, at Hoorn, Holland. Certificated teacher in Hebrew and secular instruction.

Berlin, Dr. M. *Plymouth Hebrew Congregation.* (Appointed October, 1895.) For ten years minister in Newport (Mon.). Also, formerly Head Master of Aria College, Portsea. Born March, 1849, in Hamburg. Educated under the late Chief Rabbi Stern, and at the Seminary of Dr. Hildesheimer and the Royal University College of Berlin. Ph.D. of Halle (Prussia).

Berliner, B. *St. John's Wood Synagogue.* Born in London on September 4th, 1848, and Educated at Jews' College. Also undergraduate of London University. Has occupied position of Reader of the Law to the German Synagogue, Head Master of the Borough Jewish Schools and Minister of the Bristol Hebrew Congregation.

Chaikin, A. *Sheffield Congregation.* Formerly Rabbi of the Polish Jews in Paris, and also in Rostov-sur-le-Don. Born in 1852 at Shklow, Mohilev. Educated at St. Petersburg. Fully qualified. Author of *Apologie des Juifs* (Paris, 1885).

Chotzner, Rev. Dr. *Belfast Hebrew Congregation* (appointed 1870), with a break, from 1880, of twelve years, during which he officiated as Hebrew Master at Harrow School. Born in Austria and educated at Breslau Rabbinical College and Breslau University. Has contributed to the "Jewish Quarterly Review," "American Review," etc., etc.

Cohen, Francis L. *Borough New Synagogue* (appointed 1886). Formerly of Dublin Hebrew Congregation and South Hackney. Born at Aldershot on November 14th, 1862. Educated at Jews' College (two scholarships), and University College, London. Jewish Chaplain to British Army and Volunteer Force. Authority on ancient Hebrew Melody.

Cohen, Harris. *Nottingham Hebrew Congregation* (appointed 1890). Also Hebrew Lecturer to Nottingham University College. Formerly of Merthyr Hebrew Congregation. Born Wilkowisk, Poland, July 1st, 1868. Educated at Manchester Jews' School, and Jews' College, London. Delivered many lectures on Talmudic and Biblical subjects.

Cohen, M. M. *Leicester Hebrew Congregation.* Born 1864, in Bialystock, Russia. Educated in Provincial Realschool and the Wolozin Seminary. Is a regular contributor to the Hebrew paper *Hameliz*.

Cohen, Susman. *Dayan of the United Synagogue.* Born in Kinishin, Province of Grodno, Russia. Educated at Kowno. Received Rabbinical Diploma at the age of twenty, has occupied the position of Principal of the College at Sinee and also the Kirslave College. Has been Rabbi to the Manchester Jewish Community for eighteen years.

Davids, Hermann. *Western Synagogue.* Also of Sheffield. Born at Warsaw in 1849. Educated at Government Schools. Early developed a taste for Music and singing, and at the age of fifteen conducted choirs at several synagogues, being known as the "Boy Chazan." Has composed both synagogal and other music.

Friedeberg, S. *Liverpool Old Hebrew Congregation* (Elected March, 1891). Formerly minister to Newcastle-on-Tyne Congregation, and visiting minister to the Shields and Hartlepool Congregations from 1886-1891. Born 1862. Educated at Stepney Jewish Schools. Trained for the Jewish ministry at Aria College, Portsea.

Fürst, J. *Edinburgh Synagogue* (Park-place). Previously of Hull and Middlesbrough Hebrew Congregations. Born in 1847 at Polangen, Kurland, Russia. Educated in Jewish College at Wilna. Appointed Edinburgh Synagogue, 1878.

Fyne, Simon. *Southampton Synagogue.* Born and educated at Kowno, Russia. Certificated teacher (Jews' College) religion and Hebrew.

Gaster, Dr. Moses. *Haham of the Spanish and Portuguese Congregation* (appointed 1887). Born at Bucharest, Roumania, 1856. Educated at the Rabbinic Seminary, Breslau. Exiled from Roumania, 1885. Ilchester Lecturer at Oxford 1886 and 1894. Has written "Literatura Popularea Rumana," "Greeko-Sclavonic Literature," "Chrestomatha Roumana" and has contributed papers to many learned journals. Is on the Council of the Asiatic Society and Folk Lore Society.

Goldston, Nehemiah. *South East London Synagogue.* Also Hebrew Master at Westminster Jews' Free School. Born in Great Yarmouth, December, 1866. Educated at Jews' Free School, Spitalfields.

Gollancz, Hermann. *Bayswater Synagogue* (appointed 1892). Has also been Minister at Hambro', St. John's Wood, New, South Manchester, and Dalston Synagogues. Born November 30th, 1852, at Bremen. Educated at Jews' and University Colleges. M.A. Lond. Edited Anglican version of the Bible for use in Jewish families. Has contributed to the *Asiatic Quarterly Review* and other periodicals.

Gollancz, S. M. *Hambro' Synagogue* (appointed 1854). Formerly Rabbi at Bremen. Born at Witkowo, near Posen, about 1822. Studied under R. Akiba Eger Gins in Posen. Invited to London 1854.

Gouldstein, Julius A. *North London Synagogue.* Born in Australia, February, 1858. Educated at Jerusalem and Jews' College.

Green, A. A. *Hampstead Synagogue* (appointed 1892). Has also been Minister of Sheffield and Sunderland Hebrew Congregations. Born London, September 18th, 1860. Educated at Jews' and University Colleges.

Harris, Isidore. *West London Synagogue.* Formerly Minister of North London Synagogue. Born London, June 6th, 1853. Educated at Jews' and University Colleges, M.A. Lond. Has contributed to *Jewish Quarterly Review* and *Chambers' Encyclopædia*.

Harris, R. *Bayswater Synagogue* (appointed 1863). Has also been Secretary to the Liverpool Old Hebrew Congregation. Born in London on January 14th, 1835. Educated privately.

Hast, M. *Great Synagogue.* Born in Warsaw in 1841. Educated there. Has composed several oratorios and other musical works, mostly sacred.

Hyamson, M. *Dalston Synagogue.* Has also been Minister at Swansea and Bristol, and Head Master at Dalston Schools. Born at Suwalk, Russia, on August 25th, 1863. Educated at Jews' and University Colleges, B.A. Lond. Lecturer to the Royal Institute of South Wales.

Joseph, Morris. *West London Synagogue* (appointed 1893). Formerly North London Synagogue 1868-74, and Old Hebrew Congregation, Liverpool. 1874-82. Born in London 1848. Educated Westminster Jews' Free School and Jews' College. Author of "The Ideal in Judaism" (Sermons), published 1893, etc., and contributor to the *Jewish Quarterly Review*.

Levy, I. A. *Hull Hebrew Congregation.* (Appointed 1881.) Formerly of Manchester Congregation, Western Synagogue, London, and Sunderland. Born in London 1824. His studies in Hebrew and the Talmud were under the supervision of a former Chief Rabbi, Rev. Solomon Herschell.

Levy, Solomon. *New Synagogue* (appointed 1895). Formerly of Newcastle-on-Tyne, where he was born in 1872. Educated at Jews' and University Colleges, B.A. Lond., with honours.

Manne, A. S. *Hampstead Synagogue* (appointed 1892). New Dalston Synagogue from 1888. Born at Cracow 22nd May, 1858, at which place he was also educated.

Marks, Professor D. W. *West London Synagogue* (appointed 1841). Previously Secretary of the Liverpool Synagogue. Born in London 1811. Educated at Jews' Free School. Goldsmid Professorship of Hebrew Literature at University College London. Has published three volumes of Sermons.

Mendelsohn, Rev. L. *Dublin Hebrew Congregation* (appointed 1895). Formerly Head Master (1888-90) West and East Melbourne Hebrew Schools, Minister of Newcastle-on-Tyne, Bristol. Born 1868. Educated Jews' College and University College, graduated with honours.

Munz, Simon. *North London Synagogue* (appointed 1883). Formerly Chazan of the New Synagogue, for seven years. Born February 8th, 1850, at Warsaw. Educated there. Composer.

Phillips, Isaac. *Portsea Hebrew Congregation.* Born in London 1845. Educated Edmonton, City of London School, and Jews' College.

Phillips, Jacob. *Sunderland Synagogue.* Formerly of Tredegar (Monmouth) and Swansea Hebrew Congregations. Born February 25th, 1868, at Portsmouth. Educated at Aria College, Portsmouth. Undergraduate University of Durham and member of Durham College of Science. Author of "A Peep into the Talmud" and "Jewish Rites and Ceremonies."

Price, Harris L. *St. John's Wood Synagogue* (appointed 1891). Formerly preacher to the Swansea Congregation. Born at Wilna on October 10th, 1864. Educated at Manchester Jews' School and Owens College.

Roco, S. J. *Spanish and Portuguese Synagogue*, Bevis Marks (appointed 1869). Born June 6th, 1844, at Amsterdam. Educated at Portuguese Congregational School and trained as Minister at the Portuguese Seminary, also in Amsterdam. Underwent conscription at the age of 19. Also holds the post of Hebrew Master at the Gates of Hope School.

Rosenbaum, M. *Newcastle-on-Tyne Hebrew Congregation.* Formerly of Poplar Synagogue (London) and the Hanley (Staff.) Hebrew Congregation. Also Jewish Chaplain to the North-Eastern Infirmary, Netherton. Educated Jews' and University Colleges. Hollier Scholarship for Hebrew at London University.

Rosengard, B. H. *Synagogue, Great Grimsby.* Born in Suwalk, a town in Russo-Poland, in 1865. Educated at Jews' Free School, and City of London College. Previously Minister of Belfast and Merthyr Hebrew Congregations.

Salomons, Bernard J. *Chatham Memorial Synagogue* (appointed July, 1885). Previously Minister at Oxford, and Stockton-on-Tees. Born in Poland, November 7th, 1862. Qualified Minister by the British Ecclesiastical authorities. Contributes to local press, and is a frequent lecturer.

Samuel, I. *Bayswater Synagogue* (appointed 1864). Appointed Jewish Chaplain to Colney Hatch Lunatic Asylum by London County Council in 1892, where he was instrumental in obtaining the provision of Kosher food, etc. Born March 9th, 1833, in London. Educated privately.

Singer, Simeon. *New West End Synagogue* (appointed 1879). Formerly Head Master of Jews' College School, and afterwards Minister of the Borough New Synagogue. Born in London 1848. Educated at Jews' College. Editor of the "Authorised Daily Prayer Book."

Simmons, Professor L.M., LL.B., B.A. *Synagogue, Cheetham, Manchester.* Born in London, educated at City of London School and Breslau Rabbinical Seminary. Obtained Arts Degree at London University in 1873. Law Degree Victoria University. Lecturer in Hebrew and Arabic at Owens College, Manchester.

Simon, Isidore. *South Manchester Synagogue* (appointed 1885). Formerly of Southampton. Born June 1849, at Suwalk, Russo-Poland, where educated.

Spero, Emanuel. *Central Synagogue.* Formerly Second Reader Hambro' Synagogue. Born Svenborg, Denmark, on August 25th, 1854. Educated Liverpool Jews' Free School. Gold Medallist and Associate of the London Academy of Music.

Spiers, B. *Dayan of the United Synagogue* (appointed 1876). Has also occupied the position of Rabbi and Preacher in the Duchy of Posen, and Principal of a London Collegiate School. Born at Schleschin, Poland. Educated at various Rabbinical Colleges in Poland (Yeshiboth). Obtained the Rabbinical Diploma at the age of 20. Published several Rabbinic Works.

Stern, J. F. *East London Synagogue.* Born January 2nd, 1865, at Bedford. Educated at Jews' and University Colleges. Undergraduate, London University, Associate Jews' College, Hollier Hebrew Scholar University College.

Wolfers, Philip. *Swansea Hebrew Congregation.* Formerly Barberton and Johannesburg, South Africa, and Hanley, Staffordshire. Born in London 1861. Educated Jews' Free School, and Jews' College. Certificated teacher.

JEWISH PEERAGE, BARONETAGE, AND KNIGHTAGE.*

PEERAGE.

ROTHSCHILD, BARON (Sir Nathan-Meyer Rothschild), of Tring, co. Hertford, and a Baronet, Baron of the Austrian Empire, Lord-Lieutenant and Custos Rotulorum co. Buckingham, M.P. for Aylesbury, 1865 to 1885; *b.* 8 Nov. 1840 : *m.* 17 April, 1867, Emma-Louisa, dau. of Baron Charles de Rothschild, Member of the German Parliament, and has issue,

I. LIONEL-WALTER, lieut. Buckinghamshire yeo. cav., D.L., *b.* 8 Feb. 1868.
II. Nathaniel-Charles, *b.* 9 May, 1877.
I. Charlotte-Louisa-Adela-Evelina, *b.* 3 April, 1873.

He *s.* as 2nd bart. at the death of his uncle, Sir Anthony de Rothschild, 4 Jan. 1876, and as Austrian Baron at the death of his father, 3 June, 1879. He was raised to the peerage 1885.

Lineage.

MEYER-AMSCHEL ROTHSCHILD, the Founder of this great commercial family (*see* BURKE'S *Rise of Great Families*), was father, by Gertrude Schnapper, his wife, of a 3rd son,

NATHAN-MEYER DE ROTHSCHILD, of Frankfort, afterwards of London, *b.* 19 Sept. 1777, who received letters patent of denization, dated 12th June, 44 GEORGE III.; and was advanced, by imperial letters patent dated at Vienna, 29 Sept. 1822, to the dignity of a Baron of the Austrian Empire. He *m.* 22 Oct. 1806, Hannah, 3rd dau. of Levi-Barent Cohen, merchant, of London, and had issue,

I. LIONEL-NATHAN, a Baron of the Austrian Empire, M.P. for London; *b.* 22 Nov. 1808: *m.* 15 June, 1836, Charlotte, dau. of his uncle, Baron Charles de Rothschild, of Naples, and *d.* 3 June, 1879, having had by her (who *d.* 1884),

---

* From Burke's "Peerage, Baronetage and Knightage," by kind permission of Messrs. Harrison & Sons.

1 NATHAN-MEYER, 2nd bart., created LORD ROTHSCHILD.

2 Charles-Alfred (Halton, near Tring), D.L. for London, Consul-General for Austria, *b.* 20 July, 1842.

3 Leopold (Ascott, Leighton Buzzard), D.L., *b.* 22 Nov. 1845; *m.* 25 Jan. 1881, Maria Perugia, of Trieste, and has Lionel-Latham, *b.* 26 Jan. 1882; Anthony-Gustav, *b.* 26 June, 1887; Evelyn-Achille, *b.* 6 Jan., 1886.

1 Leonora, *m.* 4 March, 1857, to her cousin, Baron Alphonse de Rothschild, and has issue.

2 Evelina, *m.* 7 June, 1865, to her cousin, Baron Ferdinand-James de Rothschild, of Lodge Hill, near Aylesbury, co. Buckingham, J.P. and high sheriff of the co. 1883, 2nd son of Baron Anselm de Rothschild, of Frankfort, and *d.* 4 Dec. 1866.

II. ANTHONY (Sir), created a Baronet.

III. Nathaniel, *b.* in 1812; *m.* in 1842, Charlotte, dau. of James Rothschild, of Paris, and *d.* 1870, leaving issue, James-Edward, *d.* Oct. 1881, and Albert.

IV. Meyer-Amschel, of Mentmore, Bucks, J.P. and D.L., M.P. for Hythe, *b.* 29 June, 1818; *m.* 26 June, 1850, Juliana, eldest dau. of Isaac Cohen, Esq., and *d.* 6 Feb. 1874, leaving by her (who *d.* 9 March, 1877) an only child and heiress,

Hannah, *m.* 1878, Earl of Rosebery, and *d.* 19 Nov. 1890.

I. Charlotte, *m.* to her cousin, Anselm de Rothschild, son of Baron Anselm de Rothschild of Frankfort, and *d.* 1859.

II. Hannah-Meyer, *m.* 1839, Hon. Henry Fitzroy, and *d.* 2 Dec. 1864.

III. Louisa, *m.* 6 April, 1842, to Meyer-Charles Rothschild, of Frankfort.

Baron Rothschild *d.* 28 July, 1836. His 2nd son,

SIR ANTHONY DE ROTHSCHILD, a Baron of the Austrian Empire, *b.* in May, 1810; *m.* in March, 1840, Louisa, dau. of Abraham Montefiore, Esq., and had issue,

I. Constance, *m.* 23 Nov. 1877, to Cyril, 1st Baron Battersea.

II. Annie, *m.* 12 Feb. 1873, to the Hon. Eliot Yorke (4th son of the Earl of Hardwicke), who *d.* 21 Dec. 1878.

Sir Anthony was created a Baronet 12 Jan. 1847, with limitation, failing his own male issue, to the sons of his elder brother Lionel, and dying without male issue, 4 Jan. 1876, was *s.* by his nephew, Sir NATHAN-MEYER DE ROTHSCHILD, 2nd baronet, created BARON ROTHSCHILD.

Creation—Baron, July, 1885; Baronet, 12 Jan. 1847.

Arms—Quarterly, 1st, or an eagle displayed sa., langued gu.; 2nd and 3rd az., issuing from the dexter and sinister sides of the shield, an arm embowed, ppr., grasping five arrows, points to the base arg.; 4th or, a lion rampant, ppr., langued gu., over all an escocheon gu., thereon a target, the point to the dexter, ppr. *Crests*—Centre, issuant from a ducal coronet or, an eagle displayed sa. Dexter, out of a ducal coronet or, between open buffalo's horns, per fesse or and sa., a mullet of six points or. Sinister, out of a ducal coronet or, three ostrich feathers, the centre one arg., and the exterior ones az. *Supporters*—On the dexter side a lion rampant, or, and on the sinister a unicorn arg. *Motto*—Concordia, integritas industria.

By royal licence dated 16 June, 1838, Lionel Rothschild, eldest son and heir of Nathan-Meyer Rothschild, was authorized and the heirs male of the body of the said father (upon whom the dignity of a baron of the Austrian Empire shall descend in virtue of the limitations of the letters patent or diploma granted to the said Nathan-Meyer Rothschild, dated at Vienna, 29 Sept. 1822), being respectively natural born subjects, to accept the dignity of a baron of Austria, and to bear the arms annexed thereto.

Seat—Tring Park, Herts.

Town House—148, Piccadilly, W. *Clubs*—Brooks's; St. James's; Turf Marlborough.

WANDSWORTH, BARON (Sydney-James Stern), of Wandsworth, co. Surrey; educated at Magdalene Coll., Camb.; J.P., cos. Surrey and London; hon. col. 4th vol. batt. East Surrey regt.; unsuccessfully contested Mid. Div. of Surrey, 1880 and 1884, the Borough of Ipswich, 1886, and the Tiverton Div. of Devonshire, 1885; elected M.P. for Stowmarket Div. of Suffolk, 1891, and sat for that constituency until his elevation to the Peerage; created a Viscount of the Kingdom of Portugal; *b.* 1845. His lordship is the eldest son of Viscount de Stern, of London, by Sophia, his wife, dau. of Aaron-Asher Goldsmid, Esq., of Cavendish Square, and niece of Sir Isaac Lyon Goldsmid, 1st bart.

Creation—19 July, 1895.

Arms—Or, on a pile, sa., a lion rampant of the last, a chief, gu., thereon two horses' heads erased, arg. *Crest*—A lion passant, ppr., gorged with a collar flory counterflory, gu., resting the dexter forepaw on an escocheon of the last charged with a horse's head erased, arg. *Supporters*—On either side a horse, arg., charged on the shoulder with an estoile within an annulet, all gu. *Motto*—Vincit perseverantia.

Seats—Bolney, Sussex; Hengrave Hall, Bury St. Edmunds. *Town Residence*—10, Great Stanhope Street, Mayfair, W. *Clubs*—Reform; Bachelors'; St. James's.

PIRBRIGHT, BARON (Henry de Worms, P.C., F.R.S.), of Pirbright, co. Surrey, J.P. for Surrey, and J.P. and D.L. for Middlesex, County of London, and Westminster, Barrister-at-Law, Fellow of King's Coll., London, a Royal Commr. of Patriotic Fund, M.P. for Greenwich 1880-85, and for East Toxteth Div. of Liverpool 1885-95, was

Parliamentary Sec. to Board of Trade, June, 1885 to Jan. 1886, and July, 1886 to Feb. 1888, and Under Sec. of State for the Colonies 1888-92, Member of Her Majesty's Privy Council 1888, President of International Conference on Sugar Bounties 1888, and as Plenipotentiary, signed the abolition treaty for Great Britain; *b*. 20 Oct. 1840 ; created a peer, 1895 ; *m*. 1st, 5 May, 1864, Fanny, eldest daughter of Baron Von Todesco, of Vienna, and by her has issue,

I. Alice-Henrietta-Antoinette-Evelina, *b*. 2 April, 1865 ; *m*. 1st, 28 April, 1886 John-Henry-Boyer Warner, Esq., of Quorn Hall, co. Leicester, D.L., who *d*. 1891. She *m*. 2ndly, 28 July, 1892, David-McLaren Morrison, Esq. of Calcutta.
II. Dora-Sophia-Emmy, *b*. 9 June, 1869.
III. Constance-Valéric-Sophie, *b*. 28 April, 1875 ; *m*. 4 Nov., 1895, Count Maximilian, Carl F. von Loewenstein Scharffeneck, Chamberlain at Court of Bavaria.

His lordship *m*. 2ndly, 25 Jan., 1887, Sarah, only dau. of Sir Benjamin-Samuel Phillips. He is the 3rd son of Solomon Benedict, Baron de Worms, by Henrietta, his wife, eldest dau. of Samuel-Moses Samuel, Esq., of Park Crescent.

Lineage.
(*See* DE WORMS, *Foreign Titles*.)

Creation—Nov. 15, 1895.
Arms—(Blazon in Patent from FRANZ JOSEPH I., Emperor of Austria). Quarterly : 1st and 4th, az., a key in bend, or; 2nd, or, an eagle displayed, sa.; 3rd, or, an eagle displayed respecting the sinister, sa., on an escutcheon of pretence, gu., a right hand couped ppr., grasping three arrows, two in saltire and one in pale, barbs upwards, or, barbed argent. *Crest*—Out of a ducal coronet, or, a plume of five ostrich feathers, 1st, 3rd and 5th, or, 2nd, gu., 4th, az. *Supporters*—Two lions rampant or, langued gu., collared az., chained gold, pendant from the collars, two escutcheons arg., each charged with a squirrel sejant on a branch of hazel turned up behind its back cracking a nut, ppr. *Motto*—Vinctus non victus.
Seat—Henley Park, Guildford, Surrey. *Town Residence*—42, Grosvenor Place, S.W. *Clubs*—Carlton ; Junior Carlton ; St. Stephen's.

FOREIGN TITLES.

GEORGE DE WORMS, BARON DE WORMS, an Hereditary Baron of the Austrian Empire, of Milton Park, Egham, D.L. and J.P. for Surrey, Middlesex, and Westminster, Knight Grand Commander of the I. and R. Austrian Order of Francis Joseph, *b*. 16 Feb. 1829 ; *m*. 18 April, 1860, Louisa, only dau. of the late Baron de Samuel, and has issue,

I. ANTHONY-DENIS-MAURICE-GEORGE, *b*. 4 Jan. 1869.
II. Percy-George, *b*. 3 Nov. 1873.
I. Henrietta-Emmy-Louisa-Amelia, *b*. 17 Aug. 1875.

Lineage.

SOLOMON-BENEDICT DE WORMS, D.L. Middlesex, *b.* 8 Feb. 1801; son of Benedict Worms, of Frankfort-on-the-Main, by Jeanette Von Rothschild, his wife, eldest dau. of Mayer-Amschel Von Rothschild, of that city, and sister of the late Baron Nathan-Mayer de Rothschild, of London. Created hereditary baron of the Austrian empire by imperial letters patent, dated at Vienna, 23 April, 1871, and by royal licence, 10 Aug., 1874, was granted by H.M. Queen Victoria, permission that he and his descendants should use the title in th's country. He *m.* 11 July, 1827, Henrietta, eldest dau. of Samuel-Moses Samuel, Esq., of Park Crescent, by whom (who *d.* 24 Jan. 1815) he has,

I. GEORGE, present baron.

II. Anthony-Mayer, *b.* 12 Oct. 1830, *m.* 1 July, 1860, Emma-Augusta, dau. of Baron Frederick Von Schey, of Vienna, and *d.* 2 Nov. 1864, having issue,
    1 Nina, *b.* 17 April, 1861; *m.* 19 July, 1880, to Baron George-Henry Levi, of Florence.
    2 Laura, *b.* 11 June, 1862; *d.* 3 March, 1863.
    3 Gertrude, *b.* 16 Dec. 1863; *d.* 2 Nov. 1889.

III. Henry (Rt. Hon.), P.C., F.R.S., created Baron PIRBRIGHT, 1895 (*see* that title).

I. Ellen-Henrietta, *b.* 13 Jan. 1836; *m.* 25 March, 1857, to Adolf Landauer, of Vienna (who *d.* 1885), and *d.* 29 Sept. 1894, leaving issue, one son and four daus.

Baron de Worms *d.* 20 Oct., 1882.

Arms—Quarterly: 1st and 4th, az., a key in bend, dexter, wards downwards, or; 2nd and 3rd, or, an eagle displayed, sa., over all, an escocheon, gu., a dexter arm, fe-sewise, couped at the wrist, ppr., the hand grasping three arrows, one in pale and two in saltire, arg. *Crest*—Out of an Austrian baron's coronet, five ostrich-feathers, or, gu., or, az., and or. *Supporters*—On either side, a lion, collared and chained, or. *Motto*—Vinctus non victus.

Seat—Milton Park, Egham, Surrey. *Town Residence*—17, Park Crescent, W. *Clubs*—Carlton; Conservative; Junior Carlton; City of London; Constitutional.

BARONETAGE.

GOLDSMID, The Late RIGHT HON. SIR JULIAN, Bart., of St. John's Lodge, Regent's Park, Middlesex; Baron de Goldsmid and de Palmeira, P.C., D.L. Sussex, M.A., Vice-Chancellor London Univ., barrister, M.P. for St. Pancras, previously M.P. for Honiton 1866 to 1868, and for Rochester 1870 to 1880, *b.* 8 Oct. 1838; *d.* 7 Jan. 1896; *s.* his uncle as 3rd bart. 1878; *m.* 31 March, 1868, Virginia, elder dau. of A. Philipson, Esq., of Florence, and by her (who *d.* 22 May, 1892) had,

I. Violet, *m.* 26 Nov. 1889, Sidney-Francis Hoffnung-Goldsmid, Esq., late Hawaiian Chargé d'Affaires, and has issue.

II. Edith, *m.* 15 July, 1890, Sir Charles Jessel, 1st Bart., and has issue.

PEERAGE, BARONETAGE, KNIGHTAGE. 105

III. Margherita, *m.* 9 Jan. 1894, William-George Raphael, Esq.
IV. Beatrice.
V. Maud, *m.* 20 Dec. 1894, Herbert M. Jessel, Esq., 17th lancers. (*see* JESSEL, Bart.)
VI. Theresa.
VII. Grace-Catherine.
VIII. Nora-Octavia.

Lineage.

This family was originally of Emden, in Germany, and settled in England in the early part of the last century.

BENEDICT GOLDSMID settled in Hamburg *circa* 1700, and had issue ; Moses, *d.* at Amsterdam, without issue, March, 1779 ; and Aaron. The 2nd son,

AARON GOLDSMID, of Leman Street, Goodman's Fields, co. Middlesex, and of the city of London, merchant, *m.* March, 1740, Catherine, dau. of Abraham De Vries, of Amsterdam, M.D. (who *d.* in 1780), and *d.* 3 June, 1782, leaving,

GEORGE, of Leman Street, *b.* in 1741 ; *m.* in 1763, Rebecca, dau. of Jonas Cohen, of Amersfort, near Utrecht, in Holland ; and *d.* 11 Dec. 1812, leaving issue.
ASHER, of whom hereafter.
Benjamin, of London, and Roehampton, co. Surrey, *b.* in May, 1755 ; *m.* Jesse, dau. of Israel-Levien Solomons, Esq., of Clapton ; and *d.* 11th April, 1808, leaving issue.
Abraham, of Finsbury Square, and Morden House, co. Surrey, *b.* 17 Dec. 1756 ; *m.* 17 Jan., 1783, Ann, dau. of Benjamin-Elias Daniel, Esq., of Amsterdam ; and *d.* 28 Sept. 1810, leaving issue. His eldest son, Aaron, *d.* 30 Oct. 1869.
Pearl, *m.* to Magnus-Joachim Moses ; and *d.* in 1821.
Esther, *m.* 1st, to Elias Joachim, Esq., of Great Prescot Street, Goodman's Fields ; and 2ndly, 14 March, 1802, Nathan Salomons, Esq., of Finsbury Square, and *d.* in 1811.
Polly, *m.* to Lyon de Symons, Esq. ; and *d.* in 1841.
Sarah, *m.* to Daniel Eliason, Esq. ; and *d.* in Dec. 1833.

The 2nd son,
ASHER GOLDSMID, Esq., of Finsbury Square, and of Merton Grove, co. Surrey, *m.* Rachel, dau. and heir of Alexander Keyser, Esq. of London (which lady *d.* in 1815), and *d.* 1 Nov. 1822, leaving issue.
ISAAC-LYON, created a Baronet.
Alexander, *b.* Oct. 1770 ; *m.* 12 Jan. 1814, Elizabeth, dau. of John Israel, Esq. of London, and by her (who *d.* in Jan. 1829) he left issue at his decease, in Jan. 1843.
Aaron-Asher, of Cavendish Square, *b.* in June, 1785 ; *m.* 19 March, 1817, Sophia, eldest dau. of Levy Salomons, Esq. of London, and of Frant, co. Sussex (who *d.* in April, 1835), and has issue.
Moses-Asher, *b.* in Jan. 1788 ; *m.* 1st, 22 Oct. 1817, Eliza, 2nd dau. of Levy Salomons, Esq., of London, and of Frant aforesaid (which lady *d.* 28 April, 1837) ; and 2ndly, 7 Nov. 1839, Sarah, sister of Sir Moses Montefiore, Bart., and dau. of Joseph Montefiore, Esq., of London, and *d.* 30 March, 1864, having had issue by his first wife.
Annie, *b.* in Jan. 1782 ; *d. unm.* in Nov. 1811.
Julia, *b.* in May, 1783 ; *m.* 25 Aug. 1813, to Philip Samuel, Esq. of Bedford Place, Russell Square ; and *d.* in 1823.

The eldest son,
I. ISAAC-LYON GOLDSMID, Esq., was created a baronet 15 Oct. 1841 ; he was also made Baron de Goldsmid and de Palmeira in Portugal, and was authorised, in 1846, by royal licence, to use his Portuguese honours in this country ; he was an officer of the Rose of Brazil ; and was invested with the Order of the Tower and Sword ; he was *b.* 13 Jan. 1778 ; *m.* 29 April, 1804, Isabel, 2nd dau. of Abraham Goldsmid, of Morden, Surrey, and by her (who *d.* 17 Nov. 1860) had issue,

I. Benjamin, *b.* in 1807 ; *d.* in the same year.
II. FRANCIS-HENRY, 2nd bart.
III. Daniel, *b.* in July, 1809 ; *d.* in Oct. 1815.
IV. Charles-Harrington, *b.* in 1811 ; *d.* in the same year.
V. Frederick-David, of Somerhill, Kent, M.P. for Honiton, *b.* 31 Jan. 1812 ; *m.* 23 July, 1834, Caroline, only dau. of Philip Samuel, Esq. of Bedford Place, and *d.* 18 March, 1866, having by her (who *d.* 24 Aug. 1885) had,
1 JULIAN, 3rd and present bart.
2 Walter-Henry, *b.* 17 Feb. 1840 ; *d.* 25 April, 1865.
3 Albert-Abraham, *b.* 9 March, 1841 ; *d.,* 1864.
1 Helen, *m.* 1855, Lionel Lucas, Esq., who *d.* 1862.

2 Mary-Ada, *m.* 29 Oct. 1856, Frederick-D. Mocatta, Esq.
3 Isabel.
4 Flora.
5 Emma-Catherine.
VI. George, *b.* May, 1813; *d.* Oct. 1815.
I. Anna-Maria, *d.* 8 Feb. 1889, aged 83.
II. Augusta, *m.* in Sept. 1835, to Elias Mocatta, Esq. of Chester Terrace, Regent's Park, and *d.* 23 Jan. 1838, leaving a dau., Constance.
III. Rachel, *m.* 24 June, 1840, to Count Solomon-Henry Avigdor, who *d.* 1871.
IV. Caroline.
V. Emma, *m.* 7 May, 1850, to Nathaniel Montefiore, Esq. (who *d.* 1883), and her second but eldest surviving son, Claude-Joseph Montefiore, assumed by Royal Licence dated 22nd Feb. 1883, the surname of GOLDSMID in addition to and before that of MONTEFIORE, and the arms of Goldsmid quarterly.
VI. Julia, *d.* at Nervi, near Genoa, 8 March, 1870.

Sir Isaac was D.L. for Middlesex and Sussex, and J.P. for the former. He *d.* 27 April, 1852, and was *s.* by his son.
II. SIR FRANCIS-HENRY GOLDSMID, Q.C., M.P. for Reading, *b.* 1 May, 1808; *m.* 10 Oct. 1839, Louisa-Sophia, only dau. of Moses-Asher Goldsmid, Esq. of Gloucester Place. Sir Francis, who was Baron de Goldsmid and de Palmeira in Portugal, *d.* 2 May, 1878, and was *s.* by his nephew, SIR JULIAN GOLDSMID, the 3rd and present bart.

Creation—15 Oct. 1841.

Arms—Per saltire, erminois and ermine, on a chief, gu. a goldfinch, ppr., between two roses, or, (being the family arms); over all an escocheon, gu., charged with a tower, or, and ensigned by the coronet of a baron of Portugal. *Crest*—1st, out of the coronet of a baron of Portugal, ppr., a demi-dragon with wings elevated, or, holding in its claws a rose, gu., slipped, ppr. 2nd a demi-lion, arg., in the paws a bundle of twigs erect, or, banded, az. *Supporters*—Dexter, a lion, arg., ducally crowned and charged on the shoulder with a rose, gu., Sinister a wyvern with wings elevated, or, and charged on the shoulder with a rose, gu. *Mottoes*—Over crests, "Quis similis tibi in fortibus, Domine?" *Exod.* xv. 11. Under the arms, "Concordiâ et sedulitate."

Seat—Somerhill, Tunbridge. *Town House*—105, Piccadilly, W. *Clubs*—Athenæum; Brooks's; Reform; St. James's; Devonshire; and Burlington.

JESSEL, SIR CHARLES-JAMES, Bart. of Ladham House, Kent,

M.A., barrister, D.L. Kent, *b.* 11 May, 1860; created a baronet 1883; *m.* 15 July, 1890, Edith, dau. of Sir Julian Goldsmid, 3rd Bart., M.P., and has issue,

GEORGE, *b.* 28 May, 1891.
Nina-Dorothy, *b.* 2 July, 1893.

Lineage.

THE RIGHT HON. SIR GEORGE JESSEL, Knt., M.A., Master of the Rolls, *b.* 13 Feb. 1854, youngest son of Zadok-Aaron Jessel, Esq. of Putney, was educated and graduated at the London University; called to the Bar by the Hon. Society of Lincoln's Inn in 1847. He was made a Queen's Counsel and a Bencher in 1865, appointed Solicitor-General in 1871, nominated MASTER OF THE ROLLS in 1873, and chosen Vice-Chancellor of the London University in 1880. He represented Dover in parliament from 1868 to 1873. He *m.* 20 Aug. 1856, Amelia, eldest dau. of Joseph Moses, Esq. and had issue,

I. CHARLES-JAMES, created a Baronet in 1883.
II. Herbert-Merton, lieut. 17th lancers, b. 27 Oct. 1866.
I. Emma, b. 27 Aug. 1857 ; m. 27 June, 1877, Ludwig-Nathan Hardy, Esq.
II. Constance, b. 6 Oct. 1858 ; m. 24 Aug. 1883, Edward-David Stern, Esq.
III. Lucy, b. 25 Nov. 1870.

Sir George Jessel, one of the most eminent lawyers of his time, d. 21 March, 1883. Shortly after, in recognition of his great services, a baronetcy was conferred on his son.

Creation—25 May, 1883.

Arms—Az. a fesse raguly erm. betw. three eagles' heads erased arg., in the centre chief point a torch erect and fired ppr. *Crest*—A torch fessewise, fired ppr., surmounted by an eagle volant, arg., holding in the beak a pearl also arg. *Motto*—Persevere.

Seat—Ladham House, Goudhurst, Kent. *Town Residence*—27, Lowndes Square, S.W. *Clubs*—Brooks's ; Garrick.

MONTAGU, SIR SAMUEL-, Bart. of South Stoneham House, co. Southampton, and of Kensington Palace Gardens, co. London, M.P. for the Whitechapel division of the Tower Hamlets, J.P. and D.L. for co. London, and J.P. for co. Southampton. By Royal Licence, 8 June, 1894, he and his issue were authorized to continue the surname of Montagu ; m. 5 Mar. 1862, Ellen, dau. of Louis Cohen, Esq. of Gloucester Place, Portman Square, London, and by her has issue,

I. LOUIS, b. 10 Dec. 1869.
II. Edwin, b. 6 Feb. 1879.
III. Gerald, b. 29 Sept. 1880.
IV. Lionel, b. 8 Sept. 1883.
I. Henrietta, m. 1885, Ernest-Louis Franklin, Esq., of Pembridge Gardens, London, and has issue.
II. Florence, m. 15 July, 1889, Montefiore-Simon Waley, Esq. of Dawson Place, Bayswater, London, and has issue.
III. Marion.
IV. Ethel, m. 12 April, 1893, Henry-D'Arcy Hart, Esq., of Pembridge Gardens, Bayswater.
V. Lilian-Helen.
VI. Elsie.

Lineage.

LOUIS-SAMUEL, Esq., of Hunter Street, Brunswick Square, co. Midx., formerly of Liverpool, co. Lancaster : b. 1794 ; d. 24 Aug. 1859 ; m. 17 Nov. 1819, Henrietta, dau. of Israel Israel, Esq. of Bury Stret, St. Mary Axe, London, and by her had, with other issue,

SIR SAMUEL, created a baronet, 23 June, 1894.

Creation—23 June, 1894.

Arms—Or, on a pile azuro between two palm trees eradicated in base proper, a tent, argent. *Crest*—A stag statant, holding in the mouth a sprig of palm, proper, in front of a flag-staff erect, gold, therefrom flowing to the dexter, a banner, azure, charged with a lion rampant, or. *Motto*—Swift, yet sure.

Seat—South Stoneham House, Southampton. *Town Residence*—12, Kensington Palace Gardens, W. *Clubs*—Reform ; National Liberal.

MONTEFIORE, SIR FRANCIS-ABRAHAM, Bart. of Worth Park, Sussex, D.L., High Sheriff co. Kent, 1889 and 1894 ; co. Sussex, 1895 ; *b.* 10 Oct. 1860 ; created a Baronet, 16 Feb. 1886 ; *m.* 14 Aug. 1888, Mlle. Marianne von Gutmann, of Vienna.

Lineage.

MOSES VITA MONTEFIORE, of the city of London, who *d.* 13 Nov. 1789, and was buried at Mile End, left, by Esther, his wife, dau. of Mossaod Racah, four sons and two daus., viz.,

DAVID, of London, *b.* 21 Sept. 1755 ; *d. s.p.*
Samuel, *b.* 9 Feb. 1757 ; *m.* Grace, dau. of Abraham Mocatta.
JOSEPH, of whom presently.
Eleazer, *b.* 4 April, 1761 ; *m.* 5 July, 1797, Judith, dau. of Jacob-Joseph Levi, and had issue. His 2nd son, Joseph-Barron, *d.* 4 Sept. 1893, aged 91.
Judith.
Sarah.

The third son,

JOSEPH MONTEFIORE, of London, *b.* 15 Oct. 1759 ; *m.* Rachael, dau. of Abraham Mocatta, and by her (who *d.* 27 Aug. 1841, aged 81) left at his decease, 11 Jan. 1804 (with four daus.), three sons,

I. MOSES (Sir), Bart. of East Cliffe Lodge, Isle of Thanet, Kent ; *b.* 24 Oct. 1784 ; *m.* 10 June, 1812, Judith, dau. of Levi-Barent Cohen, Esq., which lady *d.* 24 Sept. 1862. Sir Moses, who served as sheriff of London and Middlesex in 1837, and as high sheriff of Kent in 1845, was knighted at Guildhall, 9 Nov. 1837, on the occasion of the Queen's visit to the city, and was created a baronet, 23 July, 1846. He *d.* 28 July, 1885, when his title became extinct.
II. ABRAHAM, of whom presently.
III. Horatio-Joseph, of London, *m.* 1823, Sarah, dau. of Daniel Mocatta, and *d.* 4 Sept. 1893, aged 91.

The second son,

ABRAHAM MONTEFIORE, Esq., of Stamford Hill, Middlesex, who *m.* 1st, Mary, dau. of George Hall, and by her had one dau., Mary, *m.* B. Mocatta, and *d. s. p.* He *m.* 2ndly, Henrietta, dau. of Meyer-A. Rothschild, of Frankfort, banker, and by her (who *d.* 19 Feb. 1866) left issue,

I. JOSEPH-MEYER, of whom presently.
II. Nathaniel, *b.* 23 Sept. 1819 ; *m.* 7 May, 1850, Emma, dau. of Sir Isaac-Lyon Goldsmid, 1st bart. of St. John's Lodge, and *d.* 28 March, 1883, having had, Leonard, *b.* 1853, *d.* 6 Sept. 1879 ; Claude-Joseph, assumed by Royal Licence, dated 22 Feb. 1883, the surname of Goldsmid, in addition to and after that of Montefiore, and the arms of Goldsmid and Montefiore quarterly ; Charlotte, *m.* Sept. 1884, to Lewis MacIvor, Esq.
II. Louisa, *m.* 1840, to Sir A. de Rothschild, Bart., who *d.* 1876.

The eldest son,

JOSEPH-MEYER MONTEFIORE, Esq , of 49, Stanhope Street, Mayfair, and Worth Park, Crawley, Sussex, J.P. and D.L., high sheriff 1870, *b.* 16 May, 1816, *m.* 1 Feb. 1860, Henriette-Francisca, dau. of S.-B. Tickel, Esq., and *d.* 9 Oct. 1880, leaving two sons,

FRANCIS-ABRAHAM, now SIR FRANCIS-ABRAHAM MONTEFIORE, Bart.
Edward-Mayer, b. 16 April, 1862.
Creation—16 Feb. 1886.
Arms—Arg., a cedar-tree, between two mounts of flowers, ppr.; on a chief, az., a dagger, erect, ppr.; pommel and hilt, or, between two mullets of six points, gold. *Crest*—Two mounts, as in the arms, therefrom issuant a demi-lion, or, supporting a flag-staff, ppr., thereon hoisted a forked pendant, flying towards the sinister, az., inscribed Jerusalem, in Hebrew characters, gold. *Supporters* (by Royal Warrant, dated December 10, 1886)—*Dexter*, a lion guardant, or. *Sinister*, a stag proper, attired, or, each supporting a flagstaff, proper, therefrom flowing a banner to the dexter, azure, inscribed "Jerusalem" in Hebrew characters, gold. *Motto*—Think and thank.

Seat—Worth Park, Crawley. *Town Residence*—42, Upper Grosvenor Street, W. *Clubs*—Carlton; Marlborough; Bachelors'.

SALOMONS, SIR DAVID-LIONEL, Bart., of Broomhill, Tunbridge Wells, co. Kent, M.A., barrister-at-law, J.P. and D.L. for co. Kent, and High Sheriff, 1881, mayor of Tunbridge Wells, 1895, b. 28 Jan. 1851; s. his uncle as 2nd bart., under a special limitation, 18 July, 1873; m. 20 July, 1882, Laura, dau. of Baron de Stern, of 4, Hyde Park Gate, London, and has,

I. DAVID-REGINALD-HERMAN-PHILLIP, b. 13 Oct. 1885.
I. Maud-Julia.
II. Sybel-Gwendolen.
III. Vera-Frances.
IV. Ethel-Dorothy.

Lineage.

LEVY SALOMONS, Esq. of Bury Street, St. Mary Axe, and Frant, co. Sussex (son of Solomon Salomons, Esq.), was b. 16 Jan. 1774, and m. 1795, Matilda de Mitz, of Leyden, in Holland, and by her (who d. 19 Feb. 1838) had issue,
  I. Philip, of Brunswick Terrace, Brighton. b. 30 May, 1796; m. 10 April, 1850, Emma, dau. of Jacob Montefiore, Esq. of Sydney, N.S. Wales, and d. 28 Jan. 1867, having by her (who d. 2 June, 1859) had issue,
    DAVID-LIONEL, present baronet.
    Laura-Matilda, m. 29 May, 1873, to Edward Lucas, Esq.
    Stella-Rosalind-Jeanetta, m. 1877, George-Edmond Paget, Esq.
  II. DAVID, created a baronet.
  III. Joseph, b. 17 April, 1802; m. 20 Oct. 1824, Rebecca, dau. of Joseph Montefiore, and d. Jan. 1829, having by her (who d. 8 July, 1869) had issue, 1 Sophia, m. 20 April, 1852, to Aaron Goldsmid, Esq. of Bryanston Square; 2 Henrietta-Rachael, m. 17 Jan. 1849, to Lionel-Benjamin Cohen, Esq., and d. 29 April, 1859; 3 Matilda, m. 28 July, 1847, to Jacob Waley, Esq., barrister-at-law.
  I. Sophia, m. 19 March, 1817, to Aaron-Asher Goldsmid, Esq. of Cavendish Square, who d. 2 Nov. 1860.
  II. Eliza, m. 22 Oct. 1817, to Moses-Asher Goldsmid, Esq. of Glcucester Place, Portman Square, and d. 28 April, 1837.
  III. Esther, d. unm. 17 Oct. 1841.
Mr. Salomons d. Jan. 1843; his 2nd son,

DAVID SALOMONS, Esq., M.P. for Greenwich, J.P. and D.L. for Kent, Sussex, and Middlesex, an alderman of the city of London, barrister-at-law, *b.* 22 Nov. 1797; *m.* 1st, 18 April, 1825, Jeanette, dau. of Salmon Cohen, Esq. of Canonbury House, Middlesex, but by her (who *d.* March, 1867) had no issue; and 2ndly, 23 Sept. 1872, to Cecilia, widow of P.-J. Salomons, Esq. of Upper Wimpole Street. She *d.* 23 March, 1892. Sir David was sheriff of London and Middlesex, 1835-36; high sheriff of Kent in 1839-40; Lord Mayor of the city of London 1856-57; he was created a baronet 26 Oct. 1869, with limitation, in default of male issue, to his nephew, the present SIR DAVID-LIONEL SALOMONS, Bart. Sir David *d.* 18 July, 1873.

Creation—26 Oct. 1869.

Arms—Per chevron, gu. and sa., a chevron, vair, between (in chief) two lions rampant, double queued, or, each holding between the paws a plate, charged with an ermine spot, and in base a cinquefoil, erminois. *Crest*—A mount, vert, thereon issuant out of six park-pales, or, a demi-lion douł lequeued, gu., holding between the paws a bezant charged with an ermine spot. *Motto*—Deo adjuvante.

Seat—Broomhill, Tunbridge Wells, Kent. *Clubs*—Grafton; City of London; City Liberal; and Savage.

SASSOON, SIR ALBERT-ABDALLAH-DAVID, Bart., C.S.I.,

of Kensington Gore, London, and of Eastern Terrace, Brighton, late Member of the Legislative Council of Bombay, *b.* 25 July, 1818; *m.* in 1838, Hannah, dau. of Meyer Moses, Esq. of Bombay, and by her (who *d.* Jan. 1895) has had issue,

I. Joseph-Albert, *b.* 24 Feb. 1843; *m.* June, 1875, Rebecca, dau. of Jacob-A. Hyeem, Esq. of Calcutta, and *d.* 27 March, 1884.
II. EDWARD, capt. Middlesex yeo. cav., D.L. co. Sussex, *b.* 20 June, 1856; *m.* 19 Oct. 1887, Aline-Caroline, dau. of Baron Gustave de Rothschild, and has issue, Philip-Albert-Gustave-David, *b.* in 1888; Sybil-Rachel-Betty-Cécile, *b.* 20 Jan. 1894.
I. Aziza, *b.* 8 Dec. 1839; *m.* 17 Jan. 1853, Ezekiel-J. Abraham.
II. Rachel, *b.* 13 April, 1841; *m.* 8 Sept. 1856, Aaron-M. Gubbay.
III. Mozelle, *b.* 13 Oct. 1853; *m.* 6 Sept. 1870, Elias-David Ezra, who *d.* 3 Feb. 1886.

Sir Albert was made a C.S.I. in 1866, received the honour of Knighthood in 1872, and was created a Baronet in 1890. He has the Persian Order of Lion and Sun.

Lineage.

DAVID SASSOON, of Bombay, East Indies, Merchant and Banker, *b.* 1793, at Bagdad, naturalised at Bombay, *d.* at Poona, 7 Nov. 1864, and was buried there; *m.* 1st at Bagdad, 1808, Hannah, dau. of Abdallah Joseph, of Bagdad, and by her (who *d.* 1826), had with other issue an elder son,

PEERAGE, BARONETAGE, KNIGHTAGE. 111

ALBERT-ABDALLAH-DAVID, who was created a bart. as above.
Creation—22 March, 1890.
Arms—Or, a palm tree eradicated ppr. between on the dexter a pomegranate, also ppr., and on the sinister a branch of laurel fructed, vert, both ppr., on a chief az. a lion passant of the first, in the dexter paw a rod erect, gold. *Crest*—On a mount vert, a fern brake surmounted by a dove volant, having in the beak a laurel branch all ppr., the wings semé of estoiles, or. *Motto*—Candide et constanter.
Residences—25, Kensington Gore, S.W.; 1, Eastern Terrace, Brighton; Sans Souci, Bombay; Garden Reach, Poonah.

KNIGHTAGE.

BENJAMIN, SIR BENJAMIN, Knt. (1889), Mayor of Melbourne 1887 and 1889; son of Moses Benjamin, Esq., of Melbourne; *b* 1834; *m*. Fanny, dau. of —— Cohen, Esq., N.S.W.

SIR ISRAEL HART, Knt. (1895); Alderman of Leicester, and Mayor of that borough 1884, 1885, 1886, and 1893; J.P. for Leicester; son of M. Hart, of Canterbury, Kent, by Frances, his wife, dau. M. Moses, of Cheltenham; *b*. 16 Feb. 1835; *m*. 7 April, 1875, a dau. of Samuel Moses, late of Pembridge Square, Bayswater. ——Ashleigh, Knighton, Leicester.

SIR AARON-HENRY ISAACS, Knt. (1887), J.P. for City of London; Alderman of London, 1883-91; Sheriff of London and Middlesex, 1887; and Lord Mayor of London, 1889-90; son of Michael Isaacs, by Sara, his wife, dau. of Aaron-Enrique Mendoza; *b*. 15 Aug. 1830; *m*. Sept. 1848, Eleanor, dau. of Alexander-McDonald Rowland, Esq., of the 9th Regt.——The Hawthorns, Crescent Road, Sydenham, S.E.; City Carlton Club.

SIR GEORGE-HENRY LEWIS, Knt. (1893); admitted a solicitor, 1856; son of James Graham Lewis, Esq., by Harriet, his wife, dau, of Henry Davis, Esq.; *b*. 21 April, 1833; *m*. Feb. 1867, Elizabeth, dau. of Ferdinand Eberstadt, Esq. of Mannheim, Germany.——88, Portland Place, W.; Ashley Cottage, Walton-on-Thames; Portland and Devonshire Clubs.

SIR PHILIP MAGNUS, Knt. (1886), Director and Sec. of the City and Guilds of London Technical Institute; educated at Univ. Coll., London, and Berlin Univ.; B.A. 1863; was Professor of Mechanics at the Catholic Univ. Coll., Kensington; Member of the Roy. Commn. on Technical Instruction, 1881-84; Principal of the Finsbury Technical Coll., 1883-85; Gov. of Univ. Coll. London; son of John Jacob Magnus, Esq.; *b*. 1842; *m*. 1870, Kate, dau. of E. Emanuel, J.P. of Southsea.——16, Gloucester Terrace, W., and Tangley Hill, Chilworth, co. Surrey; Savage, and Athenæum Clubs.

NATHAN, SIR GUSTAVUS, Knt. (1891), was Consul (unpaid) at Vienna, 1877-83; and Consul-General, 1883-91; son of N. P. Nathan, Esq.; *b.* 1835; 24, Queen Anne's Gate Gardens, S.W.

SIR JULIAN-EMANUEL SALOMONS, Knt. (1891); called to the Bar, Gray's Inn, 1861; Q.C.; is M.L.C. and Ch. Justice of New South Wales; only son of Emanuel Salomons, Esq. of Birmingham; *m.* 1862, Louisa, dau. of Maurice Salomons, Esq.—— Sydney, N.S.W.

SIR SAUL SAMUEL, K.C.M.G. (1882), C.M.G. (1874), C.B. (1886), appointed a magistrate of territory of New South Wales, 1846; and elected a M.C.L. of that colony, 1854, was an M.L.A. 1857-72; in 1872 he was nominated to a seat in the Legislative Council, in which chamber, as Vice-Pres. of Executive Council, he represented the Govt.; was Min. for Finance and Trade in 1859, 1865, 1866, 1868, 1869, and 1870; and Postmaster-Gen. 1872-75, 1877, and 1879-80; since when he has been Agent-Gen. for N.S. Wales in England; represented in 1870 at Melbourne, and in 1873 at Sydney, the colony of N.S. Wales at Conferences of Delegates from all the Australian colonies to consider matters of common interest; while Postmaster-Gen., in 1873, as Special Commr. visited New Zealand, England, and United States of America to arrange for establishing a mail service between the United Kingdom and the Australasian colonies, by way of United States of America, and in the same year made a postal convention with United States Government: son of Sampson Samuel, Esq.; *b.* 2 Nov. 1820; *m.* 1st, 1857, Henrietta-Matilda, dau. of B.-G. Levein, Esq. of Victoria; *m.* 2ndly, 1877, Sara-Louise, dau. of E. Isaacs, Esq., J.P. of Auckland, New Zealand. ——15, Courtfield Gardens, S.W.; 5, Westminster Chambers, Victoria Street, S.W.; Whitehall Club.

SIR JOSEPH SEBAG MONTEFIORE, Knt. (1896); Consul General for Italy; nephew of the late Sir Moses Montefiore, to whose estates and heirlooms he succeeded; President of the Jewish Board of Deputies, 1896; *b.* 1822; *m.* Adelaide dau. of the late Louis Cohen, Esq., of Gloucester Place, Portman Square. ——4, Hyde Park Gardens, and East Cliff Lodge, Ramsgate.

SIR JOHN SIMON, Knt. (1886); educated at Univ. Coll. London (LL.B. 1841); Barrister-at-Law, 1842; created a serjeant-at-law 1864, and received patent of precedence 1868; has for several years retired from practice at the Bar; was 2nd Counsel in the State trial of Dr. Bernard, 1858, for complicity in the Orsini conspiracy to assassinate NAPOLEON III.; was M.P. for Dewsbury, 1868-88; son of Isaac Simon, Merchant, by Rebecca, his wife, only dau. of Jacob-Orobio Furtado, of Jamaica; *b.* 9 Dec. 1818; *m.* 12 July 1843, Rachael, dau. of Simeon-K. Salaman, Esq. of London. ——36, Tavistock Square, W.C. Reform, and Cobden Clubs.

SIR JULIUS VOGEL, K.C.M.G. (1875), C.M.G. (1872); educated, at London Univ. Sch.; elected a Member of the House of Representatives, New Zealand, 1869; has filled there the offices of Colonial Treasurer, 1867-73; Postmaster-Gen. 1873-75; Commr. of Customs and Prime Min., 1876; Agent-Gen. for New Zealand in London, 1876-81; and Colonial Treasurer and Postmaster-Gen. of New Zealand, 1884-87; son of Albert-Leopold Vogel, Esq. of London, by Phœbe, his wife, eldest dau. of Alexander Isaac, Esq. of Hatcham Grove, Surrey; *b.* 1835; *m.* 1867, Mary, dau. of W. A. Clayton, Esq., Colonial Architect, of New Zealand.——Junior Carlton, and St. Stephen's Clubs.

JEWISH MEMBERS OF PARLIAMENT.

COHEN, BENJAMIN LOUIS (C.), of 30, Hyde-park-gardens, W., son of Mr. Louis Cohen, founder of the firm of Louis Cohen and Sons, of 31, Throgmorton-street, E.C., born 1844, educated privately, and is a partner in the firm of Louis Cohen and Sons, and a member of the London Stock Exchange. Is a D.L. for the City of London, Governor of St. Bartholomew's, Bridewell, and Bethlehem Hospitals, member of the London County Council for the City from 1888, president of the Jewish Board of Guardians, a president of the London Orphan Asylum, vice-president of the Orphan Working School, and of the United Synagogue. *M.*, 1870, Louisa Emily, only daughter of the late Mr. Benjamin M. Merton. M.P. East Islington from 1892. 4,383 votes.

JESSEL, HERBERT. Successful Unionist Candidate by majority of 1,256, at bye-election to fill vacancy at South St. Pancras left by death of Sir Julian Goldsmid; second son of the late Sir Charles Jessel, M.R.; *b.* October 27th, 1866; *m.* Maud, fifth daughter of the late Sir Julian Goldsmid. Was at the time of his election Lieut. 17th Lancers, but has since resigned.

MARKS, HARRY HANANEL (C.), of Loudoun-hall, Grove-end-road, St. John's-wood, son of the Rev. Professor D. W. Marks, of Dorset-square, Regent's-park, by Cecilia, daughter of Mr. Mosley Wolff, of Liverpool, born 1855, educated at l'Athénée Royale of Brussels, and at University College, London, and is a journalist. Was for some time engaged in journalism in the United States, and is now editor and chief proprietor of the *Financial News*, which he established in 1844. Has written "Small Change, or Leaves from a Reporter's Note-Book," and a *brochure* on the Metropolitan Board of Works, and was a member of the first London County Council for East Marylebone, and since 1895 for St. George's-in-the-East. *M.*, 1884, Annie Estelle, daughter of the late Mr. William Benjamin, of Montreal. M.P., St. George (Tower Hamlets). 1,583 votes.

MONTAGU, SIR SAMUEL, Bart. (R.), of 12, Kensington-palace-gardens, W., and South Stoneham House, near Southampton, son of the late Mr. Louis Samuel, of London, but who established himself early in the century at Liverpool as a watchmaker and silversmith, born 1832, receiving the name of Montagu as his surname, educated privately, and at the High School of the Mechanics' Institution, now the Liverpool Institute. The family returned to London in 1847, and in 1853 Mr. Montagu established the firm of Samuel Montagu and Co., foreign bankers, 60, Old Broad-street, of which firm he continues the head. Is a J.P. for London and Hampshire, a D.L. for the Tower Hamlets, for many years a member of the Jewish Board of Guardians, is a member of the Board of Deputies, of the Council of the United Synagogue, and of other Jewish Institutions. In 1875 visited Jerusalem, in 1882 Galicia, in 1884 United States, and in 1886 Russian Poland, for philanthropic purposes. Created a baronet 1894. *M.*, 1862, Ellen, youngest daughter of the late Mr. Louis Cohen, of the Stock Exchange, and a grand-niece of the late Sir Moses Montefiore. M.P. Whitechapel division of Tower Hamlets from 1885. 2,009 votes.

ROTHSCHILD, BARON FERDINAND JAMES de (L.U.), of Waddesdon Manor, near Aylesbury, and 143, Piccadilly, second son of the late Baron Anselm de Rothschild, born 1839. Is a J.P. and D.L. for Buckingham (High Sheriff 1883). *M.*, 1865, his cousin Evelina, youngest daughter of the late Baron Rothschild, but was left a widower the following year, and subsequently founded the Evelina Hospital for Women and Children in her memory. Elected M.P. for the Borough of Aylesbury on the elevation of his cousin to the peerage in 1885, and has represented the Aylesbury division of the county from 1885. Unopposed.

SAMUEL, HARRY S. (C.), of 87, Lancaster-gate, Hyde-park, son of the late Mr. Horatio S. Samuel, by Henrietta Montefiore, niece of the late Sir Moses Montefiore, Bart., born 1853, educated at Eastbourne College and St. John's College, Cambridge (B.A. 1875), and has held a commission in the 1st Middlesex Volunteer Royal Engineers. *M.*, 1878, Miss Rose Beddington. M.P., Limehouse (Tower Hamlets), 1895. 2,661 votes.

STRAUSS, ARTHUR (L.U.), son of Mr. Strauss, of Mayence, born 1847, and educated at a German University (first prizes in mathematics and Latin and Greek). Is a metal merchant, member of the firm of A. Strauss and Co., of 16, Rood-lane, director of several Cornish and foreign tin mines, well known in metal circles for breaking the powerful tin-smelting ring, as also for his successful opposition to M. Secretan's tin and copper ring, being the largest tin and copper merchant. M.P., Camborne division, 1895. 3,166 votes.

JEWS IN THE NAVY, ARMY, AND AUXILIARY FORCES.

THE following provisional list of Jewish officers has been kindly compiled for this Year-Book by the Rev. F. L. Cohen, Acting Jewish Chaplain of the Aldershot District. He remarks that it is extremely difficult to draw out such a list, as many officers, having names strictly Jewish, are not willing to be included. With regard to the number of men serving in the ranks, it is impossible to get any returns worth considering, as the official numbers only refer to the "rankers" who declare themselves as Jews. Mr. Cohen makes the following rough maximum estimate of the numbers of all ranks serving in the various branches of Her Majesty's Forces:—

Royal Navy	20 Jews.	(2 on the books 1st January 1896.*)
Regular Army	160 ,,	(51 on the books 1st January, 1896.†)
Royal Marines	10 ,,	
Hon. Artillery Company	12 ,,	
Militia	40 ,,	(12 on the books 1st January, 1896.†)
Yeomanry Cavalry	12 ,,	
Volunteers	350 ,,	

Jewish officers now serving 1896:

Royal Navy.

Lieut. Yates	H.M.S.
Lieut. H. E. Blumberg	Royal Marine Light Infantry.

Regular Army.

Colonel A. E. W. Goldsmid	Commanding 41st Regmtl. Dist.
Second Lieut. H. J. J. Stern	13th Hussars.
Major E. N. Henriques	Royal Artillery.
Captain F. L. Nathan	ditto.
Lieut. H. S. Seligman	ditto.
Major J. J. Leverson	Royal Engineers.
Major G. F. Leverson	ditto.
Captain M. Nathan	ditto.
Lieut. W. S. Nathan	ditto.
Second Lieut. O. G. Brandon	ditto.
Lieut. H. A. Leverson	Royal Inniskilling Fusiliers.
Lieut. F. D. Behrend	West Riding Regiment.
Second Lieut. W. E. Drielsma	ditto.
Lieut. F. G. E. Cannot	South Staffordshire Regiment.
Lieut. F. M. Raphael	South Lancashire Regiment.
Captain E. S. D. Goldsmidt	Welsh Regiment.

---

* Kindly communicated by the First Lord of the Admiralty.

† These figures have been kindly supplied by the Secretary of State for War.

Major F. P. Lousada	York and Lancaster Regiment.
Captain D. E. Mocatta	Indian Staff Corps.
Brigade-Surgeon-Lieut. Colonel S. M. Salaman, M.D.	Indian Medical Service.
Surgeon-Lieut. A. Leventon	ditto.
Captain H. S. Samuel	Army Pay Department.
Assistant Surveyor A. P. Durlacher, A.M.I.C.E.	Civil Staff, Royal Engineers.
Rev. F. L. Cohen	Acting Chaplain.

Militia.

Major B. Lewis-Barned	Kent Artillery.
Captain G. E. Joseph	Lancashire Artillery.
Lieut. H. S. Oppenheimer	3rd Bn. Royal Lancaster Regt.
Captain R. P. Jessel	3rd Bn. Middlesex Regiment.
Captain E. C. Oppenheim	3rd Bn. Royal Irish Rifles.
Captain E. C. Arnold	4th Bn. Royal Irish Rifles.
Lieut. C. F. Drielsma	3rd Bn. Royal Irish Fusiliers.
Second Lieut. A. F. Joseph	7th Bn. Rifle Brigade.

Yeomanry Cavalry.

Captain W. J. Levi	Buckinghamshire Yeomanry.
Lieut. Hon. L. W. Rothschild	ditto.
Captain E. D. Stern	Berks Yeomanry.
Captain H. M. Jessel, M.P.	ditto.
Captain E. A. Sassoon	Middlesex Yeomanry.

Volunteers.

Captain C. A. Emanuel	1st Hampshire Vol. Artillery.
Captain E. A. Behrend	1st Lancashire Vol. Artillery.
Captain H. D. Behrend	ditto.
Second Lieut. B. Stern	ditto.
Captain S. G. Goldschmidt	7th Lancashire Vol. Artillery.
Lieut. O. B. Goldschmidt	ditto.
Major B. S. Jacobs	2nd East Yorkshire Vol. Artillery.
Lieut. P. Hildesheim	2nd Middlesex Vol. Artillery.
Captain C. Q. Henriques	1st Middlesex Vol. Engineers.
Lieut. C. S. Montefiore	ditto.
Second Lieut. C. S. Mendl	ditto.
Lieut. W. Oppeheim	2nd Lancashire Vol. Engineers.
Major D. de L. Cohen	2nd Tower Hamlets Vol. Engrs.
Second Lieut. J. J. de L. Cohen	ditto.
Second Lieut. D. A. H. Levy	ditto.
Capt. G. R. Murray Campbell	4th Vol. Bn. Rl. West Surrey Regt.
Capt. F. Murray Campbell	ditto.
Lieut. L. G. Marcus	ditto.
Capt. A. M. Brown	1st Vol. Bn. Royal Fusiliers.
Major M. A. Blumenthal	2nd Vol. Bn. Royal Fusiliers.
Capt. A. Levy Lever	ditto.
Capt. P. Carlebach	ditto.
Lieut. A. Pam	ditto.

Second Lieut. H. D'A. Blumberg	3rd Vol. Bn. Liverpool Regt.
Hon. Col. Lord Wandsworth	4th Vol. Bn. East Surrey Regt.
Capt. H. D. Sichel	3rd Vol. Bn. West Riding Regt.
Major M. Emanuel	2nd Vol. Bn. Hampshire Regt.
Second Lieut. B. A. Elkin	1st Middlesex Vol. Rifles.
Second Lieut. J. W. Cohen	13th Middlesex Vol. Rifles.
Capt. E. Parker	22nd Middlesex Vol. Rifles.
Major H. H. Montagu	3rd London Vol. Rifles.
Lieut. J. H. Montagu	ditto.
Second Lieut. C. D. Enoch	ditto.
Capt. S. L. Mandleberg	4th Vol. Bn. Manchester Regt.
Second Lieut. M. C. V. Hertz	ditto.
Second Lieut. H. T. Dreschfeld	5th Vol. Bn. Manchester Regt.
Lieut.-Col. F. A. Lucas	20th Middlesex Vol. Rifles.
Surgeon.-Capt. H. Dutch	1st Tower Hamlets Vol. Rifles.
Lieut. B. Samuel	1st Cadet Bn. King's Royal Rifle Corps.

Colonial Volunteers.

Several, headed by Colonel Harris, of Kimberley.

There are some Jewish Native Officers in the Bombay Infantry.

JEWISH CELEBRITIES OF THE NINETEENTH CENTURY.

THE following list was originally compiled in 1885, and for the purpose of comparative estimate of Jewish ability ("Journ. Anthrop. Soc.", 1887). It is now published with additions up to date. The principle on which it was compiled was only to include those Jews who had found their way into recognised lists of celebrities, such as Cooper's "Men of the Times," Vapereau's "Dictionnaire," and works of similar standing. This must be held as excuse for the admission of some names, and omission of some others. I have to thank Dr. Adler, Prof. Bacher, Dr. Liebermann and Mons. Théodore Reinach for kind revision and completion. When only one date is given, it is that of birth; where none, the name does not occur in the ordinary authorities. Asterisks mark those who have been converted; an obelus, persons who had but one Jewish parent; and italics, Jewesses.

Abraham, E.	1833	French Dramatist.
Adam-Solomon	1818	French Sculptor.
Adler, Felix		U.S. Ethical Society.
Adler, Dr. Hermann	1839	Hebrew Scholar.
Adler, Dr. N. M.	1803–90	Hebrew Scholar.
Aguilar, Grace	1816–47	Writer.
Alexandre, A.	1766–1850	French Chessplayer.
Alexandre, J.	1804–76	French Manufacturer, Organs.
Alkan, C. V. M.	1803	French Musician.
Altschul, E.	1812	Dr., Homœopath.
Antokolski	1833	Russian Sculptor.
Arton, G.	1829	Italian Diplomatist.
Ascoli, G. I.	1829	Italian Scholar, Sanskrit.
Asser, T. B. C.	1838	Dutch Jurist.
Auerbach, B.	1812–82	German Novelist.
Bacharach, G.	1810	German Translator, into French.
Bacher, W.	1850	Orientalist.
Bamberger, L.	1823	German Politician.
Bandmann, D. E.	1839–89	Actor.
Bardeleben, H. A.	1819	Surgeon.
Barach, M.	1818	Journalist ("Dr. Märzroth").
Barnay, L.	1842	German Actor.
*Basevi, G.	1795–1845	Architect.
Bebel, F. A.	1840	Socialist.
*Beck, K.	1817	Austrian Poet.
Bedarride, J.	1804–69	French Jurisconsult.
Bedarrides, G. E.	1817	Politician.
Benamozegh, E.	1822	Hebraist. Cabbalist.
*Benary, F. F.	1805–9...	Orientalist.
Bendavid, L.	1762–1832	Mathematician.
*Benedict, Sir J.	1805–85	Musician.
*Benfey, Th.	1809–82	Scholar, Sanskrit.
Benisch, A.	1811–78	Jewish Journalist.
Benjamin, J. P.	1811–84	Lawyer, Politician.

Benloew, L.	1818	Philologist.
Bernays, J.	1834–82	Phil., Classic.
*Bernays, M.	1834	Literary Critic.
*_Bernhardt, S._	1844	Actress.
*Bernhardy	1800–75	Scholar, Classic.
Bernstein, A.	1812–87	German Novelist, pop. sc.
Bernstein, J.	1839	Physiologist.
Berson	d. 1894	German Aeronaut.
*Biesenthal, J. H.	1800	Hebrew, Convert.
Binger, L. G.	1856	Explorer of Senegal.
Bischoffsheim, L. R.	1800	Banker.
Bleichroeder, Gerson v.	1821	Banker.
Bloch, M.	1815	Hung. Phil., "Ballagi."
Block, M.	1816	French Statistician.
*Blowitz		"Times" Correspondent, Paris.
Blum, E.	1836	French Actor.
Blum, J.	1812	French Mathematician.
Blumenthal, O.	1805	Literateur, Journalist.
*Booth, J. B.	1776–1852	Dramatic Actor, U.S.
*Börne, L.	1786–1837	Litterateur, German. [Nelson."
Braham, J.	1774–1856	Singer, Composer of "Death of
Brandes, E.	1847	Danish Scholar, Sanskrit.
Brandes, G.	1842	Danish Literary Critic.
Breal, M.	1832	French Philologist.
Bresslau, Harry	1848	German Historian.
Bruch, Max	1838	Musician.
Brull		Composer "Golden Cross."
†Burnel, A.	1840–83	Indian Palæographer.
Busch, M.	1821	Bismarck's Boswell.
†Byron, H. J.	1835–87	Dramatist.
Cahen, S.	1796–1862	French Hebraist.
Canstatt, K. F.	1807–50	Doctor, "Jahresbericht."
Cantor, G.		Mathematician.
Carmoly, E.	1805–75	Hebraist.
*Cassell, P.	1827–93	German Christian Divine.
*Chwolson, D.	1815	Arabist.
Coen, G.	1847	Bibliographer.
Cohen, Georg	1845	German Political Economist.
Cohen, Hermann	1840	Philosopher, authority on Kant.
Cohen, Joseph	1817	French Journalist.
Cohen, Jules	1835	French Musician.
Cohn, A. ("August Metz.")	1819	Littérateur, Journalist, Dramatist, [all languages.
Cohn, F.	1828	German Botanist.
Cohn, H.	1838	German Physiologist of eyes.
Cohn, H. ("Père Hermann")	1821	Violinist.
Cohnheim, J.	1839	German Physiologist of nerves.
Comparetti, Domenico		Folklorist, Italian Scholar.
Consolo, B.	1815	Hebraist.
*Costa, Sir M.	1810–84	Musician.
Cowen, F. H.	1852	Musician.
Cremieux, Adolphe	1796–1881	Politician.

Cremieux, H. J.	1828 ...	Dramatist.
Cremona, L.	1830 ...	Mathematician.
*Da Costa, J.	1798–1860	Dutch Historian of Jews.
Daniel, H. J.	1804 ...	Sculptor.
Darmesteter, A.	1846–89	Philologist, Fr. Lexicographer.
Darmesteter, J.	1849–93	French Orientalist, Zend, Eng-
David, A. L.	1811–31	Philologist, Turkish. [lish.
David, F.	1810–73	Violinist.
David, F. B.	1796–1879	French Politician.
Davis, N.	1812–1882	Traveller, "Carthage"
Dawison, B.	1818–72	German Actor.
De Benedetti, S.	1820 ...	Hebraist.
D'Ennery	1815 ...	French Dramatist.
Derenbourg, J.	1811–95	French Hebraist, Arabist.
Deutsch, E.	1829–73	Orientalist, Hebraist.
*Disraeli, B. (Lord Beaconsfield)	1804–81	Novelist, Politician.
Disraeli, I.	1766–1848	Literary Critic, "Curiosities.'
Dollfus	1800 ...	Manufacturer.
*Dollfus, C.	1825 ...	French Politician.
*Dollfus, D. Ch.	1827 ...	French Litterateur.
Dreyfus, A.	... ...	French Dramatist.
Dreyfus, F.	... ...	French Politician.
†Ebers, G.	1837 ...	Egyptologist, Novelist.
*Eichthal, G. d'	1804 ...	Politician, Communist.
Emden, M. (Princessa de la Rocca)	1810 ...	Novelist (Sister to H. Heine).
Emin Pasha (Schnitzler)	1840–93	Traveller.
Feldmann, L.	1802 ...	Austrian Comedian.
Filipowski, H.	1817–72	Hebraist, Mathematician.
Fould, Ach.	1800–67	French Politician.
Franck, A.	1809–92	Littérateur, Philosopher.
Frankel, Z.	1801–75	Hebraist.
Frankl, L. A. (Ritter v. Hochwarth)	1810 ...	Austrian Poet.
†Franzos, K. E.	1848 ...	Novelist.
Freund, W.	1806 ...	Classic, Latin Dictionary.
Friedlander, D.	1834 ...	Jewish Scholar.
Friedlander, L.	1814 ...	German Classic Scholar, "Sitten-
Friedlander, M.	1833 ...	Hebraist. [geschichte Roms."
Fulda, Ludwig	1862 ...	German Dramatist.
Fürst, J.	1805–73	Hebraist.
*Gans, E.	1798–1839	Jurist.
Geiger, A.	1810–74	Hebraist, Theologian.
Geiger, Laz.	1829–70	Philologist.
Geiger, Lud.	1848 ...	Historian.
Glaser	... ...	Arabian Explorer.
Goldmark, K.	1832 ...	Musician "Queen of Sheba."
Goldschmidt, H.	1802–66	German Astronomer, discoverer of 14 Asteroids.
Goldschmidt, M.	1819 ...	Journalist, "Nord und Süd."
Goldsmid, Sir F.	1808–80	Politician, Philanthropist.
Goldsmid, Sir Julian	1838–96	Politician, Philanthropist.

JEWISH CELEBRITIES.

Goldstücker, T.	1819–72	Sanskritist.
Goldziher, I.	1850 ...	Orientalist, Arabist.
Goltz, Bogumil	1801–70	Humorous Writer.
Gompertz, B.	1778–1865	Mathematician.
Gomperz, T.	1853 ...	Hellenist.
Goodman, W.	1838 ...	Painter.
Goudchaux, M.	1797–1862	Dutch Politician.
Graetz, H.	1817–91	Jewish Historian.
Gross, Ferd.	1849 ...	Press, Dramatist.
Gumprecht, O.	1813 ...	Musical Critic.
*Halevy, J. E. F.	1799–1862	Musician.
Halevy, Joseph	1827 ...	Assyriologist.
†Halevy, Leon	1802–83	Littérateur.
*†Halevy, Lud...	1834 ...	Dramatist.
Hart, J. T.	1810–77	U.S. Littérateur.
Hart, S. A.	1806–81	Painter, R.A.
Hartmann, M.	1821 ...	Litterateur.
*Heine, G. (Ritter v. Geldern)	1805 ...	Journalist.
*Heine, H.	1799–1856	Poet.
*Heine, M.	1807 ...	Doctor, Court St. Petersburg
Heine, S.	1766–1844	Banker, Philosopher.
Heller, St.	1813 ...	Musician.
*Hellmuth, Bishop	1820 ...	Hebraist.
Hertz, Henrik	1798–1870	Salon.
Herz, H.	1806–88	Pianist.
Herz, Heinrich	... ...	Physicist.
Herz, J. S.	1797–1880	Pianist.
Herzberg, G. F.	1826 ...	Greek Historian.
Hiller, F.	1813 ...	Musician.
Hiller, Sel.	1831–92	Poet "Ahasver."
Hirsch, A.	1817 ...	Doctor, History, Geography, Pa-
Hirsch, Abr.	1828 ...	French Architect. [thology.
Hirsch, Baron M. de	1839–96	Financier, Philanthropist.
Holdheim, S.	1802–60	Hebrew Scholar.
Horrwitz, O.	1823–85	Chess Player.
*Herschel, C. L.	1750–1848	Astronomer.
†Herschel, Sir J. W.	1771–1851	Astronomer.
*Herschel, Sir W.	1738–1832	Astronomer.
†Heyse, P.	1830 ...	Novelist.
Israels, J.	1824 ...	Dutch Painter. [bians."
*Jacobi, C. G. J.	1804–51	German Mathematician, "Jaco-
Jacobs, J. A. M.	1812 ...	Painter.
Jacobson, E.	1833 ...	German Comedies.
Jacobson, H. F.	1804–68	Lawyer.
Jacoby, J.	1805–77	German Politician.
*Jaffe, P.	1819–70	Historian. (First Jewish Prof. Pruss. "Regesta Pontificum.")
Jeitteles, J. ("Julius Seidlitz")	1814 ...	Litterateur, Journalist.
Jessel, Sir G.	1824–83	Lawyer, M.R.
Joachim, J.	1831 ...	Musician.
Jellinek, A.	1821 ...	Hebraist.

Josephson, J. A.	1818	Musician.
Jonas, Em.	1827	French Musician.
Jost, J. M.	1793–1866	German Jewish Historian.
Judith, Mdme.	1827	French Actress.
Kalisch, D.	1820–72	Comedies.
Kalisch, L.	1814	Litterateur, Poet.
Kalisch, M. M.	1828–85	Hebraist.
Kaufmann, D.	1852	Hebraist, Orientalist.
Kayserling, M.	1828	Jewish Historian
†*Keeley, Mrs.*	1806	Actress. [Dramas."
Klein, J. L.	1810–76	Litterateur, "Geschichte des
Kohn, S.	1825	Novelist, "Gabriel."
Kolisch, Baron	1837	Chess Player.
Kompert, L.	1822	Novelist.
Körösi, J.	1844	Statistician.
Krochmal, N.	1785–1840	Hebraist.
Kronecker, L.	1823	German Mathematician.
Kuh, E.	1828–76	Litterateur.
Kuranda, J.	1811–84	Hungarian Politician.
Lambert, Gen.	1825–96	French Soldier.
Landau, M.	1837–90	German Italian Scholar.
Lasker, E.	1839–89	German Politician, Leader of [National Liberal Party.
Lassalle, F.	1825–63	Lawyer, Politician, Social Demo-
Lattes, M. (U.S.)	1846–84	Hebraist. [crat.
Lazarus, E.	1851–79	Poetess, U.S.
Lazarus, M.	1824	German Philosopher.
Lederer, J. ("Ichneumon")	1810	German Littérateur.
Leeser, J. (U.S.)	1806–68	Hebrew Scholar.
Lehmann	1819	Painter.
Lehmann, L. T.	1814	Painter.
Lehrs	1802–73	Classicist.
Leitner, G. G.	1840	Traveller, Orientalist, "Kaiser-i-
Levi, C. L.	1852	Journalist. [Hind."
Levi, D.	1740–1799	Hebraist.
Levi, D.	1821	Poet, "Il Propheta."
Levi, V. Nac. M.	1840	Lawyer.
Levi-Alvares	1794–1870	Educationalist.
Levison, Olive ("Silvia Bennett")	1847	Littérateur, Novelist.
Levy, Calmann	1819-94	French Publisher.
Levy, Em.	1826	Painter.
Levy, G.	1819	French Engraver.
Levy, Hermann	1839	German Musician, Conductor.
Levy, H. L.	1840	Painter.
Levy, Julius ("Julius Rodenburg")	1831	Journalist.
Levy, M. A.	1817–72	Hebraist, Orientalist, Numism.
Levy, Maurice	1833	Prof. Math. Collége de France.
Levy, Michel	1821–75	French Publisher.
Levy, U. P.	1719–1862	Admiral, U.S. Navy.
Lewald, Fanny	1811–89	Novelist.

JEWISH CELEBRITIES.

Lewis, Sir G.	1833	Lawyer.
Liebermann, M.	1849	German Painter.
Liebrecht, Felix	1812–90	Folklorist.
Liebreich, F. R.	1830	Doctor, Oculist, "Eye-mirror."
Liebreich, M. E. O.	1839	Doctor, "Chloralhydrate."
Lindau, P.	1839	Journalist, Novelist.
Lindau, R.	1829	Diplomatist, Traveller.
Lipiner, S.	1855	Poet, "Entfesselte Prometheus."
Lippmann, C.		French Physicist, Colour Photo-
Loewe, F. L. F.	1816	German Actor. [graphy.
Loewe, L.	1809–87	Orientalist.
Loewe, W.	1814	German Publicist.
Loewe, Ludwig		Manufacturer, German Politician.
Loewy, M.	1833	French Astronomer.
Lombroso, C.	1836	Italian Doctor, Alienist.
Löw, L.	1811–75	Jewish Scholar, Journalist.
Lowenthal, J. G.	1810–76	Chess Player.
Lucca, P.	1840	Singer.
Lumbroso, A.	1813	French Doctor.
Lumley, B.	1812–75	Manager.
Luzzati, I.	1847	Italian Lawyer.
Luzzati, L.	1843	Italian Economist.
Luzzato, F.	1839–54	Orientalist, Assyriologist.
Luzzato, S. D.	1800–65	Italian Hebraist.
Maimon, S.	1753–1800	Philosopher.
Mandl, L.	1812	French Doctor.
†Manin, D.	1804–57	Italian Patriot, Defender of
Manuel, E.	1823	French Poet. [Venice.
*Margoliouth, M.	1820–82	Hebraist.
Marx, K.	1818–83	Social Economist.
Massarani, T.	1826	Italian Poet, Politician, Painter.
Mayer, A.	1814	French Doctor, Inventor.
Meldola, R.	1754–1828	Hebraist.
Meldola, R.	1849	Chemist.
Mendeleieff, D.	1834	Chemist, "Periodic Law."
*Mendelssohn, D. (Dorothea Schlegel)	1769–1839	Salon.
*Mendelssohn, F. B.	1809–47	Musician.
Meyer, L.	1820	Classical Philologist.
Meyer, Victor	1848	Chemist.
Meyerbeer, J.	1794–1864	Musician.
Meyerbeer, W.	1797–1850	Astronomer, Map of the Moon.
Meyr, Melchior	1810–71	Philosopher.
Millaud, A. P. A.	1836	French Dramatist.
Millaud, E. B.	1834	French Senator.
Millaud, M. A.	1829	French Journalist.
Mocatta, F. D	1827	Philanthropist.
Mond, Ludwig	1830	Chemist.
Montefiore, Sir M.	1784–1885	Philanthropist.
Morgenstein, Tina	1830	German. Woman's Rights.
Morpurgo, E.	1840–85	Italian Economist, Statistician.
Mortara, M.	1815	Hebraist Rabbi.
Moscheles, J.	1794–1870	Musician.

Mosenthal, S. H.	1821–77	Dramatist.
Munk, I.	1852 ...	Professor of Physiology, Berlin.
Munk, S.	1805–66	Doctor, Arabist.
Naquet, A.	1834 ...	French Doctor, Politician, Divorce.
Naquet, E.	1819 ...	French Journalist.
Nathalie, Zairic M.	1816 ...	Actress.
Nathan, J.	1792–66	Musician "Hebrew Melodies."
Nathanson, M. L.	1780–1868	Danish Journalist.
*Neander, G. A. W.	1789–1850	Christian Divine, Church Historian.
Neubauer, A.	1832 ...	Orientalist, Hebraist, Arabist.
Nordau, Max	1849 ...	Journalist, "Degeneration."
Nordmann, J.	1820 ...	Journalist.
Norsa, D.	1807 ...	Theological Litterateur.
Nort, M. M.	1785–1851	Journalist, Author, Dramatist.
Offenbach, J.	1819–1882	Musician.
Ollendorf, H. G.	1805–65	Philologist.
Oppenheim, H. B.	1817–80	Politician.
Oppert, G.	1836 ...	Traveller.
Oppert, J.	1825 ...	Orientalist, Assyrian.
*Palgrave, Sir F. C.	1788–1861	Historian.
Pereire, E.	1800–75	Banker, Philanthropist.
Pereire, J.	1806–80	Banker, Philanthropist.
Phillips, Sir B. S.	1811 ...	Politician, L. M.
Phillips, L. B.	1842 ...	Dictionary, Biographical Reference.
Philipsohn, L.	1811 ...	Jewish Journalist.
Pringsheim, M.	... ...	Professor of Botany, Berlin.
Pulitzer, T.	... ...	"New York World" "T.P."
Rachel, F.	1820–58	Actress.
Raffalovitch, A.	1855 ...	French Political Economist.
Rahel (Van der Euse)	1771–1833	Salon.
Rapaport, S. A.	1790–1867	Hebraist.
Raynal, T.	1819 ...	French Politician.
Reinach, J.	1856 ...	Politician.
Reinach, S.	1858 ...	Archæologist, Philologist.
Reinath, T.	1860 ...	Archæologist, Historian.
Reiss, P. T.	1831–83	Physicist, First Jew Berlin Academy.
Remak, R.	1816–65	Doctor, Physiology.
*Ricardo, D.	1772–1823	Economist.
Riesser, G.	1806–63	Litterateur, Journalist.
Ring, M.	1817 ...	Novelist.
Romanelli, S.	1757–1814	Italian Poet.
Romanin, S.	1803–61	Historian of Venice.
Rosenthal	1826 ...	Physicist.
Rothschild, Edmond	1826 ...	French Banker, Philanthropist.
Rothschild, James	1844 ...	French Banker.
Rothschild, M.	1743–1812	Banker.
*Rubinstein, A. G.	1829–89	Musician.
Salaman, C. K.	1814 ...	Musician.
Salomon, H.	1831 ...	French Politician.
Salomons, Sir D.	1797–1873	Politician.
Salomons, Sir D. L.	1851 ...	Electrician.
†Salvador, Joseph	1796–1873	Jewish Historian.
Sanders, D.	1819 ...	Lexicographer.

JEWISH CELEBRITIES. 125

Saphir, M. G.	1795–1858	Comic Writer.
Schapiro, M.	1816	Hebraist.
Schlesinger, Sigmund	1825	Comedian,
Schrader, A.	1815–78	Novelist.
Schreiner, Olive	...	Novelist.
Schuster, A.	1851	Physicist, F.R.S.
Schwalbe, G.	1846	Physiologist.
See, Germain	1818–96	French Doctor.
Senator, Hermann	1834	Professor of Medicine, Berlin.
Simson, B. von.	1840	Historian.
Simson, Mt.	1810	Lawyer, Politician.
Singer, E.	...	German Socialist Leader.
Soave, M.	1820–83	Hebraist.
Solomon, S.	1840	Painter.
Solomon, S. J.	1860	Artist.
Sonnenthal, A.	1834	Actor.
Stein, Ludwig	1859	Philosopher.
Steinitz, W.	1837	Chess Player.
Steinschneider, M.	1816	Hebraist, Orientalist.
Steinthal, H.	1823	Philologist, Philosopher.
Stern, Alfred	1846	Historian.
*Strauss, J.	1825	"Waltz King."
Strousberg, B. H.	1828–84	German Manufacturer.
†Sullivan, Sir A.	1844	Musician.
Sylvester, J.	1814	Mathematician.
Traube	1818–76	German Doctor.
Torquem, O.	1782–1862	Mathematician.
Touro, J.	1775–1854	Philanthropist, U. S.
Ulmann, B.	1829	French Painter.
Valentin, G. G.	1808–83	Physiologist.
*Vambery, H.	1832	Oriental Traveller.
Verne, Jules	1828	French Novelist.
Waldteufel, E.	...	German Musician.
Weil, G.	1808	German Orientalist, Arabic
Weil, H.	1818	Classic. [Historian.
Weill, Alexandre	1813	French Littérateur, Journalist.
Wilh, L.	1817	German Poet.
Wolff, A.	1825–93	Journalist, "Doyen" of French
Wolff, E.	1814	French Sculptor. [Press.
Wolff, E.	1802	French Sculptor.
*Wolff, Joseph	1795–1862	Hebraist, Traveller, Convert.
Worms, J.	1832	French Painter, [Novelist.
Zangwill, I.	1864	Critic, Humorist, Dramatist,
Zeissl, H.	1817–84	Dermatologist, Vienna.
Zimmern, H.	1846	Littérateur.
Zukertort, J. H.	1842–90	Chess Player.
Zunz, L.	1794–1887	Hebrew Scholar.

JEWISH BOOKS OF REFERENCE.

[THE following list makes no pretension to completeness, but only attempts to give some indication of the most accessible sources *in English* on the various subjects referred to.]

Bibliography.

JACOBS & WOLF, "Bibliotheca Anglo-Judaica," a Bibliographical Guide to Anglo-Jewish History. 1888. ("Jewish Chronicle" Office.) 7s. 6d.

Jewish Literature.

M. STEINSCHNEIDER, "Jewish Literature." 1857. (Longman.) *Out of print.*

M. STEINSCHNEIDER, "Catalogus Librorum Hebræorum in Bibliotheca Bodleiana." 1859. Oxford. *Out of print.*

J. ZEDNER, "Catalogue of the Hebrew Books in the British Museum." 1867. Supplement by J. Van Strahlen. 1894. 52s. 6d.

A. NEUBAUER, "Catalogue of the Hebrew MSS. in the Bodleian Library." 1886. Oxford. 52s. 6d.

A. LÖWY, "Catalogue of the Hebraica and Judaica in the Guildhall Library." 1892.

MARGOLIOUTH, D., "Hand List of the Hebrew MSS. in the British Museum."

The Talmud.

MIELZENER'S "Introduction to the Talmud." 1894. (Nutt.) 10s. 6d.

E. DEUTSCH, "Literary Remains." 1874. (Longman.) *Out of print.* (Contains the celebrated article on the Talmud, which appeared in the "Quarterly Review," October, 1867.)

POLANO, "Selections from the Talmud" (Chandos Classics). 2s.

Rabbinic Literature (Translated).

C. TAYLOR, "Ethics of the Fathers." 1877. (Pitt Press.) 10s. 6d.

MAIMONIDES, "Guide for the Perplexed." Translated by Dr. M. Friedlander. 1882. (Trübner.) *Out of print.*

BENJAMIN OF TUDELA, "Travels." Translated by A. Asher. 1841.

SOLOMON IBN GABIROL, "Choice of Pearls." Translated by H. B. Ascher. 1859.

ABRAHAM IBN EZRA, "Commentary on Isaiah." Translated by Dr. M. Friedlander. 1873.

A. NEUBAUER, "Fifty-third Chapter of Isaiah according to Jewish Interpreters." 1876. (Oxford.)

MRS. H. LUCAS, "Songs of Zion." (Dent.) 1894.

Theology.

N. S. JOSEPH, "Natural Religion." (Trübner.) 5s.

M. FRIEDLANDER, "The Jewish Religion." 1891. (Keegan Paul.) 5s.

S. SCHECHTER, "Studies in Judaism." 1896. (Black.) 7s. 6d.

A. BENISCH, "Judaism Surveyed." 1874.

Sermons.

ABRAHAMS & MONTEFIORE, "Aspects of Judaism." (Macmillan.) 3s. 6d.

Dr. H. ADLER, "Sermons on so-called Christological Passages." Translated into Marathi. *Out of print.*

M. JOSEPH, "The Ideal in Judaism." (Nutt.) 4s. 6d.

"The Jewish Pulpit." 1886. ("Jewish Chronicle" Office.)

B. ARTOM, "Sermons." 1876.

D. W. MARKS, "Sermons," 3 vols. 1851-84. (Trübner.) *Out of print.*

Jewish History.

D. CASSEL, "Manual of Jewish History." (Macmillan.) 2s. 6d.

LADY MAGNUS, "Outlines of Jewish History." (Kegan Paul.) 4s. 6d.

H. GRAETZ, "History of the Jews," 5 vols. (Nutt.) 50s. The Standard History.

I. ABRAHAMS, "Jewish Life in the Middle Ages." (Macmillan.) 7s. 6d. net.

Anglo-Jewish History.

TOVEY, "Anglia Judaica." 1738. *Out of print.*

J. JACOBS, "Jews of Angevin England" (up to 1206). (Nutt.) 4s. net.

B. L. ABRAHAMS, "Expulsion of the Jews, 1290" (Oxford Prize Essay, 1895). 3s. 6d.

J. PICCIOTTO, "Sketches of Anglo-Jewish History." (Trübner.) *Out of print.*

Publications of the Anglo-Jewish Historical Exhibition. £1. 1s.

Trans. Jewish Historical Society of England. (Wertheimer, Lea & Co.) 10s. 6d.

Biography.

MORAIS, "Eminent Israelites of the Nineteenth Century." (Philadelphia.) $2.

[See also "Bibliotheca," Nos. 821 to 1262.]

Essays.

LADY MAGNUS, "Jewish Portraits." (Unwin.) 4s. 6d.

J. JACOBS, "Jewish Ideals." 1896. (Nutt.) 6s. net.

S. SCHECHTER, "Studies in Judaism." 1896. (Black.) 7s. 6d.

Jewish Novels.

G. AGUILAR, "The Vale of Cedars."

F. DANBY, "Dr. Phillips."

MRS. ANDREW DEAN, "Isaac Leeser's Money." (Unwin.) 2s. 6d.

K. FRANZOS, "The Jews of Barnow." (Blackwood.) 6s.

GERARD, "Orthodox." (Blackwood.) 2s.

"GEORGE ELIOT," "Daniel Deronda." (Blackwood.) 7s. 6d.

LORD BEACONSFIELD, "David Alroy." (Longmans.) 2s.

AMY LEVY, "Reuben Sachs." (Macmillan.) 3s. 6d.

I. ZANGWILL, "The Children of the Ghetto." (Heinemann.) 6s.

I. ZANGWILL, "The King of the Schnorrers." (Heinemann.) 6s.

Statistics and Anthropology.

J. JACOBS, "Studies in Jewish Statistics." (Nutt.) 6s. net.

Alien Immigration. (*See* List, p. 224.)

Almanacs.

E. H. LINDO, "Jewish Calendar for 64 Years." 1838. *Out of print.*
P. VALENTINE, "Hebrew and English Almanack." (Valentine.) 6d. (From 1854 in progress.)

Ritual.

Sephardic Rite.
"Forms of Prayer," with an English Translation by D. A. de Sola. 5 vols. 1860.

Ashkenazic Rite.
S. SINGER, "Authorised Daily Prayer Book." (Wertheimer, Lea & Co.) 1s.
D. A. DE SOLA, "Festival Prayers." 6 vols. (Valentine.) £1. 18s.

Reform Rite.
"Forms of Prayer used in West London Synagogue." 5 vols. 1859.
B. H. ASCHER, "Book of Life." 1861.
B. H. ASCHER, "Dedication of the House."
A. ASHER, "The Jewish Rite of Circumcision." 1873.
A. P. MENDES, "Service for the First Night of Passover." 1862.
E. SPIERS, "Hagadah for Passover." 1887.
BARONESS L. DE ROTHSCHILD, "Prayers and Meditations." 1884.
A. L. COHEN, "Prayers," Hebrew and English. (Privately printed.) 1884.
L. MONTAGU, "Prayers for Jewish Workgirls." 1894.

Synagogue Music.

E. AGUILAR, "Ancient Melodies of the Spanish and Portuguese Jews." 1857. (Longman.) *Out of print.*
SALAMAN & VERRINDER, "Music of the West London Synagogue." 1861.
M. HAST, "Collection of Sacred Jewish Hymns and Prayers." 1874.
F. COHEN & B. L. MOSELEY, "Handbook of Synagogue Music." (Novello.) 5s.

Newspapers.

Jewish Chronicle, 2, Finsbury Square, E.C. 2d. weekly.
Jewish World, 8, South Street, Finsbury Pavement. 1d. weekly.
Jewish Express (Jargon), Office of *Leeds Express*, Quebec-street. 1d. weekly.

Review.

Jewish Quarterly Review. Edited by I. ABRAHAMS and C. G. MONTEFIORE. (Macmillan.) 3s. quarterly, 10s. 6d. annual subscription.

ACTS OF PARLIAMENT RELATING TO JEWS.

1702. An Act to oblige the Jews to maintain and provide for their Protestant Children. 1 Anne cap. 30.
   [Repealed in 1846.]

1740. An Act for Naturalising such Foreign Protestants and others therein mentioned (including Jews) as are settled or shall settle in any of His Majesty's colonies in America. 13 Geo. II. cap. 7.

1753. An Act to permit persons professing the Jewish Religion to be Naturalised by Parliament, &c. 26 Geo. II. cap. 26.

   An Act to repeal an Act of the Twenty-sixth year of His Majesty's Reign, intituled An Act to permit Persons professing the Jewish Religion to be Naturalised by Parliament, &c. 27 Geo. II. cap. 1.

1820. BARBADOS.—An Act concerning the Vestry of the Hebrew Nation resident within the Island. S. sh.
   [For electing five representatives to settle taxation.]

1830. Copy of a Bill which has recently passed the House of Assembly in Jamaica.
   [Repealing the clauses disabling Jews from being elected members of the Corporation of Kingston.]

1845. An Act for the Relief of Persons of the Jewish Religion elected to Municipal Offices. 8 & 9 Vic. cap. 52.

1858. An Act to provide for the Relief of Her Majesty's Subjects professing the Jewish Religion. 21 & 22 Vic. cap. 49.
   Sec. 1 empowers either House of Parliament to modify the form of oath, so as to enable a Jew to sit and vote. By sec. 3 Jews are precluded from holding certain offices. By sec. 4 the right of presenting to any ecclesiastical benefice possessed by Jews is to devolve on the Archbishop of Canterbury.

1860. An Act to Amend the Act of the Twenty-first and Twenty-second years of Victoria, Chapter Forty-nine, to Provide for the Relief of Her Majesty's

Subjects professing the Jewish Religion. 23 & 24 Vic. cap. 63.

[Repealed by 29 & 30 Vic. cap. 19, which removed the words " on the true faith of a Christian" from the oath.]

1870. An Act for Confirming a Scheme of the Charity Commissioners for the Jewish United Synagogues. 33 & 34 Vic. cap. 116.

MISCELLANEOUS CLAUSES IN ACTS.

1694. 6 & 7 Wm. III. cap. 6 sec. 63.
Jews cohabiting as man and wife to pay the duty imposed by this statute on marriages.

1753. 26 Geo. II. cap. 33.
Lord Hardwicke's Act for prevention of clandestine marriages. Sec. 18 exempts Jewish marriages.

1823. 4 Geo. IV. cap. 76. Repealing Lord Hardwicke's Act.
Sec. 31 exempts Jews.

1836. 6 & 7 Wm. IV. cap. 85. An Act for Marriages in England.
Sec. 2. Jews may contract marriage according to Jewish usages, provided that both parties are of the Jewish religion, and that the Registrar's certificate has been obtained.

1836. 6 & 7 Wm. IV. cap. 86. An Act for Registering Births, Deaths, and Marriages in England.
Sec. 30. The President of the London Committee of Deputies of the British Jews is to certify to the Registrar-General the appointment of Secretaries of Synagogues to act as marriage registrars.

1840. 3 & 4 Vic. cap. 72. An Act to provide for the Solemnization of Marriages in the Districts in or near which the Parties reside.
Sec. 5. Jews exempted from operation of the Act.

1844. 7 & 8 Vic. cap. 81. An Act for Marriages in Ireland.
Sec. 12. Jews may contract marriages according to their usages, provided they give notice to the Registrar and obtain his certificate.
Sec. 13. Jewish Registrars to be certified by the President of Jewish Board of Deputies.

1846. 9 & 10 Vic. cap. 59. An Act to relieve Her Majesty's Subjects from certain Penalties and Disabilities with regard to their Religious Opinions.

Sec. 2. Jews are to be subject to the same laws as Protestant Dissenters with regard to their schools, places of religious worship, education, and charitable purposes, and the property held therewith.

1847. 10 & 11 Vic. cap. 58. An Act to remove Doubts as to Quakers' and Jews' Marriages, solemnized before certain periods.

Declares all marriages amongst Jews solemnized in England before the 1st April, 1837, or in Ireland before the 1st April, 1845, according to their usages, are good in law, if both parties were Jews.

1855. 18 & 19 Vic. cap. 81. An Act to amend the Law concerning the certifying and registering of Places of Religious Worship in England.

Sec. 2. Synagogues may be certified as such to the Registrar-General, and to be exempt from the provisions of the Charitable Trusts Act, 1853, with certain exceptions.

1855. 18 & 19 Vic. cap. 86. An Act for securing the Liberty of Religious Worship.

Sec. 2 provides that 9 & 10 Vic. cap. 59 (*vide supra*), is to be construed with reference to this Act.

1856. 19 & 20 Vic. cap. 119. An Act to amend the provisions of the Marriage and Registration Acts.

Sec. 21. Marriages of Jews may be solemnized by license.

Sec. 22. Twenty members of the West London Synagogue of British Jews, or of any Synagogue in connection therewith, may certify a Secretary to the Registrar-General, as a Registrar of Marriages.

1872. 35 & 36 Vic. cap. 33. The Ballot Act.

Schedule 1, sec. 26. If a Parliamentary election takes place on Saturday, the presiding officer may mark a Jewish elector's ballot-paper for him.

1878. 41 & 42 Vic. cap. 16. An Act to consolidate and amend the Law relating to Factories and Workshops.

Sec. 50 provides means by which Jewish manufacturers closing on their Sabbath may employ young persons and women in such a way as to make up the lost time.

Sec. 51. Jewish employés in factories or workshops are permitted to be employed on Sunday, subject to certain restrictions.

TRIALS AND LEADING CASES.

1673. Lilly's Practical Register, I., p. 3.
> Religion of Jewish plaintiff was pleaded as a bar to an action for debt. Judgment for plaintiff.

c. 1678. BARKER *v.* WARREN.—2 Modern Reports, 271.
> Venue changed from London to Middlesex, to suit convenience of Jewish witness, who would not attend on Saturday.

1680. ROBELE *v.* LANGSTON.—2 Keb., 314.
> Jews sworn on Pentateuch; validity of evidence confirmed on appeal.

EAST INDIA COMPANY *v.* SANDYS.—2 Shower, 371; State Trials, vii. 540, 563 (Cobbett's Edition, x. 408, 444).
> Jews regarded by English law as "alien friends," and were in England by an implied license.

1701. PARISH OF ST. ANDREW'S UNDERSHAFT, LONDON *v.* JACOB MENDEZ DE BRETO.—1 Lord Raymond, 699.
> Father ordered to pay to converted daughter an allowance, under 43 Eliz. ii. 7: order quashed, as no proof of her needing assistance.

1718. VINCENT *v.* FERNANDEZ.—1 Peere Williams, 524, Vin. Abr. tit. Jew, sect. 12.
> A Jewess turned Christian sued for maintenance from her father's executor, as no legacy was left her: order that the Master make inquiry if the charities given by the will might not be under some secret trust for her if she turn again.

1727. The Case of Mr. Anthony Da Costa with the Russia Company. 1 sh. fol.
> Claiming to be admitted. Claim refused as he was a Jew. Attorney-General declared he ought to be admitted, but the Company still refused, and petitioned Parliament to modify their charter in that sense. The above broadsheet was a protest against the charge.

1737. ANDREAS *v.* ANDREAS.—1 Hagg. Cos.
> Restitution of marital rights: Jewess married *more Judaico* has marital rights.

1737. VILLAREAL *v.* MELLISH.—2 Swanst. 538.
> A Jewish widow having turned Christian, recovers custody of her children from her father, guardianship not being transferable.

1743. DA COSTA v. DE PAS.—Ambler's "Report of Cases in Chancery," 228. 2 Swanst. 487.
A bequest of £1,200 for founding a "Jesuba" declared invalid, as being for a superstitious purpose.

1744. OMYCHUND v. BARKER.—1 Atkyns, 21.
Jew's evidence legal, if sworn on Old Testament.

1783. ISAAC v. GOMPERTZ.—Ambler's Rep. 228, 7 Ves. 61.
Will of Benjamin Isaac for support of Jewish charities at "Bromsall" and London held valid.

1791. GOWER v. LADY LANESBOROUGH.—Peake's Cases, 25.
A Jewess may be permitted to give parol evidence of her own divorce in a foreign country, according to the custom of the Jews there.

1795. LINDO v. BELISARIO.—1 Hagg. Cos. Rep. 216.
Jewish Marriage Law to be ascertained by testimony of its Professors.

1794. VIGEVENA SILVERIA v. ALVAREZ.
Question of legitimacy: marriage by Jewish rite held to be valid.

1794. D'AGUILAR v. D'AGUILAR.—1 Hagg. Cos. Rep. 776
First divorce suit between an English Jew and Jewess.

1795. REX v. GILHAM.—1 Espinasse's Reports, 1895.
A Jew, who had not formally abjured Judaism, sworn on the New Testament, held to be an admissible witness, though when sworn he had stated he considered himself a member of the established religion.

1798. GOLDSMID v. BROMER—1 Hagg. Cos. Rep., 324.
[Validity of a Jewish marriage decided by the Beth Din.]

1807. HORN v. NOEL.—1 Campbell's Reports, 61.
Witnesses present at the marriage ceremony not sufficient to prove Jewish marriage; written contract of marriage also necessary.

1815. JONES v. ROBINSON—2 Phillimore's Reports, 285.
If Jews are married according to Christian rites, they must conform to the ordinary regulations of Marriage Acts.

1818. ISRAEL AND OTHERS v. SIMMONS.—Starkie's Nisi Prius Reports, ii. 356.
Synagogue declared to be a lawful establishment; also that lessees could sue for rent from holders of seats.

1818. *In re* TRUSTEES OF THE BEDFORD CHARITY —2 Swanston, 470.
Jews not entitled to benefits of the Bedford Charity.

1826. EDENBOROUGH *v.* ARCHBISHOP OF CANTERBURY.—2 Russell's Reports, 119 (note).
: Jews were entitled to vote in the election of a vicar, but not Roman Catholics.

1837. STRAUS *v.* GOLDSMID.—8 Simon's Reports, 611.
: A bequest to enable Jews to observe the rites of Passover held to be good, notwithstanding the decision in Da Costa *v.* De Pas.

1839. BENNETT *v.* HAYTER.—2 Beavan's Reports, 1881.
: Under "a bequest to the Jews' poor, Mile End," ordered that fund be applied *cy pres* between Jews' Hospital and Beth Holim.

1844. DAVIS *v.* LLOYD AND OTHERS.—1 Carrington & Kirwan's Reports, 275.
: The entry by the Chief Rabbi in the Synagogue register book of the circumcision of the plaintiff, a Jew, held not admissible as proof of his age.

1852. MILLER *v.* SALOMONS.—7 Exchequer Reports, 475.
: Alderman Salomons, M.P., took his seat, after taking the oath, intentionally omitting the words, "on the true faith of a Christian"; was declared liable to penalties under 1 George I. statute 2, cap. 13, sec. 17.

1859. GOODMAN *v.* GOODMAN.—33 Law Times Reports, Chancery Appeals, 70.
: A Jew and a Christian woman, who have cohabited as man and wife for twenty-eight years, presumed to be married.

1860. MICHEL'S TRUST.—28 Beavan's Reports, 39.
: A bequest by a Jew in support of learning in the Beth Hamedrash (or Divinity College), and to have the prayer called "Kadish" repeated on the anniversary of his death, held valid.

1869. *Re* ESTHER LYONS.—22 Law Times, New Series, 770.
: In the case of the abduction and baptism of a young Jewess for proselytising purposes, £50 damages recovered by father.

1882. LINDO *v.* ROSENBERG.—Annual Report Jewish Board of Deputies for 1883.
: A Jewish girl having been abducted by Roman Catholics for proselytising purposes, the Roman Catholic bishop and lady superior ordered by Court to attend there to be examined. The domicile of the girl's father being foreign, no order as to her custody could be made, but lady superior's costs disallowed.

GLOSSARY OF JEWISH TERMS.*

THE following glossary attempts to give a list of the special words most frequently used by Jews to express their religious and racial ideas and practices. It should thus cover most aspects of their life so far as it differs from that of their fellow-citizens. The greatest brevity has been aimed at, and it is to be feared that this may at times have led to obscurity or mistake. It has often been a problem which words to include, and many excluded may doubtless, by others, be considered equally entitled to a place in the list. With all its imperfections, it may be hoped that it will not prove uninstructive or uninteresting.

Great difficulty has been found in fixing upon a method of transliteration (*q.v.*), especially for the sounds indicated by *ch* and *th* (*q.v.*). This is due to the divergence between the learned and the popular pronunciation of Hebrew, and may be traced back to the influence of the Karaites in preventing the sacred tongue being written with the vowel points (*q.v.*).

Ab, Ninth of (תשעה באב).

A Fast to commemorate the destruction of both Temples, which, according to Rabbinic tradition, were destroyed on this date. It is a whole Fast beginning in the evening. If it falls on Sabbath, as in 5657, it is kept on the tenth of Ab.

Ab Beth Din (אב בית דין, lit. "Father of the House of Judgment").

The Chief or President of the Ecclesiastical Body known as the Beth Din. The term is used by Dryden.

Aboth, Pirke (פרקי אבות, lit. "Chapters of the Fathers").

A Tractate of the Mishna, containing moral precepts of the great teachers of the Law from Ezra down to the second century A.D. It is included in the Jewish Prayer Book, and is read in the afternoon services on Sabbaths between Passover and New Year. By reason of its inclusion in the Prayer Book, it has become the part of the Talmud which is best known to Jews, and deserves that distinction owing to the moral elevation and ethical fervour of most of the maxims contained in it. The original Tractate consisted of five chapters, to which a sixth, of later date, has been added and devoted to a eulogium of the Law. An excellent edition of the Pirke-Aboth has been produced by Dr. C. Taylor (Pitt Press, 1877).

Afikoman (? ἐπικομὸν or ἐπιγεῦμα, lit. "for dessert," or אפיקו מן, Chald. "dish remover").

A special Passover cake used during the Seder services (*q.v.*). Three cakes, usually thicker than the rest, are placed upon the table, and are popularly supposed to represent the three orders of Jews, being known as "Cohen," "Levi," "Israel."

---

* Copyright, 1896, in the United States. By JOSEPH JACOBS.

Half of middle cake is the Afikoman; the cake is broken in halves during the service, so as to ensure that there may be sufficient to finish the meal with some Matsa (*q.v.*). It is customary to hide one of the halves, the child finding it being rewarded for his discovery.

Akum (abbrev., lit. " worshippers of stars and planets ").

In the Talmud, and in works like the *Shulchan Aruch* derived from it, this term was applied to idolaters, towards whom Israelites were directed to take up the most uncompromising attitude. Anti-Semites have attempted to prove that the term applied to our Christian fellow-citizens, and that the Hebrew expressions used about *Akum* apply to Christians. This malicious statement has been triumphantly repudiated by Dr. Hoffmann in his work on the *Shulchan Aruch*.

Alav hashalom, Aleah hashalom (עליו, עליה השלם, lit. " on him, on her, be peace ").

It is usual to add to the name of deceased parents, or, indeed, any one deceased, the above formula, the survival of the fittest of numerous phrases of the like kind, a list of which is given in Zunz, *Zur Gesch*. English Jews generally apply the first formula to persons of either sex, and pronounce it *Olov hasholowm*.

Al Chet (על חט, lit. " for the sin ").

The recurrent opening words of a succession of confessions in the service of the Day of Atonement. Each particular sin is specialised in a long list beginning with these words, and it is customary for pious Jews, as they are pronounced, to beat their breasts for each sin.

Aleph Beth (א״ב, lit. " A, B ").

These two words are the names of the first two letters of the Hebrew Alphabet, which are identical with those of the Greek Alphabet, which is the source of all European letters. Both the Hebrew and the Greek are derived from the Phœnician. As the letters were originally intended to be carved upon rocks, it was at first incised, both in Greek and Hebrew, from right to left, so as to leave the hammer-hand free. When Greek began to be written upon papyrus or vellum, the order of writing was changed, but the more conservative Hebrew still retains the practice of writing from right to left, and, for the same reason, Hebrew books " begin at the end." Alpha Beta are simply the same words as Aleph Beth, the Aramaic ending " a "—Alph*a* B*e*t*a* —showing that it came to the Greeks from some Aramaic-speaking folk.

memar (probably Arabic).

The name given to the reading desk in a synagogue. The scrolls of the Law are carried and placed upon it when the lesson of the day is read. The name is Arabic, though it is used now equally by German and Spanish Jews. In Talmudic times it was called by the Greek term *Bēma*.

Amen (אָמֵן, lit. "verily").

This term is as frequent in Jewish prayers as in the Christian Church, which derived it from the Synagogue. Owing to the fact that there were very few prayer-books accessible in the mediæval Synagogues, it became customary for the congregation to repeat "Amen" and to regard this as equivalent to saying the whole prayer recited by the Chazan (*q.v.*). Later developments of the Cabbala laid mystical stress upon the significance of this word (*see* Hogg, in *Jewish Quarterly Review*, VIII.). The word is an excellent example of the various ways in which Hebrew words can be pronounced. While the Low Church calls it "Eh-men," and the High Church "Ah-men," the Sephardim (*q.v.*) pronounce it as if "Ah-main," while to the Ashkenazim it is familiar as "Oh-mine."

Am Haaretz (עַם הָאָרֶץ, lit. "people of the earth").

This term is used to signify those unlearned in the Law. It has been conjectured that it referred originally to the country folk, and in this case the history of the term is similar to that of "pagan" or "heathen." It is now used as indicating ignorance of Jewish matters, and a curious noun has been formed from it, "Amhaaretsuth."

Amidah (עֲמִדָה, lit. "standing").

This term is applied to that portion of prayers containing the eighteen blessings (*q.v.*). It is generally said under their breath by the congregation while standing up, and then repeated by the Chazan (*q.v.*).

Angel.

The simpler angelology of the Bible was developed, in later Judaism, into an elaborate hierarchy of angels, derived, as has been shown by Dr. Kohut, from Persia. This was still further developed by the Cabbala, which fills the world with their activity. As the messengers of God, their potency was of an entirely benevolent kind, and except in one case, the Angel of Death (*see* Malach Hamovath), the Jewish folk have paid little attention to angels, reserving their reverence for the Shedim (*q.v.*) or demons.

Anglo-Yiddish.

The German and Polish Jews use a curious jargon, mainly composed of archaic German and a sprinkling of Hebrew words, like those contained in this glossary. This is known as Yiddish (*q.v.*). The Jews of England, the majority of whom are Pollackim (*q.v.*) themselves, or descendants of Pollackim, have adopted a certain number of Hebrew words with phonetic modifications which deserve scientific investigation that cannot be spared for it here. All we need to remark is that these Anglo-Yiddish words are often mistaken by English Jews for pure Hebrew, while, on the other hand, many of the Hebrew words contained in this glossary are thought by them to be merely Yiddish.

Anti-Semitism.

In 1875, a number of the Roman Catholic journals of Germany attacked the Jews, who were mostly of the opposite political party, the National Liberals. The German Jews unwisely answered with great heat, and, as a result, the movement against them spread widely. To avoid the appearance of religious intolerance, it took upon itself the name of Anti-Semitism, emphasising the racial difference between Germans and Semitic Hebrews. The movement has spread to Russia, Roumania and Austria, where it has always been endemic, and even to liberal France. It is a curious combination of intolerance, envy and Chauvinism, which directs itself against all Jews without discrimination. That Jews give some grounds for this almost universal dislike cannot well be denied. All clannish and successful people, as, *e.g.*, the Scotch, are apt to be disliked, and when to this is added the sudden rise to riches of so many Jews without a corresponding rise in their state of culture, the feeling against pushful parvenus adds to the effect. But it is a phenomenon which defies analysis, and has been repudiated by all the leading men of Europe throughout the century.

Anussim (אנוסים, lit. "compelled").

The Hebrew name for the secret Jews, who kept up their Jewish sympathies and practices, whilst nominally Christians. *See* Marranos.

Aramaic.

A generic term applied to all the North Semitic languages, like Chaldaic (*q.v.*), Syriac, etc.

Arba Kanfoth (ארבע כנפות, lit. "four corners").

According to Deut. xxii. 12, the Jews are commanded to wear fringes upon the four corners of their vesture, and this command is observed to the present day by wearing a special garment with these fringes, generally hidden by the ordinary clothes. According to Numbers xv. 37-41, the ends should be mixed with blue thread, but authorities are divided as to the exact shade of this.

Ark.

In imitation of the Temple with its Holy of Holies, the Synagogue preserves its most sacred object, the Scroll of the Law (*q.v.*), in an Ark placed at the east end of the synagogue (*see* Misrach), which is, as it were, the home of the Siphre Torah (*q.v.*). It is generally covered with a Parecheth (*q.v.*) or curtain. Besides the Ark fixed in the synagogue, many Jews have their own private Scrolls of the Law, which they keep in smaller and portable Arks. These are often richly decorated. (*See* Illustrated Catalogue of Anglo-Jewish Exhibition.)

Ascama, pl. Ascamot (אסכמה or הסכמה, lit. "agreement").

Bye-laws of the Congregation. The term is only used by Spanish and Portuguese Jews. Those of the London Congregation have been printed, at first in Portuguese, and later on in an English version. In the form *hascama* it is commonly used to mean *approval* or *license*.

Ashkenazim.

The term applied to the Jews of German-speaking and Sclavonic-speaking countries, as distinguished from the Sephardim (*q.v.*) or Spanish and Portuguese Jews. The mediæval Jewish geographers called Germany Ashkenaz, after Genesis x. 3, so that the term as applied to Jews implies only that they dwell in the land known as Askenaz, not that they are descendants of Japheth. *See* Pronunciation.

Avoda Zara (עבדה זרה, lit. " stranger ").

By this term is meant idolatry in its grosser forms, against which the Jews have always been a standing protest. The greatest care is taken that nothing in Jewish ceremonial shall border upon the worship of material images. (*See* Akum.)

Baal-ha-Bayith (בעל הבית, lit. " Lord of the House ").

The Head of a Jewish household has certain duties and privileges in his capacity as Baal-ha-Bayith. In modern times the term has become equivalent to seatholder of a Synagogue, pronounced in Anglo-Jewish jargon Balbōs or even *Babōs*.

Baal Kore (בעל קורא, lit. " Reader ").

This term is applied to the person who reads the lessons from the Scrolls of the Law in the Synagogue. This is usually done by the Chazan (*q.v*).

Baal Shem (בעל שם, lit. " Master of the Name ").

According to the practical Cabbala (*q.v.*), some persons become acquainted with the mystical signification of each letter of the Tetragrammaton and other Names of God (*q.v.*), and are capable of controlling the course of nature, and of foreseeing the future of any individual's life. They are regarded with great reverence by superstitious Jews. The most celebrated of these was one Israel Baal Shem, who founded the sect of the Chassidim (*q.v.*) at the beginning of last century. At the end of it there appeared in England one Rabbi Falk, who was also known as a Baal Shem, and is reported to have had a mystic influence over the fate of the Goldsmid family.

Bachur, plural Bachurim (בחור, lit. " young man ").

The students of the Beth Hamedrash who intend to devote themselves to the study of the Law, are so termed up till the time they are married. Among the Sephardim an unmarried man is called up as a "Bachur" to the end of his days, however long he may live.

Badge.

The Lateran Council of 1215, under Pope Innocent III., ordered that all Jews should be distinguished from the rest of the population by a badge. This took various forms : in France and Italy that of a quoit ; in England, a representation of the Two Tables of the Law. It has been conjectured that the custom was derived from the Mahommedan custom introduced in the Pact of Omar. Full details, with illustrations, are given by Ulysse Robert, *Signes d'Infamie* (Paris, 1891).

Bar Mitzvah (בר מצוה, lit. "Son of the Covenant").

The title applied to a Jewish boy on attaining the age of 13 years. A boy of that age is considered to have reached his religious majority and to be responsible henceforth for his own actions. For all religious purposes, as, *e.g.*, for constituting Minyan (*q.v.*) or for certain forms of grace after meals, he is reckoned of full age. In olden times this age was the legal "majority." Since the 14th century it has been customary to mark the occasion of a boy entering upon his 14th year by a religious ceremony in the synagogue. He is "called up" to the Law on the Sabbath succeeding his (Hebrew) birthday, and it is usual for him to read a part or the whole of the portion of the Law with the customary cantillation (*see* Parasha). The occasion is made a family festival, even in synagogue, where the father of the boy, if alive, has the privilege of acting as Segan (*q.v.*).

Bedika (בדיקה, lit., "examination.")

The examination of the lungs of an animal slain for food to ascertain if it is kosher (*q.v.*). It has been suggested by the late Dr. Behrend ("Communicability of Diseases by Animals to Men," 1884) and others that this examination ensures that no food tainted with tuberculosis is eaten by Jews, who are accordingly remarkable for freedom from phthisis. But it is doubtful how far this method is efficacious for that particular purpose. (*See* Dembo, "Jewish Methods of Slaughter.")

Benching.

This term is applied to the recital of the blessing after meals. It is really derived from the Jewish German "Benschen," which itself is merely a popular form of the Latin "Benedicere."

Benedictions, Eighteen. *See* Shemone Esre.

Beni-Israel.

The title given to the Jews of India, who are said to have been established there since 490 A.D., when one Joseph Rabban conducted a band of refugees from Persia to Kranganor. They are divided into two classes or castes, which do not intermarry—the white Beni-Israel and the black, who are supposed to be descendants of former proselytes. There are now some 14,000 of them in the neighbourhood of Bombay.

Berachoth (ברכות).

Literally and actually "blessings," for which there are specified forms for every occasion in life, from seeing a king to hearing thunder. These all commence with the formula: "Blessed art Thou, O Lord our God, King of the Universe!"

GLOSSARY OF JEWISH TERMS.

Berith Milah (ברית מילה, lit. "covenant of circumcision").

Initiation into the rite of Abraham (Gen. xvii. 10-14). The custom is world-wide (*see* Ploss, "Das Kind," I., pp. 342-72), and was known among the Egyptians as early as the 15th century B.C. The ceremony is performed on the eighth day after birth, but can be postponed if there is any danger to health.

Beth Chayim (בית חיים, lit. "House of Life").

This euphemism is the ordinary Jewish name for a graveyard. While so familiar, it is of late origin, Mr. Abrahams informs me, though the Talmud has a practically equivalent expression, בית עלמין, lit. "eternal house."

Beth Din (בית דין, lit. "house of judgment").

An ecclesiastical tribunal which decides cases of Jewish law, and is composed of three members known for their learning in Talmudic law. The decision of any two of them is binding. Each of the members of the Court is called Dayan (*q.v.*).

Beth Hamidrash (בית המדרש, lit. "house of instruction").

A place of study, where the Talmud and other subjects of Jewish erudition are taught. In the Middle Ages, and in Russia up to the present day, it is attended by all Jewish youths between 9 and 16 years of age, and constitutes their main education. The hours are generally very long, and great stress is laid upon studying passages where the intricacies of Talmudic logic constitute remarkable training in acuteness of intellect. The sittings of the Beth-Din (*q.v.*) are generally held at the Beth Hamidrash.

Betrothal.

The Betrothal was formerly a separate ceremony from that of marriage, though it bound the contracting parties with equal stringency. It had to be performed in the presence of the parties, who were to be willing agents, at years of discretion, which were reckoned at thirteen for a boy and twelve for a girl, and in the presence of ten persons, two of whom acted as witnesses. The operative clause consisted of a gift by the bridegroom to the bride, generally taking the form of a ring, and the formula ran, "Behold! thou art sanctified to me by this gift!" It was usual to allow twelve months to elapse between betrothal and marriage. Nowadays, however, the two ceremonies are combined, only separated by the reading of the Kethuba (*q.v.*), or marriage contract. It is still customary for the announcement of an engagement to form the subject of a family feast when the young couple "sit for joy" and receive the congratulations of the family friends. But this has no validity according to Jewish law, and does not bind the parties as in the earlier form of betrothal, which was practically the same as marriage.

Birkath Ha Gomel (ברכת הגומל, lit. "blessing" [beginning] "he who showeth kindness ").

The blessing said in synagogue on returning from a journey, or escaping from great danger, when called up to the Law, is known by this name.

Birkath Ha Libana (ברכת הלבנה, lit. "blessing of the moon").

In the early part of the lunar month a special service is held, generally in the open air and within sight of the luminary which is known by this name.

Birkath Ha Minim (ברכת המנים, lit. "blessing of the heretics").

In the second century a special "blessing" was added to the eighteen blessings (*q.v.*), to express the distrust of the Jews of the period against the various sects into which they were tending to divide, among them probably being the Jewish Christians. It applied especially, however, to delators or informers.

Biur Chamets (ביעור חמץ, lit. "search for leaven ").

On the morning of Passover, the master of the house searches for leaven with a lighted candle in his hand, so as to explore all the dark corners. Whatever is found, is then destroyed, thrown or given away, and to this process the above name is given, though it is also popularly known as *Botul-Chomitse* (destruction of leaven).

Blood Accusation.

This term is specifically applied to the malicious report that has been current for the last eight hundred years that Jews use human blood for ritual purposes during Passover. As Jews are strictly forbidden in the Bible to eat blood, and the main object of the Shechita (*q.v.*) is to avoid doing so, it is needless to say that there is no foundation whatever for this belief. It has probably arisen from the quasi-secrecy with which the Passover meal is eaten. The first instance known in Europe is that of William of Norwich, in 1154, but wherever anti-Semitic feeling runs high, the libel is sure to be revived. The whole subject has been ably treated by Professor Strack in his monograph, *Der Blut-Aberglaube*.

Burial.

Jewish Burial still retains many traces of the influence of the Holy Land customs. Thus, it is not usual to keep the body from its last resting place longer than three days, because, in a hot climate like Palestine, this would lead to danger to health. In Jerusalem, indeed, it is customary to bury on the actual day of decease, but in this case burial only consisted in placing in catacombs where the body could be and was visited for some time after death, in case resuscitation should occur. Washing of the corpse used to be a preparation for anointing with oil. The former act is still kept up, whilst the latter has disappeared from Jewish customs. Up to the end of the first century, it was usual to clothe the body in costly garments, but this led to such scandalous waste that the Rabbis wisely insisted on a simple linen garment. This used to be of red in mediæval times, but it is now invariably white. In Talmudic times, the body was carried on a bier to the burial place, and placed in the ground so as to be in contact with it, either the side or the bottom of the coffin being removed for that purpose, but Jewish coffins are now enclosed. It was not unusual to place symbolic emblems on the coffin on its way to the grave. Thus the Scrolls of the Law would be placed upon the coffin of a distinguished teacher of it, and, for a betrothed person whom death had carried away before marriage, a Chuppa (*q.v.*) or marriage Baldachin was carried over the bier. The burial procession used to include women, frequently professional mourners, but it is not now customary for the ladies of the family to go to the burial ground. The great aim of Jewish burials is to prevent any distinction between poor and rich, when such distinctions have disappeared.

Full details are given in an interesting series of articles by the Rev. A. P. Bender, in the *Jewish Quarterly Review*, Vols. V. and VI. *See* Mourning.

Butter.

Great importance is attributed by the Jews to the command three times mentioned in the Bible not to seethe the kid in its mother's milk (Exod. xxiii. 19; xxxiv. 26; Deut. xiv. 21.). This is interpreted to mean that no milk, butter or cheese is to be eaten with meat, or even prepared in the same vessels. In order to ensure this, most orthodox Jewish families have two sets of cooking utensils and crockery.

Cabbala (קבלה, "tradition").

The mystical philosophy of the mediæval Jews, which may have elements that trace back to Talmudic or even Biblical times (mystical visions of the prophets, etc.), was developed into a system between the tenth and thirteenth centuries. It bears traces of Neo-Platonic influence, while parts of it can probably be traced back to Manichæism. Theoretically, it was an attempt to explain the creation of a material universe by the act of a spiritual Godhead, through the intermediation of powers and potencies known as Sephiroth (*q.v.*). The great text book of the Cabbala is the Sohar, a mystical commentary upon Genesis, supposed to have been written by Simon ben Yochai, but really composed by Moses de Leon, a Spanish Rabbi of the thirteenth century. Great influence is attributed to the names of God, and those who possessed a knowledge of these were supposed to obtain power over the material universe, which led up to what is known as practical Cabbala, or magic. *See* C. D. Ginsburg, *Cabbala* (Longmans). 1865.

Calling up to the Law.

The central function of the Synagogue Morning Service on Sabbaths and festivals is the lesson read from the Pentateuch, and it is regarded as a special privilege or mitzva (*q.v.*) to assist in the reading. Accordingly, each portion or sedra (*q.v.*) is divided into so many parashoth (*q.v.*), each of which is read to a separate individual who is called to the Almemar (*q.v.*) or reading desk with the formula: "Let N. N. arise." Formerly, each person thus called up himself read the portion for which he was summoned, but nowadays it is read to him by the Chazan (*q.v.*). Three persons are thus summoned on ordinary days, six on Festivals, seven on the Day of Atonement, and eight on Sabbaths. In some congregations the reading desk is lower than the seats of the worshippers, who are thus called down to the Law.

Cantillation.

The Lessons from the Law are read with a special form of cantillation, indicated by the accents (Neginoth, *q.v.*) given in the printed editions of the Hebrew Bible, but not included in the Scrolls of the Law, from which the reader intones. It is possible that the cantillation can be traced back to Bible times, and it is undoubtedly the source of the Church form of chanting.

Cautivos (Span., "captives").

Up to the bombardment of Algiers in 1800, seafarers on the Mediterranean were liable to capture by the Algerian corsairs, and this fate frequently befell Sephardic Jews connected with the Levantine trade. It was, therefore, usual in all Sephardic communities to establish a special fund, called the Cautivos Fund, from which the ransom of these captives was paid. In many places this fund exists down to the present day, and the Sephardic congregation of London has still a Warder of the Cautivos.

Ch (= ח).

As many Jewish technical terms commence with this sound, it may be desirable to point out that it is not to be pronounced like *ch* in "church." It corresponds to the eighth letter of the Hebrew alphabet, which is a strongly aspirated guttural, nearly corresponding to the *ch* in the Scotch word "loch." Only born Jews seem capable of acquiring this sound, which is, therefore a sort of Shibboleth. In a certain part of Russia, it is said, there are some Jews who cannot pronounce the ש or *sh* sound.

Chabrutha (חברותא, lit. "society").

This word is frequently used to express any set of people, as in the expression "the whole Chabrutha."

Chad Gadya (חד גדיא, "a single kid").

The Aramaic version of a German nursery rhyme, added at the end of the Hagada service (*q.v.*). It does not occur in early editions or MSS. The rhyme is something of the same character as our "The House that Jack Built."

Chaldaic.

The dialect used by the Jews in Mesopotamia, in which is written much of the Gemara (*q.v.*) as well as the Targum (*q.v.*).

Chalitza (חליצה, lit., "removal" [of shoe]).

According to old Jewish law, a man was obliged to marry his deceased brother's widow (*see* Levirate), but he was allowed to decline this duty, and the formula used on such occasions is known by the name of Chalitza. The form used in Bible times is given in Deut. xxv. 5—10. In Ruth iv. 7 the duty is refused by the nearest of kin. Theoretically, the brother-in-law can claim to fulfil the duty of the Levirate, but practically this is never done. Until Chalitza is given, however, the widow cannot legally marry any one else, and it acts as a divorce (*q.v.*). Chalitza must be given personally in the presence of the two parties. This sometimes involves a certain amount of hardship, if the brother-in-law lives at a great distance.

Chaluka (חלקה, lit. "portion").

The reverence felt by Jews for the Holy Land is mostly shown by special gifts or charitable donations made for the support of Jews who reside there. At one time, this had a distinct pauperising effect on the few Jews who lived in Jerusalem, but, owing to the large incursion of Russian Jews into the Holy Land during recent years the amount of Chaluka is no longer important enough to produce this effect.

Chamets (חמץ, lit. "leavened").

According to the Biblical command, Exod. xii. 19, no leaven must be found in a Jewish house during the Feast of Passover. Strictly speaking, this term only applies to any food formed from barley, wheat, rye, oats or spelt, which has not been baked immediately after the preparation or before any fermentation can take place; but, as some form of flour is used in many articles of food, the command is held to apply to any article in which it might have been used, and great care is taken to ensure the purity of such articles during Passover, lest they should be "chōmetstik" as English Ashkenazim say.

Chanuca (חנכה, lit. "dedication").

The chief post-Biblical Festival of the Jews, celebrated in memory of the restoration of the Temple Service during the time of the Maccabeans, 164 B.C., which is held for eight days, from Kislev 25th. It generally occurs about Christmas time. According to tradition, sacrifices were made to Zeus on the Temple altars, 167·4 B.C. The chief function connected with the festival was that of the ceremonial lighting of the Chanuca Light (*q.v.*), from whence the Greek Jews called it "The Feast of Lights."

Chanuca Light.

According to the legend, when the Israelites recovered the Temple under the Maccabeans, on Kislev 25th, A.M. 3607, they were only able to find a small cruse of oil, properly prepared for the Temple lights, yet this providentially lasted for eight days, during which fresh oil was being prepared. In memory of this the Chanuca lights were lighted each evening during the festival. According to Shammai the eight lights were lit on the first night, and one less on each successive evening, but, according to Hillel, the practice was to begin with one light and increase the number by one each evening. The Law follows Hillel. In actual form the candelabra containing the Chanuca light is generally made in a shape similar to that on the Arch of Titus, but has nine lights, as against the seven of the Sabbath lamp, the extra one above eight being to supply light to the others, and is known locally as the Shammas (*q.v.*) or beadle.

Charoseth (חרסת).

A mixture of apples, eggs, spices (specially cinnamon) and wine, which is used in the Seder Service (*q.v.*), and is a symbol representative of the bricks and mortar which the Israelites had to prepare in Egypt. The Jews of England before the Expulsion had a special mode of preparing this. (*See* J. Jacobs, *Jews of Angevin England*).

Chassidim (חסידים, lit. " pious "), sing. chassid (חסיד).

A Jewish sect founded by Israel Baal Shem at the beginning of last century as a protest against the overgrown formalism to which Rabbinism had arrived at that time. The leader laid stress upon the more mystic and the emotional sides of religion, and his followers attributed mysterious powers to him and his immediate successors. Those in the position of the Rabbis are called "Rebben" (*q.v.*). An admirable account is given of the whole movement by Mr. S. Schechter in his *Studies in Judaism*, 1896.

There was also a class of Chassidim or Pietists in the Maccabean period.

Chathan (חתן,) lit. " bridegroom," and so used.

Chathan Bereshith (חתן בראשית, pron. *Chōsen Berīshis*).

The chief part of the Sabbath service in Synagogue consists in the reading of the Law, a portion of which is read each week, so as to ensure that the whole of the Pentateuch is read through during the course of the year. On Simchath Torah (*q.v.*), when the first chapter of Genesis is read, the person called up to the Law is called the "Betrothed of Genesis" (Chathan Bereshith), and it is regarded as a special honour to be selected for this position. It is usual for the person thus honoured to keep open house on the Sabbath succeeding the last day of Tabernacles.

Chathan Torah (חתן תורה).

The person to whom the last section of the Law is read on the day of the Rejoicing of the Law. He is regarded as being the "Betrothed of the Law," in the same sense as the Chathan Bereshith (*q.v.*).

Chazan (חזן, lit. " Cantor ").

The name applied since the sixth century to the Reader at public service. His function was originally to recite the Piyutim (*q.v.*), but, later, he recited the whole of the service. Nowadays, the title is applied to the Minister of the Congregation generally, though quite recently again there has been a tendency to separate the function of the Chazan, who cantillates and recites the prayers, from that of the Preacher who preaches the sermon.

Chazars.

In the eighth century, a Tartar tribe, dwelling in the Crimea, and exercising rule over most of South Russia, became converted to Judaism, and kept it as the official religion for two centuries. It is possible that they adopted this device to avoid paying tribute or allegiance either to the Patriarch at Constantinople or the Sultan at Bagdad, but the fact of their conversion is authenticated by Arabic and Byzantine authorities, and forms the basis of the philosophical treatise written by the great poet-philosopher Jehuda Halevi, called after them *Cuzari*. It is possible that the Karaites (*q.v.*) now in the Crimea are descended from these Chazars.

Chazir (חזר, lit. "pig").

The chief thing that the outside world knows about Jews is that they do not eat the flesh of pig, which is accordingly denominated the forbidden animal, *par excellence*. As a matter of fact, there is a whole list of forbidden animals and birds given in Lev. xix., and in addition to this all food not killed according to the rules of Shechita (*q.v.*) is equally forbidden. Curiously enough, the Hebrew term for pig is mostly used symbolically. It is a term of reproach for a gourmand or one with uncleanly habits.

Cheder (חדר = "room").

The Jewish elementary school in which children are taught the elements of Hebrew and Religion. The pedagogic principles employed are very primitive, instruction being merely an exercise in memory. The sanitary conditions also often leave much to be desired. In civilised communities, the tendency has been to replace these Chedarim by schools on more modern principles, which include secular subjects in their curriculum.

Chen (חן, lit. "grace").

The specific Jewish term for humour. A person who has *chen* is a humorous person, though it also applies to a person who does this gracefully. "I'll tell you a *chen*," is the general prologue to a witty story.

Cherem (חרם, lit. "separation," derived from the same Semitic root as the Arabic "Harem").

The term is applied to the Jewish form of excommunication, which consists in the separation from the Congregation of those causing a public scandal or holding doctrines contrary to Judaism. There are three forms of this punishment, increasing in severity—*Nezipha*, for seven days, *Niddui*, for thirty days, and the Cherem, which lasts indefinitely until it has been formally removed. Before any of these forms can be carried out, the offender must be given three separate opportunities for repentance.

Chevra (חברה).

Originally, this expression was applied to any association of Jews for religious purposes, but nowadays it is restricted to the smaller congregations, which are a combination of Synagogue and Benefit Society.

Chevra Kadesha (חברא קדישא).

The duties connected with the preparation of the dead for their last home are considered to be incumbent on all good Israelites, and in most congregations it was usual for the most pious to form a rota to perform this duty. Among the Sephardim, such persons are called "Lavadores" (*q.v.*).

Chiddush (חדוש, lit. "news").

"What's the news?" is in Jewish talk represented by "What's Chiddush?" But the term is very characteristic of Jewish life, as it was originally applied to new points in the interpretation of the Law. When Jews meet together, the Law should form part of their talk. Opportunities for novel interpretation were thus afforded at every meeting of Jews. The term has, however, in ordinary talk, lost this significance entirely, and applies to anything that is new, especially of a gossiping character.

Chief Rabbi.

In some countries there is no single Rabbi who may claim spiritual prerogative over the rest of the ecclesiastical authorities. Indeed, since the disappearance of the High Priest, there has been no such central authority in Judaism, though the Geonim in Babylon exercised something of the authority of the High Priest for some centuries. But, owing to the relations of the Jews with the Government in various countries, it has happened on several occasions that one Rabbi has received special privileges beyond the rest, and thus in England, in the pre-expulsion times, there was a "Presbyter Omnium Judæorum," and in Navarre there was a "Rab Mayor" with corresponding position. In France, owing to the Constitution given to the French Jews by Napoleon, after the Assembly of the Sanhedrim, there is a Chief Rabbi of France, who is head of the whole French clergy, and even exercises some authority over the clergy of Belgium, Switzerland and parts of Italy, which were all under French rule in the Napoleonic era. In England, owing to a clause in the Act by which the United Synagogue was constituted, the Chief Rabbi has authority over the ritual and discipline of the Constituent Synagogues of that body. And this authority is practically extended over all the Synagogues of the British Empire, except those of the Sephardim (*q.v.*) and the Reformed Synagogues.

Chilul Hashem (חלול השם).

Jews, being a people of priests, any disgraceful act performed by an individual Jew, not alone brings shame upon himself, but is regarded as being a profanation of the name of God whose servant he is. Such an act is described in Jewish parlance as Chilul Hashem, "profanation of the Name." The opposite of this is "Kid-dush Hashem," which see.

Chinuch (חנוך, lit. "dedication").

When a Jew moves into a new house, it is sanctified, according to the Jewish principle of hallowing the home, by a special

Jewish ceremonial known by this title. Appropriate Psalms are read, especially Psalm xxx., and Mezuzoth (*q.v.*) are fixed upon the door posts. The word Chinuch is also applied to many other acts of "dedication" or initiation, *e.g.*, to education and training in the practice of the religious precepts.

Chol Hamoed (חול המעד).

The two festivals which last seven days, viz., Passover and Tabernacles, are kept more strictly by Jews at the beginning and end—which are days of Solemn Assembly—than in the middle period, which is known by the above name. These are practically only half holydays.

Chomash (חומש, lit. "fifth," pronounced *Chummesh*).

A popular term applied to the five Books of Moses.

Christ (from Greek χρίστος, lit. "Anointed").

The word is an English transcript, through the Latin, of the Greek translation of the Hebrew "Messiah" (*q.v.*), which is a specific Jewish conception. Indeed, etymologically, it implies much more the Jewish than the Christian Messiah, as it refers to the special mark of sovereignty, the unction which was the formal sign of a king, the term being applied in Scripture to kings like Saul and Zedekiah. Owing, however, to the crimes committed in the name, Jews have an objection to using it.

Chuetas.

The name given to the secret Jews in the Balearic Islands. They correspond to the Marranos elsewhere (*q.v.*).

Chukath Hagoyim (חוקת הגויים, lit. "custom of the Gentiles").

Jews have always jealously guarded against adopting the customs of surrounding nations, especially in religious matters. The influence of the Bible has been especially strong in this direction. Any deviation from this principle, which was almost a matter of necessity in the peculiar position of the Jews, is called a "Custom of the Gentiles."

Chuppa (חפה).

The Baldachin or Canopy under which the marriage ceremonial is nowadays performed. The top of the Chuppa is often composed of the curtain of the Ark of the Law, supported by four posts, which are held by the friends of the bride and bridegroom. In some countries a Talith (*q.v.*) is merely held over the heads of the couple. It probably represents the older withdrawing-room of the wedded pair, but it is now supposed to symbolise their future home.

Chutzpah (חצפה, lit. "presumption").

This Hebrew term is applied to a very distinctive Jewish quality. The Jew has the courage of his opinion about himself, and in displaying it, exhibits what is known among Jews as "Chutzpah." It is not really impudence, because it has a sort of backbone of ability attached to it, but it is often mistaken for impudence by others than Jews, and is one of the elements that contribute to their want of popularity. George Brandes, in his monograph on Lasalle, begins by pointing out that his chief characteristic was "chutzpah."

Circumcision (*see* Berith Milah).

Cohen (כהן, lit. "Priest"), plural, Cohanim.

This name, so frequent among Jews, invariably denotes one of the reputed descendants of the priestly caste in ancient Israel, though there are Cohanim, like Dr. Adler, the present Chief Rabbi, Mr. Shechter and the Rev. Morris Joseph, who do not bear that surname in civil life. As a consequence of their priestly descent, the Cohanim have certain privileges and disabilities. On various solemn occasions they give the priestly benediction with outstretched hands (*see* Hands of Cohanim), and they are always "called up" first to the reading of the Law, but only one Cohen can be called up at the same service, neither may a Cohen contaminate himself by being in the same place as the dead (Lev. xxi. 1-3). Hence, except in the case of near relatives, a Cohen must not enter a house when a death has occurred, or a Beth Chayim (*q.v.*). They must not marry a divorced woman (*see* Lev. xxi. 7, and the first part of *Children of the Ghetto*), or a proselyte. Hence, it is probable that the Cohanim, at any rate, are direct descendants of the ancient Jews.

Confirmation.

Up to the present century, while the religious majority of Jewish boys was and is celebrated by a special ceremony (*see* Bar Mitzvah), there was no definite celebration for Jewish girls. But recently it has become customary in some synagogues to confirm Jewish girls who have gone through a training in the principles of the Jewish religion. The ceremony is not confined to one individual, but includes all those who have passed the required course during the year.

Crypto-Jews.

Owing to persecution, many Jews have only been able to preserve their distinctive rites in a secret fashion. *See* Anussim, Gedid al Islam, Chuetas, and Marranos.

Daggatouns (Arab., lit. "traders").

A tribe of Jewish descent residing among the Touaregs dwelling in the Desert of Adgad, Sahara. They do not inter-marry with the Touaregs. They were visited by Rabbi Mordecai Abi Serour in 1880. They acknowledge their descent from Jews, but are now Mahommedans.

Darshan (דרשן, lit. "explain"), plural Darshanim.

Preachers who explain the Holy Scriptures, and make this the main subject of their discourse, are called by this term.

Dates.

Jews reckon by the era of the Creation, which they place 3,760 years before the Christian Era. This era was adopted at about the 10th century. Before that time, the Greek Era of the Seleucids (169 B.C.) is usual in Jewish documents under the title of "The Era of Contracts." The Jewish year, beginning in the autumn, covers part of two whole years. Thus, 5657 corresponds to part of 1896 and part of 1897. To reduce the ordinary date to the Jewish, subtract 1,240 from the Christian date, and add the result to 5,000. Some Jews have an objection to using A.D. (Anno Domini) and prefer to use C.E. (Common Era) instead of it. There is a touch of the Quaker about this, and on the same principle no reference should be made to Thursday, "the day of Thor."

Daven (Germ.), To pray, especially in public worship, and aloud.

Dayan (דיין, lit. "Judge"), plural Dayanim.

The name of the ecclesiastical assessor who decides points of Rabbinic Law at the Beth Din (*q.v.*). According to J. Jacobs (*Jews of Angevin England*, p. 372), the Dayanim were known in early England by the name of "Episcopi" or Bishops.

Derasha (דרשה, lit. "explanation").

Originally applied only to such sermons as are devoted to interpretation of the Scripture, but nowadays used popularly as the title of all sermons, or even exhortations, as in the expression, "He gave us a *derasha*."

Derech Eretz (דרך ארץ, lit. "way of").

The Jewish title for courtesy. One of the minor tractates of the Talmud has this title.

Din (דין, lit. "judgment").

As the whole of a Jew's life has an appropriate action for each of its stages, it is of importance for a Jew to know the law for each act. This is expressed by the term *Din*, which really means a reference to some former legal decision given upon the special act. As contrasted with Torah (*q.v.*) Din may be compared to Judge-made law in relation to statutes, or as bye-laws as contrasted with main laws.

Divorce.

According to Mosaic legislation (Deut. xxiv. 1), a man could divorce his wife if he were not pleased with her. In later periods this laxity was considerably reduced. In the first place, a man was not allowed to divorce his wife until he had paid the settlement mentioned in the Kethuba (*q.v.*). It was further decided, c. 1000 A.D., when monogamy was established among Western Jews, that the wife could not be divorced against her will, unless for a specific cause, as, *e.g.*, adultery, or barrenness after ten years of married life. A wife who obstinately refused to follow her husband to a new home, was also liable to divorce. There is no indication that a Jewess could demand a divorce in Biblical times, but the Rabbis allowed her to do so if ill-treated by her husband, or if he changed his religion, or if he had to leave his country to avoid the consequences of crime.

The formula of divorce consists in the husband handing or sending a "bill of divorce" to his wife (*see* "Get"). In western Europe divorce is only granted after the marriage tie has been severed by the Civil Courts.

Duchan (דוכן, lit. "platform").

The Priestly Benediction which was performed in the Temple strictly in accordance with the enactments laid down in Numbers vi. 21–27, with the traditional and sacrosanct pronunciation of the Tetragrammaton. In the Synagogue, the blessing is divided into three separate portions, separated from one another by the responses of the congregation, the Tetragrammaton is replaced by "Adonai," and the blessing is pronounced with covered head and uplifted hands, (*See* Hands of Cohanim.) It is customary not to look at the priests during the performance of this function, and according to popular belief blindness would result if this injunction were disobeyed. The priests must be in a state of ritual purity when performing this office, and, for that purpose, it is preceded by solemn lavation of the hands, during which the laver is held by Levites.

Elijah's Chair.

A seat put aside for the prophet at a Berith Millah (*q.v.*). The Sandek (*q.v.*) often sits in it nowadays when he holds the child.

Elijah's Cup.

During the service of Passover night, a special cup is laid for the prophet Elijah, which is filled at a certain stage of the ceremony. According to popular belief the prophet, who did not die, sometimes makes his appearance among men to warn them from evil, or aid them in some good action. But it is probably in his position as forerunner of the Messiah that he is expected on Passover night, and the cup may, therefore, be connected with the wish, "Next year at Jerusalem." There was a tradition that the Temple would be rebuilt at the time of Passover.

Epicurus.

Heretics or persons lax in their religious observances are spoken of by many Jews by the name of the Greek philosopher, who, with them, as with others, became the synonym for selfish indulgence.

Erubim (ערובים).

Owing to the certain inconvenience which a very strict and literal observance of the Sabbath would involve, the Rabbis admit certain modifications, which are signified by this term. They are mainly as follows, (1) The extension of all Sabbath journeys to four thousand paces instead of two thousand paces for the purpose of performing a Mitzvah (*q.v.*). (2) Preparation of food for Sabbath on the holyday immediately preceding it, if such preparation is only continued from the Thursday. (3). Permission to carry out articles from a private place into the street, by considering a district inhabited entirely by Jews as a "private place." (*See* Reshuth.)

Evil Eye.

No signs of the existence of this superstition among Jews is to be found in the Bible or in the Mishna, but several references in the Gemara show that the Jews shared in this superstition. In particular it was believed that the decendants of Joseph were not liable to be injured by the Evil Eye. Ashkenazim at the present day use the German expressions "*umbeschrien*" and "*umberufen*," whenever they praise anything or anyone in whom they are interested, and thereby unconsciously express their belief in witchcraft, the former expression being equivalent to the English "*beshrew me*."

Execution, Four modes of.

According to the Bible, there were four modes of executing criminals—strangulation, stoning, burning and beheading. The Rabbis made some of these much milder. Instead of burning, the criminal was strangled, and a lighted taper placed for a moment in his open mouth. In the case of stoning, the criminal was cast down from a height. The four forms were thus reduced to two, strangling and beheading, as in English law. Crucifixion was never Jewish, but only a Roman punishment, which was applied in the case of slaves, and those not possessing Roman citizenship.

Falashas (lit. "emigrants"; *cf*. Philistines).

A Jewish sect of Abyssinia, who are probably descendants of the old Jewish Himyarite kingdom of South Arabia. They are not Jews in race, but their ritual is distinctly Jewish, though written in the Gez language. They number some 50,000, and were visited by Mons. J. Halevy, on behalf of the Alliance Israélite.

Fast of Esther.

The 13th of Adar, being the day appointed by Ahasuerus through the instigation of Haman for the slaughter of the Jews, is kept as a minor fast, beginning in the morning.

Fasting.

On the Day of Atonement the Israelites were commanded to "afflict their souls," and this has been interpreted by Jewish tradition to mean a concomitant strict abstention from all nourishment. This interpretation is confirmed by Ps. xxxv. 13. The abstinence is of the strictest kind, not a morsel of food, solid or liquid, being allowed to enter the lips during the fast.

Fasts.

In addition to the Day of Atonement fasts are kept on the day before Passover (Fast of the Firstborn), Tammuz 17th, Ab 9th, Tishri 3rd (Fast of Gedaliah, *q.v.*), Tebeth 9th, and Adar 13th (Fast of Esther). Besides these days, fasts are kept up by some on the first and second Monday and the first Thursday of Iyar and last of Cheshvan, to atone for sins they may have committed on the holy days of the preceding months. Also it was customary, for mystical reasons, to fast on Sabbath afternoons. In the various congregations during the Middle Ages, in addition to these, fasts were kept locally on the days on which persecutions and martyrdoms had occurred in the districts.

Finta (Portuguese).

The word used by the Sephardim for the taxes paid to the Synagogue.

Fried Fish.

Amongst English Jews, a special form of fish fried in oil is a favourite food during the chief festivals and on Sabbaths. This may be thought a general Jewish custom, and might even be referred to the liking for fish shown by Jews in the Biblical times ("We remember the fish which we did eat in Egypt freely," Num. xi. 5), but, as a matter of fact, the favourite dish of the Continental Jews is Shalet (*q.v.*), and it is probable the liking for fried fish in England is derived from the Dutch Jews, among whom it is likewise found.

Frimsel.

A particular form of soup in much favour among English Jews. It is formed of a very thin vermicelli, and the term is itself a corruption of that Italian word.

"Froom."

Pious Jews are said to be "froom," which is simply an English adaptation of the German *fromm*.

Gabbai (גבאי, lit. "collector").

The two wardens of the Synagogue are termed respectively Parnass (*q.v.*) and Gabbai, the latter being technically, and often really, the treasurer. The late Professor Hatch was of opinion that the office of Bishop was originally derived from the office of Gabbai, the literal meaning of Bishop being "overseer."

Gallery, Synagogue.

For various reasons, women have always been separated from men during public service. They used even to worship in a separate room communicating with the main building of the synagogue. It has, however, become usual for the ladies to have their seats in a gallery raised above the floor of the synagogue; and, until recently, this was itself hidden from view behind a *grille*.

Gaon, pl. Geonim (גאון, lit. "excellence").

The title applied to the religious leader of the Jews at Bagdad, after the conclusion of the Talmud. The most celebrated of the Geonim was Saadia, a great philosopher and exegete. The last of them was Hai Gaon, and up to the present day, in complimentary addresses, great Rabbis are often entitled "Gaon."

Gedaliah, Fast of.

After the first fall of Jerusalem, a number of the more pious Israelites were assembled together under Gedaliah, the son of

Ahikam, protector of Jeremiah, and the grandson of Sophan, one of the leaders of the revival under Josiah. It seemed possible that, through Gedaliah's influence, the kingdom of Judah might have been reconstituted, but this hope was destroyed by his assassination by Ishmael (Jer. xl. 2). In memory of this event, which had fatal consequences on the future of Jews, the fast is kept by pious Jews on Tishri 3rd. The Fast begins in the morning.

Gehinnom (גיהנום, lit. "Valley of Hinnom").

The rubbish of Jerusalem used to be cast out into the Valley of Hinnom and there burnt. Here, too, the bodies of the dead were burnt. For these reasons, the name was adopted by later Jews for the Biblical Sheol (*q.v.*).

Gelilah (גלילה, lit. "rolling up").

When the Scroll of the Law (*q.v.*) is removed from the Ark (*q.v.*), its appurtenances have to be removed before it can be unrolled and placed upon the reading desk. When it is to be returned to the Ark, it must, of course, be rolled up and covered with the mantle, and this process is called "gelila." It is considered a special privilege or mitzvah (*q.v.*) to perform this function.

Gemara (גמרא, lit. "learning" or "completion").

A commentary of the Mishna (*q.v.*), giving in many instances the discussions and developments of the various laws and other matters contained in the text. The Mishna and Gemara, taken together, constitute the Talmud (*q.v.*).

Gematria (גמטריא, lit. "geometry").

As the Hebrew letters are used also for figures (*see* Numerals), words with different meanings may often represent the same numerals. A curious system has grown up, chiefly under mystical influence, of interchanging such words. A classical instance of Gematria is the number of the Great Beast in Revelations, where 666 represents Nero Cæsar. On the same principle Chronograms are used in Hebrew books, sentences with certain of the letters printed in different type being often employed to express their dates.

Geneza (גניזה).

It being considered indecorous to destroy any document having the Name of God printed on it, there used to be attached to most Synagogues a receptacle for torn or otherwise injured pieces of MS. written in Hebrew. Of recent years, this custom has led to the discovery of many valuable documents, though of course in a very fragmentary state, in the Genezoth attached to the various Eastern Synagogues.

Ger (גר, lit. "stranger"), plural Gerim.

The term applied to a Jewish proselyte. In earlier days, a distinction was made between "Proselytes of the Gate" and proselytes pure and simple, the former only undertaking to refrain from idolatry, the latter being obliged to conform to all Jewish customs, especially, in the case of a male, the rite of circumcision. There were a large number of proselytes of the gate in the early Roman Empire (*see* Juvenal, ed. Mayor, notes on x. 63 *seq.*), but most, if not all of these, went over to Christianity under the influence of St. Paul, who made a special appeal to them. A female proselyte is called *qeyurith* or *qeyurista*.

Get (גט, lit. "document").

The ceremony of divorce consists in the handing of the husband, in the presence of ten witnesses, to his wife, a written bill of divorce, which is called Get. The man is first asked whether he has made any vow forcing him to the act from which he could be freed. The woman is also asked whether she is willing to accept the divorce. The woman cannot marry for ninety days after the divorce, or, in certain cases, not before twenty-four or twenty-five months. The bill of divorce is written with special care and in a prescribed form, which must be exactly followed, or else the divorce is not legal.

Gevatter (Germ. "godfather," "gossip").

At the ceremony of circumcision one of the relatives or friends of the father holds the child, and is called Gevatter, a German term which corresponds to Godfather in the ceremony of baptism.

Ghetto.

The term applied to the quarter of the city in which Jews most do congregate. In the Middle Ages, this restriction of residence was compulsory, but even nowadays, when there is no legal restriction of the kind, it is customary for Jews to dwell near one another for convenience and choice. The term is supposed to be derived from the Getta, or Foundry of Venice, where the first Ghetto was established in 1516.

Goluth (גלות, lit. "exile").

Since the destruction of the Temple and the dispersion of the Jews, they regard themselves as living in exile, to which this term is applied. They regard their present position as the natural result of their exile.

Gonoph (גנב, lit. "thief").

This term has passed into English slang in its original Hebrew meaning. It deserves a place in this List, as it is the only Hebrew word that passed into middle English from contact with the pre-expulsion Jews of England. Chaucer uses it in the second line of his "Miller's Tale," in the curious form "a riche gnof." which puzzled all Chaucerian scholars till Mr. I. Gollancz elucidated its meaning. Dickens also uses it in "Bleak House" and "Sketches by Boz."

Goy, fem. Goya, plural Goyim (גוי, lit. "Gentile").

This term is applied in the Bible to the surrounding nations, but in modern Jewish parlance it simply means a non-Jew. There is, perhaps, a certain touch of contempt about the name when used by Jews, corresponding to the similar connotation of Jew among *les autres.* A curious adjective has been formed to distinguish Gentile customs or things, viz., "Goyish," which is a combination of the Hebrew Goy, and the German termination "isch." Among Jews themselves, "goy" is an opprobrious epithet, meaning "unobservant of the ceremonies."

Hagada (הגדה, lit. "telling").

This term has two meanings in Jewish practice: (1) The method of interpretation of the Scripture which deals with the more imaginative parts of it, and as contrasted with the legal parts of it known as Halacha (*q.v.*); (2) The service for the first two nights of Passover, which consists mainly of a telling of the story of the Exodus, is also known by this name. Many Hagadas are illustrated by woodcuts or, in MSS., by illuminations. It is supposed that the communion service of the Church is mainly derived from the Hagada. (*See* Seder.)

Hagbaa (הגבהה, lit. "elevation").

At the beginning or conclusion of the Lesson from the Law, the Scroll upon which it is read is lifted and shown to the congregation, who stand up in its honour. This process is known by the name of Hagbaa, and is a special privilege or Mitzvah (*q.v.*).

Haham (חכם, lit. "wise").

The term applied by the Oriental Jews, and the Sephardim, or Spanish and Portuguese Jews, to their Chief Rabbi. It is variously spelled when transcribed into English or other languages, as, *e.g.*, Chacham, Chakam, Cacam, Jaxam (old Spanish).

Halacha (הלכה, lit. "direction").

A name applied to the legislative portion of Talmudic and Rabbinic literature. As new cases arise which are not definitely determined by Biblical enactments, they are decided by the Rabbis on principles which mainly depend upon a peculiar interpretation of the Biblical texts. This method of interpretation and its results, as applied to practical Jewish life, is known by the name of Halacha.

Hallel (הלל, lit. "praise").

Psalms of Praise, *e.g.*, ciii.-cvii. are known by this name, and occur as integral parts of the ritual on several occasions, *e.g.* in the Seder service.

"Haman's Ears."

Cakes of flour, eggs, olive oil and cinnamon, cut in the shape of a human ear and eaten during Purim (*q.v.*), as a further remembrance of the arch-traitor of the day.

Hands of Cohanim.

The chief sacred function which the Cohen (*q.v.*) has to perform nowadays is the solemn blessing bestowed by him upon the congregation before the last portion of the Amida (*q.v.*) on festivals which do not occur on the Sabbath. During priestly benediction, the heads of the Cohanim are covered with the Talith (*q.v.*), and in addition to this the hands are raised with the fingers separated by a division between the middle and ring finger. This position of the fingers, which is somewhat difficult to acquire, is regarded as characteristic of the Cohanim, and is often embroidered on the Talith, or carved upon the tombstone. It may be conjectured that the similar position of the hand used by a Bishop in giving the Episcopal Benediction is derived from this. Various explanations are given of this peculiar position, one of them being that the fingers in that position represent the Hebrew letter "Shin" standing for שדי, or "Almighty." Another explanation is that the four fingers represent the Tetragrammaton (*q.v.*). It has been suggested that by these means the Shekinah is conducted down to the earth.

Haphtorah (הפטרה).

In addition to the lesson from the Pentateuch read from the Scrolls of the Law, there is a second lesson, taken from the Prophets and known by the above name. The tradition goes that during the tyranny of Antiochus before the Maccabean war, the Jews were not allowed to have Scrolls of the Law, and had to content themselves with readings from the Prophets.

Hatorath Hora-ah (התרת הראה).

When the practice of Ordination (*q.v.*) was given up, there was substituted for it a plan of giving a certificate of competence in the Law, known by this name, and conferring upon a Rabbi (*q.v.*) the right to Pasken (*q.v.*). This can be granted by one who has himself obtained the degree.

Hebrew.

Abraham is spoken of as an Hebrew (Gen. xiv. 13), and the Jews, as descendants of Abraham, may also claim to be Hebrews; but as this term might also apply to descendants of Ishmael and Esau, it is not very appropriate, and is mainly used as a stylistic synonym. It would, perhaps, be more correct if "Hebrew" was used only to describe the Children of Israel up to the foundation of the Monarchy, "Israelite," from that time till the return from the exile, and "Jews" from that eventful date up to the present day. (*See* Israelite, Jew.) On the other hand, the term Hebrew is appropriately applied to the language used by the Israelites when in their own land. (*See* Leshon ha-kodesh.)

Hep! Hep!

The cry of the Crusaders as they attacked the Jews, said to be derived from the initials of the three words "Hierosolyma est perdita" (Jerusalem is lost) but more probably from the German,

"Hab," Hab." The expression is often used with reference to Anti-Semitic outbreaks at the present day.

Hesped (הספד).

It is usual to deliver an oration over the tombs of great Jewish scholars or worthies, expatiating on their merits. Such orations are known by this name.

Hofjude (German, lit. "Court Jew").

During the depressed condition of the Jews in Germany in the last century, a few exceptional individuals were exempted from most of the disabilities placed upon their co-religionists, almost invariably because they had rendered assistance of some sort to the reigning monarch. Hence they were called Court Jews. The father of the late Baron de Hirsch was one.

Hoshana Rabba (הושענא רבה).

The seventh day of the Feast of Tabernacles, so called because many prayers beginning with Hoshanna are recited, during the performance of which seven processions round the Synagogue are made. On this day it is customary to beat leaves off twigs of willow, possibly as a symbol of the evanescence of life, though much superstition is connected with the custom, it being sometimes thought that the leaves represent sins.

Ikkarim (עקרים, lit. "principles"). *See* Thirteen Articles.

Israelite.

Descendant of Israel. This term is, strictly speaking, more general than "Jew" (*q.v.*), applying to the twelve tribes, whereas Jew, even in its more extended signification, only applies to three. When Jews were persecuted on the Continent and in England, they preferred for some time to be called Israelites rather than Jews, but this custom is dying out.

Jahrzeit (pronounced Yartsite. German, lit. "Anniversary").

It is customary for the Jews to say Kaddish and keep a burning light in the house on the Jewish anniversary of the death of a parent. It is probable that the latter custom was derived from Christian influence.

Jehovah.

This term, as is well known, is due to a mistake. After the fall of the Temple the true pronunciation of the Tetragrammaton (*q.v.*) was lost, and wherever it occurred in the Ritual or in Scripture the word "Adonai" was pronounced instead of it. When the vowel-points were introduced into Hebrew writing, the vowels proper to Adonai were added to the consonants of the Tetragrammaton, to indicate that that form should be uttered instead of the sacred word itself. When Christian theologians began to study Hebrew, they thought that the vowels belonged to the word itself, and so transliterated it "Jehovah."

Jewry (old Fr. collective term *Juifverie*).

This word is applied to the place where Jews most do congregate, and corresponds in England with the Ghetti and Judengassen (*q.v.*) of the Continent. Of recent years, it has become customary to apply the term to the inhabitants of the Jewry as a collective term, thus reverting to the original meaning of the word.

Jews (Etym., "Descendants of Judah").

This term is nowadays applied to all existing descendants of Israel, though, strictly speaking, it only applied to the tribe of Judah. It is really a survival of the division of the old kingdom of Israel into two parts, the Northern and the Southern, Israel and Judah. The kingdom of Israel comprised ten tribes who were never restored to the Holy Land (*see* Ten Tribes). The kingdom of Judah was reconstituted by Cyrus as a semi-dependent republic, and the two tribes of Judah and Benjamin, which composed it, restored to their land. In addition to these the sacred tribe of Levi also came back, so that the term "Jew" includes members of the two tribes of Benjamin and Levi as well as Judah.

The etymology of the English word is somewhat curious. Thus, it is derived from the old French, *Juieu*, which was a popular condensation of the Latin *Judæus*, derived from the Greek Ἰουδαῖος, as found in the LXX. The old French made the feminine form *Juiue*, and from this the modern French, *Juif*, is formed as masculine (*see* Darmestetter's "Dictionnaire," *s.v.*).

The moral significance of the word has also somewhat changed. It used to be employed as a term of contempt, and for a time Jews were somewhat chary of claiming the name, calling themselves Israelites by preference; but, with the recent revival of nationalist feeling, the national name has come into favour again, and Hebrew and Israelite have almost disappeared in common use among Jews.

Jubilee.

According to the Mosaical enactments (Lev. xv. 9, 10) after seven Sabbatical years (*q.v.*), the fiftieth year should be the "Sabbatical year of Sabbatical years," and in addition to entire liberty for the land to recover its fertility, all slaves became free, and each man came into his hereditary property. The command was given "for *all* the inhabitants," and the Jews, after the exile, considered that this freed them from this injunction, which was regarded by them as only being valid while *all* Israelites were in the Holy Land.

Judaism.

To express the distinctive practice and creed of Jews, this term has come into use, corresponding to the word Christianity as summing up the creed of Christians.

Judengasse (lit. "Jews Alley").

The Ghetti of the German Jews are generally known by this name, and from the signs attached to the shops in the Judengasse of Frankfort, many Jewish families, notably the Rothschilds (Red Shield), obtained their name.

Judenhetze (German, lit. "Jew-baiting").

When Anti-Semitism appeared in Germany, the friends of toleration called it by the above name to signify its true character.

Judenhut (German, "Jew's Hat").

In some parts of Germany, in addition to the Badge (*q.v.*) Jews were obliged to wear a hat, generally of a fixed colour, and with horns on each side.

Jus Chazaka.

As the Ghetti were so confined in space, while the Jewish population within them naturally increased with every generation, the landowners would have been able to rackrent the inhabitants but for an understanding among them that they should not compete with one another, and that the tenant right of a Jew should pass on to his children. This principle was known by the above name, which is a combination of Hebrew and Latin. It is fully described in Mr. Israel Abrahams' *Jewish Life*.

Kaddish (קדיש, lit. "holy").

A prayer of the Jewish Liturgy, recited at the end of any section of the Synagogue Service and at the end of Rabbinic lectures; also, and chiefly, a prayer recited by orphans for the welfare of the souls of their deceased parents. It merely consists of praise of God's goodness, and is thus a pathetic development of Job's great word, "The Lord hath given, the Lord hath taken away. Blessed be the Name of the Lord." Part of it is written in Aramaic and various forms of it exist. It is said by orphans for eleven months after the death of a parent and on every Jahrzeit (*q.v.*) succeeding. Much superstition is connected with the saying of this prayer, which is supposed to relieve souls from purgatory, somewhat after the fashion of the Catholic Mass, which may be connected with it. It is not said for more than eleven months, as that would imply that the parent was worthy of Gehinnom (*q.v.*).

Kaftan.

The long outer garment, reaching to the heels, worn usually among the Polish Jews. It was once the national costume of Poland, and it has been preserved by the conservative Polish Jews, who consider it distinctive of their creed.

Kalla (כלה), "bride," and so used.

Kaluth rosh (קלות ראש, lit. "lightness of the head").

The Jews keep up the Eastern custom of keeping the head covered, especially during prayer, and it is considered indecorous for a person of great piety or learning in the Law to appear with "a lightness of the head," *i.e.*, without a covering on it. This often consists of a silk or velvet cap, which is placed upon the head as soon as the ordinary hat is removed.

Kal vachomer (קל וחומר, lit. "light and heavy").

This is one of the technical terms of Rabbinic logic, by which they deduce one principle from another. It is practically the argument *à fortiori*.

Karaites or Karaim (lit. "Readers [of Holy Writ]").

The Protestants of Judaism. In the eighth century a reaction took place against the Talmudic developments of the Halacha (*q.v.*), and, under the leadership of a Rabbi, named Anan, a sect was formed which professed to return to the Pentateuch as the sole source of Jewish legislation. As a matter of fact, the Karaites found it necessary to have an Oral Law of their own, which was mainly borrowed from the Rabbanites (as the rest of the Jews are called in contradistinction to the Karaites). The chief seat of the Karaites was in the Crimea, where it is probable they found many adherents among the Chazars (*q.v.*). They still exist there to the number of some three thousand, and their peculiar form of Judaism is recognised by the Russian State as a tolerated creed, chiefly in order to emphasise the Russian attitude towards the rest of the Jews. A few Karaites also exist in Hungary and at Jerusalem.

Kasher (כשר, lit. "fit" or "clean").

The term applied to food properly prepared according to Jewish law and custom. According to the Mosaic legislation Jews are restricted, as regards animal food, to ruminants, and with regard to the inhabitants of the sea, to such fish as have gills and scales. But before even the former can be eaten, it has to be prepared in a special way, and it is mainly in regard to this that the term "Kasher" (pronounced "Kōsher") is applied. The animal must be killed in such a way as to remove all the blood (*see* Shechita), and must, when killed, answer the requirements of Bedika (*q.v.*), and even then, before being cooked, it has to remain in water and in salt. (*See* Melicha.) Any food which does not answer to these various requirements is called "Trepha" (*q.v.*).

Kashya (קשיה, lit. "difficulty").

One of the means by which the Rabbis encouraged the study of the Talmud was to invent difficult problems to be solved by the peculiar Talmudic rules. Each of these was known as Kashya. (*See* Chiddush.)

Kavod (כבוד, lit. "glory").

The feeling of honour is expressed by this term, which is also used to signify a honour conferred. A person or family who are in this sense honourable are entitled "bekovet."

Kedushah (קדושה, lit. "holiness").

The term applied to a prayer as read in the third paragraph of the Amida (*q.v.*). It derives its name from the recital of the cry of the Seraphim, "Holy! Holy! Holy!" from Isaiah vi. 3. It occurs as the Trisagion in the Church Liturgy.

Kehilla (קהלה), lit. "congregation," and so used.

Ke niah (קמיעא, perhaps Caméo).

Though, strictly speaking, Judaism sets itself against anything like amulets, it is frequently the practice among superstitious Jews to possess such things. These are inscribed with the names of angels, etc., or with Cabbalistic signs and formulæ, which are supposed to bring good luck to the wearer.

Keri u-Kethib (קרי וכתיב, lit. "read and written").

This is a term of the Massora (*q.v.*) which is used to indicate that in certain passages of the Bible a different reading is to be adopted to that indicated by the *consonants* of the text. This is shown by writing the vowels of the Keri or word which is to be read under the consonants of the Kethib or word as written. (*See* "Jehovah.")

Kethuba (כתובה, lit. "writing").

The Marriage Contract, which constitutes one of the essential parts of a Jewish wedding, and contains the bridegroom's promise to honour and support his wife, and to present her with a certain sum as a settlement of not less than 200 sus (100 in the case of a widow), besides the dowry of the bride. This sum is to be paid in the case of the husband's death or in the case of a divorce, and is thus a check upon a too easy resort to that expedient.

Kevana (כונה).

This term is applied to the devotion with which prayers should be said, and hence to any zealous performance of duty. Prof. Steinthal has written a fine analysis of the feeling in his essays *Zu Bibel und Religionsphilosophie* (Berlin, 1891).

Kiddush (קדוש, lit. "sanctification").

The ceremony by which the coming in of Sabbaths and Festivals was sanctified in synagogue and in the home. According to the Jewish principle of hallowing the home, all causes for rejoicing are connected with religion, and Kiddush is thus a characteristically Jewish ceremonial. It consists of drinking from a cup of wine after an appropriate benediction. According to the Talmud, "the prayer of Kiddush belongs to the meal" (Pes. 101, a.). From this it would seem that there is no justification for the Kiddush in synagogue, but it is probably a survival of the time when meals for strangers used to be prepared in the synagogue, or in adjoining rooms.

Kiddush Hachama (קדוש החמה, lit. "Sanctification of the Sun").

Every 28 years, the vernal equinox recurs at exactly the same point of time in the Jewish year, and this occasion is celebrated by a special service and blessing.

Kiddush ha-Shem (קדוש השם, lit. "Sanctification of the Name").

As any disgraceful act done by a Jew brings disgrace not only upon himself, but upon his religion (*see* Chilul Hashem), so any noble deed was regarded as redounding to the greater glory of God. Hence, martyrs who suffered for their faith, or who committed suicide rather than forswear their faith were regarded as performing their heroic actions for the "Sanctification of the Name."

Kiddushin (קדושין).

The term applied to the first stage in the ceremony of marriage, and hence to marriage generally (*q.v.*).

Kinnui (כנוי).

The secular name by which a Jew is known among his fellow-citizens is called his Kinnui, while the name with which he is called up to the Law, and identified in Hebrew deeds—his holy name—is called his Shem Hakodesh.

Kinoth (קנות, lit. "lamented").

The term applied in synagogal poetry to elegies, specially to those on the Fast of Ab.

Kippur (כפור).

See Yom Kippur.

Kiss.

Owing to the beautiful Rabbinic tradition in regard to the death of Aaron through a Divine kiss, mystical influence has been attributed to the kiss by the Cabbalists (*q.v.*). It is possible also that the kiss of peace of the early Christian Church was influenced by this tradition.

Kneeling.

Jews do not kneel at prayers except on New Year's Day and the Day of Atonement, when the rarity of the act makes it more impressive. The only reason given for this reluctance to kneel is that it is Chukath Hagoyim (*q.v.*).

Kol Nidre (כל נדרי, lit. "all vows").

Before the actual beginning of the Atonement Service, three Jews of reputed piety and knowledge of the Law ascend the reading desk, and constituting a Beth Din (*q.v.*), recite three times a formula releasing Jews from all vows which they might lay upon themselves during the succeeding year. It was probably intended as a warning against hurtful vows which would probably be entered upon during the excitement of the most solemn day of the year, and would be against the third commandment, but the enemies of the Jews have interpreted it as releasing them from the consequences of a legal oath, to which, of course, it has no application, having reference only to vows laid upon oneself in regard to one's own character. Another explanation is that the recital referred to the permission for Jews to pray in the presence of reverts to the faith.

Kupah (קופה, lit. "cup").

Beside the Tamchui (*q.v.*), or gift in kind, it was customary among mediæval Jews to have a poor-box, in which gifts of money can be deposited, which is known as Kupah.

Ladino.

Just as the German Jews speak a certain dialect of their own (*see* Yiddish), so the descendants of the exiles from Spain in 1492 still speak a certain dialect of Spanish which is known as above. This preserves many archaic Spanish words and expressions, and a tolerably large literature has been printed in it. A full account has been given by Dr. Kayserling in Ersch and Gruber, and a chrestomathy was published in 1896 by Dr. Grünbaum. Like Yiddish, Ladino is mainly printed in Hebrew characters.

GLOSSARY OF JEWISH TERMS.

Lag b'Omer (ל״ג בעמר, lit. "33 in Omer." Properly, ל״ג לעמר).

Between Passover and Pentecost, the Omer (*q.v.*) is counted, and during most of that time (from Iyar 1st) no marriages can be performed except on the 33rd day of Omer. It is conjectured, with much probability, that this custom was derived by the Jews from the Romans, who did not marry during May.

Lamp, Perpetual (נר תמיד).

In every synagogue a lamp is kept burning perpetually, immediately in front of the Ark. This is done in memory of the Temple service, where such a Lamp was lighted every night (Ex. xxvii.) as is known from the Maccabæan legend of the Feast of Dedication (*see* Chanuca). It is usually a swinging lamp, supplied with oil.

Lavadores.

The term used among the Spanish Jews for members of the Chevra Kadisha (*q.v.*), who perform the sacred office of preparing the dead for burial. The late Sir Moses Montefiore was for a long time member of this body, and frequently performed the duties.

Laver.

Before performing the Priestly Benediction (*q.v.*), the Cohanim have to purify themselves ritually by solemn lavation, in which they are assisted by Levites. Most synagogues have a special Laver for this purpose in reminiscence of the Temple Service.

Laynen (German).

The term used to express the public cantillation (*q.v.*) of prayers.

Leibzoll (Germ., lit. "body tax").

In Germany the Jews were regarded as Kammer Knechte (*q.v.*) of the Emperor, and afterwards of the various princes under whom they dwelt. On the death of any of these they had to pay the Treasury a capitation tax known by the above name.

Leshon Hakodesh (לשון הקדש, lit. "holy tongue").

The use of Hebrew as a means of communication among Jews is still sufficiently wide-spread, especially in the East. Many pious Israelites will only speak Hebrew on Sabbaths and Holydays. With the frequent wanderings of Jews it sometimes happens that a man will have forgotten the tongue of his native land, and not fully acquired that of his place of sojourn, while his acquaintance with the "holy tongue" has been kept up throughout, so that it is to him at least a living language. On the other hand, however, the study of Hebrew is being neglected by Western Jews, who are often lamentably ignorant of their sacred language.

Levi, Levite.

The members of the tribe of Levi, not having a special portion of the Holy Land allotted to them, returned after the exile to

Jerusalem, where they had special duties appointed to them in connection with the Temple, and in subordination to the members of the priestly families. (*See* Büchler, "Priester und Leviten," 1895.) Their descendants remain distinct even up to the present day from the rest of the Jews, and have certain privileges and special obligations. They are invariably "called up" to the Law second in order, and have the privilege of assisting the Cohanim or priests in ritual lavation before the Priestly Benediction (*q.v.*) and are exempt from Pidyon haben (*q.v.*).

Levirate (*from* levir, Lat., "brother-in-law").

This is a technical term much used by Biblical scholars and modern anthropologists to express the Biblical Law, Deut. xxv. 5–10, according to which a man is bound to marry his deceased brother's widow, if no child has resulted from the previous union. Should issue result, the child is known as the child of the deceased husband. This custom is found among other nations (Hindoos, Persians, Gallas, etc., *see* McLennan, "Patriarchal Theory"), with whom it is connected with the theory of reincarnation of a parent in his children. The practice was carried out in Biblical times, as is illustrated in Genesis xxxviii., but already a method of dispensation had been elaborated, the formula for which is given in Deut. xxv. 7–10. The Talmudical Law developed the principle of dispensation till at last it became the prevalent practice, though the Levirate marriage still remains legal amongst Jews. For the formula of dispensation, *see* Chalitza.

"Link."

The opposite of "Froom" (*q.v.*), and is applied to those Jews who are not very strict in their religious observances. The exact origin of the word is unknown, but it is probably derived from the German *link*, "left," meaning wronghanded.

Litvok (Polish, lit. "Lithuanian").

All Jews from the East of Europe are lumped together by those of the West as Polish. But among them there are various distinctions of custom and dialect, the most prominent being that between the Pollak (*q.v.*) and the Litvok or Lithuanian Jew of the neighbourhoods of Wilna, Grodno, etc.

Lulab (לולב).

A Palm Branch used in the synagogue service during the Feast of Tabernacles. It is generally bound with sprigs of myrtle and willow, and exhibited with a citron, or ethrog. Much ingenuity is devoted in Rabbinic homiletics to explain the symbolic meaning of the combination. (*See* Lev. xxiii. 40.)

Maariv (מעריב).

The Evening Service, which commences with the setting of the sun, is called by this name. The Talith (*q.v.*) is not worn during it, except on the Day of Atonement.

Maase (מעשה, lit. "story").

Jews, when they get together, tell one another stories, and each of these is called a *Maase*, which is generally of a comic or amusing character. A certain number of these have been collected together, and printed in Yiddish, under the title of "Maase-Buch."

Machzor (מחזר, lit. "cycle").

The term applied to the Prayer Books containing the Festival Prayers. These used to be included in one book formerly, but now it is the custom to have the prayers for each festival issued in separate volumes, those for the Day of Atonement filling two volumes with the translation. A very old Machzor (12th century) is known as the Machzor of Vitry, having been compiled by R. Simcha, of Vitry about 1100, and has recently been published in Berlin.

Maftir (מפטיר, lit. "Concluder").

In addition to the regular number called up to the Law, an additional person is summoned, to whom the last portion is read. It is customary in many congregations for the Maftir to read the Haphtorah.

Magen David (מגן דוד, lit. "Shield of David").

Two interlaced equilateral triangles, forming a six-pointed star. This is connected with the practical Cabbala, and is supposed to act as an amulet, but is often used in decorations without any superstitious intent. It must be distinguished from the Shield of Solomon, which is the well-known pentagram or Drudenfuss, and is not Jewish in origin.

Maggid (מגיד, "teller"), pl. Maggidim.

Jewish preachers are in the habit of enlivening their discourses by tales and anecdotes, often of an amusing character. Those preachers who become renowned for their stock of stories are called "Maggidim." The term is also applied by Cabbalists to renowned interpreters of dreams.

Mahamad (מעמד, "Assembly").

The Council of the Elders of the Synagogue, according to the Spanish and Portuguese Jews, always elected from the Yahidim.

Maiminen

When the false Messiah, Sabbathai Zevi, was converted to Islam, a number of his adherents followed him, and became Moslems, but retained a large number of their Jewish customs and traditions. The descendants of these kept together for a long time at Salonica, and a certain number of them still remain separated from the Moslem population, and are known by the title "Maiminen."

Malach ha-Moveth (מלאך המות, lit. "Angel of Death").

According to popular Jewish tradition no man can die unless the Angel of Death summons him. As he is supposed to have a writ from the Most High, in which the person who is to die is mentioned by name, as a last resource, in very rare instances, it is customary for Jews to have their names solemnly changed when at their last gasp (*see* Name, Change of).

Ma Nishtana (מה נשתנה, "What is the difference?").

The Seder (*q.v.*), or Home Passover Service, is opened by the youngest son of the house asking his father a series of questions commencing with the above two words, and asking why this night, apart from all other nights, is distinguished by certain peculiarities of food and posture.

Marrano.

When the Inquisition was introduced into Spain, a number of Jews nominally adopted Christianity, in order to avoid the many disabilities which their position as Jews produced, but they kept up secretly their Jewish faith and practices, and these crypto-Jews became known as Marranos. Most of the Sephardim (*q.v.*) of Holland and England are descended from Marranos.

Marriage.

See Kiddushim, Chuppa, Monogamy, Shadchan, Shidduchim, Seven Blessings, Unterführer.

Marshallik.

The licensed buffoon of the Polish Ghetti. Probably he was originally the person who led the revels on days of rejoicing, like Purim, and was thus a sort of "Lord of Misrule." He got his name from marshalling the revels. A similar position is held by the Badchan.

Martyrs.

The persecution of the Jews in the Middle Ages resulted in a large number of martyrs for the sake of the faith, or as the Jewish phrase goes, "for the sanctification of the Name." (*See* Kiddush Hashem.) It has been calculated that over a quarter of a million of Jews suffered death for their faith during the Middle Ages. It was customary to preserve the names of these heroes of Judaism in special lists (*see* Memor-Buch), and they are always referred to as Saints (*Kedoshim*).

Massa u-Mattan (משא ומתן, lit. "taking and giving").

This term is the common phrase to express business among Jews, who generally pronounce it "Mossomotton."

Massora (מסרה, lit. "tradition").

The Hebrew text of the Bible as we now have it was fixed by the labours of the Massoretes of the sixth to tenth century. These counted the number of letters in the Pentateuch (304,045 according to Blau in *Jewish Quarterly Review*, VIII.), recorded when large and small letters were to be exceptionally used (there are no capitals in Hebrew), recorded curious forms and in every way arranged that the text should not be altered; to use a typographical metaphor, they locked up the formes of the Bible. Their settlement of the text was often founded on a traditional interpretation of it, and is thus of exegetic value even apart from the text. Thus the נ or ב of the name Manasseh, in Jud. xviii. 30, is raised above the line, to indicate that the name was once Moshe or Moses. (*See also* Keri u-Kethib.)

Matsa (מצה, lit. "unleavened"). Generally pronounced Motso.

In memory of the fact that the Jews had no time to leaven their bread on leaving Egypt, the Jews only eat unleavened bread during the Passover. It is made and baked with special precautions against anything of a leavening character being mixed up in it, and is made in round thin wafers, generally a foot in diameter, but smaller ones are often made, and different shapes have been from time to time adopted. The wafer of the Communion Service is derived from this.

Mazal (מזל, lit. "station").

The signs for the Zodiac for the stations where the sun apparently rose at different periods of the year were known to early Hebrews as Mazal. Afterwards this term became applied to all stars. Then owing to the spread of astrological beliefs among the Jews, each star was supposed to have influence upon an individual life, and this influence is expressed in modern Jewish terminology by this word, which, when used alone, indicates fortunate influence ("What a Mazal!"), or with the German "schlimm" added to it, refers to misfortune.

Mazal Tov (מזל טוב, lit. "good star").

Stars are supposed to have influence upon individual life (see Mazal), and a piece of luck is called a Mazal Tov. It is also a form of congratulation.

Megilla, pl. Megilloth (מגלה, lit. "scroll").

On the Feast of Purim, the Book of Esther is read in Synagogue and in the home from a scroll which is known by the above Hebrew name. As a matter of fact, the scroll of Esther is only one of the five scrolls or Megilloth, viz., Ruth, Lamentations, Song of Songs, Esther and Ecclesiastes.

Melicha (מליחה, lit. "salting").

In order to remove every vestige of blood from meat used in Jewish households, it is laid in water and in salt for half an hour. This process is known as melicha. It has probably a very early origin, and may have possibly something to do with the use of salt in the Temple sacrifices.

Memor-Buch (Germ., lit. "Book of Memorial").

It was customary in the German congregations to record the names of martyrs who had fallen for the faith during the outbreak of persecution in special lists, to which the name of Memor-Buch was given. Many of these have been recovered and reprinted during the last few years.

Meshores (משרת, lit. "attendant").

Some Rabbis are accompanied by an assistant who is always prepared to do their bidding, and incidentally acts as a guard to their reputation, e.g., the late Chief Rabbi was never without his Meshores.

Meshorrer (משורר, lit. "Singer"),

Who stood by the Chazan, and sang with him.

Meshugge (משוגע, lit. "mad").

This term is pure Hebrew, and means simply mad, but in Jewish parlance it is used often to express great mental excitement. It corresponds to the French "*tête montée.*"

Meshummad, pl. Meshmodim (משמד, lit. "baptized").

The term applied to perverts from the Jewish faith. There is a curious mixture of contempt and sympathy felt by Jews towards Meshummodim. They are felt to be still in some sort Jews, because no Jew can imagine that another can sincerely change his faith, and yet they are felt to have given up their high privilege as the bodyguard of God for the sake of lucre. There is a curious contrast in the attitude of Jews towards the voluntary Meshummad and the forcibly converted Marranos (*q.v.*). A curious German adjective " Geschmed " has been formed from this word.

Messiah (משיח, lit. "anointed").

The term used in the Bible for the Anointed Prince who shall restore the Jews to their old land, convert the world to a belief in one God, and bring about universal peace. Modern Jews are much divided as to the exact interpretation to be given to this part of their belief. Some regard the expression as indicating an age rather than a person, while others keep strictly to the literal interpretation of the prophecies. Some Jewish authorities distinguish between a Messiah who shall be the descendant of David, and another Messiah who shall precede him, and who shall be known as the Messiah Ben Joseph, who shall lead back the Ten Tribes to the Holy Land. It is part of the Jewish belief that the appearance of the Messiah will be preceded by that of Elijah.

Messianic Texts.

There are a number of texts in the Old Testament which Christians take to indicate prophetically the coming of their own Saviour, but are explained differently by Jews, *e.g.*, Isaiah vii. 14, "A virgin shall conceive," is undoubtedly a mistranslation of Hebrew words signifying " A young woman is with child." (This interpretation is accepted by all modern Christian interpreters of Hebrew.) Isaiah liii.: The mystical servant of God foretold by the Prophet Isaiah, is regarded by Jews as a prophecy of their own fortunes among the nations. Psalm ii. 12 is translated " Worship in purity," instead of " Kiss the Son." Micah v. 5, " Peace shall be," instead of " This *man* shall be *our* peace."

Mezuza, pl. Mezuzoth (מזוזה).

The Israelites were commanded (Deut. xi. 20) to bind the Law upon the door-posts of their houses. This has been taken literally, and a piece of parchment, with Deut. iv. 6, 9, and 13, 21 written upon them, and enclosed in glass or metal cases, are fixed up upon the right-hand post of the door of the house, and of each dwelling room. They are put up slanting and, as it were, pointing to the house or room. Much superstition has gathered about this custom, (*e.g.*), it has been regarded as a sort of amulet against evil spirits, but, in its inception, it was doubtless a strict and literal fulfilment of the Biblical command.

Midrash (מדרש, lit. "explanation").

The extreme reverence for the Scriptures led in post-Biblical times to an enormous development of its interpretation. This general tendency is known by the name of "Midrash," which technically divides itself into legislative and imaginative—Halacha and Hagada (*q.v.*); but in actual usage the term is mainly applied to the latter form, and is thus to a certain extent equivalent to Hagada (*q.v.*) in its first meaning. A great collection of the Midrash is a continuous exposition of the Pentateuch and the Five Megilloth, which is known by the name of the "Midrash Rabba."

Mikvah (מקוה, lit. "gathering [of water]").

According to the Biblical enactment (Lev. xv. 19, *seq.*) a bath is obligatory upon Jewish women at certain periods. In most congregations facilities for this are afforded and are known by the above name. The name is now restricted to baths devoted to female use, but in Biblical times baths were used by both sexes to ensure ritual purity, and it was one of the acts by which a proselyte became initiated into Judaism; hence, probably, the origin of baptism in the Church.

Mincha (מנחה).

The Afternoon Service is known by this term. Jews are supposed to say the Amida (*q.v.*) three times a day, and this service forms the second occasion.

Minhag, pl. Minhagim (מנהג).

Beside the Mitzvoth (*q.v.*), or enactments actually laid down in the Pentateuch, and the prescriptions derived from them according to the Oral Law, customs have established themselves among Jews of various localities, which are felt by them to be almost equally as binding as the former, and more binding than the Dinim (*q.v.*). These are known as Minhagim, and even now are still being added to and at times given up.

Minim. *See* Birkath ha-Minim.

Minyan (מנין, lit. "number").

Public prayer among Jews can only be recited in the presence of ten males above the age of religious maturity (*see* Barmitzvah). Such a collection of ten is known collectively as a Minyan, and it is considered a Mitzvah (*q.v.*) to help to form a Minyan. In many Synagogues Minyan men, who could not otherwise afford to attend, are engaged so as to ensure that public service shall be held, but public opinion, at least in England, is against this practice. The main object of the expedient is in order to allow orphans to say Kaddish (*q.v.*) at public service, which would often be impossible if no organised means were adopted to ensure a Minyan.

Misheberach (מי שברך, lit. "He that blessed").

These words are the beginning of a prayer read out when offerings are made in the Synagogue (*see* Schnoder). The blessing is called down upon living persons on occasions of festivity.

Mishna (משנה, lit. "repetition").

In post-Biblical times many of the Levitical enactments were found to require supplemental Bye-laws, which were worked out by the Rabbis up to the second century A.D. This was not written down, but, towards the end of the second century, the great Rabbi Jehuda, in order to prevent the possibility of loss, compiled the Mishna, which contains a summary of these developments of Biblical Law. It is divided into six sections, dealing respectively with Worship, Festivals, Marriage, Justice, Sacrifice, Purity, and, together with the Gemara, constitutes the Talmud (*q.v.*).

Mishpacha (משפחה), lit. "family," and so used.

Mitzva (מצוה, lit. "command"), plur. Mitzvoth.

The commands of God are regarded by Jews as special privileges for them to perform; hence this word, which literally means "command," has come to mean "privilege," as it gives the doer of the Mitzva an occasion for adding to his sanctity. Any of the special functions of the Synagogue ceremonial are regarded as special privileges, and at one time it was even customary to pay for the privilege, and a sort of auction was held to dispose of them to the highest bidder. The plural Mitzvoth is applied also, and chiefly, to the commands laid down in the Law, as distinguished from the Minhagim (*q.v.*) or customs.

Mizrach (מזרח, lit. "East").

When they pray Jews turn to Jerusalem (hence the orientation of churches). To mark the aspect in private houses, an ornamental piece of writing is placed upon the eastern wall, which is often in the form of the two tables of Stone or a Magen David (*q.v.*).

Mohel (מהל).

The official who performs the rite of Abraham. In Germany these have to be qualified surgeons, but, except a little elementary instruction, there is no qualification required, according to Jewish custom. In England, however, certificates are now given after a certain amount of examination as to the qualifications of the candidates.

Molad (מולד, lit. "birth").

The exact moment of conjunction of sun and moon, constituting new moon. The molad of Tishri determines the Jewish year (*see* Explanation of Jewish Calendar).

Monogamy.

The Israelites of the Bible, like most eastern nations, were polygamists. From Talmudic times, however, the tendency towards monogamy has grown stronger and stronger, and, about 1000 A.D., R. Gershom laid it down as a stringent rule that the Jews of Europe should only have one wife at a time. This is effective among European Jews and their descendants at the present day, but the Jews of the East still regard themselves as authorised by the example of the patriarchs (and of their neighbours) to have more than one wife. There are cases known, in the Middle Ages, where special permission was obtained from the kings of Spain for a Jew to have two wives.

Moror (מרור, lit. "bitter").

To symbolise the bitter sufferings of the Jews in Egypt, part of the appurtenances connected with the Seder Service (*q.v.*) is a piece of horseradish. This is technically known as "Moror." In an illustrated edition of the Hagada (*q.v.*) the head of a family is represented as pointing to his wife as the Moror.

Motso Kleis.

A small dumpling made of Motso with egg and seasoning. It is boiled in soup and forms a favourite dish during Passover. Kleis is probably the German "Klöss," dumpling.

Mourning.

After the death of a relative and before the burial (*q.v.*), it is customary for the mourners to abstain from wine and meat. On the return from the funeral, they partake of a meal which has been prepared for them by their neighbours. An egg, as a symbol of life, is generally made part of this repast. In Bible times, the mourners used to rend their clothes and sit in dust and ashes. As a modern equivalent, the outer garment of all mourners is cut and left unbound for the thirty days of mourning. Also it is customary during the Shiva (*q.v.*), for the mourners to sit on low stools or cushions. The mourning for a parent is for a full year, and the Kaddish (*q.v.*), is said for eleven months after the death. Beside this, a lamp to represent the soul of the deceased (*cf.* Prov. xx. 27) is kept alight day and night generally during the first month or during the whole first year of the mourning, and is relighted every Jahrzeit (*q.v.*).

Musaph (מוסף, lit. "additional").

On Sabbaths and Festivals in addition to the morning prayers, there is a complementary service to which this name is given. It includes Amida (*q.v.*).

Name, Change of.

It is a curious Jewish custom to change the name of a person nearly upon the point of death in the hope that by these means he will avoid the attention of the Malach ha-Moveth (*q.v.*), it being supposed that the man was doomed by name. No adequate explanation has ever been given of this curious custom, which has many analogues in savage folk lore.

Names.

During the Middle Ages, Jews had no surnames, but were known as the sons of their fathers, the two names being simply joined together by the term Ben ("son of"), or, in Arabic speaking countries, Ibn. But, as the Jews gradually became emancipated, and mixed more with their fellow citizens, it became usual for them to adopt civil surnames. The Marranos (*q.v.*), being nominally Spanish Christians, of course, had surnames mainly derived from their cities of origin, like Aguilar, Castro, etc. A distinction gradually grew up between the sacred name used in Synagogue and in Hebrew deeds, as distinguished from the Kinnui, or secular name, by which the Jew was known among his fellow citizens. The first, or "Christian" names, are generally the same as those of their neighbours, but, when surnames were adopted, they were mainly derived from (1) the place of origin, as, *e.g.*, Berliner, Polack, etc.; (2) a synonym for the Hebrew name, as Hart or Hirsch, instead of Zevi; (3) a name current in the country resembling the sacred name, as Lewis for Levy, Davis for David, etc.; (4) quite artificial names, like Rosenbaum, Greenberg. These last were often given by the German officials when acts were passed forcing the Jews to adopt surnames, though attempts have been made, formerly in Prussia, and at the present day in Russia, to prevent Jews from adopting names not strictly Jewish.

Names of God.

According to the practical Cabbala, great power is possessed over the forces of Nature by those who have become acquainted with the mystical names of God. Besides the Tetragrammaton (*q.v.*), there were names known to the Cabbalists, one composed of 12 letters, and another composed of 72 letters. (*See* Baal Shem.)

Nasi (נשיא, lit. "Prince").

The head of the Jews in the Holy Land was dignified with the title of Prince or Nasi. The best known of these was Rabbi Jehuda, who compiled the Mishna (*q.v.*).

Nebbich = "alas!"

This term is used by Ashkenazic Jews to express their sympathy with misfortune, and may be taken as the characteristic word summing up the charitable instincts of Jews. (*See* Rachmoneth.) Its etymology is doubtful; Zunz states that it is the Polish for "alas!"; others derive it from the German "Nie bei Euch" (may it never happen to you).

Neginoth (נגינות, lit. "musical notes," hence "accents").

Hebrew was originally written with only the consonants, without any vowel points, but, when these were added, points were also given showing the place where the accent or stress was to be laid, and likewise indicating the manner in which a word was to be pronounced during the cantillation. These Neginoth are different for the prose books of the Old Testament and for the poetical books. They were probably written at the top of the words in early times, but are now almost invariably placed at the bottom of the consonants along with the vowels.

Neila (נעילה, lit. "conclusion").

The concluding portion of the Service for the Day of Atonement is called by this name. It begins with the opening of the Ark, which is a special Mitzvah conferred upon one of the most respected members of the synagogue. The service concludes with a rehearsal of the same service as is performed when a Jew is dying, and, coming at the close of a long day of fasting, is perhaps the most impressive ceremony known in any religion.

New Moon.
See Molad and Rosh Chodesh.

New Year of Trees.
According to the decision of Hillel, the 15th of Shebat is reckoned as the New Year of Trees, with reference to the question of tithes, and also with reference to the command (Lev. xix. 24, 25).

Nidda (נדה, lit. "separation").
The term indicating the separation of the women according to the Levitical injunction (Lev. xv.). Much stress is laid upon this in Jewish life, and many hygienic and biostatic consequences are said to be derived from it, as, for example, the greater number of boys among Jewish births.

Niddui (נדוי, lit. "separation").
A shorter Cherem (q.v.), lasting thirty days.

Numerals.
Jews have never adopted the Arabic figures in their Hebrew books, and still continue to cypher (if one can use the word where there is no nought) with letters instead of figures (see Gematria). The first ten letters are taken for the units, the next eight for the succeeding tens from 20 to 90, and the last four give the first four hundreds, the others being formed by additions. The numbers from 1 to 30 can be observed in every Jewish calendar. It will be remarked that 15 and 16 are represented by טו טז, so as to avoid any appearance of repeating the Tetragrammaton (q.v.). All higher figures than 400 must be made up by adding the signs or by actually naming them.

Oath: more judaico.
In the Middle Ages many ludicrous precautions were taken by the Civil Courts to ensure that a Jew, when being sworn, used a formula which would really bind his conscience. A Scroll of the Law was sometimes brought into court, which the witness had to hold in his hand while swearing, and the formula of the oath covered every possible means of evasion. Nowadays, it is only customary for a Jew to swear with his head covered and holding an Old Testament in his hand.

Offerings.
Instead of the sacrifices offered in the Temple, it has become customary for Jews to make money offerings on festival occasions in synagogue towards the support of the institution, or of charities connected with it. These are generally offered when a person is "called up to the Law," but as this has led to much ostentation, and seems somewhat derogatory to the sacred ceremony, it is becoming customary to commute these offerings into an annual payment, or to introduce them at a less sacred portion of the service.

Omer (עומר).

Between Passover and Pentecost, seven weeks should elapse, during which no marriages are performed, except on the 33rd day (*see* Lag b'Omer). Every day during this period an announcement of the number of days which have elapsed since the first day of Passover is made, and this is called "Counting the Omer."

Oral Law.

According to Jewish theory, beside the enactments laid down in the Pentateuch, God in addition instructed Moses with their various applications. These developments of the Law are supposed to have been handed on by Moses to the seventy elders, and from them continuously on until the time of the Sanhedrim, from whom they ultimately passed to Rabbi Jehuda, who wrote them down in the Mishna (*q.v.*). Hence, the enactments of the Talmud are considered of equal force with those of the Pentateuch, as coming from the same source.

Osur (אסור, lit. "forbidden").

Things forbidden by Jewish law are termed Osur (often pronounced Osir). Some things are forbidden to be eaten but not to be dealt in, in other things both are prohibited.

Pale of Jewish Settlement.

The Jews of Russia are an inheritance from Old Poland. They were forbidden to stop on Russian soil by a ukase of Catherine II., but when Russia, at the three successive partitions of Poland, became possessed of the lands in which Jews most do congregate, an arrangement was come to that they should be kept within the bounds of the territories thus acquired. These constitute the ten provinces of Poland itself, and fifteen other provinces bordering upon Poland and once belonging to it. Technically speaking, these last are called the Pale of Jewish Settlement, within which Jews born in Russia must confine themselves, only skilled artisans, persons of University education and merchants of the First Guild being allowed to move beyond the Pale. Owing to the "May Laws" of 1882, the Jews of the Pale are still further restricted by being only allowed to live in the towns and burghs.

Parasha (פרשה, lit. "portion").

The lessons from the Pentateuch read on the Sabbaths, called Sedras (*q.v.*), are divided up into small sections, each of which is called a Parasha. Originally they were read by the different persons who are called up to the Law for that purpose, and in the case of a Barmitzvah (*q.v.*), it is usual for him to cantillate the particular portion to which he has been called up, but at present the reader recites the portion, and the person called up only pronounces a blessing before and after. Some Jews, *e.g.* the Sephardim, apply the term to the whole of the lesson.

Parnas (פרנס, lit. "presider").

The head of a congregation for the time being is called Parnas, who may be described as a Synagogue Warden. He presides over the meetings of the Council of the synagogue, and directs the distribution of Mitzvoth during service, and, together with the Gabbai (*q.v.*), and a Council of Members, may be regarded as the ruler of the congregation. In most synagogues a pew is provided for the Wardens, and is known as the Parnass box.

Paschal Lamb.

Only the Samaritans (*q.v.*), continue actually to sacrifice the Paschal Lamb on Passover. With ordinary Jews, this is represented in the Seder service by the roasted shank bone of a lamb.

Pasken (Heb. with German ending).

To decide disputes according to Rabbinic Law.

Peloni (פלוני).

This expression is equivalent to the initials which are used to indicate that a name is unknown. Thus R. Peloni would be equal to Mons. Tel in French, or Mr. So-and-so in English.

Penitential Days.

The ten days from the New Year to the Day of Atonement, both included, are regarded as a period of penitence.

Perocheth (פרוכת).

The curtain before the Ark of the Law, which is often very richly decorated. Thus the arms of the Montefiores are first found embroidered on a Venetian Perocheth of last century.

Pesach (פסח, lit. "Passover").

In obedience to the Biblical command, the seven days between the 15th and 22nd of Nisan are kept as a holy festival in remembrance of the Exodus from Egypt, and, outside Palestine, an additional day is added to ensure that all Jews throughout the world shall keep the festival during the same absolute period of time. During the Festival, Matzoth (*q.v.*) are eaten, and every precaution is taken to prevent anything of a leavened character being used in the house (*see* Bittul Chamets). Outside Palestine the first two and the last two days of the Festival are kept as strict Holy Days of Solemn Assembly.

Pethecha (פתיחה, lit. "opening").

To remove the curtain from before the Ark is one of the mitzvoth (*q.v.*), and to that act this term is applied. The greatest privilege that can be conferred in synagogue is the Pethecha Neila, the opening of the Ark at the Conclusion Service of the Day of Atonement.

Peyoth (פאות, lit. "corners").

According to the Biblical command (Lev. xix. 27) Jews are not allowed to round the corners of their heads, which was probably a superstitious custom among the Canaanites. The Jews of Poland believe they are acting in accordance with this precept when they let grow down in front of their ears long ringlets known by the above name.

Phylacteries (Greek, "guards"). *See* "Tephillin."

Pidyon ha Ben (פדיון הבן, lit. "Redemption of the Firstborn").

In accordance with the Biblical precept (Exod. xxxiv. 20), the firstborn son, when not that of a Levite, is redeemed when one month old by giving 5 shekels to a Cohen or priest. The ceremony is known by this name.

Pilpul (פלפול, lit. "grains of pepper").

Owing to the continued expulsion of the Jews from Western Europe, the head centre of Talmudic learning became fixed, in the sixteenth century, in Poland, where the Talmud became the great subject of Jewish study. Owing to this excessive devotion to one subject, extreme minutiæ of discussion were introduced, importance was attached to hair-splitting distinctions, and peculiar methods of controversy and discussion became prevalent in the study. Talmudic disquisitions conducted on this method are known by the name of Pilpul.

Piyutim (פיוטים, lit. "poems").

From the eighth century onward, sacred poems were written by the Rabbis to celebrate the various occasions of Jewish ceremonial. Thousands of these poems exist, many of them displaying considerable religious fervour, as well as ingenuity in working in suitable Biblical passages, and the proper Rabbinical ideas relating to the festivals, etc. Many of these were added to the Machzor and, owing to the conservative instincts of Jews, became regarded as an essential part of the service, which was considerably lengthened by their insertion. In the present century, however, there has been a tendency to remove these Piyutim as much as possible from the Prayer Books, especially as, now and then, they contain ideas not in consonance with modern notions.

Pollack, plural, Polláckim (lit. "a Pole").

The term applied to Jews born in Poland but now resident in other countries. In appearance, manners and customs, they differ somewhat from the Jews of Lithuania (*see* Litvock), and those of South Russia, but, in common talk, all these are banded together under the general appellative. Ever since the terrible persecution of Chmielnicki in 1648, Jews from Poland have formed a regular stream of poverty towards Western Europe, which they have at the same time furnished with a continuous supply of orthodox piety, strenuous industry, and keen intellect sharpened by Talmudic dialectics.

Porging.

According to the Biblical story (Gen. xxxii.) the Angel only overcame Jacob at the brook Jabok by causing the sinew of his thigh to shrink. In memory of this, no animal food is considered kasher (*q.v.*) unless that sinew has been removed, and this process is known by the above name. Porging means further the removal of the forbidden fat, and also of the veins in which blood might remain.

Posuk (פסוק, lit. "division").

A verse of the Prophets or Hagiography is meant by this term.

Prelatoes.

A favourite cake, made only at Passover time, of potato flour without any ferment.

Priestly Benediction. *See* Duchan and Hands of Cohanim.

Pronunciation.

Great varieties of pronunciation of Hebrew occur among different sections of Jews. To the expert ear, even the Lithuanian Jew can be distinguished from the Polish one by certain peculiarities of pronunciation, but the chief distinction is that formed by the opposing pronunciations of the Sephardic and Ashkenazic Jews, especially with regard to the Hebrew vowels. The following table gives the most marked differences :—

Vowels.		Sephardim.	Ashkenazim.
Kamets	ָ	ā (in father)	o (in bone)
Cholem	ֹ	o (in bone)	ow (in prow)
Tsere	ֵ	e (like a in mane)	i (in mine) or e (as a in mane)

Consonants.			
Taw	ת	t	s *or* t
'Ain	ע	gn (nasalised)	rough breathing

As will be observed, the Sephardic pronunciation approximates more exactly to that of scholars, which is based upon the comparative philology of the Semitic languages, but the question is not yet decided whether in some points, as the Kamets and Taw, the Ashkenazic pronunciation does not resemble more closely that of the ancient Hebrews. These differences of pronunciation are represented by differences of transliteration (*q.v.*).

Prosbul (from the Greek προσβούλη, lit. "before the judgment").

According to the Biblical enactment, no debts could be recovered after the entry of the Sabbatical year (*q.v.*). The great Rabbi, Hillel, however, to avoid the great inconveniences which resulted from the exact fulfilment of the enactment, invented a legal instrument by which it could be avoided. This was a declaration before the Court that the debtor guaranteed to put the creditor at once in possession of a piece of land of equivalent value to the debt. This is generally cited as an instance in which the later legislation of the Rabbis evaded the prescriptions of the Bible.

Proselyte. *See* Ger.

Purim (פורים, lit. "lots").

A feast instituted to celebrate the events related in the book of Esther, but which forms the Carnival of modern Jewry. It is considered a duty to drink an extra quantity of wine on the feast, and exchange presents with one's neighbours. It thus forms a very general occasion for conviviality and the reconciliation of enmities. The late Professor Lagard attempted to show that the name and the feast were both alike derived from a Persian custom.

Purim Play.

From the seventeenth century onwards, it has become customary to celebrate Purim by amateur theatricals resembling somewhat the mummers' play of old English country life. The chief characters are, of course, Ahasuerus, Esther, Mordecai, and Haman, the latter being greatly ill-treated during the performance, somewhat after the fashion of the pantomime policeman.

Rabbanites.

The name given to ordinary Jews, who believe in the Rabbinical tradition, to distinguish them from the Karaites (*q.v.*).

Rabbi (רבי, lit. " my master ").

This term was originally applied as a mode of address to persons learned in the Law, but it then became applied to all Jews who were supposed to be thus learned. For example, every person called up to the Law is called Rabbi.

Rachmonuth (רחמנות, lit. " mercy ").

In their social relations, Jews are more a people of mercy than of rigid justice. One of their favourite synonyms for God is "Father of mercy," and their charity is not merely that of the pocket. All this is summed up for them in the word Rachmoneth, and "to have R." or "ask R." are current expressions.

Rambam (רמב״ם).

A popular abbreviation for the name of the greatest of the mediæval Jewish Rabbis, Moses Maimonides. The initials of the words "Rabbi Moses ben Maimon" are taken and formed into a fresh word as above. In a similar way, Moses Nachmanides is known as Ramban, Rabbi Isaac Alfasi as Rif, etc. *See also* Rashi.

Rashi (רש״י).

An abbreviation of the name of the greatest Jewish commentator of the Middle Ages, Rabbi Salomon ben Isaac. The Talmud is invariably printed with his commentary by the side of the text, without which it would be scarcely intelligible, and his commentary upon nearly all the books of the Bible is almost equally prized. These are generally printed with somewhat different letters from the ordinary square Hebrew characters, and this form of type is itself known by the name of Rashi.

Rav (רב, lit. "Master").

This is the noun from which Rabbi is derived, but it is now applied solely to the Chief Rabbi (*q.v.*) of a town or country.

Rebben,

The term applied by the Chassidim (*q.v.*) to their Rabbis or clergymen.

Reformers.

At the end of the last century, the enlightened influence of Moses Mendelssohn and his school tended to raise the Jews from the mediæval ignorance in secular knowledge into which they had been plunged by the persecutions of the preceding two centuries. One of the results of this influence was a movement which began in the early days of this century, in Germany, to reform the ritual of the synagogue in the direction of making it more intelligent and more outwardly decorous. In particular, there came a tendency to restrict Jewish customs to those mentioned in the Pentateuch. This movement spread to England about the year 1840, and led to the secession of a number of English Jews, mainly members of the Sephardic congregation, who denied the authority of the Talmud, refused to keep the Second Days of the Festivals (*q.v.*), introduced instrumental music into the Synagogue, and adopted a ritual less encumbered with Piyutim (*q.v.*) than the ordinary prayer-book of the Jews. The movement has not spread much in England, and there has been a marked rapprochement of recent years between reformers and orthodox. In many ways, indeed, the reformers have shown themselves less capable of reform than the orthodox. In America there are synagogues in which services are held on Sunday, the congregation are seated, male and female side by side, and the men do not wear their hats during service, and discard the Talith (*q.v.*).

Resh Galuta (Chaldee, ריש גלותא, lit. "Head of Exile").

The descendants of David who lived in Babylon after the Dispersion were regarded as the chief authorities in Israel, and they were supported by gifts sent to Bagdad till the line disappeared in the tenth century. The fullest account of them is given in Brüll's *Jahrbuch*, x.

Reshuth (רשות, lit. "ownership").

On Sabbath Jews may not carry things from a private place (רשות היחיד) into a street (רשות הרבים), but by the principle of Eruvim (*q.v.*) they are allowed to regard any district inhabited by Jews as a private place.

Reuben and Simeon

Are the John Doe and Richard Roe, of Jewish legal works, standing for plaintiff and defendant, or any other legal relations under discussion.

Rishuth (רשעות, lit. "badness").

This term, usually pronounced *rishus*, is applied to Anti-Semitic feeling, and a person who displays the feeling is known as a Roshe (רשע, lit. "bad").

Rosh Chodesh (ראש חדש, lit. "head of the month").

The first day of each Jewish month is known by this name, and is distinguished by a special service, which includes the Hakel (*q.v.*). In those months of the year which contain thirty days, the last day is also kept as a Rosh Chodesh.

Rosh Hashona (ראש השנה, lit. "head of the year").

The Jewish New Year is known by this name as well as by several others, as:—Day of Sounding (the Shofar (*q.v.*), יום תרועה), Day of Remembrance (יום הזכרון), and Day of Judgment (יום הדין). The day is regarded as a specially solemn day and preparatory to the great Day of Atonement. Indeed, according to Jewish tradition, the great books of judgment are opened on this day, and closed ten days afterwards. Additional solemnity is given to it by the repeated flourishes on the Shofar (*q.v.*), which form a distinctive portion of the service of the day.

Sabbath (שבת, lit. "rest")

Is kept by the Jews from the eve of the sixth to the eve of the seventh day of the week. Its advent and departure can be celebrated by home ceremonials (*see* Kiddush, Habdala). Great care is taken to ensure that no work of any kind is done upon the day, nothing that might reasonably lead to work should be attempted, or in some cases nothing may be done which, though harmless in itself, might seem to be breaking the Sabbath, and lead to similar infractions by others. Nothing approaching a business character is to be done or even spoken of on the Sabbath, no money to be used and nothing to be carried about in public. Some Jews are even so strict in this matter that they will not carry a stick or umbrella on the Sabbath. No fire or light may be kindled. But, while kept within such stringency, the day is by no means one of gloom, being rather the chief day of rejoicing throughout the week. Chess is allowed by many to be played, though not cards; and it is the chief day for the interchange of visits among Jews. In other words, the "Judaic Sabbath" is not a Puritanical Sabbath. Even the inhabitants of Gehinnom (*q.v.*) are said to rest and rejoice every seventh day.

Sabbath Goy.

As no fire may be lighted on the Sabbath, it has become customary to hire the services of non-Jewish neighbours to come into the house and keep the fires lit during the Sabbath. Some Jews are even too strict to adopt this method. The Rabbis allow it, on the ground that, in saving a person's life, one is permitted an infringement even of the Day of Atonement (the Sabbath of Sabbaths), and that, in cold climates like those of the North, to forbid fire would be to cause danger to life in many cases.

Sabbath Hagadol (שבת הגדול, lit. "Great Sabbath").

The Sabbath before the Feast of Passover. Formerly the Sabbaths before all three great festivals were so termed.

Sabbath Journey.

Jews must not walk more than 2,000 paces beyond the town where they dwell on the Sabbath. (*See* Erubim.)

Sabbath Shuba (שבת שובה, lit. Sabbath of "Return" or "Repentance").

The Sabbath between New Year and the Day of Atonement is

called by this name, because the Haphtara for the day is taken from Hosea xiv. 1, *seq.*, which begins with this word. It is appropriate for the Sabbath of the season of repentance.

Sabbatical Year.

According to Exodus xxiii. 10–12, the land of Israel was to be left entirely untouched every seventh year. It is by no means an unusual arrangement in village communities where there is a redistribution of the common lots of the manor every seven years. Mr. Fenton (in his *Early Hebrew Life*), has also found similar instances in Scotland, almost up to the present day. Combined with this in Biblical times, was an arrangement by which all debts ceased at the end of seven years' period. This would also naturally correspond with the arrangements of the village community, but the latter command was found to press heavily upon persons seeking loans when the position of the Israelites had advanced a stage beyond that of a village community, and Rabbi Hillel invented a form known as the Prosbul (*q.v.*) to mitigate the difficulty. With regard to the seventh or fallow year, modern Jews regard this as only applicable to the Holy Land. (*See* Shemita.)

Sacrifice.

In the later periods of the Jewish monarchy, all sacrifices had to be brought to the Temple, which became the only place where they could be legally offered. When the Temple was destroyed, the Rabbis introduced the pious principle that prayer had replaced sacrifice, basing this upon the Biblical passage, "We will compensate with our lips for the bullocks" (Hos. xiv. 30). It is a moot point among Jews whether the Return to the Holy Land will be accompanied by a reversion to the older system of sacrifice.

Samaritans.

After the return of the Jews from exile under the patronage of Cyrus, the inhabitants of Schechem, or Samaria, "a mixed multitude" of Assyrian settlers and remnants of the ten tribes, did all they could to prevent the building of the Second Temple and the walls of Jerusalem. This produced mutual aversion between the Jews and their Northern neighbours, which has lasted almost down to the present day. The Samaritans regard the Pentateuch alone as constituting the Bible, and have a special text of it written in the old Hebrew characters, and with several portions from the ordinary text, especially passages relating to Schechem, especially manipulated in order that they may claim for it the privileges given to Jerusalem in the sacred text. They have their own liturgy, and a high priest, and still sacrifice up to the present day. At every Passover, the high priest of the Samaritans, now resident at Nablus, on the site of ancient Samaria, sacrifices a Paschal Lamb according to the ancient ceremonial. They were declared to be not Jews by the Rabbinic authorities of the third century. The Samaritans are slowly dying out, and only number about 150 at the present day.

Sambatyon.

The name of a mythical river beyond which the Ten Tribes (*q.v.*) are supposed to have retired. It is supposed to flow equably for six days and then to suddenly disappear and to leave its bed dry on the Sabbath (*see* Josephus, *Wars*, VII. v.). Pliny also refers to this Sabbatical river (*Hist. Nat.*, XXX. xi.).

Sandek (Gr., σύνδικος or σύντεκνος).

The Gevatter (*q.v.*), or godfather, is also known by this term. His chief privilege is to hold the child during the Berith Milah (*q.v.*), but the Gentile custom of presenting the child with a silver cup has of recent years spread to the Sandek.

Sanhedrin (or Synhedrion, סנהדרין; Gr. συνέδριον).

The chief court of the ancient Jews during the later periods of the separate existence of the Jewish state. It consisted of a body of twenty-three members in a small Sanhedrin, and in the great Sanhedrin of Jerusalem consisted of seventy-one members, which tradition was connected with the seventy elders of Moses' time, with the addition of Moses himself. It has been suggested that the Sanhedrin was really composed of three sets of twenty-three, taken from the three different sections of Israelites—Priests, Levites, and ordinary Jews. Vacancies were filled up from the pupils of the Sanhedrin, who sat under the regular members and studied the procedure of the court. It is a doubtful question whether the High Priest was the formal President of the Sandedrin, or whether there was a special President, as the Ab Beth Din (*q.v.*). The term Sanhedrin was applied by Napoleon to an assemblage of Jewish notables which he summoned together at Paris in 1809 chiefly to settle the organisation of the French Jewry. It still continues on the lines he then laid down.

Satan (שטן, lit. "adversary").

The Satan of Job is no malevolent fiend but a divine instrument for the spiritual elevation of the individual. He corresponds more particularly to the Advocatus Diavoli of the Papal Courts. In post-Biblical times, there was a tendency to identify Satan with the Angel of Death, Malach-ha-Moveth, and the Yetser Hara (*q.v.*).

Schnoder (שנדר, lit. "who has vowed").

Though prayer was accepted in the Temple in place of sacrifice, the mundane needs of synagogue organisation led to money offerings being promised for synagogal purposes, chiefly by persons called up to the Law. Such persons are said to Schnoder.

Schnorrer.

The technical name for the Jewish beggar, who is distinguished from all other beggars by his Chutzpa (*q.v.*). Duties to Jews are their privileges (*see* Mitzvoth), consequently your Jewish Schnorrer regards himself as doing you a favour in giving you the opportunity of performing the duty of helping the poor, and his gratitude is considerably mingled with a feeling of condescension. These characteristic traits have been admirably portrayed in Mr. Zangwill's "King of the Schnorrers."

Searching for Leaven.

On the Eve of Nisan 14th it is customary for the head of every Jewish family to search throughout the house to see that there is no leaven in it. He does this with a lighted taper in his hand, so as not to let any pieces escape. The search is preceded, like all the religious duties, by a special blessing. Any leavened bread found must be destroyed or given away, and a declaration is made by the Baal-ha-Beth (*q.v.*) that he resigns the ownership of any Chamets (*q.v.*) which may be in the house unknown to him.

Second Day of Festivals.

In order to ensure that all Israel should be worshipping God at the same time on the great festivals of Jews outside Palestine, it has become the custom to celebrate the two days of the chief Festivals instead of the single one commanded in the Bible, with the exception of the Day of Atonement, where the sacrifice involved would be too great. This is merely a Minhag (*q.v.*), or custom, but, being of universal acceptance, has nearly the same weight as any of the Mitzvoth or Commands. Reformers, however, keep only one day, and this example is being largely followed.

Seder (סדר, "Order" of Service).

The service on the first two nights of Passover is known by this name, and is given in the Hagada. Among English Jews, therefore, the first night is known as the Seder night, or as they mostly pronounce it "Cyder" night.

Sedra (Chaldaic סדרא, "Order").

The principal function in the Sabbath morning service consists in reading a section of the Law, which is called the Sedra. In early days the Pentateuch used to be distributed through a triennial cycle, which has recently been discovered and restored by Buchler (*Jewish Quarterly Review*, Vol. VI.), but, according to another method still in use, the whole of the Pentateuch is read through annually. Each Sedra or portion is known by a name corresponding to the first word or words of the Biblical text, and is divided up into a number of sections each called Parasha (*q.v.*).

Segan (סגן, Lord, Prince).

During the service in synagogue, one of the most delicate tasks is to apportion to suitable persons the various Mitzvoth (*q.v.*) which occur during the service. This privilege generally devolves on one of the wardens of the synagogue, but, on special occasions, is given to some person who has a private festivity, such as a wedding or Barmitzvah, about to occur. In these latter instances, the person is said to act as Segan.

Selichoth (שלכות, lit. "Penitentials").

During the days of tribulation many elegiac poems were composed by the Jewish poets which are called Selichoth. Many of them have found a place in the Jewish prayer books, mainly in the prayers recited during a certain period before New Year and the first ten days of Tishri, which are thus known by this name.

Semicha (סמיכה, lit. "Laying on [of hands]," hence Ordination).

The formal act of consecrating a teacher of the law is known by this name. A Biblical instance occurs in the case of Joshua, Deut. xxxiv. 9. The chief act consisted of the laying on of hands, which has been taken over by the Christian Church in the ordination of ministers. At first, ordination was granted by one teacher to a pupil, but it was afterwards held to be necessary that a Beth Din should grant the privilege. It was held that the full act of ordination could only be performed in Palestine, and in the fifth century the custom altogether died out, though an attempt was made to revive it by no less an authority than Maimonides, and in the sixteenth century by Jacob ben Rab. (*See* Hatarath Horaah.)

Sephardim (ספרדים)

The land Sepharad, mentioned in Obadiah 20, is identified with Spain, hence the Spanish Jews are known by the name of Sephardim, as distinguished from the Ashkenazim (*q.v.*). They differ from the latter in pronunciation (*q.v.*) of Hebrew and in minor points of ritual.

Sepher Torah (ספר תורה, lit. "Scroll of the Law").

The Law is read in the Synagogue from special written Scrolls, containing the five books of the Pentateuch. These are written on sheepskin in long columns without points or accents, but with divisions indicating the Sedra or Masoretic paragraph, and the ends of the Scroll are attached to handles or rollers of wood upon which they are rolled up. When not in use, they are bound by a binder and covered with a mantle, while the two tops of the handles or rollers are covered with a crown of silver or gold, or with gold or silver bells. When read from, the place is indicated by a Yad, or pointer (*q.v.*), which is often decorated with jewels. The Scroll may not be printed or lithographed, but must be written by a Sopher (*q.v.*). It is a special privilege to roll up or bind together the Sepher Torah. *See* Hagbaah, Gelilah.

Sephiroth (ספירות).

The Cabbalistic name for the various emanations from God which mediate between Him and the creation. They form the subject of mystical interpretation, for which *see* C. D. Ginsburg "Kabbala," 1864.

Seven Blessings.

The actual ceremony of marriage, besides the formula mentioned, consists of the recital of seven special blessings *sub voce* by the officiating minister.

Shaaloth u Teshuboth (שאלות ותשובות, lit. "Questions and Answers").

The intricacies of Jewish law led to many doubts of the minutiæ of Jewish practice (*see* Kashya). These points used often to be put to learned Rabbis, who subsequently published both questions and answers under the above title, which exactly corresponds to the Responsa Prudentum of Roman law.

Sha-atnez (שעטנז).
It is forbidden in the Bible to wear a garment "of divers sorts" (Deut. xxii. 11). This is taken to include the prohibition as to the use of linsey-woolsey, as the old theologians called it, that is, the use of wool and linen together. Jews still keep to this prohibition by only using silk thread with linen, but as a rule this injunction is practically disregarded at the present day.

Shabuoth (שבועות, lit. "weeks").
The Feast of Pentecost occurs exactly seven weeks after the second day of Passover, and is known by this name. It is now associated with the giving of the Law on Mount Sinai, which was supposed by Jewish tradition to have occurred on this day, but it is also a reminiscence of the Harvest Festival, and it has become customary to decorate the synagogue on Shabuoth with plants and flowers.

Shacharith (שחרית, lit. "morning").
The prayers said at the morning service are known by this name.

Shadchan (שדכן, lit. "matchmaker").
Owing to the early age at which marriages used to be solemnised among Jews, it became customary to have the matches made up by the relatives or friends, and ultimately a special person undertook to bring appropriate parties together with a view to marriage. Also, from the same cause, the chief circumstance to be considered in the matter was the dowry and the settlement to be given by the bridegroom, and the Shadchan, or matchmaker, gradually devoted his chief attention to these mundane matters. In reward for his trouble, it became the custom for him to claim a certain percentage of the settlement. Many Rabbis were glad to act as Shadchanim without any remuneration, as it is a special mitzvah to promote marriages among the daughters and sons of Israel. The institution of the Shadchan often leads to much dissatisfaction, which at times finds expression in the civil courts.

Shaitel.
As early as Tertullian it had become the custom for Jewish married women to wear wigs. The reason of this curious habit has not been fully explained, but it has been suggested that it was a means of protection in times of persecution, when the removal of the wig would secure immunity from insult. The custom is still current in Poland and Galicia, and one of Franzos sketches in the "Jews of Barnow" turns upon the Shaitel. To have the hair uncut was a sign of maidenhood.

Shalat (Old French, "chauld" = hot).
As Jews were not allowed to light a fire upon the Sabbath, it was customary for them to keep warm a savoury stew known by this name, which has received peculiar honour from Heine. The old Talmudical word was *Chamin* (lit. "warm"), a word still retained by Arab-speaking Jews. In Chamin haricot beans are a chief ingredient.

Shamash (שמש).

The beadle of the synagogue is known by this name, which indicates, however, a much more important functionary than an ordinary beadle. Owing to the social character of the synagogue in the Middle Ages, and the fact that he assessed the members according to their means, the Shamash had to possess an intimate knowledge of the means and position of every member of the congregation, and in this instance knowledge gave power. He was a sort of permanent Under-Secretary-of-State, who governed while the Parnas (*q.v.*) was supposed to rule. Some of the glory of the Shamash has, however, disappeared in modern times, when the social bonds which bound together all the members of the synagogue have been somewhat relaxed. In England and abroad the word is usually pronounced *shames*. The term is also applied to the extra Chanuca Light (*q.v.*).

Shas (ש"ס, abbreviation for ששה סדרים, "six orders").

The familiar name by which the Talmud is generally known, referring to the six orders or books of which it is composed. (*See* Mishna.)

Shechinah (שכינה, lit. "dwelling").

The visible Presence of the Almighty was considered to rest in the Holy of Holies in the Tabernacle and the Temple. The term was further extended to the Omnipresence of the Deity, and it was considered that the Shechinah was brought nearer by acts of piety, and removed by acts of sin.

Shechita (שחיטה, lit. "slaying").

Animals which are to form the food of Israelites must be killed in a certain fashion, or else the food is not Kosher (*q.v.*). The main object is to entirely remove the blood, and for this purpose, the throat of the animal must be cut with an excessively sharp knife to make the cut instantaneous, and when the carcase is cut up a special examination of the lungs must take place in order to ensure that these important organs are in a sound condition (*see* Bedika). Of recent years, certain objections have been taken by Anti-Semites to the method of Shechita, which have led to restrictions on the practice in Switzerland.

Shedim (שדים, "demons").

Like all Eastern peoples, Jews believed in the existence of malevolent beings haunting ruins and deserted places. Many modern customs and superstitions have been due to this belief, as *e.g.*, amulets (*q.v.*).

Shekel (שקל, lit. "weight").

A well-known ancient Jewish coin, which still retains a certain amount of currency among modern Jews in the ceremony known as Pidyon ha Ben (*q.v.*), in which the eldest son is redeemed for the sum of five shekels, the modern equivalent of which is taken in England at 15s. or 12s. 6d.

GLOSSARY OF JEWISH TERMS.

Shelach Manoth (שלח מנות, lit. "sending of presents").

One of the means in which Purim (*q.v.*) is kept up is by an interchange of presents between friends, and this is often used as a delicate way of relieving distress.

Sheliach Zibbur (שליח צבור, lit. "Messenger of the Congregation").

Every Jew is a priest, and therefore, theoretically, there is no need for a special minister for the synagogue service, which can be performed by any member of the congregation; who in such case was considered the Messenger or Agent of the Congregation.

Sheloshim (שלשים, lit. "thirty").

For thirty days after the funeral Jewish orphans keep their rent garments untouched, and keep stricter mourning than during the rest of the year of mourning. This period is known as the Sheloshim.

Shema (שמע, lit. "hear").

The solemn declaration of the Divine Unity contained in Deut. vi., "Hear, O Israel: The Lord is our God, the Lord is One." This is the first passage taught in Hebrew to a Jewish child, and the last words that should be uttered by a Jewish man or woman. The solemn conclusion of the Yom Kippur (*q.v.*) also includes this declaration of Faith (*see* Neila).

Shem ha Mephorash (שם המפורש, lit. "Ineffable Name").

The Tetragrammaton is known among Jews by this name, which, owing to the Cabbala, has passed into use among Christian mystics.

Shemine Atsereth (שמיני עצרת, lit. "eighth, concluding" feast).

The eighth day of Tabernacles is known by this name, but is really a separate festival, which is kept for two days like most festivals outside Palestine, the second day being known as the Simchath Torah (*q.v.*). On this festival the prayer of thanks for rain is inserted, though the direct prayer for rain does not occur till two months later, when the pilgrims to Jerusalem were supposed to have returned to their homes.

Shemita (שמטה).

The practice of the Sabbatical Year (*q.v.*) led to the lying fallow of land every seventh year, but this is supposed only to apply to the Holy Land, where it is still kept up by the Jewish colonists established there by Baron Rothschild. It causes one of the greatest difficulties in the way of their prosperity.

Shemone Esre (שמנה עשרה, lit. "eighteen").

The chief portion of the daily prayers is composed of a series of nineteen blessings, which are known by this name. The additional benediction is practically an imprecation against Minim (*q.v.*). The reference in Daniel to the three prayers said every day is taken by Jewish tradition to refer to the Shemone Esre, which should be pronounced three times a day by every Jew, elaborate rules being given for the division of the day during which each recital should be made.

Sheol (שאול, lit. "pit").

The Hebrew name for Hell, which has recently been adopted in the Revised Version. According to Jewish belief, the punishment of Hell is by no means eternal, indeed, some Talmudic authorities state it only lasts for twelve months, with which probably the saying of the Kaddish (*q.v.*) for eleven months may be connected.

Shetar, pl. **Shetaroth** (שטר, lit. "contract").

The business or legal deeds of mediæval Jews, mostly written in Hebrew, are known by the above name. A whole volume of these records of the Jews of England before their expulsion was published by the Anglo-Jewish Historical Exhibition in 1888. It has been conjectured that the Star Chamber received its name from being originally the room in which the Shetaroth were kept by the King's officials.

Shidduchin (שדוכין, lit. "betrothals").

The preliminaries of the wedding, at which settlements are fixed, are known by this name, hence "to make a Shidduch" is the appropriate phrase for making up a match, in which the services of the Shadchan (*q.v.*) are often called into play.

Shiva (שבעה, lit. "seven").

For seven days after burial the mourners abstain from work, sit upon the ground or low seats (*see* Mourning). This period is known as the Shiva, and the mourning as the "Sitting Shiva." The Sabbath, however, is a welcome break in the days of gloom, for, during it, the mourners do not sit upon the ground.

Shlemihl (perhaps derived from the Hebrew proper name שלומיאל)

It is curiously disconsonant with the ordinary idea of the universality of Jewish success that one of the most characteristic figures among Jews is the Shlemihl, who invariably fails in whatever he undertakes. Whatever he touches turns out a failure, and yet it is not his own fault.

Shochet (שוחט, lit. "slaughterer").

The Jewish butchers who are acquainted with the Laws of Shechita (*q.v.*), are each called Shochet. In many small congregations they also perform the duties of Chazan (*q.v.*) and Mohel (*q.v.*). In England, as in other countries, they have to receive a licence from the Rav or Beth Din (*q.v.*).

Shofar (שופר, lit. "ram's horn").

The trumpet sounded on New Year's Day, which none can hear without feeling fear (Amos iii. 6), is usually made of ram's horn, simply hollowed out, and only emits very primitive and ear-piercing sounds. It is very difficult to perform on this instrument. In the Sephardic Ritual the Shofar is also used on Hoshana Rabba, and the conclusion of the Atonement Service is announced by a single note upon the Shofar. Among the Ashkenazim the Shofar is blown every morning (except Sabbath), and in some synagogues every evening during the month of Ellul.

Shomer (שמר, lit. "guard").

In order to ensure the ritual purity of food consumed by Jews, there is attached to every shop selling kosher meat and food a Shomer, who sees that no infringement of Jewish Law occurs during the process of preparation.

Shool (German, "schule"; Latin, "scola"; lit., "school").

The synagogue is appropriately known by this name, as it is very frequently used as a Jewish school during the weekdays. Curiously enough, in the Latin documents of the Middle Ages the synagogue was also termed Scola, apparently because the Latin scribes did not choose to recognise the synagogue as a place of worship.

Shulchan Aruch (שלחן ערוך, lit. "spread table").

The title of the celebrated code of Jewish Law drawn up by R. Joseph Karo in the 17th century, which is the real guide of Jewish life at the present day. It is really a further re-arrangement of the Tur by R. Jacob Asheri, which again is a selection of the same kind as Maimonides' "Mishne Torah." Maimonides drew up his code from the enactments of the Talmud, so that this codification of the Dinim (*q.v.*) can be traced back to the Talmud. It is divided into four portions.

Simchath Torah (שמחת תורה, lit. "Rejoicing of the Law").

Practically the ninth day of the Feast of Tabernacles, though theoretically it is the second day of the Shemine Atsereth (*q.v.*). On this day the annual reading of the Law in Sedras (*q.v.*) is concluded, and the beginning of Genesis is also read. The person to whom the last portion is read is known as the Chathan Torah (*q.v.*) and he to whom the beginning of Genesis is read is the Chathan Berashith.

Siyum (סיום, lit. "conclusion").

It is customary among students of the Talmud for the feast known by this name to be held at the conclusion of the study of a Tractate of the Talmud, and it is also customary on this occasion for the problems suggested by the Tractate to be discussed.

Sobotniki (Russ. "Sabbatarians").

A subdivision of the Jewish sect of Molakani, or Milk Drinkers, who, in the sixteenth century, adopted many Jewish customs, *e.g.*, circumcision and the Jewish Sabbath. They call themselves "Believers in the Bible of Moses" and are found even at the present day in Palow and Bobrow in Poland as well as in the Don district. In Silistria, in Bulgaria, they intermarry with Jews, and Jews with them.

Solachte (סלכתי, lit. "I have forgiven").

In one of the best-known hymns recited on the Day of Atonement, each verse finishes with this refrain. It is composed of 20 verses, each beginning with the successive letters of the Hebrew alphabet. Its author was Rabbi Yomtob, of Joigny, who was the leader of the English Jews at the celebrated massacre of York, 1190. A translation of the hymn by Mr. I. Zangwill may be found in J. Jacobs' *Jews of Angevin England*.

Succa (סוכה, lit. "booth").

The Tabernacle in which Jews were commanded to pass the seven days of Succoth (*q.v.*). Up to quite recently it was customary for Jews, even in northern climates, to have a Succa attached to their houses, in which they spent at any rate the daytime. Those who could not afford this extra convenience, were accustomed to remove a portion of their roof, and cover it with boughs sufficiently sparsely to allow the stars to be seen through it during the night. It is now usual for a Succa to be attached to the Synagogue and to be visited by the members of the congregation, Kiddush (*q.v.*) being said in it at the conclusion of the service.

Succoth (סכות, lit. "booths").

The Feast of Tabernacles commanded in Lev. xxiii. 34-42. It was intended to remind the Israelites of their dwelling in booths during their wanderings in the Wilderness. It is probably the old Harvest Home of Israel. It is now extended to nine days by the counting in Shemine Atsereth (*q.v.*), and the festival Simchath Torah (*q.v.*), and is kept by dwelling in or visiting a Succa (*q.v.*). The palm branch and citron, the willow and the myrtle, are also used during service on this feast. The booth is not dwelt in after the seventh day, called Hoshana Rabba (*q.v.*).

Swaying the Body.

Jews are accustomed to sway the body in prayer or study. This may be a natural outlet for their nervous energy, but it is supposed to fulfil the statement of the Psalm, "All the bones of my body praise thee." Others explain the practice as having arisen when there was only one book for all the worshippers or students, who had therefore to take their turn at looking at it.

Synagogue (Greek, lit. "assembly").

As the name implies, the origin of this institution can only be traced back to the Greek period. Though there are references to Houses of Prayer in Isaiah lvi. 7, it is probable they came into use after the monopoly of the sacrifices by the Temple at Jerusalem. They had evidently become a popular form of religious worship even before the fall of the Temple, and it was by their means that this event had such little disturbing influence on the development of Judaism. The old synagogues used to be built with the seats at one end arranged in the form of a semi-circle, and a reading desk in the middle, called a Bema, while the Scrolls of the Law were kept in a receptacle at the west end of the buildings. Nowadays it is usual for the seats of the audience to be on three sides of the building. On the fourth side, facing the east, is placed the ark where the Scrolls of the Law are kept, before which the perpetual lamp is kept burning. In the Middle Ages, the synagogue was more than a house of prayer, being used as a school (*see* Shool), and even as a communal inn (*see* Kiddush). The form of the synagogue is not fixed, being sometimes round and at other times octagonal, but the sexes are kept apart, the women being in a gallery (*q.v.*), above the floor of the building.

Synod.

During the Middle Ages, especially in Germany and France, it became customary for Assemblies of Rabbis to be summoned when any important question arose affecting the whole of the Jews, which were decided by the votes of the majority. Thus, on one occasion, under the Presidency of R. Tam, it was decided not to appeal to the Gentile courts on questions pending between two Jews. It has been suggested that many of the burning questions of modern Judaism might be similarly settled by the summoning of an Œcumenical Synod.

Szombatosok (Hung., "Sabbatarians").

A Judaising sect of Transylvania founded by Andreas Eossi in 1558, but given the specific Jewish term by Simon Pechi (1576-1642), who introduced Jewish prayers, festivals and customs which he had learned from the Sephardic refugees in Transylvania. Not only did they keep the New Year and Day of Atonement, but even adopted such customs as having the hair of their married women shaved, and wearing Arba Kanfoth (*q.v.*). Having kept their Jewish practices for nearly three centuries, many of them openly professed Judaism after the Edict of Toleration, December 27th, 1867.

Tables of the Law.

Jewish synagogues are left almost entirely without ornament, but on the side where the ark (*q.v.*) is placed there is generally a board on which is printed or incised the Ten Words, the opening word or words of each of the Ten Commandments. These are called the Tables of the Law.

Tachlith (תכלית, lit. "end" or "aim").

The practical tendency of the Jewish genius is shown by the use of this word, which is practically equivalent to the Aristotelian τελός, the ethical end, but is used by Jews to imply some material gain to be made by any action of theirs.

Taggin (תגין.)

On the top of the Hebrew letters written on the Siphre Torah or Megilloth are small strokes which are called by this name, and without which the Scroll is regarded as *pasul*, or not properly inscribed.

Tahara (טהרה, lit. "purification").

The cleansing of the corpse when preparing it for the coffin.

Talith (טלית, lit. "scarf").

The scarf used by Jews during public prayer in the daytime is called by this name, the etymology of which is uncertain, though Baron de Gunzburg has given reasons for believing that it is ultimately derived from the Latin, *trilix*, or three-threaded cloth which is the root of our *trellis*. It has Tsitsith (*q.v.*) at each corner, and is worn in order to carry out the Biblical command (Deut. xxii. 12), see Arba Kanfoth (*q.v.*). It is not worn at the evening service, except by the minister or by a mourner who says Kaddish (*q.v.*), and on Kol Nidre (*q.v.*), when the whole congregation wear it.

Talmud (תלמוד, lit. "learning").

The Mishna, or Oral Law, of the Jews, together with the Gemara (*q.v.*), its commentary, are both included under this title, which sums up the whole development of Jewish doctrine and practice after Biblical times up to nearly the fifth century. There are two recensions of the Gemara, one made in Babylon, which is the fuller, and one in Jerusalem, which is the earlier. The former is known familiarly as the Babli, the latter as Yerushalmi. The Talmud, together with the Midrash (*q.v.*), is the chief source of information as to Jewish thought and practice during the first Christian centuries, and the important light it throws upon the early history of Christianity, has been increasingly recognised, especially since the celebrated article on the Talmud by E. Deutsch, in the *Quarterly Review*, 1867.

Talmud Torah (תלמוד תרה, lit. "learning of the Law").

It is incumbent upon an Israelite to learn the Law, and this technical term is applied to that duty. As a rule, there are in most Jewish communities, schools in which the beginnings of this instruction are given, which are known as Talmud Torah Schools. These are preparatory to the Beth Hamidrash.

Tamchui (תמחוי)

There are two forms of organised charity among Jews, one known by this name which refers to the relief in *kind*, especially food, and another by the name of Kupah (*q.v.*).

Tamuz, 17th of (שבעה עשר בתמוז).

This day is kept as a fast in commemoration of the breach made in the wall of Jerusalem. It begins at daybreak.

Tana, pl. **Tanaim** (תנאים).

The teachers of the Law, whose activity ranged from about 200 B.C., to 219 A.D., practically include all the teachers mentioned in the Mishna (*q.v.*). They were succeeded by the Amoraim (*q.v.*), whose teaching forms the substance of the Gemara.

Taou-Kin-Kiaow (Chinese, "Extracting Sinew sect").

The Chinese name given to the Jews at Kae-Fung-Foo on the Ho-Hang-Ho in the province of Ho-nan. The reference is to the custom of porging (*q.v.*). According to their own account, they arrived in China during the Han dynasty (202 to 220, A.D.),

There were originally seven Tsung, or clans, remains of which are still left. At first, they did not intermarry with the surrounding Chinese, but only one Tsung still keeps up this restriction to the present day. They were last visited in 1865, when it was found that none of them knew any Hebrew, and had only a dim memory of their religion or origin. From their ritual, MSS. of which have been brought to Europe, it has been ascertained that they must have originally come from Persia. (*See* Dr. Neubauer, in *Jewish Quarterly Review*, Vol. VIII.). It would appear that some of this sect reside at Hong Kong. A full account of this "orphan colony of Jews" with full bibliography, has been compiled by the great Sinologist Cordier, in "Les Juifs en Chine." Paris, 1891.

Targum (Aram., lit. "Translation," תרגום).

The Aramaic translation of the Old Testament is known by this name, the portion containing the Pentateuch being known as the Targum Onkelos, and is attributed to one Onkelos, a convert to Judaism. The Targum of the prophets is attributed to one Jonathan Ben Usiel, but there is also another Targum of this portion of the Scriptures known as the Jerusalem Targum. These Aramaic versions are important, owing to their early date and to their containing the traditional Jewish interpretation of the Scriptures. There is, for instance, a tendency to reduce the anthropomorphism of the original texts. It was customary in the synagogues of Babylon for the Reading of the Law to be accompanied verse by verse with a reading of the Aramaic version by the Methurgeman.

Taryag (תרי״ג, lit. "Six hundred and thirteen").

Rabbi Simlai, one of the doctors of the Talmud, stated in a sermon that there were 613 commands mentioned in the Law. He went on to say that they could all be summed up in the one statement "Fear the Lord." But later doctors, taking his words more literally, have endeavoured to enumerate the commands making up the 613, 365 of which are negative, and 248 positive, the former giving the days of the year and showing that God's commands apply to every day of the year. The latter number is supposed to indicate the number of bones in the body, and shows that our whole frame is to be devoted to the service of God. Various enumerations have been made of these commands, but all of them contain a number relating to the High Priest and the King, and to special circumstances of Palestinian life, so that in actual practice the number can probably be reduced to 100 precepts which form the basis of Jewish practice.

Tashlich (תשליך, lit. "Thou wilt cast").

It is customary on the afternoon of the first day of New Year to visit a running stream or the sea shore. This custom has received its name from Micah vii. 18-21, in which the word Tashlich occurs. Superstition has connected itself with the practice.

Tchifout (Turkish).

The name given by the Turks to the Jews.

Tebeth, Tenth of (עשרה בטבת).

This day is kept as a fast in commemoration of the announcement of the siege of Jerusalem. It begins at daybreak.

Tehillim (תהלים, lit. "Praises").

The Psalter is popularly known among Jews by this name, and to "say Tehillim" is a favourite practice among more pious Israelites. Thus, to give a Jewish bull made in one of the English Prayer Books:—"Those who sleep in Shool on Kol Nidre night, say Tehillim."

Tekana, pl. Tekanoth (תקנה, lit. "Ordinance").

For the due regulation of congregational practice, the leaders of the various Jewish communities have from time to time issued laws known as Tekanoth. They deal with every aspect of life from tenant's right (*see* Jus Chazaka) to playing cards. They are known among the Sephardim as "ascamot."

Tekupha (תקופה, "cycle").

Each of the four seasons is known by this title. Also the solar cycle.

Tenach (ת"נ"ך abbrev. for תורה, נביאים, כתובים).

The whole Bible is known by this term, which is made up of the initial letters of the Hebrew words indicating the Law, the Prophets and the Hagiography.

Ten Tribes.

The Kingdom of Israel was composed of nine tribes, but one of these, the tribe of Joseph, was divided into two, Ephraim and Manasseh, and thus the number ten was made up. As these never returned to the Holy Land after the Assyrian Exile, whilst frequent mention is made in the prophecies about "Israel," a whole crowd of conjectures have been made as to their fate. They were settled in Mesopotamia, and the most probable claimants for the honour of being the lost Ten Tribes are the Yezidei or Devil Worshippers, who are resident in that district, and who have a tradition that they are so descended. There is, however, a very numerous sect among Englishmen, who consider that the English people have even greater claims, because it was promised in the Bible that Israel should "dwell in the isles," "extend to the ends of the earth," "speak a strange tongue" and "spread a knowledge of the Lord to the heathen." What nation on earth, ask the Anglo-Israelites, answers to this description, if not the English people. The argument is unanswerable from the standpoint of literal prophecy.

A full account of the Jewish views with regard to the Ten Tribes was given by Dr. Neubauer in *Jewish Quarterly Review*, vol. I.

Ten Words.

The Commandments are described in the Bible as the Ten Words, and they are divided by the Jews on a somewhat different method from that usual among Christians, the announcement "I am the Lord thy God" being taken as the first Commandment. According to Jewish tradition, the Ten Words were delivered at the Festival of Shabuoth (*q.v.*).

Tephilla (תפלה, lit. "prayer").

This term is applied to the Prayer Book, and indicates that it contains the daily prayers, as opposed to the Machzor (*q.v.*) which contains the Festival prayers, or the Hagada (*q.v.*) which contains the special service for the first nights of Passover.

Tephillin (lit. "head ornaments." Aramaic for the Hebrew טטפות, Exodus xiii., 16).

Small capsules covered with leather, and containing pieces of parchment on which are written Exodus xiii. 1-10, xi. 1-16; Deut. vi. 4-9 and xi. 13-14. These are bound round the head and the left arm and hand during morning prayer on weekdays, not on Sabbaths or Festivals. By this means is literally carried out the command in Deut. xi., 18, "Thou shall bind them for a sign upon thy hand, and they shall be a frontlet between thine eyes." Several Jewish Exegetes, *e.g.*, Rashbam, have taken this as metaphorical, but this cannot apply to the following injunction to "write them upon the doorposts of thine house," so that it is probable that the literal development of the command was carried out. At an early stage mystical importance was attributed to the wearing of the Tephillin, which was regarded as a means of protection against evil spirits, whence their Greek name Phylacteries (*q.v.*).

Terra Santa (Port., "sacred earth").

Among the Sephardim it is customary to place in the coffin a handful of earth brought from the Holy Land, and the custom is far from uncommon among Ashkenazim. It is a part of Jewish belief that the last Judgment will take place at Jerusalem, and that all Jews buried outside Palestine will have to burrow their way thither to attend the final summons.

Tetragrammaton (Greek, lit. "four-lettered").

A technical, theological term applied to the four unpunctuated Hebrew consonants which give the specific Jewish name of the Deity, and have been wrongly transliterated Jehovah (*q.v.*). The Jewish expression for this name is Shem ha-Mephorash (*q.v.*). Instead of it Jews pronounce the word as Adonai (My Lord).

Th (ת)

One of the chief difficulties in transliterating Hebrew words is caused by the variation of pronunciation of the letter ת. When it is aspirated, it is pronounced by Ashkenazic Jews as simply "s"; by the Sephardim, who make no difference according to the aspiration, as "t," and by the learned as "th." We have in this work followed the custom of the learned, but most Jewish readers of the present list will more quickly recognise the terms given in it if they will pronounce "th" as "s."

Thirteen Articles.

Maimonides summed up the Jewish faith in thirteen articles, which practically constitute the creed of Judaism, though never formally adopted by Jews. They are given shortly in the well-known hymn, Yigdal (*q.v.*).

Tithe.

Since the loss of the Holy Land, the Biblical command to give a tenth of all agricultural produce to the Priests and Levites has become obsolete, but many Jews of the present day keep up the practice by devoting one-tenth of their annual income to charity, connecting the practice with Deut. xiv. 29.

Tombstones (מצבה).

It would seem that in Biblical times the only form of tombstone was a cairn raised over the grave, and, as most interments were in rock sepulchres, it was natural that a superscription on the rock itself would answer the purpose of a tombstone. Tombstones are first mentioned in Jewish records in the eleventh century. Among the Sephardim they are placed lengthwise on the grave, but the Ashkenazim have erect headstones. Till quite recently they were exceedingly plain, but at Amsterdam the Marranos introduced the more elaborate tombstones with heraldic bearings, to which they had been accustomed in Spain.

Torah (תורה, lit., "instruction").

In general Jewish parlance this term is commonly applied to the Pentateuch. In strict theological significance, it is extended to the whole of the Scriptures, and refers to the spirit as much as to the letter of the Law.

Tosaphoth (lit. "Additions").

The school of Rashi (*q.v.*) further extended his comments on the Talmud, and their additions are known by the name of Tosaphoth (תוספות), and are printed on the outer margin of the text of the Talmud. The authors are known generally as the Tosaphists.

Transliteration.

Owing to the variations of pronunciation among the different sections of Jews, there has been great difficulty in transliterating the Hebrew words in such a way that they shall be recognised in that transliterated form by those who know the original Hebrew. This difficulty is further increased by the Rabbinic terms, which are mostly printed without the vowel points. In the present list, a sort of compromise has been adopted between the strictly learned form of transliteration and the popular one, which will, doubtless, please neither party.

Trepha (טרפה, lit., "torn").

Strictly speaking, this term only applies to the flesh of animals that have met a violent death, but in actual practice it is applied to any food that is not kosher (*q.v.*) according to Jewish Law, especially to food that has failed to pass the requirements of Bedika (*q.v.*). *See* Shechita.

Triennial Cycle.

The law is now read through once every year, but formerly it was finished after three years. Prof. Büchler has recently discovered the actual sections read through that period (*Jewish Quarterly Review*, IV., V.).

Tsaddik (צדיק, lit. "holy").

The saints of the Chassidim (*q.v.*) are known by this name, which, however, can be applied to any very pious man.

Tsar Baale Chayim (צער בעלי חיים, lit. "pain to animals").

The tender care shown by the Biblical precept, not to take the young bird from its nest, has found an echo in Jewish hearts with its characteristic Rachmoneth (*q.v.*), which, as the above familiar phrase shows, is extended to dumb animals. The founder of the Society for the Prevention of Cruelty to Animals was a Jew.

Tsevoa (צואה, lit., "injunction").

During the Middle Ages, and perhaps earlier (*cf.* the Testaments of the Patriarchs), it became customary for learned Jews to leave a sort of ethical will giving to their children a summary of their moral experience. These form peculiarly interesting documents as throwing light upon the ideals of mediæval Jews, and a full account of them has been given by Mr. I. Abrahams in *Jew. Quart. Rev.*, Vol. III.

Tsitsith (ציצית, lit. "corners").

Attached to the corners of the Talith (*q.v.*) are four long threads drawn through a small hole about an inch from the corner. The longest of these is wound seven, eight, eleven and thirteen times round the other threads, thus giving by Gematria (*q.v.*) the words יהוה אחד. After each set of windings a double knot is made. This method of communication recalls the Mexican *quipu*. They are so placed in accordance with the command in Num. xv. 37. If the threads are torn the Talith and Arba Kanfoth (*q.v.*) is *pasul*, and must not be used.

Unterführer (Germ., lit. "guides").

The supporters of bride and bridegroom during the marriage service are called by this name, as they lead them under the Chuppa (*q.v.*).

Viddui (ודוי, lit. "confession").

Instead of the Sin Offering, after the Fall of the Temple, was substituted a Confession of Sin. This occurs as part of the public service on the Day of Atonement and privately when a Jew is near death, when the opening of the heart in this manner was held to relieve the sinner from some of the consequences of the sin if accompanied by atonement. If the person against whom the sin had been committed was alive an apology was necessary; if dead, it was the practice to attend his grave with ten witnesses and there formally acknowledge his guilt against him.

Vowel Points.

Originally, only the consonants were written down in Hebrew, but, when the Massoretes fixed the text of the Law, they invented or adopted from the Syrians signs indicating the omitted vowels. These were at one time written above the letters, and many scrolls have been discovered vocalised in this way, which is known as the "Vowels of Tiberias," but the more usual form is the subscript. These are only used in printed Bibles or in scrolls not intended for public service. During the discussions with the Karaites (*q.v.*), this sect attacked the vowel points as being unauthorised additions to the pure text of Scripture, and as a result of this attack, it became customary not to use the vowel points even in secular works, so that most Hebrew books are printed now-a-days without this aid. In the 17th century, a fierce controversy took place between Catholic and Protestant theologians as to whether the vowel points formed an integral part of the Sacred Text.

Wacher (Germ., lit. "watcher").

From the moment of death till the body is removed for burial, it is not considered decorous to leave the corpse alone, while, of course, there are many duties to be performed in preparing it for its last home. The duties of preparing the dead, and watching over them used to be performed by volunteers (*see* Chevra Kadisha and Lavadores), but nowadays these rites are mostly performed by persons who gain a living in this way, and are known by the above name.

Washing the Hands.

Great importance is attached to this practice before meals, before the Duchan (*q.v.*) and after leaving a burial ground, but the actual washing is often reduced to a mere "survival." It is possible that there is here, besides the motive of cleanliness, some survival of an old feeling with regard to taboo, water being the usual folk-lore remedy against evil influences of any sort.

Wine-Glass at Wedding.

After the conclusion of the Seven Blessings (*q.v.*), at weddings it is customary for the bridegroom to take a wineglass and break it. Formerly, this used to be the glass in which the Kiddush (*q.v.*) had been made, and it used to be thrown against the north wall of the Synagogue, but nowadays it is an ordinary wineglass, which is simply broken beneath the foot of the bridegroom. No satisfactory explanation has been given of this quaint custom.

Wunder Rabbi (Germ., "Miracle Rabbi").

The Rabbis of the Chassidim (*q.v.*) are credited with supernatural powers, and when they take the credit are known by this name. One of them at Sadagora in Hungary, lives in a state of regal magnificence from the freewill offerings of his believers.

Yad (יד, lit. "hand").

To touch a Scroll of the Law renders a person impure

according to Rabbinic notions, consequently, to point out the place during the ceremonial Reading of the Law, a Yad or pointer is used which is usually made of a precious metal or ivory, with the end in the shape of a small hand with an outstretched finger. It is sometimes adorned with jewels.

Yahid, pl. Yahidim (יחידים, lit. "individuals").

The term applied by the Sephardim to the male seatholders of the Synagogue, of certain standing, from whom the Mahamad (*q.v.*) is elected.

Year of Mourning.

For eleven months after the death of a parent it is customary among Jews to attend Synagogue morning and evening in order to say Kaddish (*q.v.*). A light is kept continually burning in the dwelling-room, and, of course, no festivities are held or joined in during the year.

Yeshiva (ישבה lit. "session").

The Rabbinic colleges in which the Talmud is studied and taught are known by this name. On one occasion a bequest left to a Yeshiva was declared inoperative by English law, as being applied to superstitious uses, and the money was handed to the Foundling Hospital.

Yetser Hara (יצר הרע, lit. "evil imagination").

Each man has within him a good and evil tendency. The latter is personified as a sort of Evil Counsellor accompanying man. Yetser Hara is identified with Satan and the Angel of Death.

Yid (pl. "Yidden").

An English adaptation of the German *Jude, Juden*, and meaning, of course, Jew, Jews.

Yiddish (German, lit. "Jewish").

This term is applied to the dialect or jargon used by Polish and German Jews. It is very nearly pure German, with a few Hebrew and still fewer Polish words included, but the German is of an archaic type and many of the words have become obsolete in modern German. In England a number of Yiddish words and phrases have become current among English Jews who cannot speak either German or the jargon, and think these words are Hebrew. (*See* "Anglo-Yiddish.")

Yigdal (יגדל, lit. "Exalted be").

A familiar hymn of the Daily Service begins with this word, and is composed of thirteen lines, each of which sums up one of the articles in the Jewish Creed. (*See* Thirteen Articles.)

Yom Kippur (יום כפור, lit. "Day of Atonement").

The tenth day of Tishri is kept as a solemn fast: "It shall be unto you as a Sabbath of rest, and ye shall afflict yourselves; in the ninth day of the month at even, from even unto even, shall ye celebrate your Sabbath" (Leviticus xxiii. 31, 32.) This affliction is taken to mean rigid abstinence from any food or drink, but the fasting is, of course, only a means to the end of repentance, to which the day is devoted. Many Jews attend Synagogue arrayed in the *Sargenas* shroud in which they will be buried, to remind them of their end, and the conclusion of the service is a sort of rehearsal of the last moments of the Israelite. The eve of the fast is known by the name of Kol Nidre (*q.v.*), and the final service goes by that of Neila (*q.v.*). The service is held continuously from early morn till dusk. This is the most solemn day of the year to Jews, and many who do not keep any of the Jewish customs still attend Synagogue and fast on this day.

Yom Tob (יום טוב, lit. "Good Day").

The name given to every Jewish holiday. A curious adjective has been formed, "Yumtuvtik," implying suitable or appropriate for a holiday, and more especially applied to Passover.

Zid (Russian, "Jew").

The Russian name for Jew, which, as might be expected, conveys a shade of contempt in its meaning.

Zohar (זהר, lit. "light").

The great text book of the Cabbala (*q.v.*), being in the form of an Aramaic commentary on Genesis, and professing to explain the Divine economy of creation. It is supposed to be written by Simeon ben Yochai, but modern scholarship has discovered that it was written by Moses de Leon, a Spanish Rabbi of the thirteenth century.

Zuz (זוז).

A Talmudic coin which is still preserved in modern Jewish custom by references in the Kethuba (*q.v.*).

A GLANCE AT 5656.

To review the history of the Jewish people during a year is practically to write the history of civilisation for that time, in other words, an impossible task. Many events do not bear on their face the importance which will be afterwards attributed to them, while much about which the world talks excitedly at the time proves too often but a nine days' wonder. Yet we that record the progress of Israel during any period of time cannot fail to have our attention attracted by events which, so to speak, shout at us, and in looking back upon the year that has passed, we can only attempt to revive attention to doings and sayings and writings that have been most in evidence before the Jewish public. Yet even here there is a distinction to be made. The peculiarity of a Jew's position is that he has world-wide interests combined with a strong local patriotism. He is interested in the Anti-Semitic movement, and at the same time he is not above attending to an opposed election at his synagogue. Where are we to take our standpoint? If we are cosmopolitan, we shall be vague. If we are parochial, we shall be narrow. Perhaps a judicious admixture of these faults may cause them to counterbalance one another.

Speaking generally, and surveying the whole fortunes of Israel during the year, one can report some slight progress. The centre of Jewish interest within the last hundred years has been Russia, where more than half of the living Israelites manage to exist. Though no formal amelioration has taken place in the condition of the unhappy Jews of Russia, it is clear that the word has gone forth to the officials that the pressure upon them is to be relaxed. The admission of some representative Rabbis at the Coronation Ceremony at Moscow and their decoration afterwards, are but slight signs, but they may possible show in what quarter the wind is blowing.

In Austria, things seem to have gone somewhat backward, but it may only mean that it is in order that they may jump forward further. The reception by the Emperor of the well-named Dr. Lueger, the chief of Austrian Anti-Semites, at first sight appears a triumph for the party, but it may be hoped that it will merely turn out that he has been given rope enough.

Roumania still evades the performance of the duties imposed upon her by the Treaty of Berlin, but, on the whole, the Jews of the Principality are not perceptibly worse off than they were when the *Shofar* last was blown. In France, less was heard of the colleagues of Mons. Drumont last year than ever before. Nowhere else in the world is the position of Jews a cause of anxiety, though ugly rumours reach one from time to time as to their social position in the States.

The death of Baron de Hirsch perhaps stands out as the most prominent event of the year in its interest for all Jewry. The magnificent scale of his charitable operations, the practical sagacity with which they were directed, and perhaps the seeming absence of any sympathetic sentiment on the part of the Baron, have attracted the attention of the world to his schemes for many years, and this attention was only intensified by his unexpected death. What will be the future of those enterprises who shall say? The Argentine scheme is still far from being decisively successful, and the death of the Baron may turn the balance in the opposite direction. But as to this, we shall probably know more before the world is a year older.

Turning to the quarter of the globe in which the readers of this Year Book would be more particularly interested, the chief event which strikes one on looking back, is also a death—that of Sir Julian Goldsmid, who may be said to have held in the Anglo-Jewish community as commanding a position as that possessed by Baron de Hirsch in the community at large. His remarkable powers of directing men were shown not alone among English Jews, but among Englishmen in general. It can have been given to but few men to have been at the same time Vice-Chancellor of the University of London, Vice-Chairman of the House of Commons, besides being chairman of numerous companies and philanthropic bodies. This versatility made the gap caused by his loss to be the wider and extend in all directions: charity, education, synagogal organisation, and the general conduct of Jewish affairs were all rendered the poorer when Sir Julian Goldsmid was carried to his last home.

The doings of the Sephardim have, perhaps, attracted more attention during the past year than for many previous decades of years. Just when new life seemed to be showing in the younger Yehidim, as was testified by the new synagogue now being built, a deplorable incident has caused much heart-burning in this ancient community, and resulted in the closing of one of their most important institutions—the Judith Montefiore College, Ramsgate. It can only be hoped that out of this evil may come the good that a competent institution for the education of the Jewish clergy of its two sections, compounded of the other institutions which have attempted to cover that ground, would prove. The amalgamation of the three institutions would be a happy consummation of an unfortunate incident.

The year has seen changes in some of the most representative of Anglo-Jewish institutions. The Anglo-Jewish Association and the Russo-Jewish Committee both lost their chief when Sir Julian Goldsmid was taken from us. Mr. Claude G. Montefiore, who, though young, has shown himself worthy of the highest positions, has succeeded him at the Anglo-Jewish Association, while Sir Samuel Montagu takes his place on the Russo-Jewish Committee, on which he has served as Treasurer from its inception. Mr. Arthur Cohen has retired from the position of President of the Board of Deputies, which he has held so long, and has been replaced by Sir Joseph Sebag Montefiore, who gained his spurs at the same time. Another great institution which has seen changes during 5656 is the Board of Guardians for the relief of the Jewish Poor, which has moved into premises in Widegate-street, more suitable for the ever-increasing good work which the Institution carries out. The very large cost which this change involved was met by a few friends of the Institution without drawing "for a penny piece," to use Mr. B. L. Cohen's phrase, upon its own funds.

One of the youngest of our institutions has given proof of renewed life. "The Maccabeans," having exhausted all Jewish celebrities or celebrated friends of the Jews to whom they could give dinners, were somewhat at a loss for further spheres of activity. They have, however, devoluted to energetic sub-committees a system of finding out rising Jewish talent in the East End, while, in another direction, they have set up an organisation known as the Jewish Boys' Brigade, to do for their muscles what the other committee hopes to do for their brains.

Another young society has had a change of *personnel*. Mr. Lucien Wolf has retired from the Jewish Historical Society of England, for which he has done such excellent work, and has been succeeded by the Chief Rabbi, who has throughout shown the keenest interest in the former history of the flock over which he presides. Mr. Wolf's presidency will always be remembered for the additional and new holiday of the Jewish Calendar, at any rate in England—Resettlement Day, February 4th. The chief topic of interest discussed in the Jewish Historical Society during the year was the authenticity of the tradition that Moyse Hall at Bury St. Edmunds was formerly a synagogue. The pundits have not yet had their last say upon this interesting point, which perhaps did not lose in interest from the fact that there were no materials accessible for deciding either one way or the other.

Another point that aroused some general interest in the community was as to the general policy of having Jewish boys educated at public schools where no Jewish house was kept; Harrow being the particular school which gave rise to the controversy. The general impression left by it was that, whatever might be said on the principle itself, the Harrovian Jewish boys were not suffering at present from being dispersed through the school.

Other points that have been attracting considerable interest have been the question of the use of English in synagogue, which aroused fierce opposition at Berkeley Street which here, as elsewhere, shows itself *plus royaliste que le roi*. The discussion raised on this topic extended into a general *mêlée* on the comparative merits of reform and orthodoxy in the United States, in which some rather curious facts were brought to light. A sign of the times was given by another controversy raised by the exclusion from a provincial synagogue of a person who had become notorious as a money-lender. One can admire the zeal while one doubts the discretion of such an exclusion. The now defunct Education Bill had its interest for the Jewish public, who would have been seriously affected by its provisions, whether for good or for ill it was somewhat difficult to discern.

The history of Israel is the history of individual Jews, and thus the slow development of enlightenment among the Jews, and toleration among others, is best expressed by individual instances of merit or of tolerance. The generations come and go, and it is often the historian's province to record the disappearance of one with the rise of another. We have recorded some of these changes, and we can now turn our attention to some of the younger generation who are gaining distinction in new spheres, and have, therefore, no need to see the oldsters disappear before they get room for their capacities. An unusual crop of University honours has fallen to Jews during the past year, the chief being the election of Mr. I. Gollancz to the newly founded post of Lecturer in English at Cambridge. Professor Alexander, of Owens College, has become Examiner in Philosophy at London University, where Dr. Sidney Phillips examines for the same body in Medicine. Dr. F. Liebermann, of Berlin, has received academic recognition of the value of his studies in early English History by the conferment of an honorary degree at Cambridge. But, in this connection, perhaps the chief distinction of the year has been the election of Mr. Solomon J. Solomon to the rank of Associate of the Royal Academy, a position rarely gained at his age.

After gains, losses. Abroad, the decease of Rabbi Elchan Spektor, the "Kowno Rav" as he was called, removed from the Russian Jews their most prominent figure. The French General Lambert, and in Germany, Dr. Joel Müller, are perhaps the two most important deaths on the Continent. Happily in England, we have to record, in addition to the irreparable loss caused by Sir Julian Goldsmid's death, only the sad death of Dr. Dyte, and the painless passing away of Mr. Jacob Montefiore, one of the founders of the English Colonial Empire.

Literature of the Year.—Thinking over the publications of the year which have interest to Jews, one feels inclined to call the year 5656 the Apocryphal Year. In the first place, the revision of the Bible, undertaken a quarter of a century ago, was brought to a close by the publication of the Revised Apocrypha. It is difficult to understand the neglect into which the Apocrypha has fallen amongst Jewish readers, since its various books contain the chief products of the Hebrew intellect for the three years before the Fall of Jerusalem, during which scarcely any other records of the Jews exist. But apart from this, their intrinsic merit often approaches that of the Wisdom literature of the Bible. It is to be hoped that the Revised Apocrypha will revive Jewish interest in these noble records of the combined influence of Hebraism and Hellenism on the Jewish mind. But the year has also been signalised by a remarkable discovery made by Mr. Schechter as to the Hebrew origin of one of the most charming of the Apocryphal books—that of Ecclesiasticus. It forms one of the romances of scholarship, that preservation for nearly a thousand years of a torn scrap of paper only to find its way into the very hands that were best fitted to convey its message to the world. By a lucky chance, Mr. Schechter had had to concern himself with the scattered passages from Ecclesiasticus, already quoted in Rabbinic law, so that he could discern at a glance the nature of the fragment when it came into his hands. Its significance cannot be over-rated and Mr. Schechter has already drawn attention to the many problems which it may help to solve.

Mr. Schechter has been much in evidence during the past year. Though so well known as a scholar, his first book appeared this year in the form of his collected "Studies in Judaism." These have revealed to the world what his friends have always known, the remarkable gifts of Mr. Schechter as a theological thinker as well as an eloquent and witty writer.

In Bible study, we have to record a reversion to the contents of the Sacred Book. The world is getting somewhat tired of the "slicing process" adopted by the Higher Criticism, and the "Rainbow" Bible is not helping to attract further attention to the revision of the text, however necessary that process may be. The tendency is now towards studying the literary and didactic value of the Bible, and Professor Moulton's "Literary Study of the Bible" and Mr. Montefiore's "Bible for Home Reading" are significant proofs of this new tendency. The chief contribution that has been made to Biblical archæology has been from Flinders Petrie's discovery of a reference to Israel in hieroglyphic literature.

Turning to more strictly Jewish literature, most of the work that has been done is of a highly specialised character, which it is impossible to enumerate in detail. The Doyen of Jewish scholars, Dr. Steinschneider, reached this year his 80th birthday, and to celebrate the occasion, a Festschrift has appeared, in which one is glad to notice that the English Jewish scholars take a prominent position. A series of elegant extracts from Rabbinic writers, compiled by Drs. Winter and Wuenche, has come to an end, and the three volumes will give to any reader of German ample material to judge of the literary productions of Jews since Bible times. Professor Bacher has added another volume to the series in which he is systematically expounding the Hagadic authors of the principles of the Talmud: while Professor Kaufmann has made a most valuable contribution to our knowledge of the inner life of mediæval Jewesses by the publication of the diary of Gluckl von Hameln. What a pity he printed it in Hebrew characters, seeing that it is written in Yiddish!

Jewish history has received an acquisition this year in Dr. Rieger's excellent history of the later fortunes of the Roman Ghetto, while Mr. B. L. Abrahams has done a model piece of work in his Arnold essay, "The Expulsion of the Jews from England." The Historical Societies, both of England and the United States, have issued volumes throwing much light upon the Jewish history of these countries.

Some attention was attracted by an Anti-Semitic article in the *Quarterly Review*, which would have been wisely left to be forgotten if Mr. Hermann J. Cohen had not played into the author's hands by contributing an article to the *Fortnightly Review* which, to say the least, did not put the Jewish case on the highest level.

Turning to more general literature, one is glad to observe that Mr. Zangwill is returning to his old love. He has produced three sketches of Jewish idealists which have shown him in some of his best aspects. "Z. Z." has also added to his laurels by a somewhat sombre but powerful book, showing how the world conquers the man.

Lastly, some notice must be taken of a remarkable pamphlet on a Jewish State, written by Dr. Theodor Herzl, who has followed up his somewhat fantastic scheme by an attempt to put it into practice. The skill of his presentation could not, however, disguise from thoughtful readers the particularly impracticable character of his ideas, and the mechanical nature of the solution it offered to the much vexed Jewish question.

NOTABLE EVENTS.
AUGUST, 1895 — JULY, 1896.

Aug. 8th.—Degree of LL.D. conferred at Cambridge upon Professor Asser, of Amsterdam.
„ 18th.—Golden wedding of Mr. and Mrs. Alphonse Hartog.
„ 24th.—Attempt on the life of Baron Alphonse de Rothschild, of Paris.

Sept. 7th.—Conference of Jewish workers at Leeds.
„ 13th.—Rev. A. P. Bender inducted into office at Capetown.
„ 26th.—Anti-Semitic Election of Municipal Council at Vienna.
„ 27th.—Baron de Worms made Peer of United Kingdom as Lord Pirbright.

Oct. 4th.—Trial of Shochet at Birkenhead.
„ 10th.—Sir Julian Goldsmid sworn in Member of the Privy Council.
„ 16th.—New Synagogue consecrated at Pontypridd.
„ 27th.—Resignation of Mr. Arthur Cohen as President of the Board of Deputies.
„ 29th.—Dr. Lueger elected Burgomaster at Vienna.

Nov. 9th.—Mr. Michael Emanuel, J.P., elected Mayor of Southampton.
„ 10th.—Degree Day at Montefiore College, Ramsgate.
„ 17th.—Mr. J. Sebag Montefiore elected President of the Jewish Board of Deputies.
„ 23rd.—Anti-Semitic interpellation in the Austrian Parliament.

Dec. 1st.—Mr. Claude G. Montefiore elected President of the Anglo-Jewish Association.
„ 15th.—Service for Volunteers held at Boro' Synagogue.
„ „ Foundation Stone laid of Sephardic Synagogue, Lauderdale Road.
„ 27th.—Panic at a Jewish Theatre in Baltimore, U.S.A.

Jan. 17th.—Dr. Theodor Herzl explains his scheme for a Jewish State.
„ 23rd.—East End Scheme adopted by the United Synagogue.
„ 24th.—Foundation Stone laid of the extension of the Hammersmith Synagogue.
„ 26th.—Lieut. H. M. Jessel elected M.P. for South St. Pancras.

Feb. 7th.—Baron Ferdinand de Rothschild elected Trustee of the British Museum.
„ 12th.—Mr. Solomon J. Solomon elected A.R.A.
„ 15th.—Maccabean Dinner to Sir Saul Samuel.
„ 28th.—German Emperor repudiates Stoecker.

Mar. 16th.—Mr. Israel Gollancz elected Lecturer in English Literature at Cambridge.
„ 22nd.—Opening of New Offices of Jewish Board of Guardians.
„ 26th.—Marriage of Mr. G. J. G. Lewis and Miss Hirsch.

Mar. 30*th*.—Eightieth Birthday of Dr. Steinschneider.
April 8*th*.—Professor Flinders Petrie announces the discovery of the name of Israel in an Egyptian inscription.
„ „ Marriage of Mr. B. L. Abrahams and Miss Joseph.
„ 10*th*.—Election Sunday.
„ 26*th*.—Montefiore College closed.
„ 28*th*.—Interview of Dr. Lueger with the Austrian Emperor.
„ 29*th*.—Discussion on the Shulchan Aruch in the Prussian House of Lords.
„ 30*th*.—Laying of Foundation Stone of Cardiff Synagogue.
May 18*th*.—Mr. J. Sebag Montefiore knighted.
„ 28*th*.—Three Jewish Rabbis attend the Czar's Coronation.
June 2*nd*.—Marriage of Rev. S. Conquy and Miss Spiers.
„ „ Jubilee of Dr. Isaac Dembo celebrated at St. Petersburg.
„ 7*th*.—Madame Furtado-Heine made an Officer of the Legion of Honour, Paris.
„ 14*th*.—Vote of Confidence in Dr. Gaster passed by the Yehidim.
„ 21*st*.—Reconsecration of the Hammersmith Synagogue.
July 1*st*.—Publication by Mr. Schechter of part of the Hebrew Text of Ecclesiasticus.
„ 6*th*.—Maccabean Dinner to Dr. Theodor Herzl.
„ 8*th*.—Golden Wedding of Mr. and Mrs. D. de Pass.
„ „ Signor Luigi Luzzatti appointed Minister of the Treasury at Rome.

OBITUARY.
August, 1895—July, 1896.

Benham, Mr. Arthur, Dramatist, ætat. 26...	September 8th, 1895.
Berman, Vassili Lazarevitch ...	March 18th, 1896.
Cowen, Mr. Lionel, Artist	August 10th, 1895.
Davis, Edward, ætat. 88, Shrewsbury	September 4th, 1895.
Dyte, Dr. D. A. ...	September 14th, 1895.
Green, Mrs. A. L.	May 17th, 1896.
Goldsmid, Rt. Hon. Sir Julian	January 7th, 1896.
Hirsch, Baron de	April 20th, 1896.
Jacob, Mr. Edward	July 1st, 1896.
Montefiore, Jacob, ætat. 94, Pioneer of Australian colonisation	November 3rd, 1895.
Müller, Dr. Joel, Rabbinic Scholar...	November 6th, 1895.
Nathan, Mr. Henry, Australian Merchant	August 16th, 1895.
Ornstien, Rev. A. F., Capetown	December 6th, 1895.
Spektor, Rabbi Isaac Elchanan (Kowno Rav)	March 6th, 1896.
Wiener, Dr. A., Oppeln	August 25, 1895.
Worms, Mr. Henry	February 15, 1896.

ALIEN IMMIGRATION.

THERE are few matters of greater import to English Jews than the vast network of questions which come under the common denomination of Alien Immigration. The almost unanimous persecution to which Jews were subjected throughout Europe, left the old kingdom of Poland the only haven of refuge to our unhappy people, and at its partition Russia took, with her share of the fallen state, the large bulk of European Jews. Russia's hereditary policy was Anti-Jewish, and it added to this the motive of compelling universal allegiance to the Greek Church. So that, ever since Poland became part of the Russian empire, there has been a migration, albeit gradual and cautious, of Polish Jews to countries in which they might enjoy the human rights of liberty and freedom.

Occasional outbursts of Russian fanaticism, or practical manifestations of Russian bigotry, temporarily swelled the emigrant ranks, but no noticeable migration took place until the year 1881. The "May laws," as they are termed, which were then promulgated, so limited the area in which Jews might live, the callings they might follow, and their means of education, as to form a practical notice to quit to any who had the chance. Casting their eyes over the world, there was one country which men less naturally shrewd would quickly have perceived as a Land of Promise. The great Western Republic, whose very *raison d'être* was the freedom these poor Jews were denied at home, in the land of their birth, was not only capable of assimilating a vast immigration, but from the nature of its people and its industries, was an ideal goal for the tenacious, sharp-witted, hard-working Polish Jew. Hence an exodus began from Russia to America, and the Jew, with his never failing adaptability, changed his allegiance from the Eagle to the Stars and Stripes, and his language from Yiddish to Yankee. So that to-day New York contains a population of upwards of 300,000 Jews—the most Jewish city on the face of the earth.

In this migration England has played no small part, nor has she remained unaffected by it. Her geographical position, and the fact that she is the heart and centre of the world's carrying trade, have made her a half-way house for the Russian emigrant to America. And at this half-way house a few of the wanderers, in comparison with the huge numbers that have crossed the Atlantic, have made their home. But those few have not been unnoticed. Like the Jew, everywhere, and at all times throughout history, the Alien Immigrant Jew has attracted an attention altogether out of proportion to his numbers, or to the real influence, either for good or for bad, which he exercises on those amongst whom he has come to settle. Alarming and alarmist reports were sedulously put about, often with a view of currying favour with the working classes at the expense of a class that were not in a position to refute the charges, as to the nature and extent of the immigration that was taking place. An "Alien Invasion" was thought to be an accurate description of the process, and a book with this taking title received a prefatory benediction by a dignitary of the Established Church. When America adopted legislative regulations of Immigration to the States, a cry was raised as to her sending back to England hordes of Russian and Polish paupers—the present Prime Minister described this as the "choking of the drain," and Great Britain was declared to be "the dumping ground" for the offscourings of Muscovite Ghetti.

The attention of Parliament was naturally called to the matter, and in 1889 a select Committee of the House of Commons was appointed to examine into the Immigration of destitute Foreigners. Amongst the Members of Parliament who served on the Committee were Baron Ferdinand de Rothschild and Mr. (now Sir) Samuel Montagu. The Committee sat in May and July, 1889, and, after hearing a considerable amount of evidence, reported *inter alia* that the immigrants "are quick at learning, moral, frugal and thrifty, and inoffensive as citizens, but generally very dirty and uncleanly in their habits." They further reported that "the number of aliens arriving were not sufficiently large to create alarm," and recommended that measures should be taken at certain ports at which aliens debark, to ascertain with accuracy

ALIEN IMMIGRATION.

their number and their destination. As a result of this recommendation the Board of Trade began to issue returns and reports upon Alien Immigration. In the same session a select Committee of the House of Lords, with Lord Rothschild as a Member, which was appointed in 1888 to consider the "Sweating System" in the United Kingdom, issued its report. The allegation had been made that the pernicious system known as "Sweating" and the prevalence of starvation wages, were peculiarly products of Immigration. The Committee, however, after sitting on 71 occasions and examining 291 witnesses, reported—so far as this allegation is concerned, "we think undue stress has been laid on the injurious effect on wages caused by foreign Immigration, inasmuch as we find that the evils complained of obtain in trades which do not appear to be affected by foreign immigration."

The circumstance of a Unionist Government being in power and those anxious for restrictive legislation being of the same political persuasion, together with the fact that the Board of Trade returns exhibited a much smaller number of Immigrants coming to this country for settlement than had been anticipated, allowed the question to remain much in abeyance till the end of 1892. In that year a General Election took place and a Liberal Majority was returned to the House of Commons, Mr. Gladstone becoming Prime Minister. The House met in January, 1893, for the transaction of general business, and Mr. James Lowther tabled an Amendment to the Address in reply, urging the necessity for the restriction of Immigration. The debate on Mr. Lowther's Amendment took place on February 11th. Amongst those who took part in it were the late Sir Julian Goldsmid, Baron Ferdinand de Rothschild and Sir Samuel Montagu. Mr. Gladstone also spoke and insisted upon the fallacy of regarding Immigrants who possessed capacity for work as paupers because they were penniless. A vote of thanks was subsequently accorded to Mr. Gladstone for his speech at a Mass Meeting of East End Jews. Mr. Lowther's Amendment was negatived by 234 to 119, and amongst those who voted in the minority was Mr. Chamberlain, who for the first time showed his sympathy with the demand for restriction. His vote brought the question from below to above the gangway in a Parliamentary sense.

In the course of the debate it had been urged that America was excluding the class whose immigration into this country it was desired to restrict. Mr. Mundella, who was then President of the Board of Trade, therefore determined to obtain a reliable account of the methods adopted by the States, and for that purpose, in February, 1893, despatched Mr. John Burnett and Mr. David Schloss to America as Special Commissioners to examine into and report upon the whole question of Immigration as they found it in the United States. The result of their investigations was presented to the Board of Trade in the Autumn of 1893, and issued as a Blue Book. Far from restricting, it was found that America encouraged Immigration, that penuriousness was not held to be a bar to the intending settler, and that the laws that the American legislature had enacted were purely sanitary precautions where they were not in obedience to America's trade protective policy. The object of such restrictive laws as had been passed appeared to be the exclusion of the morally and physically unfit, but even these were admitted under certain regulations if they had friends who would look after them. Far more strict did our Commissioners find the authorities on the other side in the case of that other class against whom the restrictive laws were directed—the contract labourers, *i.e.*, Immigrants who had come to America under a previously concluded contract to do work there. As a general result, however, it was found that in the year under review (1891-2) the immigrants admitted to the States numbered roughly 600,000, and the rejections, after deducting those who come under the head of contract labourers, was only some 1,200. Since the immigrants coming to the United Kingdom for settlement in about the same year numbered only 150,000, and those from Russia and Poland only about 7,000, if proportions can be held to be of any value, American rejections, as reported by Messrs. Burnett & Schloss, did not betoken a very large number of undesirable aliens—certainly not of Russo-Jewish ones—settling in this country.

The Board of Trade reports on Emigration and Immigration presented in April, 1894, showed that the Immigration of

Russians and Poles, which had increased above its normal figure in 1891, and had gone back to about its average in 1892, had not risen in 1893. In June, 1894, however, President Carnot fell victim to the assassin's knife, and a certain section of the French Press, anxious to satisfy its feelings towards this country, did not hesitate to declare that Santo's murderous plot was laid and perfected in England. Only a few days before, Signor Crispi just missed President Carnot's fate, and his assailant, too, was said to have been resident for some time in this country. Lord Salisbury seems to have been much impressed with these statements, and determined, "as a private member" of the House of Lords, to introduce a Bill which should give to the police and magistracy summary powers of expelling any foreigner resident here and known to be a criminal. To "improve" the occasion, and, as Lord Rosebery said, "with a view to make his Bill logically complete," Lord Salisbury tacked on a section for restricting Alien Immigration. Perhaps the logical completeness did not trouble the present Prime Minister so much as the advantage to be gained in the constituencies when the General Election, which he knew could not be then far distant, should take place. On July 6th Lord Salisbury introduced his Bill, and it was read *pro formâ* a first time. On July 17th a debate took place on the second reading, and the then Prime Minister, Lord Rosebery, offered the Bill a strenuous opposition, basing his attitude upon the unwisdom of the Anarchist portion and the absolute non-necessity of the Aliens portion. The second reading was carried by 80 to 37, and then Lord Salisbury announced his intention of not proceeding further with the measure.

Whilst Lord Salisbury's Bill however was still before the House of Lords, the Board of Trade issued its "Reports on the volume and effects of recent immigration from Eastern Europe into the United Kingdom." This Buff Book is one of the most valuable compilations published upon the subject, and should be studied carefully by all interested in the question. The conclusions to which these reports presented by Sir Robt. Giffen to the Board of Trade inevitably point are, (1) that the numbers of aliens coming to this country for residence had been grossly exaggerated; (2) that the actual numbers were paltry as compared with the general population, or taking into consideration the vast emigration that annually takes place from England; (3) that few trades were affected by immigration, since rather than "displacing" industry the alien had created large and growing home and large export industries; (4) that a ridiculously small number of immigrants could be called paupers, since so few of them ever became a public charge ; (5) that on the contrary they were in the bulk a law-abiding, peaceful, sober and industrious people ; and (6) that they assimilated with marvellous rapidity to English habits and ideas, producing, in the second generation at least, a people of whom any State might well be proud.

A report such as this from the officials of the Board of Trade would it may be thought, have effectually set the seal upon Alien Immigration as a question of pressing politics. But few people, however, read Buff Books, and Lord Salisbury did not under-estimate its value as a party cry in the constituencies. At the general election last year it formed a "plank" in the Unionist platform and proved a most valuable aid to Unionist candidates. In their addresses they linked Alien Immigration with the Importation of Foreign Prison-made goods, a probably fortuitous combination. It, however, had the effect of hinting what more than once was asserted—that the Alien Immigrants, like the Foreign goods, came here from Continental gaols. To have the one or the other competing against Free Work or Free Workers was held to be intolerable. The Trades Unions, or a majority of them, anxious like everyone else to diminish what they conceived to be competition in their own means of livelihood, carried resolutions in favour of restricting Alien Immigration, and in a deputation to the President of the Board of Trade (Mr. Ritchie) urged their view, and extracted from him an assurance that the Government would introduce restrictive legislation. The Queen's speech at the beginning of the last session of Parliament, announced, as one of the ministerial measures, a bill to "regulate" Alien immigration, but Ministers found other matters more pressing, and the Bill did not see the light of day.

There, so far as Parliament is concerned, the matter rests. So far as the Community is concerned, here as in America, the

Immigration of poor Jews is a serious burden. There are a few Jews who regard the burden as too heavy, and who for that reason favour restrictive legislation; but the great and overwhelming preponderance of Jewish opinion is strongly against it. Whilst doing all that is possible, by representations abroad and discouragement here, to prevent any large migration from Russia or Poland, the Jews of this country cheerfully endeavour to meet the call upon their pockets and their energies, involved by the arrival of the poor people on these shores. The system of relief pursued by Jewish Charitable Organisations is devised with the special purpose of assisting its recipients to self-reliance and self-help, whilst no opportunity is lost of ridding this country of those who, for one reason or another, are likely to become ne'er-do-weels, by providing them the means for repatriation or for emigration to more favourable and less crowded parts of the world. Whatever may be said about Jews, either here or in America, it must at least be conceded to them, that with splendid self-sacrificing care, they have tended and aided these poor exiles, and never for a moment have they failed to show that they recognise to the full the Brotherhood of all Israel.

The returns showing the number of Immigrants arriving from the Continent, issued by the Board of Trade, cannot be taken as exactly accurate. Nor for very obvious reasons are the returns of any value as an index of increasing or diminishing Immigration, unless taken over long periods. Nor again are they any index as to the increase or decrease in the foreign element of the country, unless read in conjunction with the returns of Emigration both to the Continent and to places out of Europe. On the other hand the returns are most valuable, since by watching them, no "invasion" of aliens could take place unknown, nor could any considerable increase in the permanent foreign population of the country occur without its being soon detected.

The Report of the Board of Trade on Immigration and Emigration during 1895, was published in May last, and it showed the net result of the passenger movement between this country and the Continent to have been that we were left with about 32 less foreigners in Great Britain at the end of the year than at the beginning.

That figure is arrived at thus :
There came in from Europe 522,449
There went out to Europe 493,946
This leaves us with a balance of foreigners on hand of 28,503.

Against this balance, however, two items must be placed, viz. :
(1) Excess of foreigners who left for non-European countries 18,641
(2) Foreign Seamen who on arriving are reckoned as immigrants, but who on going out again are not reckoned as emigrants 9,894
               28,535

Now, deducting from this Credit figure the balance of foreigners (28,503) left as the result of the Passenger Movement between the Continent and Great Britain we get the 32 less foreigners remaining in the country at the end of 1895 as compared with the beginning of that year. The report declared "that the number of foreigners who left this country in 1895 was practically about equal to the number that arrived, a result which was also noted last year in regard to 1894."

The figures given above, still, of course, leave it possible for us to have sent all other foreigners to other countries and ourselves retained "the Polish Jew." But the Board of Trade report gives no little comfort to any that are alarmed on this score. Speaking of the increase as given in the returns of Russian and Polish immigrants to 10,204 in 1895, as against 7,246 in 1894, the report says :—

"Many of these immigrants were assisted to proceed to other countries or, in some cases, to return to their former homes. Of Jews of this class in London, about 1,600 (the great majority of whom were Russians and Poles) were removed from the United Kingdom in 1895 by the action of the Jewish Board of Guardians and the Russo-Jewish and Jewish Board of Guardians Conjoint Committee.

"Deducting the number thus known to have emigrated, the number of Russian and Polish immigrants, the class most important in regard to the question of "destitute aliens" in this country, becomes somewhat under 9,000 in 1895 for the whole country, and under 6,000 for London. These figures are obviously only to be taken as "limits," below which the actual net immigration of Russians and Poles, on balance, must lie. But there are no materials for striking a balance of this kind, as no detailed accounts exist of emigrants of the several nationalities to be set against the immigrants recorded in the Alien Lists; and the cases of emigration above referred to are only those of which information is incidentally supplied through the accounts of their operations furnished by the charitable bodies specified. It has, however, been mentioned that among the aliens recorded in the Alien Lists for 1895, as arriving in London, "not stated to be *en route* elsewhere," nearly 2,000 were found, in fact, to hold through tickets for other countries, and it may be presumed that this number includes a considerable proportion of Russians and Poles, who form more than half of the total number of aliens that arrive in London from continental ports."

If from the recorded increase of Russian and Polish immigrants is deducted the 2,000 who were really transmigrants, the increase is reduced to 722. Since the error was discovered without any exhaustive enquiry, may it not be that the increase is more apparent than real? This is more than probable, for there was a decrease of 360 in the relief cases of the Jewish Board of Guardians in 1895 as compared with 1894, and 200 in the cases relieved by the Conjoint Committee. This general decrease is again borne out by the reports send to the Board of Trade by the police at various provincial centres. At practically all there was either a decrease or no increase, whilst from a number of the towns there came the specific assurance that though there were Russian and Polish settlers, "none are destitute." The general conclusion to be derived from the report, so far as Russian and Polish immigration is concerned, is that there had been a slight decrease on the whole, so far as concerns those arriving to stay. On the other hand, it would seem that Russian and Polish emigration had swollen slightly with the increase of the general passenger movement, but the trend had been further afield than England. In the tragically graphic words of one of the provincial police reports, a larger number of "tramping foreign Jews passed through" in the course of 1895 than in 1894. Let it not be forgotten that the weather last year was exceptionally mild; this, perhaps, gives the key to the increase in the volume of traffic.

The number of rejections by America of intending Immigrants to the States from this country during 1895 was shown by the

Report to have been 409 " for all causes." These of course include Contract Labour cases, which probably formed a majority. Of these 409 there were 232 of British origin, and 177 were foreigners. America during the same period admitted 70,000 foreigners who arrived there from England. The rejections thus form about a quarter per cent., and applying that to the Immigration from the Continent to Great Britain during 1895, we find that had we acted "as they do in America," we might have rejected 75 in all, assuming this country adopted a Contract Labour restriction. And upon the same assumption we admitted some 25 Russians and Poles, who by the American system, would have been sent back to the place from which they came. It must not, however, be forgotten, that the Contract Labour law is part of America's protective system, and all parties in this country, at least for the present, are wedded to the maintenance of the principles of Free Trade.

The following table will show the extent to which America has been admitting Russians and Poles :—

Years (ended 31st Dec.).	Russians (other than Poles).	Poles.	Total.
1881	8,513	6,283	14,796
1882	18,205	4,246	22,451
1883	15,014	2,151	17,165
1884	15,529	4,369	19,898
1885	16,951	3,101	20,052
1886	26,820	6,396	33,216
1887	25,815	4,960	30,775
1888	37,353	5,902	43,255
1889	33,487	4,866	38,353
1890	40,922	19,743	60,665
1891	73,271	31,301	104,572
1892	52,334	27,013	79,347
1893	51,497	6,122	57,619
TOTAL FOR 13 YEARS			542,164

These figures be it noted are not those of all inward passengers, but only refer to those Aliens who are believed by the American authorities to have the intention of permanently settling in the United States.

The foreign Emigrants to the United States from the United Kingdom rejected and sent back to this country are, it has been remarked, few in number. Here are the figures for the six years 1888-93, the rejections being "for all causes" and including contract labour cases.

Years.	Foreign Emigrants from the United Kingdom.	
	Total going to the United States.	Number rejected by the United States' Authorities.
1888	95,390	15
1889	69,792	43
1890	81,109	18
1891	95,621	71
1892	85,182	111
1893	64,263	99
Total for the six Years (1888–1893)	491,357	357

It will be seen from the above tables, that in the years 1891, 1892 and 1893, as many as 241,538 Russians and Poles emigrated to America. The number who arrived for residence in this country were by comparison a mere handful. There were declared to be:

1891	12,607
1892	7,538
1893	7,721
Total for the three years	27,866

The numbers who arrived in subsequent years are given as:—

1894	7,246
1895	10,204

but as explained above, from the latter figure must be deducted at least 2,000, being aliens who were recorded as not *en route*, but who subsequently were found to have through tickets to America or elsewhere.

The following publications will be found specially useful for consultation upon the subject of Alien Immigration :—

"Minutes of Evidence and Report of the Select Committee of the House of Commons on Immigration and Emigration," price 1s. (1889).

"Minutes of Evidence and Report of the Select Committee of the House of Lords on the Sweating System," price 1s. 2½d. (1890).

"The Alien Invasion," W. H. Wilkins, B.A., *Methuen & Co.* (1892).

"Problems of Poverty," John A. Hobson, M.A., *Methuen & Co.* (1895).

"The Jew at Home," Joseph Pennell, *William Heinemann* (1892).

"Reports to the Board of Trade on Alien Immigration to America by Messrs. John Burnett and David Schloss," price 1s. 7d. (1893).

"Reports to the Board of Trade on the Volume and Effects of Recent Immigration from Eastern Europe into the United Kingdom," price 1s. (1894).

"Statistical Tables, etc., relating to Emigration and Immigration," published annually by the Board of Trade (usually about April in each year). Price 6d. each.

The Board of Trade also publishes a monthly return, in part showing the numbers of Aliens arriving at certain ports in the United Kingdom from the Continent. The price of these is ½d. each.

"A Voice from the Aliens." Pamphlet issued by the Jewish Workers' Defence Committee, 15, Whitechapel-road.

The Annual Reports of the Jewish Board of Guardians. Offices : Widegate-street, E.C.

"Statistics of Jewish Population in London, etc., 1873-1893." Compiled by Joseph Jacobs, B.A., *Russo-Jewish Committee.* (1894).

The Annual Reports of the Russo-Jewish Committee. Offices : 61, Old Broad-street, E.C.

MOODS OF THE JEWISH YEAR.
BY
ISRAEL ZANGWILL.

THE following poems will doubtless be included in the collected edition of Mr. Zangwill's poems, but, in the meantime, he has given me permission to cull them from "Morour and Charoseth," and other sources.

ISRAEL AS BRIDE AND AS BEGGAR.

From the Hebrew of Elchanan ben Isaac, an English Jew of the 12th century.

Erst radiant the Bride adored,
On whom rich wedding gifts are poured;
She weeps, sore wounded, overthrown,
Exiled and outcast, shunned and lone.

Laid all aside her garments fair,
   The pledges of a bond divine,
A wandering beggar-woman's wear
   Is hers in lieu of raiment fine.

CHaunted hath been in every land
   The beauty of her crown and zone;
   Now doomed, dethroned, she maketh moan,
Bemocked—a byword—cursed and banned.

AN airy, joyous step was hers
   Beneath Thy wing. But now she crawls
Along and mourns her sons and errs
   At every step, and, worn out, falls.

ANd yet to Thee she clingeth tight,
Vain, vain to her man's mortal might
Which in a breath to naught is hurled,
Thy smile alone makes up her world.

YOM KIPPUR.

I saw a people rise before the sun,
A noble people scattered through the lands,
To be a blessing to the nations, spread
Wherever mortals make their home; without
A common soil and air, 'neath alien skies,
But One in blood and thought and life and law,
And One in righteousness, and love, a race
That, permeating, purified the world—
A pure fresh current in a brackish sea,
A cooling wind across the fevered sand,
A music in the wrangling market-place;
For wheresoe'er a Jew dwelt, there dwelt Truth,
And wheresoe'er a Jew was there was Light,
And wheresoe'er a Jew went there went Love.
This people saw I shake off sleep, as shakes
The lion off the dew, and hasten forth,
The rich and poor alike, the old and young,
Each from his house unto the House of God,
The whole race closelier knit that day by one
Electric thought that flashed through all the world.
And there from dawn to sunset, and beyond,
They prayed, and wept, and fasted for their few
Backslidings from the perfect way; for they
Did Justice and loved Mercy, and with God
Walked humbly; Pride and Scorn they knew not; Lust
Of Gold or Power darkened not their souls;
The faces of the poor they did not grind,
But lived as Man with Man; yet all the day
In self-abasement did they pray and fast.
The ancient tongue of patriarchs and seers,
A golden link that bound them to the Past,
They used; as woven by their saints
And rabbis into wondrous songs of praise
And sorrow; sad, remorseful strains, and sweet,
Soft, magic words of comfort. As they prayed,
They meditated on the words they spoke,
And thought of those who wrote them—royal souls

In whom the love of Zion flamed; poets clad
Not in the purple, sages scorning not
The cobbler's bench; and then they mused on all
The petty yet not unheroic lives
Of those who, spite of daily scorn, in face
Of sensual baits, kept fast the marriage-vows
Which they in youth had pledged their Bride, the Law,
Whom they had taken to their hearths; no spirit
Austere and mystic, cold and far-away,
But human-eyed, for mortal needs create,
Who linked her glory with their daily lives,
Bringing a dowry not unblent with tears—
A marriage made in Heaven to hallow Earth.
They thought of countless martyrs scorning life
Weighed 'gainst their creed; poor, simple workmen made
Imperial by their empery of pain;
Who clomb the throne of fire and draped themselves
In majesty of flame, and haughtily,
As king for king awaited Death's approach.
The inspiration of such lives as these
Was on the worshippers; the stormy passion
Of their old, rugged prophets filled their hearts
With yearning, aspiration infinite,
Submerging puny fears about themselves,
Their individual fates in either world,
In one vast consciousness of Destiny.
For other Faiths, like glowworms glittering,
Had come to lift the darkness; and were dark.
And other Races, splendid in their might,
Had flashed upon the darkness and were gone.
But they had stood; a Tower all the waves
Of all the seas confederate could not shake;
And in the Tower a perpetual light
Burned, an eternal witness to the Hand
That lit it. So all day they prayed and wept
And fasted. And the sun went down, and night
Came on; and twilight filled the House of God,
And the grey dusk seemed filled with floating shapes
Of prophets and of martyrs lifting hands

Of benediction. Then a mighty voice
Arose and swelled, and all the bent forms swayed,
As when a wind roars, shaking all the trees
In some dim forest, and from every throat
Went up with iteration passionate
The watchword of the Host of Israel,
"The Lord our God is one ! The Lord is God !
The Lord is God !" And suddenly there came
An awful silence. Then the trumpet's sound
Thrilled. . . . .
And I awoke, for lo ! it was a dream.

✺

A TABERNACLE THOUGHT.

Lovely grapes and apples,
   And such pretty flowers,
Blooming in the *Succah*,
   To tell of festive hours.

Green leaves for the ceiling
   Sift the sun and shade
To a pretty pattern,
   As in forest glade.

Cool retreat and dainty
   For a little child,
Toddling in, by prospect
   Of its joys beguiled.

Round he casts his blue eyes,
   Stretches hand in haste ;
Darling baby, all this
   Just is to his taste.

But his eyes brim over
   Soon with sudden tears.
Ah, he learns the lesson
   Of the coming years.

> For the fruit is gilded
> And the flowers are wax.
> Life's a pretty vision,
> Only truth it lacks.

THE DEATH OF ELEAZAR.

(From the Second Book of Maccabees.)

So Eleazar, bidden to the feast,
Obeyed the Grecian summons, sick at heart.
A chief among the Scribes was he, belov'd
And reverenced in all Jerusalem.
A goodly man, well-favoured; soul and body
Both beautiful, as though each mirrored each,
The silver crown of age was on his head,
But not its icy touch upon his heart,
Fire-filled, like some volcano capped with snow.
Wisdom and kindliness lit up the face
Now overset with clouds of troubled gloom.
For he had witnessed sights disconsolate,
Wanton hetairæ in the holy fane,
Riots and revelries voluptuous;
Men, women, children burnt—and, worst of all,
Jews ivy-wreath'd and bearing ivy boughs
In Bacchus' wild procession; Jewesses,
The Sabbath lamps neglected, in the train
Of flushed Bacchantes, with their touzled robes,
Loose-blowing hair with vine-leaves garlanded,
And brandishing the thyrsus. Such the sport
To which the minion of Antiochus,
From courtly Athens come, set breaking hearts;
To such a bitter feast the Scribe was bid,
A feast of sacrificial flesh of swine
To Grecian gods on Jewish altar laid.
And when he came and knew their mind, he spurned
The proffer'd flesh, clenching his teeth; but they
Derisively pulled jaw from jaw and forced

The meat within, with threats of agonies
Of fire and wheel, and promises of life,
And mild petitions that he should not quench
A vital flame which warmed e'en them, his foes,
Who knew and honoured him in nobler days.
But he, with loathing inexpressible
For such existence, self-polluted, vile,
Spat out his life ; at which, admiring, they—
The masters of the sacrificial feast—
Bade him depart, but come again the morrow,
When if he ate not he should surely die.
But in the meantime spake him privily
And said : " Wherefore, O Scribe belov'd,
Should Death, the King of Terrors, come to thee,
And all his train of tortures ? We, thy friends
Of old, would save thee now, and since we see
Thou wilt not eat our swine-flesh, come what may,
We have devised a means whereby to spare
Thy life and yet not wound thy conscience. Bring
With thee to-morrow secretly such meat
As is permitted ; when we offer thee
The swine-flesh take it, and to eat it feign.
But in its stead do thou but substitute
The scrap of flesh concealed within thine hand."
Then Eleazar pondered, as became
The excellency of his ancient years
And honour of his hoary head, and all
His training from a child in holy lore,
And after a little while made answer thus,
With courteous mien and high, majestic words :
" I thank you, sirs, for this your clemency,
And will think further on it in the grave.
It is not seemly for an aged man
Thus to dissemble ; for our youth might deem
That Eleazar worshipped heathen gods,
Although a Jew for four-score years and ten ;
And thus, deceived, they, too, might fail, while I
Should for a breath of life make vile old age,
Which asketh valour and a steadfast heart

And glad returning of the gift of life ;
Wherefore as I have lived so let me die,
A high example to our sons of love
Unquenchable, undaunted, for the Law."
He spake ; and walked towards the torture-place,
The place of torments ; and his whilom friends,
Furious and deeming him of frenzied mind,
Followed, vituperant, and when they reached
The market-place, where souls were bought and sold,
They stripped him bare and lashed him till he died.

⁂

PURIM—PAST AND PRESENT.

The *old* Jew finished his work with speed
   And hurried off to his *chevrah* small,
To hear the musical *chazan* read
   The story of Pride that precedes a fall,
   And Trust victorious over all,
The glorious tale of the saintly layman
Who would not bow before haughty Haman.

He loved to muse on the Jewish maid,
   In wedlock joined to the Persian king.
His fancy over the story played ;
   It touched a sweet, sympathetic string
   And made him ready to dance and sing.
He armed himself with a little hammer
The hated Haman to drown with clamour.

He laughed in glee when brave Mordecai
   The tables turned on his crafty foe,
And had him strung on the gallows high
   And brought his family very low,
   So over the Persians the Jews could crow,
Ah, merry sat the entire *Kehillah*
To hear twice over the whole *Megillah !*

At home he drank from the vinous flask,
   Or masqueraded in female dress,
Or hid his face 'neath a cardboard mask,
   Essaying with greater or less success
   The national merriment to express.
He sent his neighbours large *Shalachmonous*,
Expecting ditto to reach his own house.

The *new* Jew Purim at Christmas keeps
   And Christmas pudding for *creplich* cooks,
And straight from *Succoth* to *Pesach* leaps ;
   Adar's red-letter days overlooks,
   Or thinks them only kept up in books.
He keeps the great ones, but drops his nation's
Small fasts and feasts like his poor relations.

Or else he goes to a formal dance
   In swallow-tail and a minister's tie.
His thoughts recur by the barest chance
   To Esther, Haman or Mordecai
   Or (save champagne) anything so dry.
For heartiness his contempt is hearty,
And Purim is only an evening party !

SONNET ON SEDER-NIGHT.

Prosaic miles of streets stretch all around
Astir with restless, hurried life, and spanned
By arches that with thund'rous trains resound,
And throbbing wires that galvanise the land ;
Gin-palaces in tawdry splendour stand ;
The news-boys shriek of mangled bodies found ;
The last burlesque is playing in the Strand—
In modern prose all poetry seems drowned.
Yet in ten thousand homes this April night
An ancient People celebrates its birth
To Freedom, with a reverential mirth,
With customs quaint and many a hoary rite,
Waiting until, its tarnished glories bright,
Its God shall be the God of all the earth.

THE HEBREW "WACHT AM RHEIN."

I.

"Like the crash of the thunder
  Which splitteth asunder
    The flame of the cloud,
On our ears ever falling,
A voice is heard calling
  From Zion aloud:
'Let your spirits' desires
For the land of your sires
    Eternally burn.
From the foe to deliver
Our own holy river,
  To Jordan return.'
Where the soft flowing stream
Murmurs low as in dream,
  There set we our watch.
Our watchword 'The sword
Of our land and our Lord'
  By the Jordan there set we our watch.

II.

"Rest in peace, lovèd land,
  For we rest not, but stand,
    Off shaken our sloth.
When the bolts of war rattle
To shirk not the battle,
  We make thee our oath.
As we hope for a Heaven,
Thy chains shall be riven,
  Thine ensign unfurled.
And in pride of our race
We will fearlessly face
  The might of the world.
When our trumpet is blown,
And our standard is flown,
  Then set we our watch.

Our watchword, 'The sword
Of our land and our Lord'
　　By Jordan then set we our watch.

III.

" Yea, as long as there be
Birds in air, fish in sea,
　　And blood in our veins;
And the lions in might,
Leaping down from the height,
　　Shake, roaring, their manes;
And the dew nightly laves
The forgotten old graves
　　Where Judah's sires sleep,—
We swear, who are living,
To rest not in striving,
　　To pause not to weep.
Let the trumpet be blown,
Let the standard be flown,
　　Now set we our watch.
Our watchword, 'The sword
Of our land and our Lord'—
　　In Jordan NOW set we our watch."

JEWISH TABLE CUSTOMS.

BY

ISRAEL ABRAHAMS.[*]

A Lecture delivered before the Jewish Working Man's Club, Purim, 1894.

I know as well as you do the way in which I ought properly to have treated you to-night. Here I have invited you to come and see me on Purim, and offer you the very cold welcome of a table with nothing on it to eat. I felt very much inclined to say to you: "Not at home; please call again." Once Nasica called to see Ennius, and he was told that Ennius was out. Soon afterwards Ennius returned the visit, whereupon Nasica shouted out from within that he was not at home. "What!" replied Ennius, "don't I know your voice?" "You are an impudent fellow," retorted Nasica; "when your servant told me that you were not at home I believed her, but *you* will not believe *me* though I tell you so myself." Still, I was afraid that if I said I was out you might doubt my word, so I have ventured to receive you round an empty board. It is getting customary now at public dinners for the ladies and others who are supposed not to like dining to put in an appearance when the banquet is over. Well, let us to-night make believe that we have had our meal, and that the speeches are now going to begin.

I remember taking part in the once universal Shlach Monos, when I was a boy a very long time ago. But you will say what has the Shlach Monos to do with Table Customs? Let me explain. I was sent by my grandfather to take presents to his friends and acquaintances on Purim. The present consisted usually of some fruit and cakes, and for especial favourites even a bottle of wine. When I was admitted, the recipient of the gift would spread it lovingly on the table as though it was a dainty fit for a king. But he did not *eat* it, not he. This I proved by experience. For often the recipient, Mr. B. would say: "My

---

[*] *Copyright*, 1896, *in the United States, by* ISRAEL ABRAHAMS.

good boy, tell your grandfather I am much obliged; now put your parcel down and eat it youself!" Well, of course I got tired of that after I had eaten the first dozen oranges or two, and *occasionally* refused the invitation with thanks. "Ah! well," he would say, "you don't care to eat it? Well, oblige me and take it over to Mr. C. with my compliments, wishing him a happy Purim." Of course I would consent to anything rather than eat it myself, and so I became a middle man, and took my grandfather's fruit from Mr. B. to Mr. C. The climax was reached when Mr. Z., to whom my grandfather sent me later on, gave me a parcel as a return-gift to my relative. I took it home to him; he opened the parcel, when lo! it was the very same lot that he himself had sent to Mr. D. in the morning! I leave my mathematical friends to calculate how many hands that fruit had gone through before it returned to its original starting-point.

You know, of course, that it is forbidden to drink water on Purim. Some people won't leave their windows open if Purim is a rainy day, lest some water should unlawfully get in. Jews have often made a lot of pretence about getting drunk on Purim; a a matter of fact, except in the East, I don't mean the East End, drunkenness is not a Jewish vice. On Purim a little extra indulgence was, however, permissible.

When a Jew drinks wine he says לחיים, "for life!" meaning may the wine be life-giving and not make you ill. In ancient times when a Jew was put to death, the ladies of Jerusalem gave him some medicated wine before the execution, so as to deaden his senses. When he drank the wine, the people cried למיתה "for death." Many Jewish table customs are connected with wine; several of them with the Kiddush. In Turkey, the Jews, after saying the first blessing, take a cup of wine and drop some of its contents on the floor of every room in the house, saying: "Elijah the prophet, Elijah the prophet, come quickly to us with the Messiah, the son of David." Elijah was always regarded as the precursor of the Messiah, and so on the Passover eve a cup of wine is put on the table for him, because according to a Jewish tradition the Messiah is to come on the Passover. For the same reason the door is opened to let him in. Another similar custom with wine may be seen, especially in the East, on Saturday nights. The habdala wine is used to put out the light. Why? The

JEWISH TABLE CUSTOMS. 237

Talmud says that whoever has no wine spilt in his house has no blessing. That is why, at the beginning of the new week, the habdala wine is poured out as a symbol of the plenty that will fill the house during the coming days. Then the boys, and men too, dip their fingers into the habdala wine, rub them on the brows and under their eyes, expecting thereby illumination of mind. Women do not drink the habdala wine. Many funny reasons are given for this exclusion, but I have only time to tell you the real reason. One of the ingredients of the habdala is the spice, and the origin of this is connected with the exclusion of the women from the habdala wine. In ancient times, they used to have very primitive methods of clearing up a table; they all ate out of the same dish and without any knives and forks, so that they must have spilt a good deal. On the Sabbath the accumulation of refuse-food must have been particularly unpleasant; little clearing up would be done on the day of rest. Now, after every meal in Talmudic times, a vessel containing burning aromatic spices was usually brought into the room to fumigate the atmosphere a little. On the Sabbath this fumigation, while doubly necessary, would be impossible, because they could not kindle the spices on that day. But as soon as the Sabbath was ended the women would hasten to bring in the mugmar or burning spices; hence the use of spices in the habdala. Moreover, the women would have a lot to do immediately after the Sabbath; they would have to clear up the rooms, and prepare the evening meal, which they would not necessarily share. Hence the women would have no time to participate in the minutiæ of the habdala service, and thus they were first excused and afterwards excluded.

Perhaps we had better now venture to peep in at a Jewish family in Talmudic times about to take their meal. They will not think us rude or intrusive, for they were always hospitable even to self-invited guests as we shall be. It was quite against etiquette, however, to go to a friend's house for a meal uninvited. The time will be day, for the chief meal was always eaten towards the evening, and lights would be brought in only when it became dark. There was much difference of custom as to how many meals a day were to be eaten. On the Sabbath, counting the Friday night, three meals were fixed by law, but on weekdays the habit varied. Some ate in the morning, and indeed the Rabbis very wisely said : "The man who eats no breakfast but only eats later in the day, acts as one who would throw a stone into an empty wine-skin." Breakfast, however, seems never to have been a very substantial meal. In Yemen the Jewish workmen to-day go to synagogue very early in the morning and take their hot coffee to prayers with them, they sing psalms and sip the refreshing cup, and when that is done, they go straight to their work. But let us return to our Talmudic dinner-party. The guests have been invited verbally, by a servant specially sent for the purpose ; and when they arrive possibly their feet will be washed, their hair and beards anointed by their host's servants, who will put garlands over their brows. You must not think that dressing for dinner is a new or even a merely superfine European custom. Nowhere are people more careful about dressing for the meal than they are in the East nowadays ; and in ancient times also much trouble was expended in this way. The reason why will be soon apparent. When their Talmudic guests arrived the host would kiss them—of course I mean the males ; women did not join the men at table except on special occasions, and even then the sexes were separated. The host entered first, then the guests : at the end of the meal the host went out last. Now the guests would remove their tephillin in the dining-room, which was about fifteen feet square, but they would not seat themselves on chairs. They reclined at their chief meals on couches, each of which mostly held three people. They leant on their left elbows, and turned their feet away from the tables. Thus their right hands were free to use at the meal. They were not so uncomfortably placed as you might think, because they were not lying anything like full length. Moreover the table was *lower* than the couches ; a curious reversal of our practice ; but it is clear that if you are in a semi-recumbent attitude you can eat more conveniently if the food is lower than you are. The ancient Jewish meals were passed *in complete silence*, it is easy to see why. It was felt that it was dangerous to speak while eating in a lying posture, and therefore the talking did not commence until the meal proper was over. It was considered to be rather bad manners to talk during the courses, instead of at the end of the meal. Thus a certain Rabbi, named Bar Kappara, once did this to pay off a grudge. Rabbi Gamliel made a great feast and did not invite Bar Kappara. Afterwards in order to atone for his omission R. Gamliel made a special banquet in Bar Kappara's honour. A great many guests were there, and directly the first course arrived Bar Kappara began a very interesting and witty story. Everyone listened to him and laughed so much that they could not eat of what was offered them. So he did at every course, until R. Gamliel got rather angry. " Why do you do this ? " he asked Bar Kappara. The reply was : " Because I don't want you to think that I want your dinner. I was annoyed because you slighted me before ; now you may see that it was not your dainties that I was longing for."

Regular laws of precedence were followed: the chief guest sat in the centre of the couch, the next important guest sat above him, the third in rank below him. A servant would bring in water and would begin with the chief guest, who would first wash his hands and then the man above him, and so on. Hand-washing before meals was a most necessary process, for they used no knives and forks, but ate with their fingers. You will be surprised, perhaps, to hear that though they did this, some people's taste was most fastidious. The Talmud tells us that some men, if they found a fly in their wine cup would throw the whole away and would not drink the contents. In modern times it is said that you can tell a man's nationality by the way he deals with a fly that happens to fall into his food. There is a fly in the soup ; the man throws out the fly and drinks the soup : he is an Englishman. The man calls the waiter and sends the whole away in disgust : he is a Frenchman. The man drinks the lot as it is, fly and all : he is a German. The man picks out the fly, sends away the soup and eats the fly : he is a heathen Chinee. Well, our Talmudic diners would be scrupulously refined in their habits. Later Jews have not all retained these good characteristics. Some of our Russian brethren wash their hands, indeed, before meals, but in so perfunctory a manner that they only make the dirt more visible. In the East the hand-washing is a far more sincere process. Well, fish would be almost certain to be served at the meal. Jews have always been remarkably addicted to fish. In the Middle-Ages pike was the favourite fish. Poultry was also much indulged in ; from the sixteenth century the Jews have been especially fond of geese ; so much so that the goose is in Germany nicknamed " The Jew's fowl." Between the meat and the fish, the diner would drink: and one must not drink standing. He would not eat the whole of his portion, but would leave some : if he did not do so, there would be no blessing on his meal. For this reason some bread and salt was left on the table during the grace. Why salt ? Because the table was regarded as the Altar, and every meal, if properly served and enjoyed, was a sacrifice. Now at every sacrifice in the temple salt was brought, hence the salt left on Jewish tables during the grace.

If we were visiting our Jewish Talmudists on a Sabbath we should find that they had *two* loaves on which to say מוציא. This is a very old custom, and is derived from the Biblical account of the Manna ; there was a double portion לחם משנה collected on Friday. Well, the loaf would be cut but not broken off, so that the loaf remains perfect while you say the מוציא and yet you need have no interruption between the blessing and the eating. Some people only pretend to eat. It was always customary to cover the bread with a cloth during Kiddush for fear of spilling water on the bread. The Talmudists were most severe against the sin of *spoiling* food. During grace the knife was covered, because the table is in theory an Altar, and no steel was allowed to be used in constructing the Altar of God. Another reason given for covering the knife during grace is that a case was on record of a man who was saying grace and at the words בונה ירושלים he felt so overwhelmed with grief at the thought of the destruction of Jerusalem that he seized the knife and plunged it into his heart. It is impossible for me in the brief time at my disposal to mention all the rules of etiquette obeyed during the meal. First, as regards the servants who waited at table ; they were better treated than nowadays. Throughout the Talmudic Table Rules there runs a fine sense of delicacy and regard for other people's feelings. Thus no servant was allowed to take in any particularly savoury dish without *first* receiving a share. The modern custom of letting hungry servants wait at table and only afterwards getting their meal is a breach of the Biblical command not to muzzle an ox while ploughing. Again, no guest was to say or do anything that might embarrass the host. This was a most necessary rule of etiquette : you often see guests asking for things that are not in the house : in Talmudic times such an act of rudeness would have been impossible. Another rule was : No guest may take things from the table and give them to the host's children. In the first place, to do so is a tacit offence to the host, for it is as much as to say that *he* has neglected to feed his children. Secondly, what is on the table may be only just sufficient for the meal, and the host may be shamed by your giving tit-bits to the children. The Talmud enforces the rule by telling how a father once invited three guests to a meal ; it was a very hard season and food was scarce. He provided an egg each for his guests, each of whom handed the egg to their host's son. He ate all three. The father had no other food to give them, so in his anger he struck the boy, who fell down and expired. The father in his agony of remorse went to the roof and threw himself into the street, and his wife, who came up in the dark to see what was the matter, fell off the roof also. Thus a whole family perished because a rule of etiquette was not observed.

At a famous *tête-à-tête* between Sairey Gamp and Betsy Prigg, you will remember how the two worthy old ladies were imbibing from the tea-pot something stronger than tea. Unconsciously Betsy's hand strayed to the tea-pot, but her companion, indignant at this attempt on Betsy's part to get more than her proper share, feelingly remarked, Whatever you does, drink fair. Our Talmudic guests had a similar rule. If two were partaking of a meal in common neither was to begin until both were ready. Besides, if one took his hand out of the dish and drank, the other would not go on eating, but would wait for him. Again, it was looked upon as bad manners to bite your bread and then put it down on the table. It was bad manners to drink out of a glass and then pass it on to another ; it was wrong to look at another man's portion, or to watch him as he ate ; it was a sign of excessively bad breeding to speak crossly to servants at table ; it was rude to drink without turning your face away ; it was unlucky to drink *two* cups ; you might drink three, or five, and so on, but not even numbers ; it was impolite to eat or drink ravenously. If a cup of wine was given to you, you must not drink it off in one gulp, you must finish it in two ; on the other hand if you sipped it too slowly you would be regarded as a haughty fastidious person, trying to show himself better mannered than others. The Rabbis had a very correct feeling on this matter, for it is the height of impoliteness to make yourself appear daintier and more refined than those around you. A friend once said to Beau Brummell, who was the prince of good dressers, " Look at X., how well he dresses! everyone stares to look at him." "Then he is *not* well dressed," replied Brummell very truly. It was bad manners to use both hands over the food ; that looked grasping and gluttonous. In modern times we are getting more and more into the same habit of eating with only one hand. People in the East, who use no knives and forks, possess wonderful dexterity in the use of their fingers; they scoop up the gravy with their bread, and never spill a drop. I pointed out before that a refined Eastern is very clean in his table habits; some ancient Jews, especially the Essenes, took a complete bath in cold water before every meal. It was impolite with Talmudists to rise immediately the meal was over ; and of course it was forbidden to lick your fingers. After the meal was over, the hands were again washed, but first the table was removed and the floor swept. The reason was that it was considered sinful to make food look loathesome; now, if the water were spilt on the crumbs and débris, it would not look nice. For the same reason it was forbidden to throw rice and wheat at the bridal party in *wet* weather. Hence at the ordinary meal the room was first swept while the guests were still on their couches, and then the water was handed round. Afterwards came the dessert and conversation, though dessert often formed part of the meal itself.

Jews were not very fond of fruit, and you find many remarks against eating much fruit in the Jewish books. But in modern times this is changed, and fruit is in Yemen always eaten by Jews *before* the meal. On the 15th of Shebat, the new-year for trees, quite a fruit ceremony is celebrated in various parts of the East Fruits of various kinds are arranged on a table in heaps, and all the company eat the same fruit together ; when that is done they go to the next kind, singing psalms and talking in between. But certain ritual laws about fruits were most necessary. " Do not eat plums without first opening each to see if it contains a worm." As to wine drinking, I cannot give any time now to the subject ; perhaps the best thing ever said on both sides of the subject is contained in the book of Ecclesiasticus, xxxi., and I must content myself with just quoting that.

"Show not thy valiantness in wine, for wine has destroyed many; wine is as good as life to a man if it be drunk moderately; what is life then to a man who is without wine? for it was made to make men glad. Wine measurably drunk and in season, bringeth gladness of the heart and cheerfulness of the mind; but wine drunken with excess, maketh bitterness of the mind, with brawling and quarrelling; press not thy neighbour, therefore, by urging him to drink."

This, it seems to me, is better philosophy and sounder sense than milk and watery teetotalism. Over-drinking is not a Jewish vice, but over-eating, I think, is.

In my description of the Talmudical meal I spoke frequently of guests. These would be of two kinds : (*a*) ordinary friends, (*b*) the poor. Regular diners-out were hardly known among the ancient Jews, and even in more recent times the Jews have been a stay-at-home people, who have not been partial to taking meals at other people's tables. But certain banquets were regarded as mitzvoth, it was a religious duty to attend them. These were Berith Milahs, weddings and funeral meals, and redemption of first-borns. But there were limits fixed to the proportions of even such meals as these. In the year 1418, at Forli, in Italy, the Jewish authorities made a resolution to be binding on the whole congregation, in accordance with which no one was to invite to a wedding, beyond relatives to the third generation inclusive more than twenty men, ten women, five girls. Even this would make a large party enough. Again, it was at the same time arranged, that if the bride came from another town, the company that went to escort her to her new abode must not number more than ten companions on horses and four on foot. To a Berith Milah, besides relatives, not more than ten men and five women were to be invited to the banquet. Anyone infringing this law had to pay to the Synagogue a fine of one ducat for every extra guest beyond the legal number. In ancient times some of the priests and Rabbis were very lavish in their hospitality, but often the Rabbi waited himself on his guests. Rabbi Gamliel once did so in Jabne, and when he offered a cup of wine to Eliezer ben Hyrcanus, the latter refused to accept the service, whereas Joshua ben Chananya did accept it, and quoted the example of Abraham, who personally attended to the three men who came to foretell the birth of Isaac. Then another of the Rabbis who was present, Zadok, indignantly addressed the others thus: "You are making too much fuss about Gamliel's condescension. You think more of honouring a mortal man than of honouring God! the Holy One, blessed be He, at whose word the world arose, makes the winds to blow, the clouds ascend, the rain fall, the plants grow, the seas and the earth give up their bounties ; He prepares the table before everyone of His creatures. Shall Gamliel, then, not wait upon us if he feel so inclined, and shall anyone say more than Thank you to him as he says to God?" There was no toadying here, as you may see, for Gamliel was a great man, and Zadok a member of his college, yet the latter spoke his mind and the former was not offended. The Sabbath, of course, was a day for special meals, but it was not usual to invite guests on that day, except travellers and the poor, of whom we shall speak in a minute. The Sabbath was the bride, and therefore every preparation was made to receive her. The tablecloth was spread and left spread all day long, because there was no knowing at what time the bride might not be hungry. The house was illuminated, some put lights in every room and in every window. Even if a man had hundreds of servants it was his duty himself to take some share in preparing for the Sabbath meals. The Emperor said to R. Joshua ben Chananya: " Why does your Sabbath food smell so fragrant?" The Rabbi answered: " We have a spice that we call *Sabbath*, and we put it into the dish and the flavour of the contents is sweetened." " Give me some of that spice," said the Emperor. " Ah ! " replied the Rabbi, " it has no effect except with those who keep the Sabbath." The meaning was obvious.

Though, as I have said, it was not usual to entertain guests at meals on Sabbaths and festivals, still certain ceremonial visits were paid on those days by pupils to teachers and so forth. In the East the second night of Passover is chosen for the visits of friends. At the end of the first part of the Seder, just before supper is served, people go in groups to one another's houses. The tables are gorgeously spread with fruit and flowers, and a tray containing the usual Passover herbs, covered with a rich silk

handkerchief, is passed round and round by the host over the visitors' heads, after which they partake of some of the delicacies provided, and then proceed to another house, taking their host with them. I cannot say anything very full about the Passover table ceremonies, and need not do so, because you are quite familiar with them. Let me here mention one or two customs peculiar to the East, and, perhaps, less known therefore. A boy, dressed as a pilgrim, enters, with a staff in his hand and a wallet of bread on his shoulders. He enters, and the master of the house asks : " Whence comest thou, O pilgrim ? " " From Egypt." " Art thou delivered from bondage ? " " Yes, I am free and delivered." " Whither goest thou ? " " To Jerusalem." " Come in peace and go in peace," says the master of the house, " yet stay with us to share our service." Then they proceed as usual with the Seder. In other parts one of the children takes a motso, binds it in a cloth, puts it on his shoulder, and walks about the room. This is a modification of the former rite, and each refers to the departure from Egypt. At dayenu they lift up the small table and bring it down with clatter, shouting " Dayenu." On the night of the last day of Passover the following is a custom in Morocco :—
The tables are laid out with wheaten flour, leavened dough, new bread (obtained from the Moors), stalks of beans and ears of corn of the new crop, fish, honey, butter and milk in abundance. The chief food on this night is *mooflita* ; this is dough, flattened out very thin and toasted in an earthenware vessel over the fire. This is eaten with butter and honey. In many houses the rooms and passages are strewn with beanstalks and corn-ears, also with grass and wild flowers. These are brought by Moors from the country, they being instructed to do so beforehand.

But to return to our guests, I want now to say a few words on the treatment by Jews of their *poorer* visitors. On this subject I want you to clearly realise a great distinction between two periods. In the Talmudical times the entertainment of the poor was a *luxury*, in Europe of the Middle Ages it was a *necessity*. People nowadays regret the fact that West-end Jews do not regularly have the poor at their tables. But I am not so sure that this is a disadvantage. Ecclesiasticus wisely says : " Better it is to die than to beg. For the life of him that dependeth on another man's table is no life ; better is it for a poor man to eat mean food in his own cottage than to sup on delicate fare in another man's mansion." I say that to have one at your table who comes not as a visitor but because he lacks food is embarrassing both to you and to your guest. Still, it is possible to treat such guests as equals and as brothers, and the Rabbis managed to do it. I said that this reception of the poor became later on a necessity, while at first it was a luxury. The reason is simple. The great increase of guests at Jewish tables dates from the Crusaders. Impoverishment followed in the wake of the warriors of the cross; many Jewish communities were destroyed, others reduced to abject poverty, and many Jewish schools were forcibly closed. As a result there grew up among the Jews a class of travelling beggars, or begging travellers, and also a class of poor travelling students, who went from place to place to sell their wares, or to learn the Law and the Talmud. Many of these travelling students were married, and they often had to leave their wives and children behind them. On their journeys they suffered great privations, and lived on fruits and vegetables. They were nearly always poor, and when at their studies they either lived and ate together, or their teachers and the heads of the community, besides private individuals, invited them to their tables. The entertainment of these poor wayfarers became, as I said above, a *necessity*, and gradually it became habitual for these to be sent round in turn to the different householders. Reviewing the treatment of these guests as a whole, I may say that I have nothing but praise for the consideration and the delicate regard for their feelings shown by their entertainers. As to the conduct of some of the guests, a more doubtful verdict must be pronounced. They came in course of time to look upon themselves as privileged grumblers, who might find fault with their hosts and openly express their dissatisfaction with the fare supplied. A not uncommon dodge with these professional diners-out is the following. A friend of mine lives in an English town where there are only three or four Jewish families. Last Passover, by a train that arrived ten minutes before Yomtob, came a Jew who straightway found out my friend and said, "I have come to spend Passover with you." Of course we do sincerely ask everyone to come in who is hungry, but we don't invite them to make long railway journeys on purpose to honour us with their company. I merely cite these typical facts to explain in part why we provide our poorer friends by outdoor and not indoor relief. In the old days, the entertainment of the poor was not looked upon as an irksome business, however; and many touching rules were in force on the subject. You must sit long over your meals, says the Talmud, because the longer you are the greater the chance of a poor man coming in to eat. Give your poor guest not what *you* think good enough, but what *he* thinks good enough. A poor man came to Rava for a meal. The latter said; "Tell me what you usually eat, and I will give it you." The poor man said: "I generally partake of fat poultry and old wine." "Why," said Rava, "I do not myself eat such costly things; how can you have the face to put people to so much expense?" "I eat not at *their* expense," replied the guest, "but at *God's*, who giveth everyone his food in due season." While they were speaking, in came the sister of Rava, whom he had not seen for thirteen years. She brought him a gift of fat poultry and old wine. Struck with this providential coincidence, Rava turned to his guest and said: "God has provided it, sit down and eat!" Nothing was to be done that might put the guest to shame. He was to be honoured by being invited to say the grace after meals instead of the host. This, of course, was for another reason; viz., it gave the guest an opportunity of blessing his entertainer. A Mohammedan guest thanks his entertainer and blesses God; a Jew blesses his entertainer and thanks God, a very much better division of the honours. I should have pointed out above that the Jews always fed their animals before they themselves sat to table: basing their conduct on a Biblical verse. Some Jews who were neither farmers nor owners of animals, used habitually to keep a hen in the house in order to be able to feed it, before eating their own meals! Among the other rules in honour of the guest was, that he was served first; he was never asked questions that might trouble him; he was, if an honoured and learned man, first told who the other guests were before he was expected to join the meal; he was not allowed to leave the house alone, but his host accompanied him for at least a part of the way home. R. Huna always kept the door of his house open right through his meals, so that any hungry person might enter. They prayed that God would send them worthy and learned wayfarers whom it would be an honour to entertain. Women, says the Talmud, more readily gauge a guest's character than do men, a very true remark. Also, women are less freehanded to guests, an equally true remark. On the whole, then, this treatment of poor guests shows the Jews to have been a most hospitable race ; and if there is some falling away nowadays, the cause lies in the changes arising out of the new conditions of modern life. The crown of a well-spent life was hospitality. A Rabbi of the Middle Ages wrote to a friend :—" The table at which I study contains a board on which the body of my dear wife received its last honours. When I am buried my coffin will be made out of the table at which the poor sat when I entertained them with me at my meals." The table was the altar and the offerings made to the poor were offered to God.

A most important and interesting section of my subject deals with the conversation and music that accompanied Jewish meals. In this matter a great distinction still prevails between Jews of the West and of the East; I refer to the question of the separation of the sexes. In many Jewish families, where the old Oriental ideas prevail, both in Europe and in the East itself, the women and the men occupy different apartments, or at least different ends of the same apartments, at weddings and other semi-public meals. However, it is only in Hindustan that the women get the men's *leavings*. In the coast-towns of North Africa you see the two principles at work together. In the Mellah or Jewish quarter the old habits prevail : the Jews there still eat with their fingers, still sit on the ground on mattresses at meals, and eat on table-stools about 3 feet by 2 feet and 1½ feet high, covered with a cloth. In these Mellahs the sexes are rigidly separated, but in the merchants' quarter of the town, where many Europeanised Jews dwell, the men and women feast together. Music goes on in the East right through the wedding meal. This is a very old Jewish custom, and the attempt of certain ascetics to stop it after the destruction of the Temple failed, as it deserved to do. In the East, the musicians play outside during the wedding-dinner, but the meal is hardly over before every guest flocks to give his contribution or ghramah to one of the musicians, the tips ranging from a farthing to a dollar in value ; directly he gets it, the musician shouts out the name of the donor, adds innumerable compliments and flourishes with reference to the heroes of the occasion and all their relatives and friends, all the while he holds the coin, if it be one of good value, right in the air for everyone to see, and when he has finished his compliments he brings it down with a ringing clatter into the instrument of the leader of the orchestra, who holds it out for the purpose. Collections were also made on behalf of the Marshallik, the Badchan, and the actors who performed plays before the company, both on Purim and at weddings. A Moroccan friend tells me that to go to a wedding in Morocco is thus a very expensive business, as you often have to give large tips to several entertainers. So fond were the Jews of music at meals, that in the Middle Ages they employed Christian musicians to come and play to them while they ate. In Poland there is no wedding without a Shadchan, no feast without its Badchan, or funny man. He is usually a person of lively wit and ready humour; capable of rapidly extemporising jokes to suit the character of the guests before whom he appears. This licensed jester often annoyed the Rabbis by his ribald jokes, because he would not always avoid coarseness and even irreverence. In Persia, unhappily, the joke is often the other way. When a Jew marries in Persia, a rabble of Mohammedan ruffians invite themselves to the ceremony, and after a scene of riot and intoxication, of shameless jokes and jests at the expense of their involuntary host, they beat the man and his relatives, insult the women, and only leave the Jewish quarter when they have slept off the drink swallowed at the cost of their unwilling entertainer. Even in Russia such scenes do not occur, and the subject is too odious to dwell upon. Of Jewish table-music and songs and games and amusements, the most part were connected with the Grace, with studying the Law, with choruses and riddles. I say nothing about the Grace because, though this forms a very important part of Jewish table customs, yet I am not now giving a homiletic discourse. Before beginning the Grace, the crumbs and fragments of the loaf from which מוציא was taken, are by many Jews carefully collected and eaten, some even specially saving pieces for the purpose. Studying the Law was a very important table custom; no respectable Jewish meal would be complete without it. Many content themselves with singing a psalm or two and reading two or three lines of Mishna. Others have regular discourses and discussions, and this is very ancient. The Rabbis originally gave no religious exhortations at the Chupah itself, but at the end of the wedding-meal, and this is done in some parts still. We can understand how it has become less usual, because a banquet table is not usually the best place at which to speak of sacred subjects, people's minds are bent on less serious matters, and therefore I think the religious discourse at long and elaborate meals a custom more honoured in the breach than in the observance. If a guest was a Lamdan, he was expected to address the company, but with a remarkable delicacy the Talmud forbids the host asking the guest to say some Torah unless he knew beforehand that his guest was qualified to accede. It was unlawful to shame the guest by compelling him publicly to avow his ignorance. Of all absurdities, however, in the matter of table speeches, was the Barmitzvah boy's derosha, which I regret to say still largely prevails. It grew up in Poland about two centuries ago. Boys who had been in the Cheder or Talmud school from the moment they could speak, would perhaps be able at the age of thirteen to compose and deliver an elaborate piece of pilpul with all the usual ornaments of Rabbinical learning and argumentation. But even so it must have led to much conceit on the part of those precocious infants. The worst thing was that the fathers of less learned boys would not allow their children to be behind the clever boys of rival parents, and so if their boys could not themselves write a derosha, they could at least learn one by heart. Hence it grew usual for some one else to write the boy a speech, which he would parrot-like deliver for the delectation of his admiring group of aunts and uncles. Not long ago I went to a Barmitzvah supper, and the young hero got up and delivered a very able address. Unfortunately, however, the time originally designed for its delivery was altered, and so at 11 o'clock at night he began : " My dear parents, grandparents, relatives, and friends, as we have just finished breakfast. . . ." It was far better when a regular professional darshan was employed on these occasions. It is some personal satisfaction for me to remember that I obstinately refused at my Barmitzvah to make the usual speech, though I was looked upon as a dunce for my pains. The choruses and songs at table are quite another matter, and we can have nothing but praise for them. In the Talmud is one addressed to the bride, praising her beauty unadorned.

> No dye is on her eye,
> No sham beauty does she seek;
> Her hair's her own and truly fair,
> No rouge or paint is on her cheek.
> Ah! he loves thee well,
> Thou fair gazelle.

A favourite chorus in the East is a Kabbalistic one called Bar Yochai; this is sung incessantly and it is quite endless, for there are hundreds of verses in some forms of the song, and when one singer has spent all his breath another begins it all over again, the company all joining vigorously in the chorus. A favourite form of the table-talk was the riddle. Samson in the Bible propounds riddles at tables. At weddings much genuine fun and merry wit is shown in this way even at the present time in Germany. In England our wedding parties have, unfortunately, very little that is characteristically Jewish about them, unless it be the inevitable card playing. Though here and there I have had to state objections to Jewish table customs, one would be very sorry to see too close an assimilation between Jewish and non-Jewish manners in this respect.

But I must not detain you any longer. I have left a very great deal unsaid: I have told you nothing about the curious custom of breaking a costly vessel at a wedding as a sign of grief amid tumultuous joy, just as the Egyptians introduced a coffin at their feasts. I have said nothing about smoking at table. Smoking is one of those few things about which the Talmud, for obvious reasons, is silent. Smoking spread with wonderful rapidity among the Jews, especially in the East, and in the seventeenth century it was more usual with the Jews of Cairo than of Poland. Some Jews thought it necessary to say a blessing before smoking, the dispute being whether the pleasure was one of smell or of taste. It was usually regarded in the latter sense, and thus no blessing was necessary. Curiously enough the Church raised religious objections to smoking, quoting the passage in the Gospel: "Not that which goeth into man's mouth, but that which cometh out, defiles." This obviously forbids smoking to good Christians. The Rabbis *never* raised any objections, except as regards festivals and fast days.

As a matter of fact, the Jews in the East did not give up smoking on Saturday without a struggle. They filled their hookas over night, and thus kept the tobacco alight for many hours, and claimed the right to smoke on the Sabbath as they did not kindle their pipes anew. But these questions are matters for our Rabbis, and smoking on Sabbath is forbidden by all recognised authorities. In conclusion I may point to the fact that the tobacco trade very early got into the hands of the Jews, and thus the fact that there are nowadays so many Jewish tobacconists is by no means a new thing. Another interesting matter on which I would like to speak is table decoration by Jews, which was usually tasteful and elaborate ; but I can only say two things. On the Passover the custom was to make the table look as nice as possible, and it was held lawful to exhibit on that night articles which had been left in pledge. At weddings it was sometimes customary to put on the table a vessel of water containing live fish swimming about, as a sign of blessing.

The female servant of R. Jehuda, when nothing more was left for the guests, used to say : " The can has reached the bottom of the cask, let the eagles fly away to their nests." I have come to the end of my supplies and must make a similar request. May you spend a merrier Purim next year than you have this, on more substantial and more pleasant food than the fragments I have been able to offer you.

[Some few passages from the above Lecture will be found also in my forthcoming book " Jewish Life in the Middle Ages."]

JEWISH MESSIAHS.*

IT is a mistake to think that there has been only one occasion on which a Jew has claimed or been claimed to be the Messiah prophesied in the Hebrew Scriptures. Scarcely a century has elapsed, during the Christian era at any rate, in which some Jew has not appeared and claimed to be the one who was to restore the Holy Land to Israel and peace to the world. Nothing indeed has shewn the tenacity with which the Messianic hope has lived on in Israel like the persistent way in which it revives from time to time after it has been disappointed, when some meteoric Messiah has passed across the scene of History and disappeared again. It may be of interest to refer briefly to the most brilliant of these meteors.

It was the pressure of the Romans that brought out the earliest of these Jewish Messiahs. It is a question whether Judas of Galilee, who headed a revolt against the Romans in A.D. 7, was assisted by any Messianic hopes connected with him: but there is no doubt that Theudas, who was equally unsuccessful in trying to throw off the Roman yoke about 50 A.D., claimed divine powers, for he led his followers down to the Jordan with the assurance that his mere word would part the waters. In 58 an Egyptian Jew collected together a crowd, numbering according to Josephus 30,000 Jews, and promised them that the walls of Jerusalem would fall down at his bare word, and that they should enter and possess the city. The procurator Felix intercepted him with his troops before he could ascend the Mount of Olives. It does not appear that the first fall of Jerusalem under the Romans was due to any outbreak of Messianic zeal, but its second and final conquest under Hadrian was undoubtedly connected with the remarkable career of the adventurer who was first called Barkochba, "Son of a Star," and whose want of success caused him to be known among the people as Barkosiba, "Son of Lies." Yet he was certainly greeted by R. Akiba, the noblest Jew of his time, as the Messiah promised in Num. xxiv. 18. The terrible punishment which the Romans took for the revolt of Barkochba was a severe lesson for the Jews, and for nearly seven centuries they refused to listen to any Messianic claims. In 720 a Syrian

---

* *Copyright*, 1893, *in the United States, by* JOSEPH JACOBS.

Jew, Serenus by name, promised as Messiah to recover the Holy Land and free the Jews from the yoke of Islam. Even the Spanish Jews, who had only recently come under that yoke, of their own free will listened with eagerness to his promises, and suffered the usual disappointment when Serenus was captured by Caliph Omar II. Only thirty years later similar pretensions were put forth by a Jew of Ispahan named Obaiah. It is true he only claimed to be a sort of Mahdi of Judaism, but as he asserted that this position was of equal merit with that of the Messiah, he may fairly be accounted as one of the Jewish Messiahs that failed to prove his claim, as he fell in battle and the Persian Jews had to pay the penalty of their credulity.

Times of misfortune are peculiarly prone to produce hopes of redemption, and with the coming of the Crusades a plentiful crop of Jewish Messiahs made their appearance. One appeared in France after the terrible massacres of the First Crusade in 1087. The twelfth century saw no fewer than four of these pseudo-Messiahs. We owe our knowledge of three of these to the great Maimonides. In 1171 a Jew claiming to be the Messiah had appeared among the Jews of Yemen, who accordingly wrote to Maimonides to ask his advice. He wisely recommended them to give no credence to the impostor, and in his reply states: "Forty five years ago, (*i.e.* in 1117) a man arose in Fez who gave himself out as the herald of the Messiah, pretending that the latter would appear in the same year; his words however were not fulfilled, and the Jews only suffered fresh sorrows. About ten years before that, (1107), a man had arisen in Spain, Cordova, who represented himself as the Messiah, and it wanted but little that this did not produce the ruin of the Jews."

The Cordovian Messiah seems to have counted among his adherents the great poet Jehuda Halevi, one of whose finer odes was prompted by the Messianic hopes which the impostor aroused.

The best known Jewish Messiah of that century was David Alroy, whose meteoric career attracted the attention of Benjamin Disraeli. He suffered the usual fate of these claims to Messiahship, and was brought before the Persian Sultan of the period. Legend declares that he freed himself from prison by magical means. But in his case imposture led to further imposture. Two mysterious strangers appeared with credentials from him at

Bagdad, and declared that he had appointed a certain day for the flight of all the Jews of Bagdad to Jerusalem. They were to assemble in the night on the roofs of their houses dressed in green robes, and at the appointed signal would be given the power to fly to the Holy City. When the night arrived they consulted the two emissaries of Alroy what to do with their property, and these undertook to guard it. All night was spent on the roofs, and when day broke the enthusiasts found the two rogues had decamped with all the property entrusted to them. The date was ever afterwards known to the Jews of Bagdad as the Flying Year.

We next hear of a Jewish Messiah in the year 1286, when the mere rumour of the appearance of such a claimant to divine honours caused quite an exodus of Jewish Rabbis and pious men from Germany, with the venerable R. Meir, of Rothenburg at their head. But the emperor got wind of the proposal and arrested R. Meir and his train, in order to prevent the loss of so many of his most lucrative subjects.

But it has always been from the troubled sources of mysticism that supernatural claims have arisen. The Kabbala began its triumphant career in Judaism in the thirteenth century, and one of its chief opponents, Abraham Abulafia, towards the end of his adventurous career, claimed in Sicily in so many words to be the Messiah promised in Scripture, and prophesied the year 1290 as the era of the Restoration. He seems, however, to have found more credence among Christians than Jews, and retired in dudgeon to Comino, a small island near Malta. The fateful year 1290 brought no redemption to Israel, but only an increased persecution in the expulsion of the Jews from England, and Abulafia died or disappeared in the following year. Two of his followers, however, took up the *rôle* of Messiah, and one of them succeeded in inducing the congregation of Avila to dress themselves in their burial clothes and await in the synagogue on the last day of Tammuz, 1295, the trumpet blast which should announce the beginning of the Messianic Era. Needless to say the final trump was not heard on that occasion. Nearly a century later another Spanish Kabbalist, Moses Botarel, announced himself as the Messiah, and prophesied the beginning of his triumph for Nissan, 1393. There seems to be a general law which causes these Jewish Messiahs to appear in batches, and these generally appear after some great misfortune. Thus we cannot fail to connect with the expulsion from Spain the appearance in 1502 of Asher Lemlein at Istria as a forerunner of the Messiah in Italy. For a whole year many Jews of Italy and Germany devoted themselves to preparation for the holy time coming, and were only disillusioned when the "Year of Repentance" was at an end without any signs of redemption. Twenty-two years later there appeared upon the scene one of the most remarkable of Jewish, adventurers. There came to Italy a stranger from the East who claimed to be the brother of the King of the Lost Ten Tribes. His name, he said, was David, and being of the Tribe of Reuben he is known in Jewish history as David Reubeni. He came as an ambassador from his brother, so he said, in order to enlist the help of Christian kings for descent upon the Holy Land. His advent roused Messianic hopes throughout all Jewry, and a chamberlain of the King of Portugal, Diogo Pires by name, was so impressed by David Reubeni that he openly assumed the religion of his ancestors, called himself Solomon Molcho, and fled to the East, where he attracted the attention and hopes of the large Kabbalistic circles. He even gained a convert in the great Talmudic authority, Joseph Caro, the compiler of the *Shulchan Aruch*. Venturing back to Italy he was seized by the Inquisition as a pervert, and put to death at Mantua, 1532.

But the most celebrated and influential of Jewish Messiahs was to appear in the next century in the person of Sabbatai Zevi, son of a rich Jewish merchant at Smyrna, who was born on the fateful day that lost Jerusalem to the Jews, the 9th of Ab, in the year 1626. He became early impressed with Kabbalistic views, and in 1648, the very year in which the Sohar, the text book of Kabbala, declared the Messiah would appear, he laid claim to that office by solemnly pronouncing the Tetragrammaton. He betook himself to Greece and afterwards to Egypt, gaining adherents at every congregation he visited, owing to his impressive appearance and enthusiastic nature. At Cairo he became united in marriage to a young Polish girl, whose life had been as adventurous as his own, and she on her part had always declared that she would marry none but the Messiah, though previous to her meeting Sabbatai she had lived by her charms. Her influence brought a licentious element into the movement which for a time at least added to its attractions. At length Sabbatai was publicly proclaimed Messiah on New Year's Day, 1665, in the synagogue at Smyrna, to the sound of rams' horns, the whole congregation rising and saying "Long live our King, our Messiah." His fame began to spread beyond Jewish circles, and one finds even in English pamphlets of the period references to the expected coming of the Jewish Messiah. Indeed, Sabbatai's pretensions attracted exceptional attention in London, to which the Jews had so recently returned. Jacob Sasportas, who had been Chief Rabbi of London, exerted all his influence against the new movement, but in vain. Oldenburg, secretary of the newly-founded Royal Society of London, wrote to Spinoza that all the world was talking of a rumour of a return of the Israelites. Indeed, throughout all the Jewish communities of East and West preparations were made for the return which was confidently expected for the year 1666.

But at this moment the Turkish authorities became aware of the possible danger attaching to the movement, and Sabbatai was summoned to Constantinople. Here he was cast into prison by the Sultan's orders, and after a few months the whole movement subsided and Sabbatai became converted to Islam and was appointed doorkeeper to the Sultan. He still kept up in a feeble way his pretensions to the Messiahship, but died abandoned and neglected in 1676. Notwithstanding his death his claims were still kept alive by many followers, and even spread widely through Cordova. For fifty years after his death his adherents formed themselves into a new sect known as the Chassidim or Pious Ones.

This sect received new developments with the appearance of another pretender to Messianic signs in the person of Israel Baal Shem, of whom Mr. Schechter has given an admirable account in his recently published "Studies in Judaism." With him the Messianic element was rather directed to the claim of miraculous powers than of real prerogative. The sect he founded answered in Judaism to the Welsh Jumpers or New England Shakers in Protestantism. Baal Shem was followed in his Messianic pretensions by Jacob Frank, who claimed to be the incarnation of the Messiah, and founded a sect known even to this day as the Frankists, who were put under excommunication by the great

Synod in Constantinof in 1756. With Frank the long list of Jewish Messiahs for the present comes to an end, but even to the present day there are among the Chassidim in Poland and Russia men claiming supernatural powers known as *Wunderrabbis*, and one would not be surprised if the recent troubles in Russia brought forth new names to be added to the long list.

But even when the supply of Messiahs was not equal to the demand caused by persecution, Jews have continued to expect a redemption throughout the ages, and the great Zunz has, with his usual erudition, given a list of no less than 86 dates (*Ges. Schr.* iii. 225-31) on which Messiahs were prophesied and expected. Saadia fixed the year of hope in 964, Rashi in 1352. In 1211 no less than 600 Rabbis from England and France travelled to Jerusalem because they expected the coming of the Messiah in the following year. The Sohar, as we have seen, fixed upon the fateful year 1648, or as an alternative 1840. The year 1900 was one of the dates on which Jewish hopes have been fixed, and we have even seen movements in England giving a practical direction to the conception of the return to the Holy Land. Hope springs eternal in Israel's breast for the day when his woe shall be at an end. Disappointment after disappointment has not succeeded in quenching the sacred fire which has done so much to give an ideal tinge to the otherwise sordid history of persecuted Israel.

ALPHABETICAL TABLE OF CONTENTS.

A

	PAGE
Aberdare Synagogue	64
Aberdeen Synagogue	64
Acts of Parliament relating to Jews	129
Acts of Parliament relating to Jews, Miscellaneous Clauses in	130
Advertisers, Index of	264
Aldershot, Synagogue	64
Alien Immigration	213
Almanacs	128
Anglo-Jewish Association	59
Anglo-Jewish History, Books of Reference on	127
Aria College	56
Australian Colonies	91

B

Baker-street Board School	55
Bangor Synagogue	64
Baronetage	104
Bath Synagogue	64
Baths (Mikvahs)	61
Bayswater Jewish School	53, 54
Bayswater Synagogue	34
Belfast Synagogue and Institution	64
Berkeley-street Synagogue, *see* West London Synagogue.	
Berner-street Board School	55
Beth Hamidrash	57
Beth Holim Hospital	43
Bibliography, Books of Reference on	126
Biography	127
Birmingham Synagogues and Institutions	65, 66
Blackburn Synagogue	66
Board of Deputies, *see* London Board of Deputies.	
Board of Guardians for the Relief of the Jewish Poor	43
Borough Jewish School	54
Borough Synagogue	35
Bradford Synagogue	67
Brighton and Hove Synagogue and Institutions	66, 67
Bristol Synagogue and Institutions	67
Bryanmawr Synagogue	67
Buckle-st. Jewish Infants' School	53, 54
Buck's-row Board School	55
Burnley Synagogue	67
Butchers and Poulterers	62

C

Cambridge Synagogue	67
Canterbury Synagogue	63
Cape Town	94
Cardiff Synagogue and Institutions	68
Central Synagogue	34
Charities	40, 52
Chatham Synagogue & Institutions	68
Cheltenham Synagogue	68
Chevra Kadisha	44
Chevrath Tehillim U-Mishmorim	44
Chicksand-street Board School	55
Chovevi Zion Association	60
Church-street Synagogue	37
City of London Benevolent Society	44
Clubs	57
Colonial Congregations	91
Commencement of Festivals	26
Commercial-street Jewish Infants' School	53, 54
Communal Statistics	30
Cork Synagogue	68
Coventry Synagogue	69

D

Dalston Synagogue	35
Deaf and Dumb Home	54
Deal-street Board School	55
Dempsey-street Board School	55
Derby and Burton-on-Trent Congregations	69
De Worms Family	102, 3
Domestic Training Home	45
Dover Synagogue and School	69
Dublin Synagogue & Institutions	69, 70
Dudley Synagogue	70
Dundee Synagogue and Institutions	71
Dunk Street Synagogue	37

E

East London Jewish Benevolent Society	45
East London Jewish Communal League	45
East London Orphan Aid Society	45
East London Synagogue	35
Ecclesiastical Authorities and Persons authorised by them	61
Edinburgh Synagogues and Institutions	71, 72
Educational and Literary Institutions	57
English Evening Classes Committee	58
Essays, Volumes of	127
Exeter Synagogue	72
Explanation of the Jewish Calendar	15

S 2

F

	PAGE
Fashion-street Synagogue	37
Federation of Synagogues	37
Finsbury Park Synagogue	39
Foreign Titles	103
Form of Prayer at the commencement of the New Solar Cycle	26
Four per Cent. Industrial Dwellings Company, Limited	60
Free Employment Registry	45

G

Gateshead-on-Tyne Synagogue	72
Gates of Hope Incorporated School	53
General Jewish Statistics	27
Glance at 5656, A. J. Jacobs	203–209
Glasgow Synagogues and Institutions	72, 73
Glossary of Jewish Terms	135–202
Goldsmid Family	104, 105
Gravel-lane Board School	55
Great Alie-street Synagogue	37
Great Grimsby Synagogue and Schools	73
Great Synagogue	34
Greenfield-street Synagogue	37
Guide to London Jewish Charities	40
Gun-street Synagogue	37

H

Halifax Synagogue	73
Hambro' Synagogue	34
Hammersmith Synagogue	35
Hampstead Synagogue	35
Hanbury-street Board School	55
Hanley Synagogue & Institutions	74
History, Jewish, Books of Reference on	127
Home and Hospital for Jewish Incurables	46
Home for Aged Jews	46
Honen, Dalim, Menahem Abelim, Hebrat Yetomot	43
Hope-street Synagogue	37
Huddersfield Minyan	74
Hull Synagogue & Institutions	74, 75

I

Institution for the Relief of the Indigent Blind	46
Israelite Marriage Portion Society	46

J

Jahrzeit and Barmitzvah Tables	21, 25
Jessel Family	106, 7
Jewish Books of Reference	126–8
Jewish Branch of Children's Country Holiday Fund	47
Jewish Calendar	2–14
Jewish Celebrities of the Nineteenth Century	118–25
Jewish Cemeteries	63
Jewish Children in Board Schools	55
Jewish Children in Voluntary Schools	54
Jewish Convalescent Home	47

	PAGE
Jewish Girls' Club	57
Jewish High School for Girls	53
Jewish Historical Society of England	58
Jewish History, Books of Reference on	127
Jewish Holidays and Festivals	20
Jewish Inmates at Public Institutions	32
Jewish Ladies' Association for Preventive and Rescue Work	47
Jewish Ladies' Benevolent Society	47
Jewish Ladies' Clothing Association	47
Jewish Ladies' West End Charity	48
Jewish Literature, Books of Reference on	126
Jewish Members of Parliament	113, 14
Jewish Messiahs	253
Jewish Ministers	95–9
Jewish Novels, List of	127
Jewish Peerage, Knighthood and Baronetcy	100
Jewish Religious Education Board	58
Jewish Schools	53
Jewish Table Customs, I. Abrahams	235
Jewish Tradesmen's Benevolent Society	48
Jewish Working Men's Club	57
Jewish Year, 5657, The	1
Jews' College	56
Jews' Deaf and Dumb Home	48
Jews' Emigration Society	48
Jews' Free Schools	53, 4
Jews' Hospital and Orphan Asylum	48
Jews in the Navy, Army and Auxiliary Forces	115–17
Jews of Africa	27
Jews of America	28
Jews of Asia	27
Jews of Australia	28
Jews of Europe	27
Jews of the British Empire	28
Jews of the World	28
Judith Montefiore College	56

K

Kehol Chasidim Synagogue	37
Knightage	111-113
Konin Synagogue	37

L

Ladies' Benevolent Institution	49
Ladies' Holy Vestment Society	49
Leeds Synagogues and Institutions	75–77
Leicester Synagogue and Institutions	77
Limerick Synagogue & Institutions	77
Liverpool Synagogues and Institutions	77–80
Location and Information Bureau	49
Lodz Synagogue	37
London Committee of Deputies of the British Jews	59

THE SWAN Fountain Pen.

(Reduced Facsimile.)

THREE SIZES: 10/6, 16/6, 25/-.

Consists of a Mabie, Todd & Bard Gold Iridium Pointed Pen joined to a Vulcanite Reservoir Holder, which supplies ink to the nib in an even, continuous flow.

Whether for Longhand, Shorthand, Sketching, or, indeed, for any and every purpose where a pen can be used, the **SWAN FOUNTAIN PEN** has become indispensable, if absolute satisfaction would be obtained.

ILLUSTRATED PRICE LIST POST FREE.

MABIE, TODD & BARD, 93, Cheapside, LONDON.

Branches (retail):
95a, Regent Street, W.   21, High Street, Kensington, W.

WEST HAMPSTEAD SCHOOL,
148, ABBEY ROAD, WEST HAMPSTEAD,
LONDON.

Mr. JAMES L. POLACK receives Boys either for preparation for the Public Schools (more particularly for the "Jewish House" at Clifton College), for the Cambridge University Local Examinations, or for general Commercial Education.

By a system of small classes, each boy receives the maximum amount of personal attention; thus sound and sure work is guaranteed.

Special arrangements are made for Colonial boys, who will here find a comfortable home.

Lists of successes at Clifton and Cambridge, Terms for Boarders or Day-boys, and all particulars on application.

MESSRS. MACMILLAN & CO.'S PUBLICATIONS.

Aspects of Judaism,

BEING

EIGHTEEN SERMONS BY ISRAEL ABRAHAMS AND CLAUDE MONTEFIORE.

Second Edition, including two additional Sermons.

Fcap. 8vo., 3s. 6d. net.

Jewish Chronicle.—"The study of a work by these two authors is like an intimate acquaintance with a charming and cultured person—it is a liberal education in itself, a study fertile in interest, and fruitful of good. . . . There are not many books published in the present day of which it can be said that they will do no harm, and unlimited good. But of this book it is possible to say so, and higher praise cannot be given."

THE BIBLE FOR HOME-READING.

Edited, with Comments and Reflections for the use of Jewish Parents and Children, by C. G. MONTEFIORE.

FIRST PART. To the Second Visit of Nehemiah to Jerusalem. EXTRA CROWN 8vo., 6s. NET.

Jewish Chronicle.—"By this remarkable work Mr. Claude Montefiore has put the seal on his reputation. He has placed himself securely in the front rank of contemporary teachers of religion. He has produced at once a most original, a most instructive and a most spiritual treatise, which will long leave its ennobling mark on Jewish religious thought in England." . . . . . Though the term "epoch-making" is often misapplied, we do not hesitate to apply it on this occasion. We cannot but believe that a new era may dawn in the interest shown by Jews in the Bible.

The Jewish Quarterly Review.

Edited by I. ABRAHAMS and C. G. MONTEFIORE.

Price 3s. 6d. each number. Annual Subscription, Post Free, 11s.

Guardian.—"Though designed primarily for Jewish readers, or at least for those specially concerned in Jewish studies, it has often papers of much general interest."

PERSONAL CHARACTERISTICS FROM FRENCH HISTORY.

BY

BARON FERDINAND ROTHSCHILD, M.P.

With Portraits. 8vo. 10s. 6d. net.

Times.—"Baron Ferdinand Rothschild has made a study of the leading personages in French History, and he has produced in *Personal Characteristics from French History* an extremely entertaining collection of their more famous utterings and *bons mots*; or, as he prefers to call them, their 'replies.' . . . There is not a dull paragraph in the entire book."

MACMILLAN & CO., LIMITED, LONDON.

ALPHABETICAL TABLE OF CONTENTS.

	PAGE
Londonderry Synagogue	80
Lovers of Justice and Peace Benefit Society	49

M

Maccabæans, The	57
Maiden-lane Synagogue	38
Manchester Synagogues and Institutions	80-82
Mansell-street Synagogue	37
Marriage Portion Society	49
Merthyr Tydvil Synagogue	82
Meshivath Nephesh	50
Metropolitan Institutions	34-60
Metropolitan Promoters of Charity	50
Metropolitan Synagogues not incorporated with the United Synagogue	38
Middlesbrough Synagogue and Institutions	82
Mikvah Synagogue	37
Miscellaneous Colonial Congregations	93
Miscellaneous Institutions	60
Mohelim (Authorised) in London	61
Montagu Family	107
Montefiore Family	108, 9
Moods of the Year, I. Zangwill	225
Music, Books on Synagogue	128

N

Names, Index of	259
Newcastle-on-Tyne Synagogue and Institutions	82, 83
New Dalston Synagogue	37, 39
Newport Synagogue	84
New-road Synagogue, Whitechapel	37
Newspapers, Jewish	128
New Synagogue	34
Northampton Synagogue	84
North London Synagogue	35
North Shields Synagogue	84
North West London Synagogue	39
Norwich (Eastern Counties) Synagogue and Institutions	84
Notable Events of the Year	
Nottingham Synagogue and Institutions	84
Novels, Jewish	127

O

Obituary of the Year	211
Old Castle-street Board School	55
Old Castle-street Synagogue	37
Old Montagu-street Synagogue	37
Orphan Asylum, Norwood	54
Oxford Synagogue	85

P

Peerage	100
Penny Dinner Society	50
Plymouth Synagogue & Institutions	85
Pontypridd Synagogue and School	85
Poor Jews' Temporary Shelter	50
Portsea Synagogue & Institutions	86
Princelet-street Synagogue	39
Provincial Congregations	64-90

R

	PAGE
Rabbinic Literature, Books of Reference on	126
Reading Synagogue	86
Representative Institutions	59
Returns made to Board of Deputies	33
Review, Jewish	128
Ritual, Books of Reference on	128
Rothschild Family	100, 101
Russo-Jewish Committee	50

S

St. John's Wood Synagogue	35
St. Mary-street Synagogue	37
Salomons Family	109, 110
Sandy's-row Synagogue	37-39
Sassoon Family	110, 111
Scarborough-street Synagogue	37
Sermons	127
Settles-street Board School	55
Shechita Board	60
Sheffield Synagogue and Institutions	86
Society for Providing Strangers with Meals	51
Society for Relieving the Aged Needy	51
Society for Relieving the Poor on the Initiation of their Children into the Holy Covenant of Abraham	51
Sons of Plotzkar Benefit Society	51
Soup Kitchen for the Jewish Poor	51
South African Colonies	91
Southampton Synagogue and Institutions	87
South-East London Synagogue	39
South Hackney Synagogue	38
South London Jewish School	53
Southport Synagogue and School	87
South Shields Synagogue & School	87
Spanish and Portuguese Jews' Board of Guardians	52
Spanish and Portuguese Jews' Congregation	38
Spanish and Portuguese Jews' Orphan Society	52
Spanish and Portuguese School, Heneage-lane	54
Spital-square Synagogue	37, 38
Spital-street Synagogue	37
Statistics and Anthropology	127
Stepney Jewish Schools	53, 54
Stern Family	102
Stockton-on-Tees Synagogue and Institutions	88
Stroud Synagogue and School	88
Sunderland Synagogue and Institutions	88
Swansea Synagogue and Institutions	89
Sydney, N.S.W.	94
Synagogue Music, Books on	128
Synagogues	34-39

T

	PAGE
Talmud, The Books of Reference on	126
Talmud Torah School	53
Theological Colleges	56
Theology, Books of Reference on	126
Tredegar Synagogue and Institutions	89
"Tree of Life" Mourning Benefit Society	52
Trials and Leading Cases	132-134

U

United Synagogue	34
United Synagogue Burials	31

V

Villareal Girls' School	53
Vine-court Synagogue	37

W

Watchers, Female	63
Watchers, Male	63
Waterford Synagogue	89
West Central Jewish Girls' Club	57
West End Synagogue	35
West End Talmud Torah	58
West End Talmud Torah Synagogue	37
West Hartlepool Synagogue and Institutions	90
West London Synagogue of British Jews	39
Western Hebrew Library	58
Western Jewish Philanthropic Society	52
Western Synagogue	38
Westminster Jewish School	53, 54
White's-row Synagogue	37
Wolverhampton Synagogue and Institutions	90
Wrexham Synagogue	90

Y

York Synagogue and Institutions	90

WORKS WRITTEN or EDITED by Mr. JOSEPH JACOBS,

PUBLISHED BY

DAVID NUTT IN THE STRAND.

JEWISH IDEALS. Demy 8vo, 280 pp., Cloth, 6s. net. Contents: Jewish Ideals, God of Israel; Browning's Theology; Jehuda Halevi; Little St. Hugh of Lincoln; Aaron, Son of the Devil, etc.

AN INQUIRY INTO THE SOURCES OF THE HISTORY OF THE JEWS IN Spain. Demy 8vo, xlix. 262 pp., Cloth 4.
₊ In addition to a list of documents preserved in the chief Spanish archives, a list is supplied of Spanish Jewish writers; an alphabetical list of towns with their Jewish inhabitants mentioned in documents; a Spanish Jewish Bibliography, and very full Indices locorum et nominum.

GEORGE ELIOT—MATTHEW ARNOLD—BROWNING—NEWMAN. Essays and Reviews from the *Athenæum*. By JOSEPH JACOBS. 16mo,' xxiv.-192 pp., printed in old-faced type on laid paper, Cloth 3s. 6d. Contents: Introduction—George Eliot; Matthew Arnold; Robert Browning; John Henry Newman; Lord Tennyson; R. L. Stevenson; Professor Seeley.

TENNYSON: AND IN MEMORIAM. An Appreciation and a Study. By JOSEPH JACOBS. 16mo, 108 pp. Cloth 2s.

STUDIES IN JEWISH STATISTICS, Social, Vital and Anthropometric. Reprinted from the *Jewish Chronicle* and the *Journal of the Anthropological Institute*. Pp. viii.-56, li.-18, and three plates, including composite photo of the Jewish Type. 6s. net. Contents: Consanguineous Marriages; Social Condition of the Jews of London; Occupations; Professions; Vital Statistics; Racial Characteristics of Modern Jews; Comparative Distribution of Jewish Ability; and Comparative Anthropometry of English Jews.

STUDIES IN BIBLICAL ARCHÆOLOGY. Crown 8vo, xviii.-148 pp. Cloth 3s. 6d.

THE JEWS OF ANGEVIN ENGLAND. Documents and Records from Latin and Hebrew sources printed and manuscript, for the first time collected and translated. With Appendix and Illustrations. 16mo, xxx, -452 p.p. Cloth 4s., in morocco 10s. 6d.
₊ A complete collection of all Documents relating to the History of the Jews in England during the 12th and early 13th Centuries.

THE FABLES OF BIDPAI; or, The Morall Philosophie of Doni: Drawne out of the auncient writers, a work first compiled in the Indian tongue. Englished out of Italian by THOMAS NORTH, 1570. Now again edited and induced by JOSEPH JACOBS. With a full-page Illustration by EDWARD BURNE-JONES, A.R.A. (lxxxii.-264 pp.) 1888. 12s. net.

THE FABLES OF ÆSOP, as first printed by WILLIAM CAXTON in 1484, with those of Avian, Alfonso, and Poggio, now again edited and induced by JOSEPH JACOBS, with Introductory Verses by Mr. ANDREW LANG. Frontispiece by Mr. H. RYLAND. 2 vols. 1889. 21s. net.

DAPHNIS AND CHLOE. Excellently describing the Weight of Affection, &c., finished in a Pastorall, and therefore termed the Shepheards Holidaie. By ANGEL DAY. 1587. Edited from the unique original in the Huth Library. 10s. 6d. net. Half-roxburgh, 12s. 6d. net.

THE PALACE OF PLEASURE. Elizabethan Versions of Italian and French Novels from Boccaccio, Bandello, Cinthio, Straparola, Queen Margaret of Navarre, and others. Done into English by WILLIAM PAINTER. Now again edited for the fourth time, with Introduction, Biographical Notice, Inedited Documents relating to Painter, and Analytical Table of Contents, with sources and parallels to the 102 stories of the book. 3 vols. 4to, xcv.-363, 428, 428 pages. £2. 10s. net. Only forty copies left.

THE FAMILIAR LETTERS OF JAMES HOWELL, Historiographer Royal to Charles II. 2 vols. Demy 8vo. £1. 4s. net.
₊ The first English Edition with Historical and Explanatory Notes, Full Index, Account of the Author, and Searching Discussion of the Authenticity of the Familiar Letters.

BOOKS for JEWISH READERS.

HEINRICH HEINE.

THE PROSE WORKS OF HEINRICH HEINE. Translated by CHARLES GODFREY LELAND, M.A., F.R.L.S. (HANS BREITMANN). In Eight Volumes.

The Library Edition, in Crown 8vo, Cloth, at 5s. per Volume. Each Volume of this Edition is sold separately. The Cabinet Edition, in special binding, boxed, price £2. 10s. the set. The Large Paper Edition, limited to 50 Numbered Copies, price 15s. per Volume net, will only be supplied to subscribers for the Complete Work.

THE FAMILY LIFE OF HEINRICH HEINE. Illustrated by one hundred and twenty-two hitherto unpublished Letters addressed by him to different members of his family. Edited by his nephew, Baron LUDWIG VON EMBDEN, and translated by CHARLES GODFREY LELAND. In one Volume, 8vo, with 4 Portraits, 6s.—["Great Lives and Events."]

MAX NORDAU.

PARADOXES. Demy 8vo, 17s. net.

DEGENERATION. Demy 8vo, 17s. net. Ninth Edition.

CONVENTIONAL LIES OF OUR CIVILISATION. Demy 8vo, 17s. net. Second Edition.

ISRAEL AMONG THE NATIONS. Translated from the French of ANATOLE LEROY-BEAULIEU, Member of the Institute of France. In One Volume, Crown 8vo, 7s. 6d.

THE NEW EXODUS. A Study of Israel in Russia. By HAROLD FREDERIC. Demy 8vo, Illustrated, 16s.

AS OTHERS SAW HIM. A Retrospect, A.D. 54. Crown 8vo, Gilt top, 6s.

NOVELS BY JEWS.

I. ZANGWILL.

THE MASTER. One Volume, Crown 8vo, 6s.

CHILDREN OF THE GHETTO. One Volume, Crown 8vo, 6s.

THE KING OF SCHNORRERS, GROTESQUES AND FANTASIES. With over Ninety Illustrations. Crown 8vo, Cloth. 6s.

THE OLD MAIDS' CLUB. Illustrated. Boards, 2s.

THE PREMIER AND THE PAINTER. By I. ZANGWILL and LOUIS COWEN. One Volume, Crown 8vo, 6s.

WITHOUT SIN. By MARTIN J. PRITCHARD. One Volume, Crown 8vo, 6s.

MAX NORDAU.

THE MALADY OF THE CENTURY. One Volume, Crown 8vo, 6s. Second Ed.

A COMEDY OF SENTIMENT. One Volume, Crown 8vo, 6s.

"Z. Z."

THE WORLD AND A MAN. One Volume, Crown 8vo, 6s.

A DRAMA IN DUTCH. One Volume, Crown 8vo, 6s.

London: Wm. HEINEMANN, 21, Bedford Street, W.C.

INDEX OF NAMES.

A

Aaron, Israel, 66
Aaron, Rev. N., 86
Abelson, Rev. J., 63, 96
Abrahams, Dr. B. L., 57
Abrahams, H. A., 34
Abrahams, Israel, M.A., 56, 58
Abrahams, L., 87
Abrahams, Rev. M., B.A., 75, 76, 95
Abrahams, M., 51
Abrahamson, L. S., 84
Abrahamson, M., 76
Abramovitz, Moritz, 81
Adler, Elkan N., 47
Adler, Mrs. J., 49
Adler, Mrs., 50
Adler, Rev. M., 35, 95
Adler, Very Rev. Dr., 49, 56, 61, 73, 95
Agar, M. H., 86
Agusky, H., 77
Alexander, Rev. A., 86
Alexander, B., 86
Alexander, C., 71
Alexander, J., 77
Alexander, S., 39, 44
Angel, H., 67
Ansell, J. M., 43
Antoine, A., 56
Aronsberg, W., J.P., 63
Aronson, L. H., 64

B

Balaban, B., 81
Baker, D., 80
Barczynski, Meyer, 84
Barnard, Mrs. B. J., 75
Barnett, Ernest E., 80
Barnett, J., 64
Barnett, J. H., 75
Barnett, Lionel, 65
Barnett, Phillip, 79
Barnett, Mrs. S., 68
Barnstein, Rev. Isidore, 69, 95
Battersea, Lady, 47
Barron, J., 77
Bauer, James, 81
Behrend, Henry D., 80
Behrens, Mrs., 81
Belisha, B. I., 80
Benas, Baron L., 78
Bendon, George, 34
Benjamin, S., 90
Benson, S., 70
Bentwitch, H., 44, 57
Berg, Joseph, 43
Bergensky, Louis, 70
Berlin, Rev. Dr. M., 85, 95
Berliner, Rev. B., 35, 95
Berliner, H., 37, 39
Berliner, Isidore, 68
Berlinski, J., 38
Berlyn, M., 65, 66
Berlyn, Mrs. M., 65
Bernberg, J., 47
Berner, David, 85
Bernstein, B., 67
Bernstone, Henry, 83
Besso, J. S., 80
Birn, J., 35
Birnbaum, Mrs. B., 50
Birnbaum, Bernard, 52
Birnbaum, I., 51, 60
Bischoffsheim, Mrs. H. L., 47
Birnstingl, A. L., 44
Blachman, Rev. I., 37
Blain, David, 66
Blanckinsee, A. M., 66
Blanckinsee, Mrs. A., 65
Blank, J. E., 38, 39, 49, 50
Bles, A. J. S., 81
Bles, David S., J.P., 81
Bloom, A., 88
Bloom, Mrs., 73
Bloom, Rev. E., 90
Bloomfield, I., 46, 51
Bloser, Rev. N., 87
Boas, H., 64
Bockbinder, I. M., 29
Bradlaw, R., 69, 70
Broady, Jacob, 90
Bronkhorst, Rev. S., 33
Brown, H. L., 87
Brown, Isaac, 69
Brown, S., 69
Budranzki, H., 87
Burman, Isidore, 64

C

Camrass, S., 75
Carason, D., 90
Caro, J., 84
Castello, Manuel, 43, 46, 59, 60
Castro, Joseph de, 52
Chaikin, Rev. A., 86, 87, 96
Chapman, Rev. John, 56
Chetham, N., 38
Chotzner, Rev. Dr., 64, 96
Cobe, Louis, 80, 81
Cohen, A., 68, 76
Cohen, Dr. A., 51
Cohen, Abraham, 73
Cohen, Alfred Louis, 51
Cohen, Arthur, Q.C., 56
Cohen, B., 38
Cohen, Rev. Benjamin, 88
Cohen, Benjamin Louis, M.P. 34, 43
Cohen, Benjamin, 73
Cohen, E. E., 75
Cohen, E. M., 67
Cohen, Rev. F. L., 35, 56, 96
Cohen, H. J., 57
Cohen, Harris, 66
Cohen, Rev. Harris, 84, 85, 96
Cohen, Miss Hetty, 65
Cohen, Jacob H., 67
Cohen, John A., 35
Cohen, J., 90
Cohen, L., 84
Cohen, Mrs. Louis S., 78, 79
Cohen, Rev. Mark, 76
Cohen, Marks L., 69
Cohen, Rev. M. M., 77, 96
Cohen, M., 69, 87
Cohen, Moses, 83
Cohen, M., 37
Cohen, N. L., 51, 58
Cohen, Rev. N., 74
Cohen, Philip, 83
Cohen, S., 77, 86
Cohen, Samuel I., 37, 43, 46, 52, 60
Cohen, Rev. Susman, 61, 96
Conquy, Rev. S., 37
Cook, Samuel, 67
Cormick, M., 70
Cree, David, 71
Cree, Nathan, 71
Crocker, J., 57
Cropman, D., 77
Curlender, J. L., 78

D.

Danziger, Isidor, 81.
Davies, Rev. C., 38.
Davies, Rev. M. E., 82.
D'Avigdor, O. E., 67.
Davids, Rev. H., 37, 96.
Davids, S. H., 37, 52.
Davidsohn, J., 39
Davidson, Jacob, 44

INDEX OF NAMES.

Davidson, Mrs. Louis, 44, 57
Davies, Adolph, 69
Davies, Herbert J., 80
Davis, Rev. —, 90
Davis, David, 34, 66
Davis, Felix, 57
Davis, Felix A., B.A., LL.B., 48
Davis, H., 77
Davis, Henry, 65
Davis, Joel, 58
Davis, J., 39
Davis, L., 81
Davis, Mrs. Montague, 65
Davis, S. J., 64
Davis, Woolf, 66
Davis, W., 67
Defries, I. L., 49
De Groot, M., 69
De Pass, Abraham D., 52
De Pass, C., 58
Devilliers, J. A. J., 34
Diamond, M., 85
Dight, E. A., 45
Dight, M. L., 65
Dimant, Z., 39
Dresner, Philip, 71
Dreyfuss, Mrs., 81
Drukker, M., 46
Dumoulin, Mrs. V., 75
Duparc, M., 50

E.

Edwards, Councillor Henry, 86
Ehrenberg, J., 86
Eldov, S., 38
Eliasaf, E., 70
Elkin, B.A., 51
Ellis, Barrent S., 52
Emanuel, Miss, 48
Emanuel, Alderman A. L., J.P., 56
Emanuel, Ellis, 48
Emanuel, Rev. G. J., 65
Emanuel, Lewis, 59
Emanuel, M., J.P., 87
Epriler, P., 71
Epstein, A. D., 90
Epstein, Mrs., 74
Epstein, Rev., M.A., 34
Epstein, M., 74
Esterman Harris, 71
Esterman, Max, 71
Esterson, Rev. Woolf, 38

F

Fagin, A., 77
Falk, David, 83
Falk, Michael 84
Franks, Mrs., 83
Farbstein, Dr. H., 75
Farbstein, Mrs., 75
Fay, Rev. David, 34, 53
Feinberg, H. M., 80
Feldman, E. L., 68
Feldman, S. F., 50
Fersht, B. A., 58
Finestone, Maurice, 87
Finewich, Rev. Salomon, 38
Foa, Gaston, 48
Fontyn, Jacob, 38
Foutyn, J , 39
Fox, H., 64
Frankenburg, Julian, 72
Frankenburg, Mrs., 73
Frankenburg, Miss, 73
Frankenstein, P., 80
Frankenstein, S., 51
Franklin, Arthur E., 43, 44
Franklin, Ellis A., 50, 55, 59
Franklin, Mrs. Ellis A., 44
Franklin, E. L., 47
Franklin, F. S., 44
Franklin, Leonard B., 35, 57
Franks, A., 84
Franks, B. I., 85
Franks, M., 64
Fredman, M., 85
Fredman, S., 72
Freedman, L., 38
Freedman, Marks, 85
Freedman, M., 39
Freeman, B., 71
Fridlander, A. E., 69
Friedeberg, Rev. S., 78, 79, 80, 96
Friedlander, M., Ph. D., 56
Friend, Herman, 76
Fuld, B., 38
Furiansky, B., 72
Fürst, Rev. Jacob, 71, 72, 97
Furst, J. E., 58
Fyne, Rev. S., 87, 97

G.

Gabrielsen, D., 78
Gallewski, Mrs. Jacob, 89
Gallewski, Solomon, 89
Gaster, Rev. Haham, Dr. Moses, 61, 97
Geershon, T., 64
Geffen, Rev. J. L., 35
Gershon, E. N., 67
Getz, M., 88
Gilder, S., 52
Glassman, Miss, 75
Gluckstein, N., 39
Goldberg, Barnett, 89
Goldberg, Mrs., 74
Goldberg, L., 77
Goldberg, L., 74
Goldberg, H., 39
Goldenberg, M., 90
Goldhill, J., 35
Goldman, F., 67
Goldman, H., 68
Goldman, I., 86
Goldman, P., 76
Goldman, Ralph, 84, 85
Goldring, J. W., 83
Goldsmid, Colonel Albert Edward W., 57, 60
Goldsmid, Mrs. Alfred, 48
Goldsmid, E. I., 73
Goldsmid, Rt. Hon. Sir Julian, 104
Goldstein, S., 39
Goldston, Ernest 71
Goldston, Joseph, 85
Goldston, Rev. N., 38, 97
Gollancz, Rev. Hermann, 97
Gollancz, Rev. H., 34
Gollancz, Rev. S. M., 34, 97
Gompertz, A. S., 87
Gompertz, J., 87
Goodman, B., 66
Goodman, H., 38
Goodman, Jacob E., 82
Goodman, M., 83
Goodman, W., 39
Gordon, S., 34
Gordon, Mrs. S., 65
Gottliffe, J., 76
Gouldstein, Rev. J. A., 35, 97
Graft, B., 77
Green, Rev. A. A., 35, 97
Green, A., 86
Green, J., 35
Green, Louis S., 45
Green, Michael A., 43
Green, M. J., 48
Greenberg, Mr., 70
Greenberg, Rev. I., 35
Greensweig, Eli, 88

H

Haes, Frank, 58
Haldinstein, Alfred J., 84
Halford, B. B., 51, 58
Halford, Mrs. F. B., 47
Hamburger, S., 38
Harris, A. T., 87
Harris, B., 44
Harris, E., M.A., 81
Harris, Miss Emily Marion, 57
Harris, Ephraim, M.A., 82
Harris, F., 80
Harris, H., 39
Harris, H. M., 46
Harris, Henry, 48
Harris, Henry, 37
Harris, Rev. Isidore, 52, 97
Harris, Rev. J., 80
Harris, Jacob, 74
Harris, Lionel L., 89
Harris, M., 39
Harris, Myer, 37
Harris, Nathaniel H., 80
Harris, Rev. R., 34, 97
Harris, S. M., 83, 87
Hart, Miss, 78
Hart, Alderman Henry, J.P., 68, 69
Hart, M., 86
Hart, Sir Israel, 77
Hart, P., 80
Hart, Samuel, 69
Hartman, A., 86

THE JEWISH CHRONICLE

[Reprinted from "THE SKETCH," Nov. 27, 1895.]

It is no exaggeration to say that the *Jewish Chronicle*, that substantial twopenny weekly newspaper which is to be found in almost every Jewish household on a Friday night, holds a unique place in journalism: it supplies a real want in the community; in London it may be said to link the East and West Jews; and wherever English-speaking Hebrews are settled, from South Africa to Australia; the Chinese Ports, India, and the most remote towns, there will the *Jewish Chronicle* be found. It boasts subscribers in Kingston, Jamaica; Paramaribo; St. Thomas, West Indies; Dunedin: Ondtshoorn: British Honduras; Salisbury, Mashonaland; Guayaquil; Buluwayo; Iquique; Philipopolis; Vryheid; Panama; Suva, Fiji; Zeernst—just to quote a few out-of-the-way places.

It is more than fifty years since the paper was called into being, and as may readily be imagined, it has undergone many transitions since Nov. 12th 1841, when the first number appeared.

Nowadays the *Chronicle* gives great prominence to communal intelligence, the record of births, deaths, and marriages, of successes and distinctions won by Jews, and the general personal note of interest, conduce in no small degree to its popularity. As young scholars obtained prizes and distinctions, these facts were duly noted in the *Chronicle*, and though it may seem a very small matter to announce that a boy has matriculated or passed a University local, these items form, perhaps, the first record of some life destined to be of great importance to the community. Turning over some old file, for instance, I find that Master George Jessel has won a prize, and thirty years later he is made Master of the Rolls. There is the record of Sir Francis Goldsmid's admission to the Bar; on August 1, 1856, the list of young Jews who have matriculated includes "Hermann Nathan Adler," the present Chief Rabbi; Julian Goldsmid, the present baronet, who has just been made a member of the Privy Council; and Joseph Morris Solomon, the eminent conveyancing counsel. These events, small in themselves, go to make up modern Jewish history, since the life of the community lies in its people.

Non-Jewish readers must find the advertisements of this paper somewhat curious; for instance; it is not uncommon to find a death announcement inserted three, or even four times, and couched in almost identical terms, except, perhaps, that the first announcement may conclude with the words, "Father of A, B, and C"; the second, "Brother of D, E, F"; the third alluding to some other relationship of the deceased. The explanation is that all the relatives desiring to show a mark of respect to the dead man elect to insert an advertisement, each on his own account. Again, "at home" days of middle-class Jews, on the occasion when a lad is confirmed, the date on which a tombstone will be set, and similar personalia, are advertised, since it is a recognised fact that in this way the news will certainly be conveyed to all relatives and friends. "Returns thanks" for letters and calls during a week of mourning are also advertised. Recently I was struck by a full column of "return thanks" after the death of an aged lady. There were a large family of wealthy sons, each of whom inserted a notice addressed from residences in Bayswater, Finchley Road, Hampstead, and other well-to-do parts; while brothers and sisters of the deceased lady returned thanks from the less aristocratic quarters of Whitechapel and Bow, East and West-End Jews thus set cheek by jowl.

The correspondence of the *Jewish Chronicle* of to-day is another of its interesting features Within the last few months, letters on various topics of the hour have appeared from Sir Samuel Montagu, Sir Julian Goldsmid, Mr. F. D. Mocatta, Mr. B. L. Cohen, M.P., and Mr. Zangwill, while the signatures of Lord Rothschild, the Chief Rabbi, Sir Philip and Lady Magnus, and other men and women of note, are frequently appended to letters. Contributors whose writings have appeared in this paper include Mr. Zangwill, whose clever paper on "The Growth of Respectability," in the Jubilee Supplement, Nov. 13th, 1891, has just been translated into German; the late Miss Amy Levy, Sir Philip and Lady Magnus, Mr. Joseph Jacobs, various Jewish journalists whose work is well known on other papers, and nearly every Jewish minister, from the Chief Rabbi downwards.

It may not be amiss to mention that the *Jewish Chronicle* is an entirely commercial undertaking, in the first instance; and the only time when it was not a paying concern was when it was run, nearly thirty years ago, by four of the most prominent men of the community. It is quite independent in its views, the orthodox, the ultra-orthodox, and the reform Jew being all represented. It is the accepted organ of the British Jews, and is comprehensively Semitic.

THE JEWISH CHRONICLE,

Offices—2, FINSBURY SQUARE, LONDON, E.C.

(ESTABLISHED 1820.)

WERTHEIMER, LEA & CO.

English and Foreign Printers,

STATIONERS,

ACCOUNT BOOK MANUFACTURERS, ENGRAVERS, LITHOGRAPHERS, AND TRANSLATORS.

Telephone No. 814.

WERTHEIMER, LEA & CO. possess a very large and complete Hebrew plant, and have printed and published many of the most important Hebrew works issued in this country, including the Authorised Version of the Daily Prayer Book by the Rev. S. Singer.

WERTHEIMER, LEA & CO. have a large and experienced staff, including educated men of nearly every European nation, thus enabling them to ensure accuracy in all foreign languages.

WERTHEIMER, LEA & CO print *Le Courrier de Londres*, *Londoner Zeitung*, the French edition of the *West Australian Review*, and many other English and Foreign weekly and monthly journals.

SPECIAL FACILITIES FOR THE RAPID AND PROMPT EXECUTION OF COMPANY PROSPECTUSES AND LEGAL WORK.

Newspaper, Magazine, Book, Commercial and Miscellaneous Printing of every description carefully and expeditiously executed on moderate terms.

CIRCUS PLACE, LONDON WALL,
LONDON, E.C.

INDEX OF NAMES.

Hartnet, M., 70
Hasluck, S. L., 56
Hast, Rev. M., 34, 97
Heilbron, Rev. M. J., 37
Heilbron, Mrs. S., 44
Heiser, M., 45
Henriques, E. M., J.P., 81
Henry, Abraham Lindo, 52
Henry, Alfred, 33
Henry, Miss Ethel, 83
Henschberg, S. J., 78, 79
Herr, B., 38
Hess, J., 52
Hillner, S., 66
Hindin, Rev. S. M., 77
Hirsch, S. A., Ph.D., 56, 60
Hirschkovich, J., 57
Houtman, J., 39
Hovsba, J., 77
Hush, J., 82
Hyam, David, 46
Hyam, Stephen S., 35
Hyams, Emanuel, 86
Hyams, Henry H., 46, 47, 50
Hyams, J., 87
Hyamson, Rev. M., 35, 98
Hyman, M., 75
Hyman, S., 76

I

Isaacs, Sir Aaron Henry, 111
Isaacs, Asher, 34
Isaacs, Miss F., 44
Isaacs, Rev. G., 37
Isaacs, Isaac A., 81
Isaacs, Rev. M., 90
Isaacs, Mauris, 71
Isaacs, Mrs. M., 71
Isaacs, W., 35

J

Jackson, A., 89
Jackson, Miss Sophy, 88
Jackson, Mrs. A. M., 78
Jacob, Mrs. E., 47
Jacob, Lionel, 58
Jacobs, A., 39
Jacobs, Rev. A. C., 66
Jacobs, B. S., 75
Jacobs, Mrs. B. S., 75
Jacobs, Charles, 72
Jacobs, Rev. D., 88
Jacobs, Daniel, 34
Jacobs, D., 39
Jacobs, I. L., 66
Jacobs, Mrs J., 49
Jacobs, Jacob, 66
Jacobs, Joseph, B.A., 53
Jacobs, Joseph, 34
Jacobs, J. M., 67
Jacobs, K., 64
Jacobs, M., 74
Jacobs, S. H., 67
Jacoby, B., 88, 89
Jafe, L., 70
Jaffe Otto, 64

Jessel, Sir Charles James, 106
Joel, Miss Kate, 49
Joel, M., 49
Jones, Alexander, 79
Joseph, Alexander, 65
Joseph, B. H., 65
Joseph, C. S., 51
Joseph, Delissa, 35
Joseph, Edward A., 51
Joseph, George S., 47
Joseph, Henry, 89
Joseph, Isaac A., 34, 50
Joseph, Rev. J., 84
Joseph, Rev. Morris, 45, 98
Joseph, Mrs. Morris, 45
Joseph, N. S., 44, 50
Joseph, S., 76
Josephs, L., 87
Josselson, Mr., 70

K

Kahn, Mr., 74
Kaliski, I., 44, 46, 51
Kalker, M., 69
Kantor, Rev. J., 81
Katz, Mrs. A., 79
Kilner, G. Washington, M.A., 56
Kino, Mrs. C., 65
Kishinisky, David, 71
Kossick, J., 47
Kranz, Mr., 83
Kreugel, M., 84
Krüger, Henry, 74
Kutner, S., 48

L

Lambert, Max. E., 87
Landa, C., 76
Landa, Mrs. C., 76
Landau, Hermann, 39, 50
Langdon, A. M. L., 81
Laski, N., 80
Lassman, Mr., 64
Lawrence, Rev. Z., 84
Lazaneck, J., 64
Lazaneck, S.
Lazarus, A., 67
Lemon, Miss, 81
Leon, E., 35
Lesser, Rev. J., 35
Levene, M., 64
Levensohn, H. R., 51
Levenson, A., 72
Leventon, J., 70
Leventon, Mrs., 70
Leventon, Rev. I., 69
Levett, Mrs., 70
Levi, Miss J. M., 65
Levin, Rev. E. B., 77
Levin, Rev. H., 80
Levin, T., 70
Levine, I. L., 72
Levine, J., 72
Levinsohn, H. R., 44

Levinsohn, H. R., 58
Levinson, Rev. A., 67
Levinson, H. F., 82
Levinson, L., 82
Levinstein, J., 75
Levy, Mrs. Asher, 85
Levy, Barnard, 78
Levy, Mrs. Eliot, 79
Levy, Rev. I., 75, 90, 93
Levy, J., 39
Levy, J., 82
Levy, Joseph, 88
Levy, J. M., 35
Levy, Joshua M., 37
Levy, Lawrence, Jun., 45
Levy, Lewis, 45
Levy, Lewis, 35
Levy, N., 87
Levy, Mrs. P. S., 79
Levy, Rev. S., 34
Levy, Rev. Solomon, 98
Levy, Mr., 90
Lewis, A., 76
Lewis, Bernard, 82
Lewis, Sir George Henry, 111
Lewis, Hyam, 67
Lewis, Lewis, 66
Libgott, J. M., 39
Lieberman, S., 75
Lindo, Eustace A., 37, 52
Lindo, M. A. N., 37
Lipkin, Rev. Benjamin, 87
Lipman, M., 76
Lipson, H., 87
Lipson, J., 78, 80
Lissack, J. M., 39, 57
Lissack, J. M., Jun., 35, 45.
Litovitch, Rev. I., 72
Littmah, F., 59
Littman, Rev. James, 64
Loewe, E. J., 37
Loeczen, Jacob, 49
Lotinga, M., 83
Lowe, E. J., 38
Lowenstein, Miss May, 65
Lowy, E. D., 50
Lucas, Edward, 48
Lucas, Henry, 34, 48
Lucas, Mrs. Lionel, 44, 48, 49
Lyon, G. L., 48
Lyon, J. S., 37.
Lyon, R., 52
Lyons, A., 89.
Lyons, Frank I., 35
Lyons, J. 76
Lyons, J. S., 89
Lyons, Nathaniel, 74
Lyons, S., 89

M

Mabon, Charles B., 73
Magnus, Sir Philip, 48, 111
Magnus, Lady, 57
Mallis, K., 81
Mandelberg, G.C., J.P., 80
Manne, Rev. S., 98

INDEX OF NAMES.

Manson, Rev. S., 76
Marcan, Lucien, 76
Marcan, Mrs. Lucien, 76
Marchant, L., 46
Marcus, L., 70
Marks, D., 83
Marks, Daniel, 48
Marks, I. M., 34
Marks, Mrs. R., 89
Martin, C. T., F.S.A., 53
Matthews, A., 80
Matz, Rev. Jacob, 82
May, J., 77
May, Samuel, 86
Meisels, Rev. Isaac S., 56
Meltzer, N., 83
Mendelsohn, Rev. L., B.A., 69, 70, 98
Meyer, Mrs. F., 45
Michael, H., 71
Michaels, A., 45
Michaels, M.A., 80
Michaelson, H., 84
Michelsen, C. Z. A., 88
Michelsen, Mrs., 88
Miller, S., 70
Mitafsky, M., 70
Mocatta, B. Elkin, 33
Mocatta, Edward L., 37, 52
Mocatta, F. D., 38, 46, 73
Moch, M., 37
Model, Mrs. L., 45
Montagu, Miss Lily H., 57
Montagu, L Samuel, 47, 57
Montagu, Sir Samuel, Bart., M.P., 39, 49, 50, 51, 57, 60, 107
Montefiore, Cecil Sebag, 51
Montefiore, Claude G., 59
Montefiore, Sir Francis Abraham, 108
Montefiore, Joseph Sebag, 59
Morley, Ernest, 44
Morris, A., 85
Morris, Aaron, 66
Morris, Isidor, 72
Morris, M., 78, 90
Morris, Miss, 75
Moses, A., 46
Moses, L., 39
Moses, M., 39
Moses, Mark, 44
Moses, Moses H., 44
Moses, Samuel, 35
Mosesson, Jacob, 90
Moss, Albert E., 35
Moss, David, 75
Moss, Nathan, 79
Moss, Samuel E, 34
Munz, Rev. S., 35 93
Muscat, Rev. L. I., 82
Myers, Rev. J. E., 69
Myers, Joseph, 82
Myers, Mrs. J., 71
Myers, L. M , 48
Myers, S., 72
Myers, Solomon, 90
Myers, Wolf, 34
Myerston, H., 81

N

Nabarro, A. N., 49
Nathan, Mrs. A., 45
Nathan, H., 35
Nathan, Mrs. Henry, 45
Nathan, L. A., 35
Nathan, Miss, 57
Nathan, Samuel, 63
Newman, A., 77
Newman, M., 69
Noyk, M., 70

O

Oppenheim, E., 39
Oppenheim, S. S., 29
Ornstien, P., 34, 60

P

Pass, H. L., 67
Pearlson, Rev. E., 75
Pennamacoor, F., 52
Phillips, Rev. E. P., 72, 73
Phillips, Mrs. E. P., 73
Phillips, Alderman George Faudel, 46, 48
Phillips, Harry P., 66
Phillips, H., 39
Phillips, H. J., 35
Phillips, Rev. Isaac, 86, 98
Phillips, J., 72
Phillips, Mrs. John, 65
Phillips, Rev. Jacob, 88, 98
Phillips, Moses, 64
Phillips, Mrs. P., 63
Phillips, Rev. P., 37
Phin, P., 72
Pinkers, Aaron, 66
Piperno, Rev. J., 37
Pirbright, Baron, 102
Polack, Rev. J., B.A., 67
Posener, Adolph, 35
Posener, Alfred, 35
Prag, Joseph, 82
Prashuer, S. A., 86
Price, A., 87
Price, Rev. Harris L., 35, 98
Prins, A., 37, 45, 49, 52
Pushinsky, Mrs., 70
Pyke, Alfred, 38
Pyke, Joseph, 34

R

Rabinovitch, Gershon, 84
Rabinovitch. Jacob, 84
Radnitzki, Rev. S., 85
Raisman, M., 76
Raisman, Mrs. M., 76
Raphael, Miss, 81
Raphael, Mrs. George C., 47
Raphael, R. H., 46
Reinowitz, J. D., 66
Resser, B., 86
Richardson, Harry, 50
Richardson, N., 88
Ritter, B., 39
Robinson, B., 80
Robinson, H., 67
Robinson, L., 69
Robinson, Ralph, 79
Robinson, P., 83
Robinson, S., 70
Roco, Rev. S. J., 37, 98
Rose, Mrs., 83
Rosen, I., 80
Rosen, Isaac, 71
Rosenbaum, Henry, 34
Rosenbaum, H., 50
Rosenbaum, Mrs. H., 83
Rosenbaum, Rev. M., 83, 99
Rosenbaum, S., 89
Rosenberg, Rev. —, 85
Rosenberg, J., 37
Rosenberg, J., 82, 83
Rosenberg, M., 78
Rosenberg, S., 83
Rosenblum, J., 81
Rosenfeld, A., 34, 44
Rosengard, Rev. B. H., 73, 74, 99
Rosenheim, Ernest, 80
Rosenthal, H., 39
Rosenthal, John, LL.D., 69
Rosenzweig, Rev. I., 64
Rosenzweig, Rev. Simon Wulf, 71
Rotenberg, M., 74
Rothband, H. L., 80
Rothschild, Right Hon. Lord, 34, 39, 60, 100
Rothschild, Lady, 44, 47, 49
Rothschild, Louisa, Lady de, 47
Rothschild, Leopold de, 43, 48
Rothschild, Mrs. Leopold de, 47
Rudolph, J., 90
Rutkowski, Rev. A., 78
Rutkowski, Mrs., 79

S

Saffer, A., 76
Salamans, Major, J.P., 71
Salmen, A. B., 37
Salomon, Rev. Dr. B , 80, 99
Salomon, D., 84
Salomon, E., 34, 84
Salomon, J., 80
Salomons, Rev. Bernard J., 68, 99
Salomons, Sir David Lionel, 109
Salomons, Sir Julian Emanuel, 111
Salomons, L. J., 34, 46
Samuel, B., 77
Samuel, Charles, 44, 56
Samuel, F. H. Harvey-, 59
Samuel, Gilbert E , 51
Samuel, Rev. I , 34, 48, 56, 99
Samuel, Mrs. I., 68
Samuel, Rev. J., 76
Samuel, Samuel E., 45

EDWARDS' HARLENE FOR THE HAIR

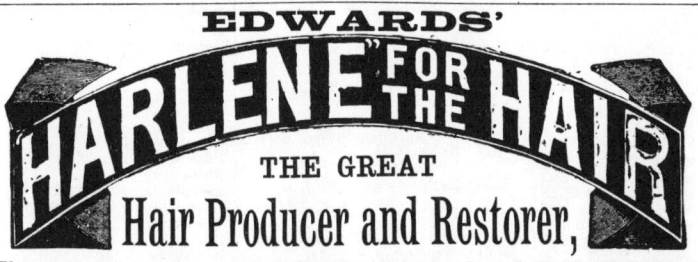

THE GREAT
Hair Producer and Restorer,

The very Finest Dressing, Specially Prepared and Perfumed, Fragrant and Refreshing.

A LUXURY AND A NECESSITY TO EVERY MODERN TOILET.

"HARLENE"

Produces Luxuriant Hair. Prevents it falling off or turning Grey.

UNEQUALLED For Promoting the Growth of the Beard and Moustache

THE WORLD-RENOWNED REMEDY FOR BALDNESS.

For Curing Weak and Thin Eye-lashes, Preserving, Strengthening, and Rendering the Hair beautifully Soft, for Removing Scurf, Dandruff, &c., also for

RESTORING GREY HAIR TO ITS NATURAL COLOUR,
IT IS WITHOUT A RIVAL.

Physicians & Analysts pronounce it to be devoid of any metallic or other injurious ingredients.

WHY NEGLECT YOUR CHILDREN'S HAIR?

Edwards' "Harlene" Preserves, Strengthens, and Invigorates it.

Prevents and Cures all species of Scurf, keeps the Scalp Clean, and Allays all Irritation.

The Hon. Mrs. Thompson's Testimony.
"Ackworth Moor Top, Pontefract.
'"THE HON. MRS. THOMPSON desires to testify to the value of 'HARLENE' for strengthening and preserving the Hair, and will be pleased to allow her testimony to be publicly used."

Proved it Herself.
"59, Elgin-crescent, Notting-hill.
"Dear Sir,—I am delighted to add my testimony to the wonderful efficacy of your hair tonic. I never could have credited the effects of 'Harlene' had I not myself proved them.—
Yours truly, "KATHERINE RAMSEY."

1/-, 2/6, & (triple 2/6 size) 4/6 per Bottle, from Chemists, Hairdressers, and Perfumers all over the World; or sent direct on receipt of Postal Orders.

Edwards' "Harlene" Co., 95, High Holborn, London, W.C.

INDEX OF NAMES.

Samuel, Sir Saul, 112
Samuel, Stuart M., J.P., 46
Samuell, Charles S., 78
Samuels, C., 72
Samuels, Edward, 71
Samuels, Jacob, 73
Sassoon, Edward, 37
Sassoon, Sir Albert Abdullah David, 110
Saunders, A., 35
Schabatt, S., 67
Schaffer, G., 82
Schar, David, 69
Schloss, David, 44
Schloss, Rev. S., 85
Schomfeld, Adolph, 72
Schwarzschild, J., 50
Schwerin, M., 90
Seligman, Charles D., 46
Shaffer, G., 80
Shane, Isaac M., 88
Shapero, M., 75
Shatz, Rev. M., 69
She r, K., 39
Shmith, H., 51
Silldeir, Mrs., 65
Silver, Rev. H. M., 78, 79
Silverberg, I., 78
Silverblatt, Jacob, 82
Silverman, J., 39
Silverston, F., 69
Simmons, Hyman, 77
Simmons, Rev. L. M., LL.B., B.A., 81, 99
Simmons, Ex-Baillie Michael, J P., 72, 73
Simon, Miss, 75
Simon, Rev. Isidore, 82, 99
Simon, Sir John, 112
Simons, S., 43
Simons, Michael, 73
Simons, Miss, 73
Simons, Philip B., 72
Singer, J., 39
Singer, Rev. S., 35, 58

Singer, Julius, 44
Smith, A. W., 51
Sockel, Abraham, 76
Solomon, A., 83
Solomon, M. H., 51
Solomon, James H., 56
Solomon, Louis, 79
Solomon, Mrs. H., 79
Solomon, Solomon, J., A.R A., 57
Solomons, M., 70
Sonnenthal, R., 35
Sperber, Solomon, 88
Spero, Rev. E., 34, 99
Spielman, Isidore, F.S.A., 58
Spielmann, M. A., 58
Spielmann, Mrs. Meyer A., 47
Spiers, Miss Lizzie, 65
Spiers, Rev. B., 58, 61, 99
Steel, B., 81
Steinheim, Dr., 38
Steinmark, B.A., 81
Stephany, M., 43
Stern, Edward D., 48
Stern, Rev. J. F., 35, 45, 99
Stoloff, W., 68
Stone, H., 75
Strelitski, S., 39
Strump, Benjamin, 73
Sumberg, Rev. S., 74
Swaab, A., 49
Symons, Mr., 84
Symons, Mrs. H. E., 47

T

Taffer, Hirsch 64
Trenner, S., 58
Tuck, Adolph, 35
Turner, S., 83

V

Vance, M., 70
Van Kleef, Nathan, 52

Veitel, M., 64
Vogel, Jacob, 38
Vogel, Sir Julius, 112

W

Wachman, E., 70
Waley, Alfred, 38
Waley, Philip S., 50
Wallmars, Rev. —, 67
Wandsworth, Baron, 102
Wartski, A. M., 34, 50
Wartski, I., 64
Wartski, M, 64
Weber, I., 39, 51
Wharman, Samuel, 50
Wilks, J., 82
Wilson, J., 82
Wolf, Lucien, 58
Wolfe, Mrs. Elias, 89
Wolfe, Mrs. J., 89
Wolfers, Rev. Philip, 89, 99
Wolff, Dr. A., 51
Woolf, Mrs. A. M., 44
Woolf, Miss D., 44
Woolf, Miss E., 44
Woolf, Jacob, 35, 83
Worms, Baron de, 103

Y

Yates, E. W., 78, 79
Yates, Mrs. E. W., 79
Yates, Ellis K., 78, 79

Z

Zacchiew, J. B., 89
Zachariah, Edward, 86
Zachariah, L., 37
Zacharias, J., 85
Zacharias, M., 67
Zamck, A., 64
Zucker, I., 72

INDEX OF ADVERTISERS.

	PAGE.
ALLEN & WRIGHT, 26, Poultry, E.C., and 217, Piccadilly, W.	iv

Founded upwards of a quarter of a century ago, this firm has an extensive reputation for the manufacture of briar pipes, etc., of the highest quality. It imports very largely Havanah cigars and Egyptian cigarettes, besides always having in stock an extensive variety of fancy articles of interest to the smoker. Messrs. Allen & Wright's "Special Flake" cigarettes have a world-wide popularity.

THE ALLIANCE ASSURANCE COMPANY, 2, Bartholomew-lane ... ii

This Company was established in 1824, its affairs being regulated by Acts of Parliament and by laws and regulations passed by the members. The immense business done by the Company is evidenced by the number of branches which it has been compelled to open. Amongst the original Directors were Sir Moses Montefiore, Bart., F.R.S., and Nathan Meyer Rothschild, Esq., Lord Rothschild being the present Chairman of the Company. One of the auditors is his son, Hon. Walter Rothschild, and the actuary is Mr. Marcus N. Adler.

THE AMERICAN LINE CO. (Richardson, Spence & Co.), 3, Cockspur-street, S.W. 297

The service between Southampton and New York has become one of the most popular for migration from England to America, thanks to the magnificent floating palaces owned by this Company, and to their splendid equipment, both in regard to comfort and speed. The owners of the steamers are the International Navigation Company, which was established originally as the Inman and International Steamship Company, in 1851. This was the first company to run screw steamers across the Atlantic. For many years Liverpool was its English port for landing and embarking passengers. In 1893 the service was transferred to Southampton, that port, by reason of its proximity to London and the Continent, being found to be more convenient. The American Line carries the large bulk of alien transients who go to America from Russia through England, and provides special facilities, such as kosher food, etc., for its Jewish passengers.

BARNETT, E. & CO., 79 & 81, Middlesex-street, Aldgate, 249, Euston-road, & 334, Essex-road, N. 287

Founded by Mr. Emanuel Barnett, the present proprietor, in 1860 at Stony-lane. Mr. Barnett has from time to time purchased cattle at, amongst other sales, those held on behalf of Her Majesty at Windsor, H.R.H. The Prince of Wales at Sandringham, Lord Rothschild at Tring, etc. Last Christmas, Mr. Barnett was commissioned by the *Daily Telegraph* to supply the Jewish cripples with the meat for their hampers. Mr. Barnett has, in addition to his business places, a farm at Great Hawkesley, near Newmarket, where he raises prize cattle and poultry.

ECONOMIC BANK, 34, Old Broad-street, E.C. 294

Was opened in 1893, for the purpose of affording persons of even moderate means the advantages of a banking account, the safety of the depositors being insured by all funds being invested under the Trust Act, 1893, and in Colonial Government securities. The bank discounts no bills, no loans are granted, no overdrafts allowed. The rapid progress which this Bank has made is the highest proof that it is obtaining, by its sound policy the full confidence of the public.

EDWARDS & CO., 95, High Holborn 273

Firm founded in 1887 by the present proprietor, at 5, New Oxford-street. In addition to the world-renowned preparation for the hair, Mr. Edwards manufactures various toilet articles of high merit.

THE JEWISH WORLD.

The Leading Organ of the Anglo-Jewish Community.

PUBLISHED EVERY FRIDAY, PRICE ONE PENNY.

Offices:

8, SOUTH ST., FINSBURY, LONDON, E.C.

Special Correspondence from the Provinces, the Colonies, and Abroad.

THE JEWISH WORLD is essentially a Jewish orthodox paper, and devotes its columns to inculcating the principles of our Holy Religion. It is the only Penny Jewish paper in English, published throughout the world, and therefore commands a wide circulation. It gives constant attention to the elucidation of communal problems.

From its extensive circulation, THE JEWISH WORLD offers exceptional advantages to Advertisers. Best Jewish Medium. THE JEWISH WORLD is forwarded free by post to any address in the United Kingdom on payment in advance of the Yearly Subscription of 6s. 6d., or the Half-yearly Subscription of 3s. 3d.

Copies may be had at all the Principal Railway Stations in London and the Provinces, or ordered through any Newsagent.

Special Rates for Trade Advertisements (displayed or ordinary) can be obtained on application to the Offices,

8, SOUTH ST., FINSBURY, LONDON, E.C.

JEWISH EXPRESS.

(Established 1895.)

EVERY FRIDAY, 1ᴅ·

A Family Newspaper for the Jewish People.

Officially recognised by the principal educational and charitable institutions of London, Manchester, Leeds, Liverpool, Glasgow, etc.

The only Newspaper for Jews printed in Judische-Deutsche Jargon in England.

The *Jewish Express* is the largest and most comprehensive Jargon newspaper in the world.

It circulates amongst the Jewish people throughout England, Ireland and Scotland.

The only medium open to English Advertisers seeking trade with foreign Jews.

For Advertisement Rates apply to the Manager, at the Chief Office, Quebec Street, Leeds.

London Office.—144, Fleet Street. *Wholesale Agent in London.*—Mr. TRAUBMAN, 8, Little Alie Street, Leman Street, E. *Manchester.*—Messrs. BLOCK & FALK, Great Ducie Street, Strangeways.

The above receive Advertisements.

Paris Agents.—M. FRIEDMANN, Reulier, 11, Rue des Rosiers; M. KREMER, 48, Rue Traversière.

Agents in every town in the United Kingdom.

The *Jewish Express* is published by W. Gavazzi King for the Leeds Express, Limited, at Quebec-street, City-square, Leeds, proprietors of the *Leeds Evening Express, Leeds Weekly Express, Leeds Daily Mid-day Tissue, Leeds Express Xmas Annual.*

INDEX OF ADVERTISERS.

	PAGE.
J. S. FRY & SONS, Bristol	iii

This world-famed firm, the products of whose vast range of factories are in truth "too sweet for words," was established somewhere about the year 1728. It is now a limited company, but the whole of the interest is continued in the family, the two chief proprietors being Mr. Joseph Storrs Fry, who is the head of the firm, and great grandson of the founder, and Francis James Fry, J.P. Messrs. Fry have branches at London and Sydney, N.S.W., and are the happy possessors of close on 200 medals and diplomas, received in various exhibitions in every part of the world for the excellence of their manufactures. The firm chiefly advertises the Pure Concentrated Cocoa, for the superiority of which they have the highest medical opinions; but they are also manufacturers of all kinds of fancy chocolates, their more expensive caskets forming presents of a most acceptable kind.

GOULD, Dr. W. E., 129, New Kent-road, S.E. 294

The pills prepared by Dr. Gould are claimed to be a sure remedy for obesity. Dr. Gould undertakes to cure corpulency by means of his preparation, without any change of diet.

GREAT EALING SCHOOL, Ealing, W. 295

Founded a century ago. Under present management since 1880. Principal, Rev. John Chapman, First B.A. London University, and Member of Jews' College, assisted by Staff of Graduates and Foreign Masters. Prepares for all University and Public Examinations, and for Commercial and Mercantile pursuits.

GREENBERG & CO., 80, Chancery Lane, W.C. 284

Established about ten years ago. Publishers of and sole Contractors for all advertisements appearing in the *Jewish Year Book*. The firm also holds Contracts for entire advertisement space in, amongst other publications, *Pick-Me-Up, Forget-Me-Not, Home Sweet Home*, and *Golf*, and has special Contract for advertisements appearing upon *Jewish Chronicle* cover. Messrs. Greenberg also undertake the insertion of advertisements at office rates in all publications anywhere throughout the world.

HEINEMANN, W., 21, Bedford-street, Strand, W.C. 266

To Jews Mr. Heinemann is perhaps best known as the publisher of Mr. Zangwill's books. The firm publishes for Max Nordau, and amongst its advertised works is M. Le Roy-Beaulieu's "Israel among the Nations."

HOBBS, HART & CO., Cheapside, E.C. 299

Founded by Mr. Alfred Hobbs, known in the early fifties as the "lockpicker," when he demonstrated the worthlessness of the Safes of best English manufacture of that day. Doors and safes of their manufacture are employed by the Bank of England, Windsor Castle, etc. Some of the largest Scotch Banks have ordered safes in large numbers from this firm. This chairman of the Company is Mr. E. B. Ellice Clark, M.Inst.C.E., and the General Manager and Secretary is Mr. Charles Lee, F.I.S.

JAMESON, W., 92, Newington-butts, S.E. 288, 289

The soap manufactured by this firm is a preparation which claims to be, not only an excellent adjunct to the toilet, but also to contain curative properties peculiarly adapted to skin trouble. The special preparation is manufactured solely by Mr. Jameson, and those desiring his products should see that the soap is stamped with his name, as there are many soaps bearing the same name on the market made by inferior makers.

"JEWISH CHRONICLE," 2, Finsbury Square, E.C. 269

The *Jewish Chronicle* was founded in 1841, and is believed to have the largest circulation of any Jewish newspaper in the world. Amongst those who have edited the paper in the past are Dr. Benisch, Mr. Michael Henry, and Mr. M. Angel (Head Master of Jews' Free School), whilst its columns have received contributions during the 55 years it has been established from every prominent English Jew.

INDEX OF ADVERTISERS.

	PAGE.
'**JEWISH EXPRESS**," Leeds...	278

An eight page weekly newspaper printed in Judische-Deutsch. It was established by the editor, Mr. Gavazzi King, in June, 1895. The *Jewish Express* claims to be the largest jargon paper in the world, and is said to have a large circulation in the colonies and various parts of Europe.

"**JEWISH WORLD**," 8, South-street, Finsbury, E.C. ... 277

This paper was established in February, 1873. It has been consistently orthodox, and took special part in unfolding the tale of the Russian persecutions through its "Special Commissioner." It is the only Anglo-Jewish (English) penny paper. Mr. Lucien Wolf at one time edited the *Jewish World*.

JOSEPH, ISIDOR, Dunedin-house, Basinghall-avenue, E.C. ... 298

After many years' practical experience with some of the leading houses in the printing and stationery trades, Mr. Joseph established himself at Dunedin-house, Basinghall-avenue. He makes a speciality of Hebrew printing, produces general commercial printing of an artistic character, and is also an inventor and maker of advertising novelties and showcards for all trades.

KILBURN CONSERVATOIRE, 4, High-road, Kilburn, N.W. ... 292

This Conservatoire of Music was founded in 1894 by Miss Gertrude Azulay, the Principal, who is perhaps the only lady in this country at the head of a Musical Institution. The particular method of training introduced has proved a conspicuous success.

LONDON HOSPITAL, Whitechapel-road, E. ... 282

The great hospital of the East-end. It contains special wards for Jews and Jewesses, medical and surgical, and is an institution largely used by the poor Jews of the East-end. It is dependent upon voluntary contributions, and has immense claims upon the Jewish community.

MABIE, TODD & BARD, 93, Cheapside, E.C. ... 261

Mabie, Todd & Bard's Factory was established in New York in 1845, and its capacity, machinery and appliances for the manufacture of Gold Pens, Pen Holders, Pen and Pencil Cases, Gold and Silver Pencils and Fountain Holders were added to and improved, and the staff of skilled workmen for the finishing of gold nibs *by hand* increased year by year, until it is now one of the largest and best reputed manufactories of its kind in the world. The Cheapside Depôt was established in London in 1881, from whence supplies are distributed throughout the Colonies, India, and the Continent of Europe; and later, branches opened at 95, Regent-street, and 21, High-street, Kensington.

MACMILLAN & CO., Bedford-street, Strand, W.C. ... 262

No firm of publishers occupies a higher position in the literary world than Messrs. Macmillan, the publications it has issued covering the widest possible range of literature, not, by any means, neglecting elementary books, in regard to which, indeed, Messrs. Macmillan hold a very special place. The firm has published a number of Jewish works, the latest being Montefiore's "Bible for Home Reading," and it publishes the "Jewish Quarterly Review."

MALTBY, JAMES, 8, Hanover-place, Upper Baker-street, W. 292

Mr. Maltby is the well-known Army tailor and outfitter, and has an extensive reputation for the best-class work.

MAPLE & CO., LTD., Tottenham-court-road, London ... 281

Founded about sixty years ago by Mr. John Maple, since when it has developed into the largest Furnishing Establishment in the World, giving direct employment to about 3,000 persons. This immense establishment to which two extensive additions in the Tottenham court-road and Gower-street have been added during the current year, comprises an area of about 20 or more acres. The busi-

MAPLE & CO

HIGH-CLASS
Second-Hand Furniture

MAPLE & CO. have set apart a series of spacious Showrooms for the exclusive display of SECOND-HAND FURNITURE of the very best class, both antique and modern. The most interesting collection of

OLD CHIPPENDALE SHERATON ADAM HEPPLEWHITE LOUIS XIV. XV. XVI. EMPIRE ITALIAN RENAISSANCE FURNITURE

IN LONDON

EVERYTHING MARKED IN PLAIN FIGURES AT COMMERCIAL PRICES

MAPLE & CO (Ltd)
TOTTENHAM COURT ROAD
LONDON W

ESTABLISHED SIXTY YEARS

LONDON HOSPITAL, E.

President:
H.R.H. THE DUKE OF CAMBRIDGE, K.G.

Treasurer:
JOHN HENRY BUXTON, Esq.

An **APPEAL** for **FUNDS** is now made to carry on the work of this, the greatest Charity of the East End, in its present efficiency.

All who are willing to assist the Committee by Contributions are most cordially asked to promise to send a donation, or to become annual subscribers. Any subscription, however small, is most cordially appreciated.

£40,000 a Year is required from Voluntary Contributions.

THE LONDON HOSPITAL ASKS FOR HELP

BECAUSE—It is the Largest Voluntary Hospital—776 beds.

- It treated 10,559 In-patients last year.
- It treated 2,412 Children under 12 years of age last year.
- It has special Wards for Jews—830 treated in 1895.
- It is a Special Hospital for Women, Cancer, Stone, &c., &c.
- Its assured Income is only £20,000 a year.
- It relieved 154,617 Patients of the poorest class in 1895.
- It is managed with the strictest economy.

All interested are cordially invited to visit the Hospital.

J. H. HALE, Esq.　　　　　G. Q. ROBERTS, M.A.,
　Chairman.　　　　　*House Governor and Secretary.*

ness became a Limited Liability Company with a capital of Two Millions in 1891. The Governor of the Company is Sir J. Blundell Maple, M.P., Conservative member for Dulwich, and member of the London County Council.

METROPOLITAN HOSPITAL, Kingsland-road, N.E. 285
This Hospital has always had a very special claim upon the generosity of those who belong to the Jewish community by reason of its having treated a large number of their poor sick and injured co-religionists. And this claim will be strengthened by a new departure, which a short while ago the committee commenced. In order to overcome the difficulty of poor Jews who do not understand English, and the better to treat this particular class of patients, the committee have set apart Tuesdays and Fridays in each week for the treatment of Jewish patients. This department is under the charge of Dr. Abraham Cohen, and we have reason to believe that this arrangement has already given great satisfaction to those for whose benefit it was inaugurated. In addition to this the committee have opened two small wards, containing 12 beds, for the exclusive reception of Jewish patients. A "Kosher" Kitchen has also been fitted up.

MINERVA COLLEGE, Folkestone-road, Dover, The Misses Hart. 294
This school has been established for seven years, and is adapted for high-class education. The many advantages offered by the College may be seen from the prospectus, for which application should be made to the principals.

NORTH LONDON HOSPITAL FOR CONSUMPTION AND DISEASES OF THE CHEST (1860), Mount Vernon, Hampstead, N.W. Central Out Patients' Department and Office, 41, Fitzroy-square, W. 286
Affords medical relief to the poor afflicted with diseases of the chest from all parts of the kingdom. An Incurable Fund and a Samaritan Fund provide help for the poorest patients on their discharge from the hospital. Admission by subscribers' letters of recommendation. Last annual income, £6,274. This Hospital is largely used by the poor Jews, and therefore has abundant claim for support upon the Jewish community.

NORWICH UNION LIFE INSURANCE SOCIETY, Head Office: Norwich. London City Office: 10, King William-street, E.C. 296
Was established on the Mutual Principle in the year 1808. In 1866 it took over the business of the old Amicable Society, which was founded by Royal Charter in the reign of Queen Anne, and the united Societies thus constitute the oldest Life Office in the world. Its new business now amounts to upwards of one-and-a-half millions sterling per annum. At the last division of profits the average bonus was at the rate of £2 per cent. per annum upon the sum assured.

NUTT, DAVID, 270, Strand, W.C. 265
This business was founded in 1829, and specially handles foreign, classical and theological publications. Mr. Nutt is publisher to the Folk Lore Society and to the Goethe Society.

OGDEN, THOMAS, LIMITED, 38, Wapping, Liverpool. 274
This business was established by the late Thomas Ogden about the year 1866. It was first formed into a limited liability company in 1890, amongst the directors being Mr. R. H. Walters, Mr. Thomas Ogden, Mr. W. B. Ogden, Mr. Percy Callaghan, Mr. J. McConnal, etc. This firm is chiefly known for their "Guinea Gold" tobacco and cigarettes.

REGENT'S PARK CYCLE STORES, 7, Hanover-place, Upper Baker-street, W. 293
Mr. Arthur Maltby, the well-known champion cyclist, is the leading spirit in this Company, who are manufacturers of the famous "Royal Park" cycles, besides being general agents for Osmond's and all the best makers.

INDEX OF ADVERTISERS.

	PAGE.
TANN, JOHN, 11, Newgate-street, E.C.	293

Claims to be the oldest safe manufacturing firm in the world. It was established by the present Mr. John Tann's father in 1795, and, during the 101 years which have elapsed, the firm has only passed through two hands. Mr. John Tann, in 1843, invented the system of making safes fire-resisting by chemical means, which is the process now adopted by all makers.

W. WALKER & SONS, Bunhill-row, E.C. 291

Established in 1843, manufacture high-class furniture, interior woodwork, wood mantel-pieces, etc. Besides their London factory and showroom, they have also factories and show-rooms at George-street Sydney, N.S.W., and Risik-street, Johannesburg.

WERTHEIMER, LEA & CO., 1½, Circus-place, Finsbury ... 270

Founded by the late John Wertheimer, in 1820, at 44, Leman-street, Goodman's-fields. The firm now, in addition to their premises at Circus-place, occupy two other factories in London, and employ over 200 hands. The firm have printed for all the chief Jewish institutions, and many of the best known publications of the community.

WEST HAMPSTEAD SCHOOL, 148, Abbey-road, N.W. 261

This School was founded in 1892 by the present Head Master, Mr. Polack, who had a previous experience of seventeen years as Assistant Master at Great Ealing School. The school provides a general education for boys. Mr. Polack boards boys if necessary.

WOMAN'S LIFE 290

Woman's Life is one of the numerous publications issued from the office of Sir George Newnes, Bart., the M.P. for the Newmarket Division in the last Parliament. Sir George Newnes' first paper was the world-renowned *Tit-Bits*, and the immense success of that publication has only been equalled in the region of more expensive periodicals by the *Strand Magazine*, which also issues from the same office.

ADVERTISEMENTS

In the *Jewish Year Book* are charged as follows:—

WHOLE PAGE	£8	0 0
HALF PAGE	5	0 0
QUARTER PAGE	3	10 0

(*Special positions by arrangement.*)

All applications for Advertisement space must be made to—

GREENBERG & Co.,

Sole Contractors for all Advertisements,

80, Chancery Lane,
London, W.C.

☞ Advertisements for the *Jewish Year Book* for next year 5658 (1897-8) must reach Messrs. Greenberg & Co. not later than 15th July, 1897.

METROPOLITAN HOSPITAL,

KINGSLAND ROAD, N.E.

(Late Devonshire Square, City).

Patron: H.R.H. THE PRINCE OF WALES.

Chairman: JOSEPH FRY, Esq. Treasurer: The Rt. Hon. LORD BATTERSEA.
Hon. Secretary: Sir E. HAY CURRIE.

This Hospital has accommodation for 160 In-Patients, but owing to want of Funds only 66 Beds are at present available.

THE Committee are anxious to bring before the Jewish community the many advantages this Hospital affords to the Jewish Poor, for whom Special Wards, with Kitchens and Food, are provided, according to their laws, and every necessary arrangement is made for compliance with their religious principles.

A Doctor (who speaks "Jüdisch-deutsch") has also been appointed for Out-Patients, and Attendance is given twice weekly.

The following were under treatment during 1895:—

In-Patients	820	
Do. (Jewish)	151	971
Out-Patients (Attendances)	87,373	
Do. (Jewish do.)	3,403	90,776

The aid of the benevolent is most earnestly solicited.

CHARLES H. BYERS, Secretary.

Bankers { GLYN, MILLS & CO.
LLOYD'S BANK, Ltd.

NORTH LONDON
HOSPITAL FOR CONSUMPTION
AND DISEASES OF THE CHEST.

Mount Vernon, Hampstead, N.W., and Fitzroy Square, W.

Established 1860, for the Reception of Patients from all parts of the Kingdom. The Charity is unendowed and entirely dependent upon Voluntary Contributions.

"The most beautiful Hospital in London."—*The Philanthropist.*

Chairman.—BENJAMIN A. LYON, Esq. | *Deputy-Chairman.*—The Lord ROBARTES

Amongst the officers of the Institution are:—The Lord ROTHSCHILD, Baron FERDINAND DE ROTHSCHILD, The Right Hon. G. J. GOSCHEN, M.P., B. L. COHEN, Esq., M.P., Miss FLORA GOLDSMID, H. L. W. LAWSON, Esq., M.P., and F. D. MOCATTA, Esq.

Sufferers from Consumption are unsuited for, and are usually rejected by, the General Hospitals. Although there is no malady so rife, less provision has been made for those who have been so unfortunate as to contract this than any other disease. Owing to the magnificent site, on very high ground in close proximity to Hampstead Heath, the **North London Hospital for Consumption** possesses advantages for the treatment of this complaint unequalled by any other Metropolitan Hospital, and unsurpassed by any Institution in the Kingdom.

Relieves a Large Number of Jewish Patients

Contributions are earnestly solicited and will be gratefully received by
W. G. FARRANCE BOSWORTH,
Offices: 41, FITZROY SQUARE, W.
Secretary.

"In want of a Subject."

THE Readers of this valuable book will, we trust, appreciate our position. We are always expected to have nice witty, "up-to-date" advertisements, but what can we possibly say about the undisputed excellence of our

MEAT AND POULTRY

For everybody tries it, everybody likes it, and everybody recommends it.

WE serve the Queen.

WE serve the Prince.

WE serve the Members of the House of Lords.

WE serve the Members of the House of Commons.

WE serve Ninety per cent. of the leading Jewish Families, Public Banquets, and Institutions.

WE are the only licensed Jewish Game Dealers.

WE have a West End Branch thoroughly and efficiently equipped for any amount of Trade.

WE have telephones all over the place.

WE deliver by our own carts as often as required to all parts of London daily free, whether for breakfast, luncheon, dinner, tea, or supper.

WE have a special supply daily of Scotch meat and Welsh mutton from Scotland and Wales.

WE make it our study because it is our business to buy and sell only the very best

MEAT AND POULTRY

E. BARNETT & CO.

79, 81 & 83, MIDDLESEX STREET, ALDGATE,

249, EUSTON ROAD, N.W.,

AND

TERRACE HALL FARM, COLCHESTER.

BY THE USE OF
JAMESON'S
Arsenical Complexion Soap

A lovely clearness, tone, and colour is guaranteed to everybody. Unsightly blotches, blackheads, pimples, black specks, sallowness, etc., disappear in a few days like magic, and the lovely pink and white and clearness of the skin will cause astonishment.

From Chemists, price **2s.** per box of **3** tablets, or direct, post free, from

W. JAMESON,
92, NEWINGTON BUTTS, LONDON, S.E.

Beware of injurious imitations, and have only JAMESON'S.

HOW LOVELY COMPLEXIONS ARE MADE.

"MY face is my fortune, Sir, she said"; and this ingenuous confession attributed to the heroine of the old-time song finds an echo in the hearts of thousands of damsels of to-day who have not, perhaps, the frankness and courage of the pretty milk-maid of old. "Beauty unadorned is adorned the most," so says the poet, and his immortal words, when not taken in too literal a sense, should govern the judgment of every sensible girl, while they convey a well-pointed reproach to misguided females who think more about bedecking themselves in all the wild vagaries of fashion than of preserving and nourishing the beneficent gifts of Nature. The desire of every rational girl, from the peasant to the princess, is the possession of a good complexion and to retain that lovely tone, pink and white colour, which constitute the essence of beauty. One has only to glance down the advertising columns of the newspapers to be convinced of this. Quacks have made fortunes by pandering to this natural female weakness, while their patients have derived little or no benefit from their nostrums. Arsenic taken in the smallest possible quantities has long been recognised as an effective, although highly dangerous, expedient to have recourse to, and many a fair maiden by partaking of the deadly drug, has gained the beautiful skin she desired at the price of ruining her health. The application of arsenic in a harmless form is what the toilet table has long required, and Dr. Jameson's Arsenical Soap appears to me to fit the bill.

Seeing how extensively it is advertised, my chief commissioned me to interview the proprietor, and if possible inspect his premises. Accordingly I called on Dr. Jameson at 92, Newington Butts, and was most courteously received. Mr. Jameson expressed his willingness to show me all over his premises, and explain as far as possible, without disclosing trade secrets, the working of his extensive business which has recently so increased that he was compelled to remove to the present commodious building. On the first floor I found a small army of clerks engaged in replying to letters and otherwise attending to the correspondence, the extent of which may be gauged from the fact that the post brings an average of 700 letters a day. Passing through the packing department, where a score of hands were engaged labelling and packing the soap in boxes ready for transmission through the post, I was shown over the several departments in which the mixing, boiling, and stamping of the soap is carried on, and in each of these departments I was much impressed with the cleanliness and excellent sanitary arrangements. I was next conducted to the wholesale and export warehouse, where men were busily engaged packing large cases of soap ready for transmission to different parts of the kingdom, as well as to America, Australia, Africa and India, with which distant parts the doctor informed me he does an extensive trade. Catching the doctor in a genial moment, I ventured to ask if the soap was really beneficial without being harmless. His answer was characteristic of the man. "I'll express no opinion myself but let you see what my customers think of it." I was escorted into the doctor's sanctum, where he raised the lid of a large chest which must have contained thousands of letters. "These are the original testimonials I have received. Dive your hand in and select a few from any part you like." I did so, and after perusing about a dozen letters from different purchasers I was compelled to admit that the valuable properties of the soap were beyond question. Some of the writers even expressed gratitude for the great benefits they had derived from the use of it. When I expressed myself satisfied, the doctor said, "to have a personal proof of its value, take this box and try it yourself." As the beauty of my complexion has long since departed and is now replaced by the bloom of the heather (real Scotch, ye ken), I did not desire to submit the soap to so severe a test. I, however, presented it to the partner of my joys and sorrows, who has since informed me that it is far and away the best soap she has ever used. Having attained my object I bid the proprietor of the Arsenical Soap factory good day, thoroughly satisfied with the genuineness of the article he manufactures, and I trust that my experience may not be without interest to the many fair readers of THE JEWISH YEAR BOOK.

Something in its pages for every member of the Household.

WOMAN'S LIFE.

NO HOME SHOULD BE WITHOUT **WOMAN'S LIFE.**

'A GEM OF LATTER-DAY JOURNALISM.'

'A WOMAN'S TRUE COMPANION.'

PRICE ONE PENNY.

CONTENTS OF INTEREST TO

The Pretty Woman
The Dainty Woman
The Homekeeping Woman
The Society Woman
The Fashionable Woman
The Gossiping Woman
The Business Woman
The Motherly Woman
The Romantic Woman
The Practical Woman
The Musical Woman
The Womanly Woman
The New Woman
The Old Woman

EVERY WOMAN.

'A WOMAN'S TRUE COMPANION.'

'A GEM OF LATTER-DAY JOURNALISM.'

PRICE ONE PENNY.

EVERY TUESDAY.

AT ALL NEWSAGENTS AND BOOKSTALLS.

Published by Geo. Newnes, Ltd., Southampton St., London, W.C.

W. WALKER & SONS,

THE LARGEST STOCK OF
HIGH-CLASS FURNITURE
IN LONDON.
ESTABLISHED 1848.

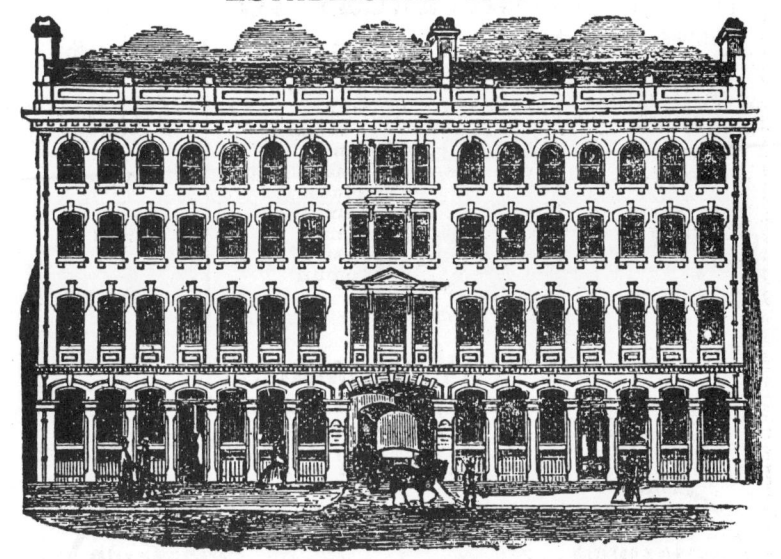

Furniture Works and Show Rooms—
BUNHILL ROW, LONDON, E.C.
Branches—
Rissik Street, JOHANNESBURG.
George Street, SYDNEY.

THE
Kilburn Conservatoire

(Russian Method).

Principal - - GERTRUDE AZULAY.

Instruction given by eminent Professors in all Musical subjects at moderate fees. Elocution and Dramatic Art Classes for children and adults. Students' Concerts take place frequently. Entrance at any date.
For Prospectus apply,

THE SECRETARY,

THE KILBURN CONSERVATOIRE, 4, High Road, Kilburn, N.W.

(Adjoining Maida Vale and two minutes from Kilburn and Maida Vale Station.)

DRESS SUITS, Lined Silk, £3. 18s.

Usually charged £5. 5s.

LIVERIES AT SPECIAL PRICES.

References permitted to Leading Members of the Community.

JAMES MALTBY
Army Tailor,
8, Hanover Place, Upper Baker Street, W.

FIRE! BURGLARS!!

JOHN TANN'S

Bent Steel
"ANCHOR RELIANCE"
SAFES,

For Jewellery, Plate, Deeds, Books, &c.

Special **BENT STEEL** £5. 5s. **SAFE** Carriage Paid.

Price Lists Free.

11, NEWGATE STREET, E.C.
ESTABLISHED 1795.

New Cycles

SENT ANY DISTANCE *on Hire.*

Agent for
OSMONDS and all BEST MAKERS.

☞ Repairs of all kinds.   Send for Catalogue.

REGENT'S PARK CYCLE STORES,
7, Hanover Place, Upper Baker Street.

THE ECONOMIC BANK,

LIMITED,

34, OLD BROAD STREET, E.C.

ESTABLISHED 1893.

Trustees.

COLONEL HENRY EYRE, C.B. | WALTER BISHOP KINGSFORD.
THOMAS LITTLEJOHN FEILD, | EDWARD CHISENHALE-MARSH.
FREDERICK ALEXANDER HAHN. | SAMUEL GURNEY MASSEY,
Managing Trustee.

Current accounts opened for small amounts.
2 % interest allowed on minimum quarterly balance of current accounts.
2½ % interest allowed on Deposits, repayable on demand.
No commissions charged for keeping accounts.
No bills discounted, no loans granted, no overdrafts allowed.
All funds invested under the Trust Act, 1893, and in Colonial Government Securities.
Full particulars on application.

MINERVA COLLEGE,

FOLKESTONE ROAD, DOVER.

HIGH-CLASS SCHOOL FOR YOUNG LADIES.

Principals - - - **The Misses HART.**

THE School premises are situated in the healthiest quarter of Dover, with the exceptional advantages of a Garden and Tennis Ground.

High-Class Modern Education, combined with a Refined Home and Careful Training. Individual care.

Special attention is given to Music, Drawing, Modern Languages, and other accomplishments. Pupils are prepared for the Local Examinations. Arrangements are made for Pupils whose Parents reside abroad.

Sea-bathing and Swimming Lessons during the Season.

A Resident German Governess and Visiting French Master.

Terms moderate and inclusive.

Mathematics taught by a Professor M.A. Special advantages for Senior Pupils who may desire to Matriculate.

FOR PROSPECTUS APPLY TO THE PRINCIPALS.

TO FAT PEOPLE.

When you have tried all known preparations to reduce superfluous fat, and have failed to get permanent relief, write for a box of

Dr. Gould's Obesity Pills,

stating age, height, weight, and whether the obesity is abdominal or general. A reduction of 6lb. a week is guaranteed to anyone, young or old, by their use. They are agreeable to take, and harmless, being entirely a vegetable preparation; the effects are lasting, and no change of diet is required, and they are highly recommended by the Medical Profession. Price 2s. 9d., 4s. 6d., and 11s. per box from Dr. W. E. GOULD, 129, New Kent Road, London, S.E.

The following are the kind of letters that are being daily received from all parts of the country, and such unsolicited testimony is far better than anything.

> *From* W. WOODHEAD, Associate of the Kennel Club,
> *To* W. E. GOULD, Esq.   Clotilton Villa, Clown, nr. Chesterfield.
>
> Dear Sir,—I beg to enclose you postal order for 4s. 6d for another box of your Obesity Pills.
>
> I must certainly acknowledge that I feel considerably better since I commenced taking them, *and am reduced over three stone.* I have recommended them to two or three others, and given them addressed envelopes to send to you.—Yours truly, W. WOODHEAD.

Others, written in a similar strain, could be quoted by the score, but the foregoing will be sufficient to show the remarkable success which has always attended the use of Dr. Gould's Obesity Pills, which have been acknowledged to be the only safe and effectual remedy for obesity or corpulency known at the present date.

Great Ealing School

EALING, W.

Principal: Rev. JOHN CHAPMAN.

1st B.A. University of London, and Member of Jews' College.

The School stands in nearly **seven acres of land**, surrounded by picturesque rural scenery, and contains Cricket Fields, Lawns, Orchards, and covered Playgrounds. Ealing owing to its remarkable salubrity has been called "**The healthiest Suburb of the Metropolis.**"

During its long and successful career, the School has been awarded nearly **400 Certificates, Distinctions, and Scholarships**; of which more than **FIFTY** have been gained during the past two years. The Pupils are prepared for every species of Public Examination, and also for Commercial and Mercantile Pursuits by a large and efficient Staff of English Graduates and Foreign Masters.

The School has achieved conspicuous success at Oxford, Cambridge, and London Universities; and also at Harrow and Clifton, for which boys are specially prepared. It has presented Pupils who have taken high honours in the examinations of the Incorporated Law Society, The Science and Art Department, the Oxford and Cambridge Local Examinations, and in the examinations of the College of Preceptors.

The Domestic Arrangements are under the careful superintendence of Mrs. Chapman. The Diet is of the best, and unlimited in quantity; the Principal and his family taking their meals with the Pupils. Foreign and Colonial Boys are specially cared for during the Vacations.

Every attention is paid to the Health, Morals, and Comfort of the Pupils, and references can be given to parents of pupils, who have been sent to the Rev. Mr. Chapman to be educated from all parts of the World. Full Prospectuses on application.

NORWICH UNION LIFE

INSURANCE SOCIETY.

Increasing Business,

Increasing Reserves,

Increasing Bonuses.

CLAIMS PAID EXCEED

£20,000,000.

Applications for Agencies invited.

Head Office - - NORWICH.

Secretary and Actuary—
J. J. W. DEUCHAR, Esq., F.S.A., F.F.A.

LONDON:
City Office—10, King William Street.

WILLIAM OATES *Manager.*

BONUS YEAR: 1896.

AMERICAN LINE.

Southampton—New York Service.

UNITED STATES MAIL STEAMERS.

TWIN-SCREW STEAMERS, "**St. Louis**" and "**St. Paul**" (11,600 tons), "**New York**" and "**Paris**" (10,800 tons), "**Berlin**" and "**Chester**" (5,500 tons) appointed to sail from **SOUTHAMPTON** to **NEW YORK** direct every Saturday. From **NEW YORK** to **SOUTHAMPTON** every Wednesday.

Special Trains leave Waterloo Station, London, on day of sailing, conveying passsengers and their baggage alongside the steamers, thereby avoiding the inconvenience, expense, and exposure incurred in embarking at other Ports by Tenders, etc.

THESE MAGNIFICENT VESSELS are amongst the largest and fastest in the world, and are well-known for the regularity and rapidity of their passages across the Atlantic.

THE SALOON accommodation and cuisine is unsurpassed on any boat. Ladies' Boudoirs Gentlemen's Sitting and Smoke Rooms, Pianos, Libraries, Barber's Shop, Bathrooms, etc., provided.

SALOON FARES by S.S. "**ST. LOUIS**," "**ST. PAUL**," "**NEW YORK**" & "**PARIS**."
  SUITE OF ROOMS .. .. £90 to £130 } and upwards, according to season
  SPECIAL DECK CABINS .. .. .. £50, £60, £75 } and numbers occupying them.
  SINGLE BERTHS .. .. £12 to £35 }
  By Other Steamers of the Line, Single £12 to £21 } according to season.

SECOND CABIN.—The accommodation is of very highest class, Smoking Room, Vestibule, Piano, Bed, Bedding, and requisite utensils being provided, and a Liberal Table provided. All Passengers from London are furnished with Railway Tickets to Southampton, FREE.

Sailings from Liverpool to Philadelphia every Wednesday. Splendid accommodation for Second Cabin and Steerage Passengers.

Apply in New York to International Navigation Co., 6, Bowling Green.

RICHARDSON, SPENCE & CO., Managing Agents, 3, Cockspur Street, S.W., and 115 & 116, Leadenhall Street, E.C., LONDON;
Canute Road, SOUTHAMPTON; 22, Water Street, LIVERPOOL.

SPECIALITY:

Hebrew Printing

ISIDOR JOSEPH,

WHOLESALE

Manufacturing Stationer,

Letterpress & Lithographic

Printer.

—•—

DUNEDIN HOUSE,

BASINGHALL AVENUE, LONDON,

E.C.

MAKER of ADVERTISING NOVELTIES

AND

SHOW CARDS.

HOBBS, HART & CO.,

LIMITED,

MANUFACTURERS OF THE

Bank of England Treasury Doors.

| These Safes are bent by Powerful Machinery from one Sheet of Steel, thus the Corners (the weakest part in all other Safes) are as strong as the sides, and cannot be wedged. |

SAFES,

DOORS

AND

GATES

TO MEET ALL RISKS for all PURPOSES.

MANUFACTURERS OF

London-Made Locks

FOR ALL REQUIREMENTS.

General Offices and Works:
ARLINGTON STREET, ISLINGTON, LONDON, N.

Show Rooms:
76, CHEAPSIDE, LONDON, E.C.